OXFORD
UNIVERSITY PRESS

Oxford University Press, Inc., publishes works that further
Oxford University's objective of excellence
in research, scholarship, and education.

Oxford   New York
Auckland   Cape Town   Dar es Salaam   Hong Kong   Karachi
Kuala Lumpur   Madrid   Melbourne   Mexico City   Nairobi
New Delhi   Shanghai   Taipei   Toronto

With offices in
Argentina   Austria   Brazil   Chile   Czech Republic   France   Greece
Guatemala   Hungary   Italy   Japan   Poland   Portugal   Singapore
South Korea   Switzerland   Thailand   Turkey   Ukraine   Vietnam

Copyright © 2013 by Oxford University Press

Published by Oxford University Press, Inc.
198 Madison Avenue, New York, New York 10016

www.oup.com

Oxford is a registered trademark of Oxford University Press

All rights reserved. No part of this publication may be reproduced,
stored in a retrieval system, or transmitted, in any form or by any means,
electronic, mechanical, photocopying, recording, or otherwise,
without the prior permission of Oxford University Press.

Library of Congress Cataloging-in-Publication Data
Llano, Samuel.
Whose Spain?: negotiating "Spanish music" in Paris, 1908–1929/Samuel Llano.
   p. cm.
Includes bibliographical references and index.
ISBN 978-0-19-985846-0
1. Music—France—20th century—History and criticism.   2. Music—Spain—
20th century—History and criticism.   3. Music—Political aspects—
France—History.   4. Nationalism in music.   I. Title.
ML270.5.L63 2013
780.946´0944—dc23   2012010290

9 8 7 6 5 4 3 2

Printed in the United States of America
on acid-free paper

Publication of this book was supported in part by the PAYS 75 Fund of the American
Musicological Society, funded in part by the National Endowment for the Humanities
and the Andrew W. Mellon Foundation.

To Rodrigo

ACKNOWLEDGMENTS

It seems hard to express in a few lines my gratitude to the people in whose personal support and intellectual worth I have found encouragement and inspiration since I began research for this book almost ten years ago. I should start thanking the people without whose close support and guidance I could not have carried out that task, let alone finalize this book. This includes Katharine Ellis, Alison Sinclair, Álvaro Torrente, Helena Buffery and Enrique Sacau.

I feel most grateful to colleagues who have read the manuscript for this book and provided me with feedback. This includes, most especially, Michael Christoforidis, whom I warmly thank for his careful reading of the whole manuscript and his extensive advice, as well as writing the foreword to this volume. I should also thank Fernando Delgado, María Cáceres, Juliane Dorsch and Ralph P. Locke for reading portions of the manuscript. Juliane has also kindly facilitated her unpublished work on Falla. I am equally grateful to Suzanne Ryan, Walter Clark, Erica Woods Tucker, Caelyn Cobb, Thomas Finnegan and the OUP editorial team for their support and dedication during the publication of this book; as well as the two anonymous reviewers for their detailed and well-informed comments.

This book is loosely based on my doctoral thesis (Universidad Complutense de Madrid, 2008), which was supervised by Emilio Casares and examined by Louis Jambou, Celsa Alonso, Yvan Nommick, Víctor Sánchez and Javier Suárez-Pajares. I would like to thank all of them for their careful comments, and to add the list the two writers of the reports with which I obtained the "Doctor Europeus" Mention, namely, Bruno Péquignot and Stéphan Etcharry. To the latter I am also indebted for his bibliographical and documentary remarks on Henri Collet and Raoul Laparra, and for facilitating my access to his doctoral thesis.

Conversations with colleagues have proved to be an invaluable source of information and support. In this sense, I am most thankful to Iván Iglesias, Sonsoles Hernández Barbosa, Igor Contreras, Tess Knighton, María Palacios, Richard Langham Smith and Alejandro Madrid for their ideas and advice in various matters.

Staff at the Music and Opera departments of the Bibliothèque Nationale de France in Paris, at the Biblioteca Nacional de España, the Archivo Manuel de Falla in Granada, the British Library and the Cambridge University Library have hugely facilitated the always-demanding task of bibliographical and archival research.

I could not have carried out the research for this book without the material support of a scholarship from the Spanish Ministry of Education and a postdoctoral fellowship from the programme Juan de la Cierva run by the same institution. Two fellowships from the Arts and Humanities Research Council, to carry out postdoctoral research at the University of Birmingham and, currently, at the University of Cambridge, have allowed me to complete the final stages of this volume.

Finally, my warmest thanks go to my family and closest friends for their constant trust and support, and most especially to my parents, Ana and Luis, and my brother, Rodrigo, to whom this book is dedicated.

TABLE OF CONTENTS

Foreword xi
Introduction xv

PART I ▪ **"SPANISH MUSIC" AS PROPAGANDA**

CHAPTER 1. "Spanish Music" as Allied Propaganda 3

CHAPTER 2. "Spanish Music" as Catholic Propaganda 49

PART II ▪ **NEGOTIATING "FRENCH" AND "SPANISH" MUSIC**

CHAPTER 3. Citizens or Savages? The Spaniards in Raoul Laparra's *La jota* (1911) 99

CHAPTER 4. Falla's *La vie brève* (1914) and Notions of "Spanish Music" 136

PART III ▪ **BUILDING THE POSTWAR ORDER**

CHAPTER 5. Domesticating Difference? *Carmen* and the "French" Canon in the 1920s 161

CHAPTER 6. Showcasing Spain at the Opéra Comique: The Homage to Falla (1928) 192

Conclusions 237
Bibliography 241
Index 263

FOREWORD

Reflecting on Spanish music at the Universal Exposition of 1889, Julien Tiersot complained that Spain was everywhere, with Paris hosting "bullfights to right and left; Spanish choral societies here, Spanish soirées there; at the Cirque d'hiver Spanish fiestas, orchestra, dance, estudiantina; at the Exposition the gypsies from Granada."[1] Such a proliferation of Spanish attractions in Paris was not a new phenomenon, and it was a situation that would continue over the next half century, during which time Paris would host multiple coexisting, interacting and evolving representations of Spanish music, which ranged in style from the popular through modernist.

Spanish artists and entertainers, and the very enactment of Spanishness, were at the heart of the Parisian culture-entertainment enterprise throughout this period. This "Spanish" identity evolved and was reconfigured according to the dictates of competing cultural, political and social factors. In the process, France became the dominant arbiter of Spanish identity and exoticism. As Paris was the principal foreign market for Hispanic musical and musico-theatrical entertainment, its preferences clearly shaped international consumption, fueling a succession of debuts, fashions and even crazes in the early decades of the twentieth century.

Hispanic musical identity and musical exoticism had been closely related since at least the Napoleonic period. Yet Spain's unique position and its enactment of cultural identity cannot be easily reconciled within current narratives of musical exoticism. In a sense, the fashion for things Spanish in Paris constituted a musical proto-exoticism, and the sustained engagement of Spaniards with this French current could even be viewed as a precursor of postcolonial discourse. Although the French had been fascinated by a number of "exotic" cultures throughout the

[1] Julien Tiersot, *Promenades musicales à l'Exposition* (Paris: Fischbacher, 1889) 276. Author's translation.

nineteenth century, it could be argued that Spain was different. Both European insider and outsider, Spain was at times politically colonized while still maintaining the semblance of a colonial Empire. In this case the exotic Other was not predicated primarily on concepts of absence and imaginary musings, as Spaniards and Spanish influence were all too present in Paris.

Parisian Hispanic musics (labeled, at times pejoratively, *espagnolades*) were therefore intricate assemblages of exotic topoi and markers of cultural identity, resulting from a process of continuous cultural exchange. Spanish musicians both informed these musics and were inspired by them; thus the perpetrators and subjects of these musical manifestations were engaged in constant, if at times uneven, dialogue. Fin-de-siècle Parisian Hispanic exoticism also coincided with the heightened search for Spanish cultural identity and an artistic renaissance in the aftermath of the Spanish-American War, further complicating the boundaries of exoticism and nationalism in music.

The phenomenon of Spanish musics in Paris has been examined from a number of perspectives, ranging from the question of exoticism and Hispanic evocations in the music of non-Spaniards to the presence of Spanish musicians in Paris, and the influence of French music on the rise of Spanish musical nationalism. To some extent the choice of perspective has reflected the different, nationally motivated concerns of French and Spanish musicologists, as well as the Francophile or Hispanist frames of reference of Anglo-American and Continental researchers. More recently, forums on *latinité* and Franco-Spanish exchanges have shed light on specific aspects of this complex relationship during the late nineteenth and early twentieth centuries. These studies coincided with a new wave of Spanish musicology, which over the past generation has seen a resurgence in the discipline and the broadening of its scope leading to further interrogation of handed-down narratives of Hispanic musical identity. Samuel Llano's work is at the forefront of such exploration.

Whose Spain? is a long-awaited text that engages with the role of Paris in the construction of Hispanic musical identity in the early nineteenth century. It deftly navigates and illuminates the often-murky categories of exoticism, nationalism, authenticity, the *espagnolade* and even auto-exoticism in relation to musical identity. Demonstrating a profound understanding of the previous research on the subject he has broached, and drawing on a varied body of European and Anglo-American literature and approaches, Llano's sustained narrative is argued through a series of case studies, each of which further illuminates this multifaceted phenomenon.

The first half of the book engages with subjects that are not usually the focus of discussions of the topic, charting the role of political propaganda and religious debates and regional identity in the shaping of Franco-Spanish relations and understandings of Spanish music. The rise of French Hispanism and its impact on musical discourse is also explored through one of its leading figures, Henri Collet. The introduction of Raoul Laparra allows Llano to unravel the arguments adopted by French composers engaging with Spanish themes and musical idioms. However, Llano does not shy away from interrogating the more usual suspects of Parisian Spanish music. He explores the French acclamation of Isaac Albéniz and Manuel de Falla, whose Parisian reception was crucial to international and Iberian constructions of Spanish music. The changing meanings accrued by *Carmen*, arguably the *espagnolade* par excellence, are examined half a century after its premiere, although by that stage Paris had lost its international leadership in mediating the opera's meanings and production styles.

Whose Spain? rightly problematizes the issue of Hispanic music in Paris, eschewing simple answers to this intractable question. This renders it an indispensable study of the forces and arguments that shaped this construction of musical identity. May it stimulate and inform the debates to come.

Michael Christoforidis

INTRODUCTION

I believe I am not the only one to have witnessed or taken part in a conversation on Spanish music, involving music lovers and professionals, in which one or more of the interlocutors bring to bear their own views on what constitutes "authenticity" in matters of Spanish music and culture. In an impassioned and/or expert tone, some of them ascribe different degrees of "Spanishness" to the music they talk about, and even argue that certain works are too "exotic," or, on the contrary, too "detached" to be considered as "authentic" specimens of Spanish music. Others will try to focus the conversation on styles and genres, and argue that the "true" music of Spain is flamenco, Manuel de Falla, the *jotas* or *sevillanas*, while others will claim that the pop songs of Mecano have the same right to wear the label "Spanish music" as more "traditional" musical forms—and in this, they will feel empowered by the term "pop español" used by the music industry. More rarely, some will even deny that such a thing as "Spanish music" exists, and argue that Spanish composers have not managed to formulate a national style without borrowing formal, harmonic and, more generally, stylistic formulae from their Italian, German and French counterparts, which they allegedly apply to folkloric melodies from the Spanish songbooks. Last, there are those who argue that only Spanish composers can successfully compose Spanish music, and that the "Spanish" works by Debussy, Ravel, Rimsky-Korsakov, Chabrier, Lalo—and a long list—are mere pastiches. I believe I am not the only one to have witnessed, or even taken part in, such conversations in which the opinion of those perceived as "native" Spaniards tends to be given more credit, unless musical proficiency or scholarship is believed to compensate for a sense of non-belongingness. In that context, therefore, "Spanish music" becomes a tentative ground on which individual or shared perceptions and conceptions about the identity of music, music practitioners and of those who talk and write about music, can be tested, and their differences played out. It could be argued that descriptions and talks about "Spanish music" reveal more about the attitudes, agendas and anxieties of those who talk about it, than about a concept that is freighted with historical, political, social and—more generally—cultural dilemmas.

This phenomenon is far from exclusive to "Spanish music," and if we were to deal with any other national or collective form of identity we would face the same uncertainties, expressed in different or similar ways. Therefore, to define "Spanish music" as a process—that is, as a varying concept that takes form through cultural performance—adds little or nothing to what we know about cultural categories. Moreover, if, as I have argued, the study of "Spanish music" as a category reveals more about its practitioners, consumers and those who, with more or less fortune, have tried to define it, it becomes necessary to situate this concept, and the cultural struggles underlying its formation, in a particular historical, social and cultural horizon.

This book aims to do so, by focusing on a key moment in the definition of "Spanish music" and identity, a moment in which a sense of national crisis triggered an urgency to search for the purported roots and essence of Spanish identity. The phenomenon was not new at the beginning of the twentieth century, but the colonial losses of 1898 and the sentiment of crisis that preceded and followed it certainly contributed to intensifying that search. Related to it, a sense of being confined to a cultural periphery took certain strands of Spanish intellectuals, musicians and artists to seek abroad and, most especially in Paris, the narrative moulds with which to build a successful literary, artistic, musical and cultural nationalism, one that would gain wide support at "home" and yet be exportable, that is, recognizable and positively sanctioned in the international arena. They entered into a negotiation with their European, and above all French, counterparts over the way in which "Spanish music" and identity could be formulated. This process developed over the background of an intense and unprecedented flow of human, cultural and economic capital across the Pyrenees, and a notorious presence of Spanish musicians, artists and writers in Paris, alongside incomers from other European and world countries. Moreover, it nourished on a similar sentiment of crisis on the part of French intellectuals, whom the Dreyfus affair, at the turn of the century, equally prompted to define French identity and its relations with its Others—a category that, as I shall argue, included Spain.

In sum, this is not a book about Spanish music in Paris, if, by that, we understand a historical and analytical account of the musical works performed in the opera houses, symphony halls and salons in that city, and the lives and fortunes of émigré Spanish musicians. A wealth of scholars have already remarkably undertaken that task, and there is little that I could add to their studies on the contributions of Spanish and French composers to what, with more or less consensus, we tend to think of as "Spanish music." Neither does this book deal with French exoticism or Orientalism, or, more particularly, with more or less clichéd representations of Spain in the work of French musicians, writers, painters, choreographers, etc.—although this phenomenon is given substantial consideration. Instead, this book aims to locate "Spanish music" in the French intellectual imaginary, that is, to account for the wide array of discursive practices that endowed the concept with meaning(s). Therefore, I intend to uncover the uses and abuses of the concept, to identify the individuals, social groups and institutions involved in their definition and to unveil their political and ideological agendas. Furthermore, I analyze how attempts to define "Spanish music" helped those individuals, groups and institutions to position themselves in the intellectual and artistic arena. By so doing, they used "Spanish music" to articulate their mutual relations and give expression to their cultural anxieties. The purpose of this book, therefore, cannot be to formulate a definition of "Spanish music." Since the agents involved in its definition were multiple and varied, "Spanish music" must be approached as a register and a catalyst of social practices. Notwithstanding this variety, however, there are certain constants that can be identified.

During the period covered by this study, the approach, development and aftermath of the First World War was the main force that shaped how different social and institutional agents imagined, represented and described Spain and its music. Spain's neutrality before and during the War was the principal source of anxiety underlying and prompting attitudes to Spain and Spanish music, and the main reason French intellectuals, critics and musicians conceived of these concepts as discursive repositories on which it was possible to test the success of French propaganda and, to some extent, rethink certain aspects of French identity. Since the artificers of French propaganda sought to find—or conjure up—cultural bondings in order to attract the Spaniards to France and drive them away from German culture, they partially tore down the ontological barriers that separated them from their southern, "subaltern" neighbors in their imagination. By so doing, they brought under question the strategies that notions of French cultural supremacy had long relied upon. As we shall see, by claiming cultural proximity to their "exotic" neighbours, while simultaneously seeking to establish a hierarchical distance and cultural prophylaxis, French intellectuals, critics and musicians complicated the phenomenological experience of defining the Self by way of representing and describing the Other. Music played a key role in this process thanks to its semantic malleability and its privileged capacity to convey a sense of place and collective identity.

A substantial endeavor, therefore, will be devoted to analyzing how the ontological distinction between "French" and "Spanish music" and culture was understood, modified and negotiated among the social and institutional agents at stake. Again, the multiplicity of political and ideological agendas entertained by these agents elicited a wide range of attitudes, which no current terminological toolkit can help to fully encompass and pin down. To begin with, "exoticism" has become a catchword that masks a variety of practices and experiences, a label lumping together an array of forms in which the Other can be imagined, conceptualized and related to shared notions of the Self. "Marginalization" and more recently "appropriation" have emerged as the most common terms to refer to what lies beyond the reach of "exoticism's" semantic vagueness, and to account for further strategies in which Otherness has been—and is—constructed and coped with. Yet, a terminological reexamination is needed since, as I shall argue, very different ends and motivations underlie the range of experiences encompassed in these terms.

Beyond the aforementioned differences, French constructions of "Spanish music" during the period under consideration here show an increasing tendency to rely on strategies of appropriation at the expense of the inherited tropes of marginalization and "exoticism" that nevertheless still persisted. As I shall argue, the need to break Spain's neutrality as the War approached took French intellectuals to reconceptualize Spanish music, that is, to start contemplating it as a national "school" (*école*), and to a certain extent to redeem it from the "exotic" status to which it had been relegated through the use of subaltern tropes of race, class and gender. Besides the needs of wartime propaganda, however, other factors played an important role in bringing about this discursive repositioning of "Spanish music" in the French intellectual imaginary. More particularly, the consolidation of Hispanism as an academic discipline endowed with its own institutional, corporative and editorial apparatus helped to imbue descriptions of "Spanish culture," and by extension "Spanish music," with a knowledgeable basis. Animated by an impulse to bring under question hackneyed stereotypes and popular myths about Spain and Spanish music, these academic *hispanistes* helped, to a certain extent, to overcome the stigmas of exoticism that, since at least the 19th century, had surrounded those very notions. Yet this attitude conflicted with the *hispanistes*' concerns about the state of French cultural hegemony, which took them to keep on relying, to a certain extent, on those very stereotypes in order to subordinate "Spanish music" and situate it at a safe distance from notions of "French music."

The work of these *hispanistes* and the way in which they conceptualized "Spanish music" will be studied in Part I. Chapter 1 focuses on the effect of anti-German propaganda on conceptions of Spanish music. It shows that the longstanding anti-German sentiment that intensified in the wake of Sedan (1870), and the experience of French critics with using music as the basis for shaping forms of propaganda, brought to bear on descriptions of "Spanish music," which they represented as a cultural ally in the fight against the hegemony of "German culture." I will devote special attention to Henri Collet, whose academic background and whose vital and professional trajectory singled him out as the intellectual most able to shape, in many ways, how "Spanish music" has been understood, until very recently, by French and Spanish musicologists. Collet's writings about Spanish music mark, to a great extent, the period here studied, as a relatively defined moment in the history of French representations of "Spanish music." From his first writings, dating from 1908, to his latest monograph about Spanish music (*L'essor de la musique espagnole au XXe siècle,* 1929), Collet put forward an evolving, yet relatively well-defined and very influential idea of Spanish music that served the interests of a certain hegemonic strand of French propaganda. This chapter also considers other French intellectuals who were hardly or not at all concerned with "Spanish music," but whose work played a substantial role in shaping the discursive framework from which prevailing notions of that concept emerged. This is the case, most particularly, of Charles Maurras, whose formulation of a "Latin race" provided the basis for prevalent conceptualizations of "Spanish music." By advocating Latin bonds with Spain, French intellectuals could serve the purposes of anti-German propaganda while preserving an agenda of racial purity that would help to curb fears of cultural miscegenation, which had significantly increased in the wake of the Dreyfus affair. In sum, French critics projected their fears of a German cultural menace onto their descriptions of Spanish music and, by so doing, construed German music as the foremost enemy of Spanish composers.

Chapter 2 analyzes how "Spanish music" became a vehicle for French Catholic propaganda, which outdid its secular rival. In order to gain the support of the increasingly influential Catholic intellectuals, institutions and powers in Spain, and elicit this country's enrollment in the Entente, the French artificers of Catholic propaganda depicted Spain as the spiritual reserve of the West, which was called upon to fight in order to save Catholicism from German Protestantism. Although French Catholic propaganda in Spain mostly targeted German culture, descriptions of "Spanish music history" in the work of French musicologists were rather opposed to Italian music. In this aspect, they followed Spanish musicologists, for whom the influence of "Italian music" came to represent a cultural invasion that had lasted approximately from 1700 to 1850. By concocting a Catholic and anti-Italian construction of "Spanish music history," French musicologists built on, and at the same time nourished, the urgency of their Spanish counterparts to create and identify a common enemy, in order to stimulate a sense of national cohesion. In other words, French musicologists helped their southern neighbors forge one of the foundational myths of "Spanish music." Again, Collet was the most consistent and influential artificer of a Catholic and anti-Italian construction of "Spanish music history." Furthermore, he was the first to map Catholicism across the national territory, as a force that created regional asymmetries and hierarchies in a way that connected with certain strands of Spanish nationalism, as we shall see.

The second part of the book presents two case studies of operas that prompted French critics, audiences and composers to question how they conceptualized and imagined "Spanish music" before the War. The study of opera in Paris of the 1910s and 1920s constitutes a privileged means for analyzing collective constructions of Spanish identity in that context. Despite the growing popularity of cinema and jazz, which came with the affluence of Americans in that city during the War,[ii] opera was still the realm of "exotic" lands, which, notwithstanding my concerns about the vagueness of the term "exotic," was the prism through which French audiences, musicians and critics regarded Spain. Furthermore, opera received more media coverage than any other music spectacle, and gave expression to a wider range of conceptions and meanings, since it gathered writers, composers, theater directors, performers and painters, among others.

Chapter 3 deals with the première of *La jota* (Opéra Comique 1911), the second opera by Raoul Laparra, a young composer who would subsequently write a substantial amount of criticism about Spanish music and culture. In this opera, Laparra sought to transcend stereotypical views of Spain and present a chapter of Spanish history that, at least for the Spaniards, was highly controversial, namely, the Carlist Wars. These wars had divided nineteenth-century Spanish society to an extent that could be compared to the effect of the Dreyfus affair in France. Indeed, one may arguably regard Laparra's opera as a reflection on the fractures of French society mirrored on an episode of Spanish history. Laparra's comparatively advanced knowledge of Spanish history, culture and music, and his keen interest in transgressing common views of that country, conflicted with his use of some of the most formulaic procedures of *verismo* (or *naturalisme*), which helped to wrap an unfamiliar subject in a more conventional package. More relevantly, Laparra resorted to such an unprecedented level of onstage violence that he not only elicited the opposition of most music critics but also helped to revive notions of Spain as a brutal and tragic country, once evoked by *Carmen*.

If *La jota* may be regarded as the foray of a "French" composer into key issues and debates of Spanish identity, the Paris première of Manuel de Falla's *La vie brève* at the Opéra Comique in 1914—following the world première in Nice a few months earlier—arguably came to represent the incursion of a "Spanish" composer into a territory the French thought they had been the first and best to tread. Indeed, *La vie brève* added to a series of "Spanish" operas by French composers performed on the stage of the Opéra Comique since the nineteenth century and, to a certain extent, could be said to have participated in the conventions that reigned in the opera house. Furthermore, the belief that French composers had been the first to discover and exploit the riches of Spanish popular music and the most successful ones in elevating it to a form of "Art" elicited attempts to appropriate the opera that some regarded as the greatest accomplishment of a living Spanish composer. Yet, in 1905, before he left for Paris (1907), Falla had won a Spanish competition with *La vida breve*, a first version of *La vie brève*

[ii] Jeffrey Jackson, *Making Jazz French: Music and Modern Life in Interwar Paris* (Durham: Duke University Press, 2003), 15–16.

based on a Spanish-language libretto, which never made it to a Spanish stage. These circumstances, plus the loss of the orchestral score of the 1905 "original" version, turned *La vie brève* into the object of anxieties and speculations about the independence of a Spanish musical school. How much had Falla adapted his "Spanish" opera in order to win the favor of the Opéra Comique audiences? Did he become a "Frenchified" composer in his seven-year Paris stint (1907–1914)? Chapter 4 tackles these and other questions.

Part III analyzes the continuities and discontinuities in the postwar evolution of the idea of "Spanish music," when French propaganda was no longer aimed at breaking Spain's neutrality. Chapter 1 showed how Collet's prewar anti-German stance was radicalized after the war; Chapter 5 locates Spain in the postwar French musical imaginaries, at a time when the need to show the world a revitalized and recovered France introduced new dilemmas in the way its relations with its Others were conceived. At the time of its fiftieth anniversary (1925), the opera *Carmen* had long been a staple of French opera houses and came to embody values of Frenchness, serving as a yardstick to assess the place of other works in the national canon. Yet, that occasion provided a new opportunity to examine the Spanish elements in *Carmen*, and to renegotiate the ontological distinction between notions of "French" and "Spanish" music.

Chapter 6 focuses on the homage that the Opéra Comique paid to Falla in 1928, with performances of three of his most emblematic works: *La vie brève, El amor brujo* and *El retablo de Maese Pedro*. These works offered very different and even contrasting images of Spain that responded to divergent, and to some extent incompatible, agendas. Although the homage was by no means the first spectacle to showcase diverse corners of Spain, it contributed to contesting images of this country that were uniformly based on stereotypes from the southern region of Andalusia. Furthermore, the works presented challenged the critics' understanding of "Spanish music." In order to cope with "difference" presented under diverse guises, they unanimously relied on a narrative of Falla's personal evolution toward a higher goal, which cast the latest of his works performed that night, namely, *El retablo*, as his most "Spanish work." However, critics conflicted with the fact that *El retablo*, which was first offered to the public after its private première of 1923, presented none of the signs that critics identified with "Spanish music," most notably folklore. This and the other works afforded a new occasion to reformulate notions of "Spanish music" and its relation with "French music." Critics regarded *La vie brève* as symptomatic of the prewar verist aesthetics and deemed it an immature work. More importantly, this work helped them negotiate their relations with an episode of French music history that was recent, but perceptions of which were mediated by the War traumas. In between *La vie brève* and *El retablo*, *El amor brujo* received wide and unanimous acclaim, as it embodied a right balance between the aesthetic traditionalism and alleged Italianism of the former work, and *El retablo*'s sharp musical and staging modernisms. The critics' liking of *El amor brujo* shows that their concept of Spain still relied on gypsy stereotypes. However, their reactions to La Argentina's neoclassical performance show that they were ready to couch "Spanish music" in the same rhetoric that they used to describe "French music," and, therefore, to bring down, if only momentarily, the ontological divide between both concepts.

Whose Spain?

PART

"SPANISH MUSIC" AS PROPAGANDA

CHAPTER 1

"Spanish Music" as Allied Propaganda: Henri Collet

The early decades of the twentieth century witnessed a significant change in how Spain was situated on the French intellectual horizon. At that moment, Spain ceased to be mostly regarded as an exotic corner of Europe, and was increasingly being used as a discursive site on which to project shared anxieties over the definition of a French identity. Although the popular imaginaries mostly relied on nineteenth-century "exotic" stereotypes of Spain, French intellectuals started to reflect their concerns over Germany's military power and cultural hegemony in their studies about Spanish culture, literature, music and the arts. This phenomenon stemmed from the fact that, unlike Spain, Germany had represented a military, diplomatic, economic and cultural rival since at least the midnineteenth-century.

As is well known, the defeat in the Franco-Prussian War in 1870 brought about the demise of the Second Empire, the loss of Alsace and Lorraine and the rise of a creeping social malaise, which led to the Paris Commune the year after; it also raised deep concerns about the scientific and cultural influence of Germany in French universities, the sciences and the cultural production that manifested itself in academic, intellectual and artistic production.[1] By contrast, Spain was conceptualized as a "low Other" in the French popular and intellectual imaginaries, as a result of its gradual loss of political and economic power. A centuries-long policy of "splendid isolationism" caused Spain to play a minor role in European politics and, unlike Germany, did not threat French plans for hegemony.[2] France had even inflicted two "humiliations"

---

[1] Martha Hannah, *The Mobilization of Intellect: French Scholars and Writers During the Great War* (Cambridge, MA: Harvard University Press, 1996), 12–13, 27–32. Hannah argues that inferiority was more a sentiment than a reality.

[2] Ángel Viñas, "Apertura exterior y modernización económica," in *España, Francia y la Comunidad Europea: Actas del Segundo Coloquio Hispano-Francés de Historia Contemporánea, celebrado en Aix-en-Provence los días 16, 17 y 18 de junio de 1986*, ed. José Ramón de Urquijo y Goitia (Madrid: CSIC, 1989), 265–277. Viñas argues that despite the efforts

on Spain in the nineteenth century, namely, the peaceful occupation by Joseph Napoléon's troupes and administration, which led to the War of Independence (1808–1813), and a military intervention aimed at restoring the Bourbon dynasty (1823). Spain's gradual loss of colonies, from the sixteenth century to 1898, further contributed to undermining its international status and eliciting "exotic" portrayals by European artists and musicians.[3] Since the Early Modern Ages, European powers had settled their colonial rivalry with Spain through a dismissive form of propaganda based on exotic and brutal stereotypes known as the "black legend."[4] Progressively, Spain was metaphorically sent to the margins of Europe, conceptualized as "the door to the Orient."[5] Despite their different roles, representations and descriptions, Germany and Spain became two interdependent discursive frameworks on the French intellectual horizon, to a degree that, though significant, has been much overlooked.

It was not until the turn of the twentieth century that concerns over German cultural supremacy started to impinge on intellectual representations of Spain. At that time, French intellectuals gained awareness that Spain could be a crucial ally in the event of a war against the Axis. France had maintained an intense, centuries-long diplomatic, economic and cultural relation with its southern neighbor, not exempt from periods of antagonism.[6] Consequently, a strand of French intellectuals came to think that Spain could be called upon to intervene in the case of war, and they carried out intense propaganda aimed at driving Spain away from Germany and toward the Triple Entente.[7] The French administration instituted and implemented a series of intellectual "missions" that toured Spanish cities and targeted particular opinion groups. Substantially different forms of propaganda were tailored to particular social, political and ideological

---

carried out by a certain strand of Spanish intellectuals during the early decades of the twentieth century, the progress in political aperturism was minimal.

[3] James Parakilas, "How Spain Got a Soul," in *The Exotic in Western Music*, ed. Jonathan Bellman (Boston: Northeastern University Press, 1998), 137–138.

[4] Ricardo García Cárcel, *La leyenda negra: Historia y opinión* (Madrid: Alianza Editorial, 1992).

[5] Hishaam D. Aidi, "The Interference of al-Andalus: Spain, Islam, and the West," *Social Text* 24, no. 2 (June 2006): 67–88. Spain's historical connections with Al-Andalus and its ensuing ambiguous position between notions of the "West" and the "Orient" has been the object of speculation and manipulation by Spanish and European intellectuals and politicians for centuries.

[6] Jover Zamora argues that during the periods in which Spain had been diplomatically cut off from Europe, it first sought the support of France, such as after the Treaty of Utrecht (1713). José María Jover Zamora, *España en la política internacional: Siglos XVIII–XX* (Madrid: Marcial Pons Historia, 1999), 60–62.

[7] Antonio Niño Rodríguez, *Cultura y diplomacia: Los hispanistas franceses y España de 1875 a 1931* (Madrid: Consejo Superior de Investigaciones Científicas, 1988), 167–179, 204–228, 257–271; Paul Aubert, "La propagande étrangère en Espagne pendant la première guerre mondiale," in *Españoles y franceses en la primera mitad del siglo XX* (Madrid: CSIC, 1986).

groups in Spain.⁸ The Republican Spaniards were shown a progressive France, which was concealed from the sight of Catholic Spaniards, and vice versa. Spain remained neutral during the First World War, given the weight of its longstanding isolationist policies and its simultaneous exposure to French and German propaganda,⁹ which reinforced its social and political inner fractures.¹⁰

The turn of the twentieth century was also the moment when the *hispanistes* emerged and consolidated their presence among French intellectuals. By *hispanistes* I refer to a loose group of professionals and specialists in various areas of Hispanic culture and history, who played a key role in shaping and spreading French propaganda in Spain. The foundation of the first chairs in Hispanic studies (Bordeaux, 1898) and the editorial expansion of this area at the end of the nineteenth century helped the *hispanistes* consolidate their position among French intellectuals.¹¹ Moreover, it invested them with a degree of scholarly authority that their discipline had not known before. Boosted by their new position, the *hispanistes* helped to challenge how French intellectuals and artists had largely understood or imagined and represented Spain during the nineteenth century. By way of their scholarly production and their concert and book reviews, they endowed images of Spain with a more knowledgeable basis. In their writings, they construed Spain as an allied, Latin and anti-German culture, and imbued their descriptions of Hispanic music with a marked anti-Teutonic character. Furthermore, they played a key role in articulating French propaganda in Spain, seeking to undermine the rise of German Hispanists as experts on Spanish literature and history, and to avoid having German replace French as the first foreign language studied by Spaniards.¹² But the *hispanistes* still relied, to some extent, on the strategies of marginalization that underpinned most nineteenth-century exotic stereotypes. They reinforced inherited views of Spain as being exotic, barbarian and backward, with the purpose of building French cultural hegemony. A compelling contradiction arose in their writings, therefore, between images of Spain as a powerful ally in

---

⁸ Niño Rodríguez, *Cultura y diplomacia*, 271–308.

⁹ On German propaganda in Spain during the First World War see Jesús de la Hera Martínez, *La política cultural de Alemania en España en el período de entreguerras* (Madrid: CSIC, 2002), 11–25.

¹⁰ On the impact of German and Spanish propaganda in musical culture in Spain, see Carol A. Hess, *Manuel de Falla and Modernism in Spain, 1898–1936* (Chicago: University of Chicago Press, 2001), 59–78. An emphasis on these divisions has led to an artificially neat distinction between two factions, known as the "mito de las dos Españas." See Enrique Moradiellos, *1936: Los mitos de la guerra civil* (Barcelona: Península, 2004) and Paul Preston, *Las tres Españas del 36* (Barcelona: Plaza & Janés, 1998), 13–25.

¹¹ Most especially, the *Bulletin Hispanique* (1899), which built on the work of the *Revue Hispanique* (1876).

¹² Antonio Niño Rodríguez, "El hispanismo científico y los intereses franceses en España a finales del siglo XIX," in *España, Francia y la Comunidad Europea: Actas del Segundo Coloquio Hispano-Francés de Historia Contemporánea, celebrado en Aix-en-Provence los días 16, 17 y 18 de junio de 1986*, ed. Jean-Pierre Etienvre and José Ramón de Urquijo y Goitia (Madrid: Casa de Velázquez, 1989), 47.

the fight against German culture, and subaltern constructions of Spanish identity. In this chapter, I shall analyze how that contradiction underpinned, in different ways, the production of the *hispanistes*, and will devote special attention to Henri Collet.

Henri Collet: Early Anti-Germanism

Although better known for having boosted Les Six at the beginning of their career, Henri Collet devoted most of his life to the composition of, and writing about, "Spanish music."[13] He wrote on that subject for journals such as *Le Ménestrel*, *Comœdia* and *S.I.M.*; authored several book-length publications; and received his doctorate at the Sorbonne in 1913 with a thesis on mysticism in sixteenth-century Spanish music.[14] He also wrote several fictional literary works, and won the French National Prize for Literature in 1929 with *L'Île de Barataria*, a novel inspired by *Don Quixote*. By way of these achievements and the reputation that came with them, he could make a decisive contribution to shaping images of Spain in intellectual and academic circles.

Collet first gained interest in Spanish culture and music in Bordeaux, where he moved with his family in 1904, and where he took his first lessons in piano and composition. Bordeaux received a substantial increase of immigrant Spanish population at the end of the nineteenth century, which introduced cultural practices and customs from Spain. The University of Bordeaux carried out the first attempts to institutionalize Hispanic studies in France, which materialized in creation of a chair (1898), the founding of the prestigious *Bulletin Hispanique* (1899) and the constitution of the first higher degree in that discipline.[15] Collet decided to take up the degree in Hispanic studies at Bordeaux, where he graduated in 1908 with a thesis on Spanish music of the sixteenth century—on which he would base his doctoral thesis.[16]

Collet undertook a serious propagandistic activity in defense of French music, as he was convinced that the Spaniards "hold a passionate admiration for the

---

[13] Selected bibliography on Collet: Stéphan Etcharry, "Henri Collet (1885–1951), compositeur: Un itinéraire singulier dans l'hispanisme musical français" (Ph.D. diss., Université de Paris-Sorbonne, 2004); Jean Gallois, *Henri Collet ou l'Espagne impérieuse* (Geneva: Editions Papillon, 2001); Miguel Ángel Palacios Garoz, *El hispanismo musical de Raoul Laparra y Henri Collet: Dos discípulos franceses de Federico Olmeda en Burgos* (Burgos: Institución Fernán González, 1999). For a complete list of Collet's writings see Christiane Le Bordays, "Henri Collet (1885–1951): Le compositeur," *Revue internationale de musique française*, no. 26 (June 1988): 109–110.

[14] Published as Henri Collet, *Le mysticisme musical espagnol au XVIe siècle* (Paris: Felix Alcan, 1913).

[15] Etcharry, "Henri Collet," 74; Niño, *Cultura y diplomacia*, 119–123.

[16] Henri Collet, "La valeur expressive de la musique religieuse espagnole au XVIe siècle" (Bordeaux: Université de Bordeaux, 1908). For a review and details on the examination see E. B. and Pierre Paris, "Chronique," *Bulletin hispanique* 11, no. 2 (1909): 227–228.

master of Bayreuth"—that is, Wagner—and entertain a "ferocious gallophobia" which "increases day by day."[17] Therefore, he tried to drive the Spaniards away from German music and culture. The bulk of his writings, however, are mostly devoted to pitting notions of "Spanish" and "German" music against each other, as he mostly addressed a French readership. Collet's anti-German conception of Spanish culture emerged briefly but acridly in his first publication on Spanish music, namely, "La musique espagnole moderne," published in 1908.[18] In reality, the main purpose of this article was to underscore Spain's cultural, regional and musical variety, in order to transcend commonplace views of that country based solely on stereotypical elements from the southern region of Andalusia. But his anti-German feelings emerge bitterly at the end: "in these days, when the spirit and the soul of the old Latin race seem to reawaken, we thought that it was the right time to remind that we are not alone in our fight against the invader."[19] Collet spares any direct reference to German music and culture, but it will become clear that they lie behind his idea of the "invader" when regarded in the context of his other writings, and more especially once the concept of the "Latin race" that he invokes is explained.

Spain and the Latin Race

The concept of "Latin race" had been taking on anti-German connotations since at least the beginning of the Third Republic. At that time, French intellectuals and politicians explained the defeat of Bismarck's Prussia in 1870 as a symptom of the alleged "decadence of the Latin race."[20] By way of this myth, their Spanish and Italian counterparts explained their colonial losses, as well as the German and British victories. Consequently, in order to boost France through its postwar recovery, and liberate it from what they believed to be its national ills, a powerful and numerous strand of French intellectuals heralded the renaissance of the Latin race, situating France at its center. By way of a series of cultural strategies, they claimed that France was the "true" and "superior" inheritor of Greco-Roman Antiquity. They manipulated the findings of Roman structures

---

[17] "Décidément les Espagnols ont pour le maître de Bayreuth une admiration passionnée"; "La farouche gallophobie des Espagnols […] va chaque jour s'accroissant." Henri Collet, "Madrid," *L'actualité musicale (supp. S.I.M. Revue musicale mensuelle)* (July 1910).

[18] Henri Collet, "La musique espagnole moderne, 1er partie," *Bulletin français de la S.I.M.* 4, no. 9 (September 1908).

[19] "En ces jours où semblent se réveiller l'esprit et l'âme de la vieille race latine, il nous a paru opportun de rappeler que nous n'étions pas seuls à lutter contre l'envahisseur." Ibid.

[20] Inman Edward Fox, "Spain as Castile: Nationalism and National Identity," in *The Cambridge Companion to Modern Spanish Culture*, ed. David T. Gies (Cambridge: Cambridge University Press, 1999), 32.

and remnants in Southern France.[21] They recuperated the myth of the *translatio studii*, which posits that Medieval Paris had inherited the world's knowledge, once accumulated in ancient Athens and Rome, turning the French capital into the center of civilization.[22]

One of the most prominent and influential advocates of the Latin construction of French national identity was the political thinker Charles Maurras. He became one of the staunchest opponents of the Third Republic and most outspoken defender of the Ancien Régime and monarchic values. He believed that France was engulfed by an identity crisis that had started with the 1879 Revolution, waning only during certain periods of authoritative rule. He proposed Greek antiquity as a model for overcoming the crisis, as a universal legacy of values such as order, hierarchy and submission to power, which, he believed, France had once embraced but subsequently lost during the Revolution.[23] He claimed that, in order to recover the interrupted French tradition, it was necessary to restore beauty by way of a return to classical aesthetics, recover truth by way of Catholicism and reestablish order, unity and harmony by way of monarchic rule. This fusion of the literary, political and religious constitutes the core of his "integral nationalism."[24] Further to grounding France on a classical tradition, Maurras urged the cleansing of non-French elements from French identity, which he named as German and Jewish. He argued that the influence of German Romanticism had diverted France from its primary function as the true inheritor of the ancient Greek tradition, as it contained the revolutionary germ of the social disorder that had brought about the demise of the Second Empire and establishment of the Republic in France.[25] He also argued that German Romantic poetry had introduced a deleterious, "effeminate" component into

---

[21] Even if by no means they outdid in number or interest their equivalent in other European countries. As Musk has shown, however, these findings also became associated with the regionalist movements in Southern France. Andrea Musk, "Regionalism, Latinite and the French Musical Tradition: Deodat de Severac's Heliogabale," in *Nineteenth-Century Music: Selected Proceedings of the Tenth International Conference*, ed. Jim Samson and Bennett Zon (Burlington: Ashgate, 2002), 234–235.

[22] Liah Greenfeld, *Nationalism: Five Roads to Modernity* (Cambridge, MA: Harvard University Press, 1992), 99–100. See also Jeanice Brooks, "Italy, the Ancient World and the French Musical Inheritance in the Sixteenth Century: Arcadelt and Clereau in the Service of the Guises," *Journal of the Royal Musical Association.* 121, no. 2 (1996): 147–150.

[23] Gaetano DeLeonibus, *Charles Maurras's Classicising Aesthetics: An Aestheticization of Politics* (New York: P. Lang, 2000), 1–7.

[24] David Carroll, *French Literary Fascism: Nationalism, Anti-Semitism, and the Ideology of Culture* (Princeton NJ: Princeton University Press, 1995), 74–78; Michael Sutton, *Nationalism, Positivism, and Catholicism: The Politics of Charles Maurras and French Catholics, 1890–1914* (Cambridge and New York: Cambridge University Press, 1982).

[25] Philippe Mège, *Charles Maurras et le germanisme* (Paris: L'Æncre, 2003), 1–25.

French, "virile" literature and hence into the nation—which he defined as an "artwork."[26] Furthermore, since he identified Protestantism with Romanticism, he embraced the Catholic faith with greater fervor. Last, he predicated French identity upon an agenda of racial purity that most conspicuously excluded the Jews, whom he conceptualized as the primary internal Other. Although he argued that his nationalism was not racist, he identified the Jews, and to a lesser degree the Masons, and more generally the *métèques*,[27] as elements of disruption in the historical narrative of the "nation-work."[28]

In addition to formulating the principles of a Latin, anti-German conception of French identity, Maurras put forward the establishment of a Latin Union of nations, with which to isolate Germany. A series of politicians and intellectuals throughout the Third Republic availed themselves of this form of propaganda, especially in the wake of the First World War. Among the several instances in which Maurras left testimony of this idea, his essay "Les forces latines" deserves special attention, as it reveals the role that Maurras granted to Spain.[29] In tune with the book's subject, Maurras starts by expressing his wish that Latin America should become part of the Latin Union, but he soon turns his attention to Spain.[30] He blames Spain's neutrality during the First World War for having spoiled a chance to forge the Latin Union (p. 9), as he argues that Spain has helped to preserve the Greco-Roman tradition that was almost destroyed by Lutheran Germany (p. 11). He then builds a history of Franco-Spanish diplomatic relations in which the periods of monarchy and governmental stability in both countries brought about prosperity and facilitated their mutual understanding (pp. 11–14). Maurras ends by extolling Catholicism, which, he argues, should provide an element of cohesion between the Latin nations.

---

[26] Carroll, *French Literary Fascism*, 79.

[27] *Métèques* is the ancient Greek term for "immigrants," which Maurras invested with a markedly xenophobic meaning.

[28] Carroll, *French Literary Fascism*, 88.

[29] Charles Maurras, "Les forces latines," in Marius André, *La fin de l'empire espagnol d'Amérique Latine*, ed. Marius André (Paris: Nouvelle librairie nationale, 1922), 1–16.

[30] The impact of Action Française in Latin America was very limited. Denis Rolland, "L'Action Française et l'Amerique Latine," in *L'Action Française et l'étranger: Usages, réseaux et représentations de la droite nationaliste française*, ed. Catherine Pomeyrols and Claude Hauser (Paris: L'Harmattan, 2001), 99–115. Collet regarded Latin America as a potential area for the expansion of French propaganda, but equally dedicated little space to the matter in his writings: "Allons nous encore négliger l'Amérique du Sud, si bien faite pour nous comprendre, en notre place là-bas sera-t-elle encore prise, comme avant la guerre, par l'Allemagne expansive […] N'a-t-on pas encore compris la force de propagande que contient en soi la musique?" Henri Collet, "La musique au Chili," *Comœdia* (September 10, 1920).

Before Maurras published "Les forces latines," his ideas had already exerted a substantial influence on certain Spanish intellectuals and musicians.[31] After the death of Debussy in 1918, Falla gave an homage conference at the Ateneo de Madrid, in which he advocated a pan-Latin union with France, which was reminiscent of Maurras's rhetoric.[32] In the same spirit, he exchanged several letters with Alfredo Casella between 1915 and 1918, discussing the possibilities of establishing an anti-German Latin alliance of the national musical societies for contemporary music in Italy, Spain and France. These societies included the Società Nazionale di Musica (1917), founded by Casella, the Société Musicale Indépendante and the Sociedad Nacional de Música (1915), which Falla helped to establish.[33]

Maurras's influential role in France and Spain was partly due to his being one of the main ideologists of the increasingly powerful league Action Française. This monarchic, far-right league was created in 1898, in the wake of the Dreyfus affair, with the purpose of destabilizing the Republic and countering the campaign in support of the Jewish General Dreyfus, who was accused of passing on secret military information to the German army.[34] Once Dreyfus's Jewish background became a political issue, his case became widely aired in the newspapers, and took the form of a public debate on the nature of French identity and its relations with its created Others. The affair helped to articulate the confrontation between republican and monarchic strands of French thinking. Action Française took the lead in the anti-Dreyfus cause and became a powerful and influential advocate of xenophobia and Maurras's ideals, until the pope banned it in 1926 for engaging in terrorist activities. Its power and verbal violence helps to understand the context in which Collet's anti-German reading of "Spanish music" emerged. It would be unfair and deterministic to attribute all the subscriptions to a Latin entente to the anti-Republican, monarchic and antirevolutionary cause of Maurras and Action Française. However, their activity left an effectual and available discursive repository on which to shape anti-German propaganda.

---

[31] Especially José Martínez Ruiz "Azorín," José María Salaverría, the five-time prime minister of Spain Antonio Maura, and Eugeni D'Ors, with whom Maurras became friends. Maurras's opponents in Spain include José Ortega y Gasset and Miguel de Unamuno. Pedro González Cuevas, "La recepción del pensamiento maurrasiano en España (1914–1930)," *Espacio, tiempo y forma* 3 (1990): 343–356. González Cuevas argues that Maurras's influence on Spanish intellectuals well precedes the first translation into Spanish of one of his books, in 1935 (p. 350). In response to the proclamation of the Second Republic in 1931, some far-right monarchists founded Acción Española, which, as its name suggests, was highly influenced by Maurras and Action Française.

[32] Although he declined Maeztu's invitation to form a Spanish version of Action Française. Hess, *Manuel de Falla*, 85, 214, 280.

[33] Chris Collins, "Falla in Europe: Relations with His Contemporaries," in *Manuel de Falla: His Life and Music*, ed. Nancy Lee Harper (Lanham, MD: Scarecrow Press, 2005), 257.

[34] Jane F. Fulcher, *French Cultural Politics & Music: From the Dreyfus Affair to the First World War* (New York: Oxford University Press, 1999), 4.

The Albéniz Obituary

Collet first gave form to a fully fledged anti-German formulation of Spanish music in his obituary of Albéniz, who died in May 1909.[35] As befits an obituary, Collet extols the qualities of Albéniz's music, but manipulates details of his biography to give them a clearly intentional anti-German meaning. Most significantly, Collet focuses on Albéniz's brief training in the Leipzig Conservatoire in 1876. In that institution, the sixteen-year-old Albéniz sought to "discipline" his previous experience and training and keenly attended the classes. For reasons that remain unclear, however, he stayed less than two months.[36] The Leipzig experience notably grasped Collet's attention, even if its impact cannot compare with that of his subsequent training in the Conservatoire of Brussels (1876–1879)[37]:

> In those Germanic milieux, which are so favorable to serious and profitable work, Albéniz acquired enough mastery to begin confronting high composition, while preserving that freedom of attitude, that charming negligence and that spontaneity by which Spain remains impervious to Teutonic pedantry.[38]

Collet overstates the import of the Leipzig episode, most likely in order to justify his otherwise awkward interest in it. He construes Albéniz as a composer innately "impervious to Teutonic pedantry," on account of his Spanish origin. Interestingly, Albéniz's penchants lay far from Hispanic music at the time he visited Leipzig, as they did not arise before he composed the *Rapsodia cubana* (1881) and the *Pavane espagnole* (1882). Nevertheless, Collet did not want so much to discuss Albéniz's aesthetic penchants as to remark on his nationality. By defining identity as a matter of birth, Collet sought to construe Albéniz's alleged imperviousness to "Teutonic pedantry" as innate and natural, rather than acquired or artificial. Thus, Collet anticipated one of the prevailing arguments of French wartime propaganda, namely, that Spain's potential enrollment in the Entente constituted a matter of national fate and patriotic loyalty that Spaniards were called upon to fulfill.[39]

---

[35] Henri Collet, "Nécrologie," *Revue musicale et bulletin de la S.I.M.* 5, no. 7 (July 15, 1909).

[36] Walter Clark, *Isaac Albéniz: Portrait of a Romantic* (Oxford and New York: Oxford University Press, 1999), 34–35.

[37] Ibid., 37–39.

[38] "Dans ces milieux germaines si favorables au labeur sérieux et profitable, Albéniz acquit assez de maîtresse pour être en état d'aborder la haute composition, tout en conservant cette liberté d'allure, cette charmante négligence et cete spontanéité par quoi l'Espagne demeure impénétrable au pédantisme teuton." Collet, "Nécrologie."

[39] Niño Rodríguez, *Cultura y diplomacia*, 204–228.

In the Albéniz obituary, Collet took the opportunity to put "Spanish music" at the service of French cultural hegemony:

> Albéniz then came to France. The modern Athens willingly smiled at him; and, thereafter, success came to his life. […] Indolent Spain still ignores the genius of one her most glorious children. Only a Parisian success could give Albéniz the popularity that he so longed for. How curious! His music, which we find to be so "Spanish" finds only a few echoes in the souls of the people from Madrid and Seville. […] Albéniz is therefore ours, despite his apparent exoticism. Listening to *Iberia*, one evokes a wealth of landscapes, impressions and feelings which a Spaniard would surely laugh about. Albéniz's impressionism often sounds like Debussy or Fauré rather than Spanish.[40]

In this excerpt, Collet casts Spain as a cultural periphery, or more particularly, a satellite of France. He describes Spain as a neglectful "motherland," which refuses to recognize and support to its own "children." On that basis, he construes Paris as a cultural Mecca or "modern Athens," the ultimate destination of the Spanish cultural "pilgrimage," or to put it even more dramatically, "exodus"; the "only" place where Albéniz could gain the "popularity that he so longed for." In sum, he masks the exercise of cultural hegemony behind the appearance of a receptive attitude toward Spanish artistic "refugees." Moreover, he conceals the power structures underlying the mechanisms of cultural production and dissemination that led to the establishment of centers and peripheries.

This form of propaganda gained pride of place in the *hispanistes*' writings, as it shrewdly and efficiently fed on the malaise of the Spanish musical avant-garde over the lack of public and private support and infrastructure.[41] Although the situation had improved since the end of the nineteenth century with the founding of orchestras and associations in a small number of Spanish cities,[42] the avant-garde

---

[40] "L'Espagne indolente ignore encore le génie d'un de ses plus glorieux enfants. Un succès parisien peut seul donner à Albéniz la popularité qu'en son cœur il désirait tant. Chose curieuse! cette musique que nous trouvons si 'espagnole' ne trouve que peu d'échos dans l'âme des Madrilènes ou des Sévillans […] Albéniz es donc nôtre, malgré son exotisme apparent. Nous évoquons en attendant son Ibéria, par exemple, bien des paysages, bien des sensations, bien des sentiments don un Espagnol souriait sans doute. L'impressionnisme musical d'Albéniz est souvent plus debussyste ou plus fauréen qu'espagnol." Collet, "Nécrologie."

[41] A statistic published in 1917 shows that the works of Spanish composers represented only 4 percent of the repertoire played at the Madrid Philharmonic Society since its foundation in 1901. Anon., "Sociedad Filarmónica de Madrid," *Revista musical hispano-americana*, May 1917.

[42] María Encina Cortizo and Ramón Sobrino Sánchez, "Asociacionismo musical en España," *Cuadernos de música iberoamericana* 8–9 (2001): 11–16; Xosé Aviñoa, "Sociedades musicales y modernidad en Cataluña en el primer tercio del siglo XX," *Cuadernos de música iberoamericana* 8–9 (2001): 277–286. Emilio Casares Rodicio, "La música española hasta 1939, o la restauración musical," in *España en la música de occidente: Actas del congreso*

still complained about the pervasiveness of *zarzuela*, which was surely the cause of Falla leaving Paris in 1907.[43] The avant-garde could not see their ambitions fulfilled until, after returning from Paris, Falla founded the short-lived Sociedad Nacional de Música (1915) with the help of the critic Adolfo Salazar.[44]

Besides replicating French propaganda, Collet tries to appropriate Albéniz's music. In the passage above, Collet describes Albéniz's music as "ours" (meaning "French"), a music that "finds only a few echoes in the souls of the people from Madrid and Seville," one that a "Spaniard would surely laugh about," and which sounds "more like Debussy or Fauré rather than Spanish." By Frenchifying Albéniz's style and describing his success as "Parisian," Collet appropriates Albéniz's "success."[45] An emphasis on the Mediterranean links between France and Spain provides the legitimate discursive framework:

> Through that contact with France, [Albéniz] also gained a fluent grace, a clear ardour, a nervous precision, which make him rather precious in the eyes of every true musician, and which would have charmed Nietzsche, who dreamt of a Mediterranean art of which *Carmen* seemed to him to be the preliminary sketch.[46]

Thus, Collet played with prevailing notions of the "Mediterranean" as being opposed to Nordic and German culture.

Since the 1890s, the notion of Mediterranean culture and identity acquired new meaning in French culture. One the one hand, it became intimately connected to the rise of political regionalism in that decade, and on the other, it became a trope of anti-German sentiments. In order to vindicate the French Midi, the leaders of French political regionalism, such as the aforementioned Maurras and Jean Charles-Brun, argued that Western civilization had originated in the Mediterranean.[47] They built upon the activity carried out, since the mid-nineteenth century, by the literary group Félibrige, headed by the Provençal poet

---

internacional celebrado en Salamanca, 29 de octubre–5 de noviembre de 1985, ed. José López-Calo, Ismael Fernández de la Cuesta and Emilio Casares Rodicio, vol. 2 (Madrid: INAEM, 1987), 267–272.

[43] Carol A. Hess, *Sacred Passions: The Life and Music of Manuel de Falla* (Oxford: Oxford University Press, 2005), 24–33.

[44] Hess, *Manuel de Falla and Modernism*, 51.

[45] As we shall see in Chapter 6, a similar strategy underpinned critical reactions to Falla's music on the occasion of the homage that the Opéra Comique paid to him in 1928.

[46] "à ce contact français il acquit une grâce fluide, une ardeur claire, une précision nerveuse, qui le rendent bien précieux aux yeux de tout vrai musicien, et qui eût enchanté Nietzsche, qui rêva d'un art méditerranéen dont Carmen lui parut être l'ébauche." Collet, "Nécrologie."

[47] Musk, "Regionalism, Latinité"; see also Pierre Guillot, "Déodat de Séverac: Quelle 'méditerranéisation' de la musique?" in *La musique dans le Midi de la France: XIXe siècle. Actes des rencontres de Villecroze, 16 au 18 mai 1996*, ed. François Lesure, vol. 2 (Paris: Klincksieck, 1996), 309–324.

Frédéric Mistral.[48] The Félibres recuperated French regional languages and opposed the cultural standardization that came with political centralization.[49] Drawing on their activity, Maurras and Action Française sought to destabilize the Republic, which, since 1789 and most especially after the 1870 Commune, relied on centralism as a guarantee of social order. The Schola Cantorum, where Albéniz taught during his last years, got deeply involved in the regionalist movement by welcoming and supporting regionalist students, and helping to fund Action Française.[50]

In the Albéniz obituary, however, Collet imbued the Mediterranean trope with an anti-German character. Like the concept of "Latin race," the "Mediterranean race" was defined in contradistinction to the North, which, in Third Republic France, principally functioned as a trope for German culture.[51] Maurras revived discourses on the superiority of Mediterranean culture that harken back to ancient Greece and Rome. Ancient Greeks and Romans sought to distinguish themselves from the rest of the world by elaborating a complex idea of Mediterranean culture that cast a pejorative light upon their Northern and Southern neighbors.[52]

Collet borrowed the use of the trope of "Mediterranean race" from Nietzsche, who conceived of *Carmen* as an epitome of Mediterranean culture. This opera elicited his oft-quoted claim that "music needs to be made Mediterranean" ("il faut méditerraniser la musique").[53] He furthermore remarked that, with *Carmen*, "we take a break from the humid North, from all the Wagnerian haze."[54] Nietzsche's anti-Wagnerian diatribes gained pride of place among French nationalists since the publication of *Le cas Wagner* in 1889—only one year after its German original. His ideas became invaluable cultural capital, since he could be regarded as a "convert" from the Wagnerian "cult" to the Mediterranean "faith." Once

---

[48] Anne Marie Thiesse, *Écrire la France: Le mouvement littéraire régionaliste de langue française entre la Belle Époque et la Libération* (Paris: Presses Universitaires de France, 1991), 23; Julian Wright, *The Regionalist Movement in France, 1890–1914: Jean Charles-Brun and French Political Thought* (Oxford: Oxford University Press, 2003), 46; Musk, "Regionalism," 227–231.

[49] Mège, *Maurras*, 22–25.

[50] Musk, "Regionalism," 231–243.

[51] Ali Nematollahy, "Nietzsche in France, 1890–1914," *Philosophical Forum* 40, no. 2 (June 1, 2009): 176; Sander L. Gilman, "Nietzsche, Bizet, and Wagner: Illness, Health, and Race in the Nineteenth Century," *Opera Quarterly* 23, no. 2–3 (March 31, 2007): 247–264.

[52] Anthony Pagden, *The Idea of Europe: From Antiquity to the European Union* (Washington, DC: Woodrow Wilson Center Press, 2002), 35–37. According to Pagden, the "radical distinction between the North and South" that emerged in that period "retained its imaginative force until at least the nineteenth century" (ibid., 36). Once could argue, however, that the anti-German connotations that notions of Mediterranean culture gained in Third Republic France constitute a telling example of the further durability of that distinction.

[53] Friedrich Nietzsche, *Le cas Wagner, suivi de Nietzsche contre Wagner*, trans. G. Colli, M. Montinari, and Jean-Claude Hémery (Paris: Gallimard, 1991), 6; also see Nematollahy, "Nietzsche in France."

[54] "Avec cette œuvre on prend congé du nord humide, de toutes les brumes de l'idéal wagnérien," Nietzsche, *Le cas Wagner*, 5.

"one of the most corrupted Wagnerians," Nietzsche turned his back on Wagner's music in 1876 and embraced *Carmen* as the epitome of a "redeeming" music that symbolizes the "return to nature, health, joy, youth, virtue!"[55] In other words, Nietzsche's testimony could help to substantiate claims over the superiority of French music.[56]

Prewar Neoclassical Aesthetics

Collet's obituary of Albéniz constituted but one of many instances of anti-German propaganda based on rhetorical strategies and the tropes of Latin and Mediterranean races. That same year of 1909, *Le courrier musical* published three articles on German aesthetics by Paul de Stoecklin, which show that an anti-German rhetoric of order, beauty and balance was at stake well before 1920s neoclassicism.[57] The impact of this unconnected series of articles was limited, especially if compared with Cocteau's *Le coq et l'arlequin* a decade later.[58] However, they deserve a detailed analysis, insofar as they offer the keys to understanding the origins of the binaries that crystallized into the aesthetics of neoclassicism after the War.[59]

In "L'Esthétique Allemande" (January 1, 1909), Stoecklin describes the German "race" as "reflective," prone to "interior life and contemplation," and credits it with having "invented subjectivism."[60] Furthermore, he characterizes German art as being "born from a theory" and affected by a "lack of spontaneity," and as one that "conveys ideas rather than emotions, seeks to be expressive rather

---

[55] "L'œuvre de Bizet, elle aussi, est rédemptrice," ibid., 5; "Le retour à la nature, à la santé, à la gaieté, à la jeunesse, à la vertu!—Et cependant j'étais l'un des wagnériens les plus corrompus…J'étais capable de prendre Wagner au sérieux…," ibid., 6.

[56] According to Nematollahy, "While the university with its official neo-Kantianism remained mostly indifferent to the arrival of Nietzsche's work west of the Rhine, the literary establishment largely appropriated Nietzsche as a 'good German' who had rejected his own country in favor of France." "Nietzsche in France," 172.

[57] Ellis traces it back at least to the beginning of the Third Republic. Katharine Ellis, *Interpreting the Musical Past: Early Music in Nineteenth-Century France* (New York, Oxford: Oxford University Press, 2005), 116, 142–143.

[58] Jean Cocteau, *Le coq et l'arlequin: Notes autour de la musique* (Paris: Ed. de la Sirène, 1918). On the impact of this essay, see Jane Fulcher, *The Composer as Intellectual: Music and Ideology in France 1914–1940* (New York: Oxford University Press, 2005), 162–167. Fulcher describes Nietzsche as the forerunner of a wartime anti-German rhetoric epitomized in Cocteau, but fails to account for the latter's pre-war antecedents, such as Stoecklin.

[59] The Italian painter Giorgio de Chirico, whose Paris exhibitions in the early 1910s elicited critical attempts to appropriate his work as "French," embraced Nietzsche's Mediterranean, anti-German rhetoric before the First World War. Ara H. Merjian, "'Il faut méditerraniser la peinture': Giorgio de Chirico's Metaphysical Painting, Nietzsche, and the 'Obscurity of Light,'" *California Italian Studies Journal* 1, no. 1 (2010).

[60] "race"; "réfléchi"; "vie intérieure et à la contemplation"; "l'Allemagne a-t-elle inventé le subjectivisme." Paul de Stoecklin, "L'esthétique allemande," *Le courrier musical* (January 1909).

than beautiful."⁶¹ These ideas anticipated views of German romanticism as being too sentimental and removed from French Enlightened ideals of beauty and order, which became widespread during the War.⁶² Stoecklin distinguishes between the "reflective" (réfléchie) and "reasoning" (raisonneuse) nature of the German and French "soul" (âme), or between German "sentimentality" (sentimentalité) and French "feeling" (sentiment). He turns more overtly anti-German when he takes issue with symbolism, which, in line with Maurras and Action Française,⁶³ he describes as "the great wound of German art," "the foolish chimera of integral art"; or with "Wagner's dramas, in which useless and cold abstractions, vacuous and pompous daydreaming hinder the development of action and sometimes chill and kill life!"⁶⁴ Stoecklin censures German cultural imperialism, describing the Germans as "the most jingoistic people on earth," whose "idealism is a Pan-Germanism without a purpose," a form of "intransigent nationalism"; they "dream of the moral conquest of the world" and "feel themselves to be superior to the rest of the world."⁶⁵

It seems ironic that Stoecklin should draw on ideas that, even though already widespread among French intellectuals, ultimately stem from nineteenth-century German aesthetics. More particularly, he takes on Schopenhauer's idealization of music as a "sublimation of emotions," or Herder's argument that in music "the whole soul of a people is contemplated."⁶⁶ However, Stoecklin acknowledges that the main source behind his thoughts is Germaine de Staël's essay *De l'Allemagne* (1810).⁶⁷ Staël wrote her essay after returning from one of her trips around Germany (1807–1808), during the exile to which Napoléon condemned her. Unlike Stoecklin, Staël did not intend to vilify German culture or glorify France. However, *De l'Allemagne* presents some of the key ingredients with which to elaborate a dichotomous distinction between German and French culture that works to the

---

⁶¹ "né d'une théorie"; "manque de spontanéité"; "traduit des idées plutôt que des émotions, qu'il recherche l'expression plutôt que la beauté." Ibid.

⁶² Scott Messing, *Neoclassicism in Music: From the Genesis of the Concept Through the Schoenberg Stravinsky Polemic* (Ann Arbor, MI: UMI Research Press, 1988), 75.

⁶³ Nematollahy, "Nietzsche in France," 176.

⁶⁴ "la grande plaie de l'art germanique"; "la folle chimère de l'art intégral"; "les drames de Wagner, dans lesquels d'inutiles et froides abstractions, de vides et pompeuses rêvasseries, entravent incessamment l'action, refroidissent et éteignent parfois la vie!" Stoecklin, "L'esthétique allemande." Stoecklin does not mention French symbolism, but one must assume that he implicitly regards it as a Germanization of French art.

⁶⁵ "le plus chauvin des peuples de la terre"; "son idéalisme est du pangermanisme sans objet pratique"; "un nationalisme intransigeant"; "ils rêvent la conquête morale du monde"; "il se sent supérieur au reste de la terre." Ibid.

⁶⁶ "mise en valeur d'émotions"; "l'âme entière d'un peuple se contemple." Ibid. On Schopenhauer's and Herder's aesthetics see Carl Dahlhaus, *Between Romanticism and Modernism: Four Studies in the Music of the Later Nineteenth Century* (Berkeley: University of California Press, 1980), 28–31, 80–90; Dahlhaus, *Nineteenth-Century Music* (Berkeley: University of California Press, 1989), 88–96, 35–40.

⁶⁷ Germaine de Staël, *De l'Allemagne* (Paris: Charpentier, 1839).

benefit of the latter. She classifies European nations in three categories, namely, Latin (France, Italy, Spain and Portugal), Germanic (Germany, Switzerland, England, Sweden, Denmark and Holland) and Slavonic (Poland and Russia)[68]; she argues that Latin nations have been more "formerly civilised than the others," since they experienced the "establishment of Christianity"[69]; and concludes that French and Germans occupy "two ends of the moral chain, given that the former consider the external objects to be the origin of all ideas, whereas the latter, take their ideas as the basis of all impressions."[70] But Staël's portrayal of Germany is far from depreciative or dismissive. Indeed, in the second chapter (pp. 17–27), which Staël devotes to analyzing "the habits and character of Germans," she establishes a balance between values she deems positive—such as "self-abnegation" (p. 18), "sincerity, fidelity" and "honesty," "power of work and reflection" of a "literary and philosophical" nature (p. 19), a zeal to cultivate the "intimacy of life" and the "poetry of the soul" (p. 20), "politeness" (p. 22), "justice," "equality" (p. 25) and "obedience" (p. 26)—and values she regards as being negative, such as "slowness," "rude manners" (p. 20), military inefficiency (pp. 22 and 24), an excessive fondness for drinking and smoking (p. 23), "imagination" (p. 24), individualism, a lack of social cohesion (p. 24), indifference toward "freedom" (p. 25), a lack of "skilfullness" (p. 26) and excessive "speculation" (p. 26).[71]

In his second contribution to *Le courrier musical*, Stoecklin acridly vilified the music of Richard Strauss.[72] The title of his article, "Chand d'Musique," parodies *Chand d'habits* (Folies Bergères, 1896), a pantomime by Catulle Mendès, one of Wagner's foremost champions in France and the author of the first book-length biography of Wagner in French.[73] "Chand d'habits" is the "marchand d'habits" or "chifonnier," the ragman or junkman who symbolized the urban intellectual in France since the 1830s. Like the "chifonnier," who recycles clothes, the intellectual "gives back to society what it has previously discarded" while he suffers from discrimination.[74] The meaning behind Stoecklin's title is not fully clear. It may obliquely refer to Mendès's Wagnerian penchant, or to Richard Strauss, the producer of "cheap junk

---

[68] Ibid., 9.

[69] "plus anciennement civilisées que les autres"; "établissement du christianisme." Ibid., 9.

[70] "deux extrémités de la chaine morale, puisque les uns considèrent les objets extérieurs comme le mobile de toutes les idées, et les autres, les idées comme le mobile de toutes les impressions." Ibid., 11.

[71] "abnégation de soi-même"; "sincérité"; "fidélité"; "honnêteté"; "puissance du travail et de la réflexion"; "littéraire et philosophique"; "vie intime"; "poésie de l'âme"; "politesse"; "justice"; "égalité"; "obédience"; "lenteur"; "formes grossières"; "imagination"; "liberté"; "habileté"; "spéculations."

[72] Paul de Stoecklin, "Chand d'musique," *Le courrier musical* (April 1909).

[73] Catulle Mendès, *Richard Wagner* (Paris, 1886).

[74] "recupera para la sociedad lo que ésta última previamente ha desechado," Dorde Cuvardic García, "El trapero: El otro marginal en la historia de la literatura y de la cultura popular," *Káñina Revista de artes y letras de la Universidad de Costa Rica* 31, no. 1 (2006): 218. In nineteenth-century France, the "chand d'habits" found his way to the works of Baudelaire, Manet, and Daumier, among others. Mendès's pantomime follows the widespread

merchandise," who only "wants […] to earn money," "the cause of his phenomenal success."[75] Stoecklin molds Strauss in contradistinction to notions of French music. He argues that Strauss is attracted by the sheer "appearance" and the "bluff" of "virtuosity," rather than its "brilliant side."[76] He argues that Strauss's language "becomes exaggerated, his polyphony turns inordinately complicated, his orchestra becomes incessantly enriched, loaded with affectation, ugly, it glows."[77] Last, Stoecklin blames Strauss's influence for having "obnoxiously destroyed the sincere work of a young French composer,"[78] an ambiguous contention that either refers to a particular case or to a whole generation of young composers.

In his third contribution to *Le courrier musical* that year ("Le germanisme et la musique"), Stoecklin tried to demonstrate that French intellectuals and artists had surpassed the greatest hallmarks of German culture.[79] He contended that Hegel's "indigestible, heavy and pretentious hodgepodge […] has become humanised, purified, mature" once it was "passed through the Latin filter"; then he describes idealism as a form of "pan-Germanism devoid of any purpose in real life."[80] Last, he dwells on the notion that Germans are "serious" and "grave," and conceive of art as a "religion whose priesthood they exercise with unction,"[81] an idea reminiscent of de Staël's contention that a moral basis underpins all the judgments and acts of the German people.[82]

Stoecklin attempts to undermine the notion of a continued German musical tradition, or to put it in his own words, "that miracle of German music, one and indivisible, which suddenly starts with J. S. Bach and carries on to the infinite through Händel, Haydn, Mozart, Schubert, Weber."[83] He argues that, because "Bach is not a first-rank star," Handel "is dazzled by the Italian sunshine" and

---

criminal version of the Pierrot myth, from the Commedia dell'Arte, carried out by the mime actor Jean-Gaspard Deburau (1796–1846) in *The Ol' Clo's Man* (1842), and revived by Théophile Gautier at the end of the century. In Mendès's *Chand d'habits*, the title character dies at the hands of Pierrot, who tries to overcome his poverty and lack of self-esteem by stealing the former's possessions and killing him. Théophile Gautier, "Shakespeare aux Funambules," in *L'art moderne* (Paris: Charpentier, 1856), 167–179.

[75] "marchandise de pacotille"; "veut […] gagner de l'argent"; "la cause essentielle de son succès phénoménal." Stoecklin, "Chand d'musique."

[76] "De plus en plus la virtuosité l'attire et dans la virtuosité, non le côté brillant qui a son attrait en soi, mais le résultat, le bluff." Ibid.

[77] "Son écriture s'exagère, sa polyphonie se complique démesurément, son orchestre s'enrichit sans cesse, s'alourdit de nouvelles recherches, s'enlaidit, rutile." Ibid.

[78] "d'avoir odieusement détruit l'œuvre sincère d'un jeune compositeur français." Ibid.

[79] Paul de Stoecklin, "Le germanisme et la musique," *Le courrier musical* (November 1909).

[80] "le fatras indigeste, lourd et prétentieux"; "s'est humanisée, épurée, mûrie"; "en passant au crible latin." Stoecklin, "Le germanisme et la musique"; "c'est le pangermanisme sans objet dans la vie pratique." Ibid.

[81] "sérieux"; "grave"; "religion dont il exerce le sacerdoce avec onction."

[82] Staël, *De l'Allemagne*, 19.

[83] "ce miracle de la musique allemande une et indivisible commençant soudainement avec J.-S. Bach et se continuant à l'infini par Haendel, Haydn, Mozart, Schubert, Weber." Ibid.

"the other Germans are Italians," "if there is such a thing as a German music it does not really begin until Haydn and Mozart, being continued by Beethoven after whom it suffers a new halt."[84] Hence, he concludes that "between Bach and Wagner, only Beethoven counts."[85] In other words, he argues that German music consists of a few names scattered over history, instead of a proper national tradition. Furthermore, he couches descriptions of their music in the rhetoric of the "Latin race." He argues that Bach's sons

> are the first to abandon the paternal traditions in order to Italianise themselves; that is, to make a lively art, an art that was needed in their time, an art that belongs to a society which one may describe as exquisite, subtle, refined, sentimental, sometimes tearful, rational, fond of elegance, clarity, of forms which are fixed but not rigid, in good taste, elegant, proper, and which does not show arrogance or affectation.[86]

Stoecklin construes Italian, Latin and, by extension, French music as a counter-portrait of his bigoted notions of German music. Adjectives such as "exquisite," "subtle," "refined" and "sentimental" stand in opposition to Stoecklin's conception of German music as being inordinately expressive and marked by affectation; he opposes "rationality" or "clarity" to alleged German subjectivism and obscure inwardness. Furthermore, the mention of "forms which are fixed but not rigid" reads like an oblique critique of the formalism attributed to the Schola Cantorum and the German canon.

Stoecklin's contributions to *Le courrier musical* during 1909 are a representative example of the critical atmosphere and discursive framework that Collet relied upon. Anti-German rhetorical strategies rubbed off smoothly on reviews of Spanish music, since Spain became the target of French propaganda. This phenomenon can be observed in Stoecklin's review of a performance by Enrique Granados, which he characterized as being marked by "sobriety" and "discretion," and showing "no signs of bad taste or useless feats, always staying musical."[87]

---

[84] "Bach n'est pas une étoile de première grandeur"; "est ébloui par le soleil italien"; "Les autres Allemands sont de Italiens"; "S'il y a une musique allemande, elle ne commence réellement qu'à Haydn et à Mozart, se continuant par Beethoven et avec lui nouvel arrêt." Ibid.

[85] "il n'y a, entre Bach et Wagner, que Beethoven qui compte!" Ibid.

[86] "sont les premier à abandonner les traditions paternelles pour s'italianiser, c'est à dire pour faire de l'art vivant, de l'art dont leur époque avait besoin, un art de société, d'une société exquise, subtile, raffinée, sentimentale, larmoyante à ses heures, raisonnante pourtant et raisonneuse, amoureuse d'élégance, de clarté, de formes arrêtées sans dureté, de bon goût, de bon ton, de bienséance, sans morgue ni raideur." Ibid.

[87] "un admirable pianiste qui ne tape pas, qui joue avec sobriété, discrétion, sans mauvais goût, sans tours de forces inutiles, demeurant toujours musical." Paul de Stoecklin, "Salle Pleyel. MM. Granados et Jacques Thibaud," *Le courrier musical* (June 1909).

Since the program was also made up of Mozart and Franck, Stoecklin may have regarded Granados's performance as an example of the "Latin filter" discussed above.

Collet and Postwar Propaganda

Following the First World War, the building of a new order in France was the opportunity to redefine certain aspects of how French identity was publicly and collectively constructed. Most intellectuals, artists and musicians aimed their cultural production at showing the world a fully revitalized France, one reemerging victorious and triumphant after the War. The War had led to a rhetorical and ideological radicalization of anti-German conceptions of French music, as became notorious, among many publications, in Jean Cocteau's anti-German and xenophobic pamphlet *Le coq et l'arlequin*.[88] In that book, Cocteau drew on prewar discourses on French identity and established what would become the basis of the anti-German aesthetics of neoclassicism (although he took on an anti-Russian and xenophobic stance that most in his circle would disagree with).[89] Since its publication, this text attracted much attention due to its rhetorical radicalism, as well as Cocteau's prominence, which was based on his direct influence on Les Six and his multiple connections with the musical and artistic avant-garde establishment. One could argue, however, that *Le coq et l'arlequin* represents hardly more than a rather personal, but in any case individual, contribution to a general state of affairs, manifest in a host of postwar publications. To take just one example, during the War Georges Jean-Aubry published his collection of essays *La musique française d'aujourd'hui* (1916), which, in many ways, anticipates Cocteau's more celebrated essay. With good reason, Jean-Aubry defined himself as one of the keenest supporters of Spanish music abroad. He organized a concert of Spanish music in his natal Le Havre in 1910, in which Falla performed his *Cuatro piezas españolas* for piano.[90] Furthermore, he wrote on Spanish music in his monograph *La musique et les nations* (1922), where he grounded differences in national musical styles on notions of race, thus reflecting a prevailing anxiety in his time.[91] He held a close relationship with Falla, Turina and Les Apaches, and played a key role in spreading Spanish music in postwar London from his position as the editor of the music journal *The Chesterian* between

---

[88] Cocteau, *Le coq et l'arlequin*.
[89] Fulcher, *The Composer as Intellectual*, 162–167.
[90] Georges Jean-Aubry: "Le Havre. Un concert espagnol." *Revue musicale SIM*, December 15, 1910.
[91] Georges Jean-Aubry, *La musique et les nations* (Paris: Éditions de la Sirène, 1922).

1919 and 1923. He was also a poet and translator of Joseph Conrad and, as we will see in Chapter 6, of Falla's libretto for *El retablo de Maese Pedro*.[92]

In *La musique française d'aujourd'hui*, Jean-Aubry presented a collection of essays animated by a ferocious anti-German character. In the introductory essay "Musique française et musique allemande," he groups musical styles according to wartime military alliances and therefore opposes French and Russian music to German music.[93] Interestingly, he added Spanish music, together with English, Italian and Hungarian, to the list of "neutral" but anti-German styles grouped around France, which "holds in itself the moral direction of the world" and represents the "very soul of the fight."[94] Moreover, he argued that "European music would not have retreated a single step should the music of Strauss or Mahler be suppressed; it is easy to feel what would be missed in our musical vocabulary if we did not have a Rimsky, Albéniz or Debussy."[95] His belligerent tone becomes even more conspicuous when he grounds French cultural hegemony on the prediction of a military victory: "a French military victory will earn us a deserved pride and will project us onto the world."[96] Most of this chapter is devoted to arguing that German music is dead after Wagner and that it is now France's turn to show the world a new musical path.[97] This stance clearly recalls the philosophy that prevailed in the Schola Cantorum, where Wagner, although a fundamental element in their curriculum, was regarded as the last valid element of the German tradition. Furthermore, it reminds one of Maurras's postulation of an anti-Teutonic cultural entente and, to some extent, anticipates the latter's article "Les forces latines" by including Spain in it.

By aligning Spanish music with its French and Russian counterparts, and situating it against German music, Jean-Aubry seems to have laid the ground for Collet's first postwar publication, "L'internationalisme musical" (1919).[98] This article shows how much his anti-German attitude was radicalized and exacerbated during the war. Indeed, despite declaring himself a "pacifist," Collet embraced "the most ferocious nationalism."[99] The imprint of Maurras and Jean-Aubry is

---

[92] Anon. "Jean-Aubry, Georges," *Dictionnaire de biographie française, vol. 18* (Paris: Librairie Letouzey et Ané, 1994) 584–585.

[93] Georges Jean-Aubry, "Musique française et musique allemande," in Georges Jean-Aubry, *La musique française d'aujourd'hui* (Paris: Perrin et cie, 1916), 1–18. For a detailed analysis of this chapter see David Bancroft, "Two Pleas for a French, French Music," *Music and Letters*, no. 48 (July 1967) 251–258; Hess, *Manuel de Falla and Modernism*, 64–67.

[94] "concentre sur soi la direction morale du monde" "l'âme même de la lutte." Jean-Aubry, *La musique française d'aujourd'hui*, 4, 12.

[95] "La musique européenne n'aurait pas reculé d'un pas si on en supprimait la production straussiste ou mahlérienne; il est aisé de sentir ce qui manquerait à notre vocabulaire musical si nous n'avions eu ni Rimsky, ni Albeniz, ni Debussy." Ibid., 12.

[96] "La victoire des armes françaises nous fera de justes orgueils et nous composera dans le monde." Ibid., 16.

[97] Ibid., 4–9.

[98] Henri Collet, "L'internationalisme musical," *Le courrier musical* (December 1919).

[99] "pacifiste"; "nationalisme le plus farouche." Collet, "L'internationalisme musical."

manifest in Collet's postulation of an anti-German cultural entente. He refers to how, after attending a recital of Russian music, he realized that "Mussorgsky had won...after the war"[100]; he sets out to undermine the two most prominent German music publishers, Breitkopf und Härtel and Peters[101]; and he builds French hegemony over the ashes of a military, morally and culturally defeated Germany: "Just as Leipzig was the headquarters of the *Internationalmusikgesellschaft* [...] Paris could become the metropolis of musical internationalism."[102] He finished his article by situating Spanish and French composers "at the head of contemporary European music," since "their audacious endeavors constitute a precious lesson for musicians from all over the world."[103] Perhaps for the first time, a French critic disassociated "Spanish music" from subaltern conceptions and granted it a significant position in the European arena.

Again, Collet's attitude reflected a more general state of mind. The celebration of the Semaine espagnole at the Petit Palais in February 1919 testifies to how the Latin Union had established itself as a dominant political discourse after the War that could, eventually, accommodate Spain. The Semaine gathered French and Spanish speakers, and was aimed at fostering exchange of students between both countries, as well as appeasing diplomatic tensions over control of Morocco.[104] During the closing ceremony, the future president Paul Deschanel called for a "Latin alliance," aimed at revitalizing the Pactes de Famille between the French and Spanish branches of the Bourbon dynasty—otherwise known as the treatises of El Escorial (1733), Fontainebleau (1743) and Paris (1761).[105] By way of these pacts, both crowns tried to curb the imperialist ambitions of England and Austria, and more particularly Spain sought

---

[100] "Moussorgski avait vaincu...après la guerre...." Ibid.

[101] Fulcher describes the campaign carried out by the French editor Durand, with the support of French composers, in order to finish with the dominion of Breitkopf and Peters. Fulcher, *The Composer as Intellectual*, 42–45.

[102] "De même que Leipzig fut le siège de la 'Internationalmusikgessellschaft' [...] de même Paris pourrait devenir la métropole de l'internationalisme musical." Collet, "L'internationalisme."

[103] "L'Espagne et la France vont à la tête de l'Europe musicale contemporaine, leurs audacieux efforts son un enseignement précieux pour tous les musiciens de l'univers." Ibid.

[104] During 1901 and 1904, tension escalated among European powers over control of Morocco and, in 1904, forced by England, France had to hand part of the protectorate to Spain. Since then, France tried to recover it, and revived the former diplomatic tension by raising the subject during the 1919 peace conference. Frederick J. Thorpe, "The French Press and the Franco-Spanish Convention of 1904 on Morocco," *French Colonial History* 3, no. 1 (2003): 157–173. Germain Ayache, "Les rélations franco-espagnoles pendant la guerre du Rif," in *Españoles y franceses en la primera mitad del siglo XX* (Madrid: CSIC, 1986), 287–293; Paul Aubert, "L'influence idéologique et politique de la France dans l'Espagne de la fin du XIXe siècle à la Première Guerre Mondiale (1875–1918)," in *España y Francia en la Comunidad Europea*, ed. Jean-Pierre Étienvre and José Ramón Urquijo Goitia (Madrid: CSIC, 1989), 58–64. Jover Zamora, *España en la política internacional*, 171.

[105] Niño Rodríguez, *Cultura y diplomacia*, 366. Indeed, some French politicians and press sectors evoked the *Pactes de famille* during the diplomatic conflict (1901–1904) in order to reach consensus with their Spanish counterparts. Thorpe, "The French Press," 166, 170.

to extend its control of Naples and Sicily.[106] The Pactes brought about a period of good diplomatic relationships between the two countries, which came to a temporary break with the 1789 Revolution.[107] In the postwar context, the revitalization of these pacts, even if just a rhetorical strategy, was surely aimed at reinforcing the cultural divide between Latin and Nordic nations. Deschanel's discourse at the end of the Semaine shows that, during the War, discourses on the Latin race became the official doctrine of anti-German propaganda. On July 14, 1921, Alexandre Millerand, the president of the French Republic, celebrated the installation, in the gardens of the Palais Royal, of a monument to the Génie Latin, sponsored by the patriotic Ligue de la Fraternité Latine, which had been founded during the War. The monument was offered "to all the nations in the Latin fraternity" and displayed a gigantic athlete holding a small Minerva in his right hand. The statue prefigures the Italian fascist statuary of the 1930s—according to Jean-Marc Delaunay—and thus aligned itself with Maurras's pre-fascist literary aesthetics and ideology.[108]

I propose, therefore, to regard Collet's postwar writings as an exacerbation of his prewar anti-German publications and a reflection of a more general state of affairs, epitomized in the writings of Jean-Aubry and, to a lesser extent, Cocteau. Rather than inventing a new form of propaganda, Collet endeavored to situate "Spanish music" in the preexistent anti-German discursive mold, as can be observed in his first postwar monograph, *Albéniz et Granados* (1926).[109] In his introductory statement of purpose, Collet manifests that he

> would like, in the pages that follow, to make more accessible to the lovers of good music, the works of Albéniz and Granados, which the theoreticians of an impeccable and insensitive construction and architecture will laugh about, but which will seduce those who consider that music is a song, and that one signs feelings rather than thoughts.[110]

Collet describes "Spanish music" as being emotional and unconstrained, and opposes it to a rational, theoretical and mechanical music that, most likely, is German.

---

[106] María Victoria López-Cordón Cortezo, "Pacte de famille our intérêts d'état? La monarchie française et la diplomatie espagnole du XVIIIe siècle," in *La présence des Bourbons en Europe: XVIe–XXIe siècle*, ed. Lucien Bély (Paris: Presses Univ. de France, 2003), 185–206.

[107] Jover Zamora, *España en la política internacional*, 78–79.

[108] Jean-Marc Delaunay, *Des palais en Espagne: l'Ecole des hautes études hispaniques et la Casa de Velázquez au coeur des relations franco-espagnoles du XXe siècle (1898–1979)* (Madrid: Casa de Velázquez, 1994), 181.

[109] Henri Collet, *Albéniz et Granados* (Paris: Felix Alcan, 1926).

[110] "Nous voudrions, par les pages qui vont suivre, rendre plus accessible aux amateurs de bonne musique, cette œuvre d'Albéniz et de Granados dont souriront les théoriciens d'une construction, d'une architecture acoustique impeccable et insensible, mais qui séduira toujours ceux qui considèrent que la musique n'est qu'un chant et que l'on chante comme l'on sent et non comme l'on pense, selon son cœur et non selon sa raison," Collet, *Albéniz et Granados*, 6.

Collet devotes most of his book to construing the music of Albéniz and Granados as anti-German cultural artefacts. His view of Granados seems encapsulated in this excerpt:

> A Latin musician. That seems to be the adjective which best suits the author of the *Canciones amatorias*, which display such a supple and pure line.
>
> Granados has been compared to Chopin, Schumann or Grieg. However, his romanticism is rather personal, creole by its melodic nonchalance, Catalan by the rhythmic contrast. He has incessantly progressed towards a greater suppleness, subtleness and expression.[111]

Collet defines Granados as a Latin musician and uses adjectives such as "supple," "pure" and "subtle" to describe his music. He also uses the expression "creole" to refer to the origin of his father, born in Cuba when it still was a Spanish colony.[112] Collet's reference to Granados's Catalan background holds more substantial implications, especially if seen in connection with the "Latin race." One should remember, however, that the Catalan intellectual Eugeni d'Ors responded to the influence of Maurras's nationalism and regionalism by spearheading a Catalan nationalist movement called *noucentisme*, which advocated a Mediterranean Classicism and situated Catalonia at its head.[113]

In his lengthy analysis of Albéniz's life and works, Collet displays a wide range of rhetorical and cultural strategies. He describes Albéniz as "an essentially meridional musician," whose music embodies "the qualities of the race that he belongs to," namely "vivacity, color, harmony, clarity and elegance."[114] Just as in the obituary, Collet renders anti-German attitudes inherent to Spanish "race," so as to dissimulate the effect of French propaganda. Collet compares Albéniz's music to a "'Moorish art,' an improvisatory art in which a pedigreed refinement replaces the necessity experienced by the serious Franc, Saxon and German

---

[111] "Un musicien latin. Tel semble être l'épithète qui convient le mieux à l'auteur des Canciones Amatorias, d'une ligne si souple et si pure. On a comparé Granados à Chopin, à Schumann, à Grieg. Mais son romantisme est bien à lui, créole par la nonchalance mélodique, catalan par le contraste rythmique. Il a progressé sans cesse vers plus de souplesse, de subtilité, d'expression." Ibid., 201.

[112] Mason complained that "both French and Spanish writers seem to have made a curious error and speak of the 'creole nonchalance' of style which he is supposed to have inherited from his father's people." A. L. Mason, "Enrique Granados (1867–1916)," *Music & Letters* 14, no. 3 (July 1, 1933): 232.

[113] Eduardo González Calleja, "Noucentisme, Catalanisme et arc latin," *La pensée de midi*, no. 1 (2000): 44–51; Hess, *Manuel de Falla and Modernism*, 9, 75–76; González Cuevas, "La recepción del pensamiento maurrasiano en España," 352.

[114] "un musicien essentiellement méridional"; "qualités de la race à laquelle il appartient"; "la vivacité, le coloris, l'harmonie, la clarté et l'élégance…" Collet, *Albéniz et Granados*, 57.

artists to 'constantly polish their work.'"[115] Associations with "Moorish art" push Albéniz's music toward the South, away from German music; however, they also evoke otherness and drive Spanish music toward the margins of "civilisation."[116] In order to compensate for this effect, he characterizes Albéniz by a "powerful autodidactic individualism, fertilized by a fresh genius which is Latin and Oriental at the same time, and which links him to other incomparable personalities of Spanish art and literature, namely, Cervantes or El Greco."[117] References to Cervantes and the Cretan painter El Greco (1541–1614)—a resident in Spain—serve to inscribe Albéniz in the Spanish literary and artistic canon that gained momentum at the turn of the century, among the mostly anti-German strands of Spanish and French nationalism. Another prominent intellectual in Action Française, Maurice Barrès, published a biographical essay on this painter in 1913.[118] With that same purpose, Collet compares Albéniz with "Don Quixote" by virtue of his "disregard for success or benefits,"[119] the marks of German greed that Stoecklin saw in Richard Strauss.

Certain aspects of Albéniz's life did not offer themselves so readily as the basis for anti-German propaganda, such as his involvement in the Schola Cantorum—given that this institution was greatly focused on Wagner and the German romantic canon, in spite of entertaining tight connections with Action Française and embracing its anti-Germanism.[120] Collet tackled this setback by vindicating Albéniz's early works, which, according to him, mostly consisted of short salon pieces marked by "an improvisatory character."[121] This stance entailed Collet's subverting widespread assessments of Albéniz's output as one that constantly progressed toward more ambitious goals. Collet takes issue with Albéniz's London operas, which "Wagnerian chromaticism contaminates—like a disease."[122]

---

[115] "art 'mauresque', art d'improvisateur chez qui la finesse racée supplée à la nécessité qu'éprouvent les lourds artistes francs, saxons, ou germains, de 'remettre leur ouvrage vingt fois sur le métier.'" Ibid., 11.

[116] Collet had already presented a similar view, applied to modern Spanish in general, in a previous article, in which he defined the "base de l'édifice sonore qu'érige le compositeur espagnol moderne." He found "çà et là, un accent qui mord ou une inflexion rauque nous rappellent que l'Afrique est proche, voilà qui peut forcer notre imagination à dépasser les limites de l'Occident et à se perdre sous les arceaux à boucles des avenues mauresques." Henri Collet, "La musique espagnole moderne," *Le courrier musical* (May 1918).

[117] "individualisme puissant d'autodidacte qui, fécondé par un frais génie à la fois latin et oriental, l'apparente à ces autres personnalités non pareilles de l'art ou de la littérature espagnols: à un Cervantès ou à un Greco." Ibid., 21.

[118] Fox, "Spain as Castile," 21–36; Fox, *La invención de España: Nacionalismo liberal e identidad nacional* (Madrid: Cátedra, 1997), 157–161. Barrès's reading of El Greco will be discussed in Chapter 2.

[119] "insouciance du succès et du gain." Ibid., 11.

[120] Fulcher, *French Cultural Politics*, 31–35.

[121] "Ainsi, Albéniz reconnaissait ce caractère d'improvisation que revêt, jusqu'à la Vega, chacune de ces célèbres pièces pour piano." Collet, *Albéniz et Granados*, 37.

[122] "le chromatisme wagnérien contamine—comme une maladie." Ibid., 92. Albéniz lived in London intermittently during the 1890s and composed several operas under commission from the wealthy solicitor and

He argues that youthful compositions for the piano, such as *Suite espagnole* (1886) and *Chants d'Espagne* (1891–1894) "still enjoy today, among the enthusiast crowds, a success which neither *La Vega* nor *Ibéria* have ever equalled."[123] Collet prefers Albéniz "with his youthful weaknesses, his bohemian independence, his boundless love for life!" since, at that time, he "was a great nomad and endured all sort of errant vicissitudes."[124] Collet underscores Albéniz's aesthetic independence by drawing on the mythologizing of gypsy freedom—here, "bohemian"—carried out by Alphonse Daudet, Victor Hugo and others in the previous century.[125] The pervasiveness of the "bohemian" and "nomad" tropes in the historiography about Albéniz has been responsible for exaggerated and distorted accounts of his peripatetic youth.[126] In this and other aspects, Collet's *Albéniz et Granados* proved to be an influential work in the way both composers were understood in the years to come.[127]

Collet's recount has a tone of resignation when he turns to commenting on Albéniz's years in the Schola Cantorum. He narrates how, once in Paris, Albéniz met Ernest Chausson, who introduced him to Charles Bordes, director of the Schola, as well as Fauré, Dukas and d'Indy, whom he describes as the "French masters of musical form."[128] He regrets that, in this milieu, Albéniz, "who was born a rhapsodist, came to detest the Russian rhapsodies, such as Rimsky's *Antar*"; "admired […] the architectures of Dukas and d'Indy"; and showed "his dislike for the picturesque masters," such as Chabrier or the Spanish musicologist Felipe Pedrell, whom most Spanish and French musicians regarded as the "father" of Spanish musical nationalism for his influential advocacy of the use of Spanish folklore in musical composition. Collet added that, while at the Schola,

---

amateur poet Francis Money-Coutts: *Henry Clifford* (Barcelona, Liceu, 1895), *Pepita Jiménez* (Barcelona, Liceu, 1896), and *Merlin* (composed between 1897 and 1902), which was to be the first part of a never-completed Arthurian trilogy. Critics and scholars regard these operas as Wagnerian. Clark, *Isaac Albéniz*, 102–108, 109, 125. On *Henry Clifford* and *Merlin*, Collet adds: "Cette ambition wagnérienne d'Albéniz a été fatale à ces deux derniers opéras." *Albéniz et Granados*, 123.

[123] "connaissent encore aujourd'hui, auprès de la foule des amateurs, un succès que ni la Vega ni Ibéria n'ont jamais égalé." Collet, *Albéniz et Granados*, 37.

[124] "avec ses faiblesses de jeune homme, son indépendance bohème, son amour éperdu de la vie!"; "fut le grand nomade et passa par toutes les vicissitudes des errants." Ibid., 29.

[125] Lou Charnon-Deutsch, *The Spanish Gypsy: The History of a European Obsession* (University Park: Pennsylvania State University Press, 2004), 58.

[126] Clark, *Albéniz*, 10–15.

[127] Anon, "Rhapsodie espagnole, Albeniz," *Le guide du concert* (February 1926). The author acknowledges Collet's influence on his view of *Rhapsodie espagnole* (1887), as evinced in the following excerpt: "Cette pièce écrite, comme la plupart des œuvres du compositeur, pour piano, appartient à sa première manière, qui a été souvent fort décriée, mais qui vaut cependant par des qualités de fraîcheur et de spontanéité que l'on ne retrouve plus à un égal degré dans Ibéria, par exemple, où la complication de l'écriture pianistique et harmonique nuit peut-être, dans une certaine mesure, à l'épanchement naturel de la veine mélodique."

[128] "maîtres français de la forme musicale." Collet, *Albéniz et Granados*, 57–58.

Albéniz "never liked Debussy" and "found *Pelléas* unpleasant," and "saved his enthusiasm for *Fervaal, Ariane et Barbe-Bleue*"—that is, the operas of d'Indy and Dukas—"and Fauré's chamber music."[129] Collet depicts Albéniz as "hypnotized by the Société Nationale de Musique," where, under d'Indy's auspices, the Schola students enjoyed a certain favoritism.[130] Collet's Albéniz was "concerned about complicating his own works—such as *Ibéria*—by way of a vain desire to imitate Vincent d'Indy." The result of that "mistake" was that Albéniz "did not manage at all to develop motives, but only to overburden" his music.[131] He concludes, rather abated, that "however it may be, it is in that milieu […] that Isaac Albéniz lived happily ever after."[132]

It seems striking that Collet did not grant Albéniz any aesthetic independence from the Schola, and described him as a sheer "imitator" of d'Indy. However, he depicts Albéniz as a politically free character who opposed the Schola's well-known anti-Dreyfus stance.[133] He recounts that, in this institution, "much was spoken about the Dreyfus affair," but that "Albéniz, naturally 'Dreyfusard,' mourned over the fate of the innocent Jew…and that always finished with a bottle of champagne."[134] In a similar vein, Collet contended that Albéniz used to "ruminate the most philosophical reflections on his name 'Isaac': Sem's race insufflated a soul in him, like so many other Spaniards."[135] Collet seemingly tries to argue that, despite allegedly entertaining Dreyfusard and pro-Semitic

---

[129] "Lui qui état né rhapsode, détestât les rhapsodies russes, telles que l'Antar de Rimsky"; "admirait […] les architectures de MM. Dukas et d'Indy"; "Son dégoût des maîtres pittoresques: Chabrier ou Pedrell était grand"; "il n'aima jamais Debussy. Pelléas lui paraissait désagréable"; "il n'eut de bravos que pour Fervaal, Ariane et Barbe-Bleue ou la musique de chambre de Fauré." Ibid., 58.

[130] "hypnotisé par la Société Nationale." Ibid., 58. Indeed, Albéniz was the first non-French composer to be played at the Société Nationale de Musique since foreign composers were accepted in 1886. During the 1900s he was one of the most played. Michel Duchesneau, *L'avant-garde musicale et ses sociétés à Paris de 1871 à 1939* (Liège: Mardaga, 1997), 22, 150.

[131] "préoccupé de compliquer ses propres ouvrages—tels qu'Ibéria—par un vain désir d'imiter M. Vincent d'Indy. Erreur sans doute, puisqu'ainsi que nous l'établirons, il ne réussit point à developper mais seulement à surcharger…." Collet, *Albéniz et Granados*, 58. Several pages below, however, Collet offered a somewhat more sympathetic view of Albéniz's late style, which marked "la première fois en Europe, depuis le XVIe siècle, que dans le 'concert' international, la voix de Espagne est admise" (p. 105). Furthermore, he stated that "*Iberia*, enfin, établissait l'indiscutable maîtrise du compositeur espagnol" (p. 75). See the impact of Collet's rhetoric in Dumesnil's view on Albéniz: "hypnotisé par la Société Nationale, il s'efforça de compliquer ses propres œuvres pour imiter ses nouveaux maîtres." René Dumesnil, *La musique contemporaine en France*, vol. 2 (Paris: Armand Colin, 1930), 70.

[132] "Quoi qu'il en soit, c'est dans le milieu de la Société Nationale et de la Schola que vécut désormais, et avec joie, Isaac Albéniz." Ibid., 58.

[133] Fulcher, *French Cultural Politics*, 31–35.

[134] "On parlait beaucoup de l'affaire Dreyfus. Albéniz, naturellement 'dreyfusard,' pleurait sur le sort de l'innocent israélite et cela finissait toujours par une bouteille de champagne." Collet, *Albéniz et Granados*, 60.

[135] "ruminer les plus philosophiques réflexions au sujet de son prénom 'Isaac': La race de Sem lui insuffla son âme comme à tant d'autres grands et authentiques Espagnols." Ibid., 87.

allegiances in a hostile environment, Albéniz was conciliatory enough to drink with his political opponents. Collet's attitude suggests that he did not believe in the full communion of aesthetic and political ideals, much as critics and musicians confused them. Collet gives proof of an ability to read beyond created binaries and posits that political independence may act as a surrogate of aesthetic freedom.

Collet's reading of Albéniz therefore reveals a somewhat contradictory attempt to construe Spanish music as an anti-German artifact.[136] In addition, it shows a multicultural and multiethnic conception of Spanish identity, evident in his comparison of Albéniz with a Moor and a Jew. Although Collet strategically imbues these associations with an anti-German character, they undeniably depart from the thinking of Maurras, which otherwise informs most of his political formulations. Furthermore, Collet somehow anticipates the hybrid formulation of Spanish identity and history that historian Américo Castro would uphold, more famously and polemically, in his *España en su historia* (1948)—written in exile from the Franco dictatorship.[137] But Collet's hybrid rendition of Albéniz cannot be considered more seriously than as an opportunistic, ad hoc strategy. Indeed, in an article published in the short-lived, Spanish-language, Paris-based journal *Gaceta musical* two years later, he showed an overtly *scholiste* and anti-Semitic stance.[138] In that article, titled "El porvenir de la Música Española" (The Future of Spanish Music), Collet argued that

> Spain is perhaps the European nation entitled to carry out the most tenacious endeavors in the name of art, and to serenely contribute a new formula, given that it did not experience the manifold troubles which affected the belligerent countries. However, that formula, which must be enriched by the most recent harmonic inventions, must be rooted in the classical Spanish tradition, which is essentially contrapuntal [...] Unfortunately, a portion of [the Spanish musical school] has been influenced by Debussysm, and, in the second place, by French Dadaists, who are neither musicians nor French, but Hebrew and Semitic and, hence, curious about harmonic voluptuousness and shivers.[139]

---

[136] However, my purpose is not so much to reveal who the "real" Collet was, as I do not believe there was one. Instead I shall try to identify how different pressures and conditionings gave shape to his arguments, especially when they contradicted each other.

[137] Aidi, "The Interference of al-Andalus," 70–71; Antonio Cascardi, "Beyond Castro and Maravall: Interpellation, Mimesis, and the Hegemony of Spanish Culture," in *Ideologies of Hispanism*, ed. Mabel Moraña, vol. 30 (Nashville, TN: Vanderbilt University Press, 2005), 141–142.

[138] Henri Collet, "El porvenir de la música española," *La gaceta musical* (May 1, 1928): 18–19.

[139] "España es acaso la nación europea que puede realizar los más tenaces esfuerzos en pro del arte, y darnos con serenidad una fórmula nueva, ya que no experimentó las múltiples inquietudes de los países beligerates.

From the focus on counterpoint to the rejection of what d'Indy variably called "Dreyfusisme artistique," "style mélodique judaïque" or "école Judaïque," this passage encapsulates much of the *scholiste* rhetoric, which was not necessarily a true reflection of the program taught at the Schola.[140] Collet strikingly leaves out Falla from the list of Spanish composers who have brought about the "current Renaissance" of Spanish music. Instead, he mentions Albéniz, Granados, Turina, Esplá, Conrado del Campo and Nin, that is, composers who have shown a *scholiste* or formalistic penchant. This stance matched the *Gaceta*'s aesthetic and political profile. Its chief editor, the Mexican composer Manuel M. Ponce, entertained a sympathy for what Collet would tag the "French masters of form." Already a prominent composer in Mexico, Ponce went to Paris (1925–1932) to train under Paul Dukas in the techniques of fugue and counterpoint, most likely—as Alejandro Madrid argues—"as a way of distancing himself from the social and cultural changes taking place in his country in an attempt to make sense of them"—an explanation that could be arguably applied to Falla's similar venture (1907–1914), as shall be discussed in Chapter 3.[141] The *Gaceta* gives testimony to Ponce's aesthetic penchants, for besides the main bulk of articles on Spanish avant-garde music the journal published dossiers on Dukas and Fauré.[142] "El porvenir" was not Collet's only publication in which he extolled the aesthetics of the Schola, as even a few years after the end of the War he published "Musique et expression," in which he quoted extensively from d'Indy's anti-Semitic *Cours de composition* in order to endorse the use of polyphonic procedures.[143]

French Hegemony in the Latin Union

The works analyzed here show that, since the beginning of the twentieth century, Collet ascribed to "Spanish music" a new place and role in the French intellectual imaginary. More specifically, he imbued "Spanish music" with strongly anti-German

---

Ahora bien: dicha fórmula, enriquecida por las modernísimas invenciones armónicas contemporáneas, ha de tener sus profundas raíces en la tradición clásica española, la cual es esencialmente contrapuntística [...] Desgraciadamente, una porción de ellos se muestra influída por el debussysmo, y luego, por el dadaísmo francés de los que ni son músicos, ni siquiera franceses, sino hebreos o semitas, y, por ende, tan sólo curiosos de voluptuosidades y escalofríos armónicos." Collet, "El porvenir," 18–19.

[140] For the *scholiste* rhetoric see Fulcher, *French Cultural Politics*, 32, 49. For a relativization of the *scholiste* rhetoric and on the teaching of harmony in the Schola see Jann Pasler, "Deconstructing d'Indy, or the Problem of a Composer's Reputation," in *Writing Through Music: Essays on Music, Culture, and Politics* (Oxford and New York: Oxford University Press, 2008), 122–139.

[141] Alejandro Madrid, *Sounds of the Modern Nation: Music, Culture, and Ideas in Post-Revolutionary Mexico* (Philadelphia: Temple University Press, 2008), 86–87.

[142] Although some widely accepted anti-German composers such as Debussy and Ravel were also represented.

[143] Henri Collet, "Musique et expression," *Le courrier musical* (December 1922).

meanings, and cast it as a cultural ally. Thus, he contributed to redeeming Spain from the stigma of exoticism. One aspect of Collet's writings, however, conflicts with the attitude just described. Just as Charles Maurras situated France at the head of the Latin Union, Collet sought to reinforce French cultural hegemony; but he sometimes did so at the expense of "Spanish music." Collet's passion for Spanish culture did not prevent his eventually prioritizing a commitment to French nationalism and, consequently, rendering a subaltern portrayal of Spain. The discursive strategies that he employed deserve close examination.

Collet most frequently resorted to the "noble savage" trope to describe the "Spanish musician." By "savage," I refer to the French category through which the "natives" of the colonies were conceptualized. Like other French cultural inventions, the "savage" was the imaginative product of a centuries-long process aimed at fulfilling a set of pressing functions at "home"; an invention that sought to empower itself through establishment of a dubious scientific basis.[144] There prevailed a twofold conception of the savage in French and European culture since the eighteenth century, namely, the so-called noble savage and what we could conceptualize as the "monstrous," "evil" or "ignoble savage." Although generally associated with Rousseau's *Discourse on the Origin of Inequality Among Men* (1754), the "noble savage" trope dates back to the seventeenth century, even if that very term was not used yet.[145] With the rise of colonialism during the Early Modern Ages, the "noble savage" became a vehicle for critiques of civilization, privileging physical strength over technology, instinct over intellect, and goodwill over knowledge. By contrast, the "ignoble savage" reinforced images of cannibalism and violence in order to present the colonial enterprise under the light of a civilizing mission. Most of the time, the "ignoble savage" trope relied on subaltern constructions of race and ethnicity. Thus, representations of Spain often included highly imaginative depictions of the Spanish gypsy, to whom Spanish intellectuals, in negotiation with their European counterparts, assigned the role of the internal low Other.[146]

Collet imbued the "noble savage" trope with anti-German meanings. In the opening pages of *Albéniz et Granados*, he described the works of these two composers as ones "which the theoreticians of an impeccable and insensitive

---

[144] Terry Jay Ellingson, *The Myth of the Noble Savage* (Berkeley: University of California Press, 2001), 11. On racism and French identity during the Third Republic France see Herman Lebovics, *True France: The Wars over Cultural Identity, 1900–1945* (Ithaca, NY: Cornell University Press, 1992) 12–50.

[145] Ellingson, *The Myth of the Noble Savage*, 1–8. Ellingson argues that Rousseau did not invent or use the concept for the first time.

[146] Lou Charnon-Deutsch, *The Spanish Gypsy*, 179–238; Charnon-Deutsch, "Travels of the Imaginary Spanish Gypsy," in *Constructing Identity in Contemporary Spain: Theoretical Debates and Cultural Practice*, ed. Jo Labanyi (Oxford: Oxford University Press, 2002), 22–40; José F. Colmeiro, "Exorcising Exoticism: 'Carmen' and the Construction of Oriental Spain," *Comparative Literature* 54, no. 2 (April 2002): 127–144.

construction and architecture will laugh about."[147] Collet seeks to undermine German "civilization" by opposing to it a "Spanish musician" who privileges instinct over intellect, knowledge and technique—like the noble savage. In a similar tone, Collet remarks that "Albéniz et Granados [...] were not and could not be impeccable technicians," since "composition responded, in them, to a need for relaxation, an almost sensual distraction rather than a preconceived intention of leaving a strong and durable work to posterity."[148] Thus Collet casts the "Spanish musician" as a nonchalant and almost hedonistic artist, and opposes him to shared notions of the German musician as one who is serious, self-indulgent, proud and vane. In addition, Collet describes the Spanish "savage" composer as one who disregards rules and methods, one who composes "outside of any European precepts of musical composition: did he not ignore the rules of counterpoint and harmony as they were taught in our conservatoires?"[149] Through the use of the "noble savage" trope, Collet sends Spain to the margins of European civilization and casts Spanish culture as subaltern.

Collet's belief in the supremacy of French culture prompts him to lower his demands on Spanish musicians in a patronizing manner. He remarks that "when one wants to assess the construction of *Ibéria*, one must not criticize it from a French point of view. The lack of a sense of time may not be censured on a Spaniard."[150] This passage rests upon perceptions of the "savage" as being oblivious to time constraints and, on that basis, associates technical incapability with a specific cultural background.

Collet's conception of the Spanish musician as a savage manifests itself, perhaps even more conspicuously, in his comments on Granados. Collet remarks that the latter composes "without order or method, but [guided] by an infallible instinct"; and produces a music characterized by "a lack of proportion and balance in the themes and phrases across the different parts, an absence of a tonal plan and a pianistic overburdening."[151] These "technical inferiorities"—Collet argues—find compensation in the skills of an "almost too fastidious engraver"; however, such care for detail "causes Granados to lose sight of the general architecture, to

---

[147] "dont souriront les théoriciens d'une construction, d'une architecture acoustique impeccable et insensible." Collet, *Albéniz et Granados*, 6.

[148] "Albéniz et Granados [...] ne furent point et ne pouvaient être d'impeccables techniciens"; "la composition répondait pour eux à un besoin de délassement, de diversion quasi sensuelle, plutôt qu'au dessein préconçu de léguer à la postérité une œuvre forte et durable." Ibid., 2.

[149] "en dehors de tous les préceptes européens de composition musicale: n'ignorait-il pas les régles du contrepoint et de l'harmonie telles qu'on les enseigne dans nos Conservatoires?" Ibid., 107.

[150] "Quant on veut juger la construction des *Ibéria*, il ne faut pas la critiquer du point de vue français. Le manque de sens du temps n'est point censurable en tant qu'espagnol..." Ibid., 166.

[151] "sans ordre et sans méthode, mais par un infaillible instinct," *ibid*. 195; "le manque de proportion, d'équilibre des thèmes et des phrases dans les diverses parties, l'absence de plan tonal, et la surcharge pianistique," *ibid*. 201–202.

deliberately sacrifice form to ornament."¹⁵² This description reveals an interesting dualism; one the one hand, it casts Granados as an unskilled and whimsical composer whose fondness for detail blinds him to other aspects of musical discourse; on the other hand, it builds upon the prevailing notion that German composers are driven by "architectural" concerns. Thus, Collet predicates the alleged anti-German qualities of Granados's music upon a critique of his technical skills. In other words, he conceives of the "Spanish musician" as an anti-German "noble savage" and, by the same token, identifies Germany with pejorative notions of "civilization."

Collet's construction of French hegemony turns more pernicious when he associates technical shortfalls with racial difference. True, comparisons of Albéniz with a "Moor" or a "Jew" gain positive, anti-German overtones in the quotations above.¹⁵³ However, in the following comment on "Jerez," from *Ibéria*, racial otherness substantiates a discourse of technical incompetence:

> Its acoustic arabesques resemble the blue volutes produced by the hookah smoke, or the stuccoes in Arab palaces. The chords can only be analyzed with reference to an extraordinarily free counterpoint. Otherwise, there is no brusqueness here. The superposition of seconds, however, render the sounds vague.¹⁵⁴

Eccentricities such as the "freedom" of counterpoint, or deficiencies such as the "vagueness" of sounds, find a deterministic explanation in the trope of racial otherness.

By couching an enthusiastic endorsement of Spanish music in the rhetoric of the widely accepted anti-German propaganda, and satisfying cultural anxieties over cultural miscegenation in France, Collet established a discursive template on Spanish music whose influence became noticeable in the decades to come. More than half a century later, in *La présence lointaine* (1983), the French philosopher Vladimir Jankélévitch offered an image of Albéniz that reproduced, to a striking extent, the racist stereotypes and the noble savage trope that Collet had used so efficiently. Jankélévitch wrote about "Albéniz's nonchalance, which rather is an Oriental laziness, an African indolence," and argued that Albéniz "is

---

¹⁵² "ciseleur presque trop minutieux"; "conduit Granados à perdre de vue l'architecture générale, à sacrifier délibérément la forme à l'ornement." Ibid., 202.

¹⁵³ And in other passages: "Albéniz est véritablement More par instinct, sinon comme il vient d'être précisé, par la volonté qui sera celle des musiciens à venir." Ibid., 158. Interestingly, he did not use the more expected trope of the "Gypsy," as he probably intended to emphasise a non-Spanish, non-European, African otherness.

¹⁵⁴ "Nous voguons en rêve avec le musicien vers des contrées lointaines. Ses arabesques sonores ressemblent aux volutes bleues des fumées des narghilés, ou aux décorations en stuc des palais arabes. Les accords ne sont plus analysables qu'en fonction des courbes d'un contrepoint extraordinairement libre. Au reste, ici, nulle brusquerie. Mais les superposition de secondes mêmes rendent des sons flous." Ibid., 175.

not an erudite […] but contents himself (if we can say that!) with being Spain, with recreating naively, existentially, joyfully, the songs and the voice of Spain," by virtue of his "childhood spirit."[155] Jankélévitch's description of Albéniz as a noble savage testifies to the endurance and efficiency of Collet's cultural strategies.

Locating "Spanish Music" in Europe

In *Albéniz et Granados*, descriptions of Spain as a nation and a subaltern culture stand in perpetual tension. This conflict manifested itself more conspicuously in Collet's last monograph on Spanish music, namely, *L'Essor de la musique espagnole au XXe siècle* (1929, The Splendour of Spanish Music in the Twentieth Century).[156] In this book, Collet elaborates a shrewd and well-articulated cultural narrative that casts Spanish music as an anti-German artifact and locates Spain as a cultural periphery of France. He depicts a panorama of aesthetic battles between the followers and the denigrators of Wagner and German music. These cleavages reign over a well-informed classification of composers by regional school and aesthetic penchant. Toward the end of the book, he declares anti-German composers as the victors and proclaims accomplishment of the Spanish musical "renaissance." He concludes that those "great artists who followed Wagner and Strauss, or César Franck" have finished by "burning what they once adored [and] have ended up descending from their ivory tower in order to join the crowd formed by their happy juniors."[157] Thus, he formulates an anti-German, subaltern, class-oriented concept of Spanish music.

Collet's strategies operate subtly but powerfully through the arguments that he uses to locate Spanish music in a European imaginary. The bottom line seems encapsulated in the opening two-page statement, which follows here abridged:

> For a musician, music does not wear a national label. It is simply music, with its laws and its forms, patiently elaborated through the centuries.

---

[155] "La nonchalance d'Albéniz, qui est plutôt une paresse orientale, une africaine indolence"; "Albeniz n'a rien d'un érudit"; "il se contente (si l'on peut dire!) d'être l'Espagne, de recréer naïvement, existentiellement, dans la joie, le chant et la voix de l'Espagne." "L'esprit d'enfance." Vladimir Jankélévitch, *La présence lointaine: Albeniz, Séverac, Mompou* (Paris: Editions du Seuil, 1983), 10, 24, 30.

[156] Henri Collet, *L'essor de la musique espagnole au XXe siècle* (Paris: M. Eschig, 1929).

[157] "de grands artistes formés par Wagner et Strauss, ou par César Franck"; "brûlant ce qu'ils avaient adoré, ils ont fini par descendre de leur tour d'ivoire pour se joindre à la foule de leurs heureux cadets." Collet, *L'essor*, 131. Other passages express this same idea in other forms: "La guitare espagnole populaire a remplacé l'ancienne vihuela aristocratique. Elle possède une richesse et une variété de timbres inconnues des autres instruments, en dépit de son manque de volume sonore, de son 'intimité.'" Ibid., 164. Collet would dwell on this idea in other publications: "Ils sont légion ceux qui, suivant l'exemple de Nin, ont résolument abandonné l'enseignement germanique pour revenir à l'éternelle vérité latine." Henri Collet, "Espagne (1)," *Le ménestrel* (June 1929).

However, one could say that, considered from that perspective, music fatally leads to a dead end. Once the musical matter is deprived from any particular color and offered to anyone, one senses that, with the enormous concurrence of international artisans, that matter wears off after having dried up in the formal combinations to which it is subjected […]

After several years, the highbrow symphony reveals itself with all its wrinkles, irredeemably outdated. That is the case of Beethoven, Mendelssohn, Schumann and Franck. […]

By contrast, the free poems for orchestra and the lyric works based on popular elements preserve all their flavor. The magnificent productions of the Russian school, as well as those of the young Spanish school, have gained the approval of the musical élites as well as the masses, and seem to have defied the passage of time.[158]

Collet exhorts Russian and Spanish composers to use distinctive folklore in order to assign their music a specific location in the international arena. Thus, he casts Russia and Spain through the trope of cultural "difference" and, indirectly, implies that France is entitled to predicate its identity upon the normative trope of "universalism." This distinction relies on the way in which supremacy was historically understood in Europe. Since the eighteenth century, French and German intellectuals had grounded the construction of cultural hegemony upon a narrative of cultural universalism. They based their cultural production on codes and values that, they claimed, held universal meaning.[159] In order to debunk their German rivals, most French intellectuals distinguished between good and bad forms of universalism. They argued that German universalism constituted a form of cultural imperialism that developed and spread at the expense

---

[158] "Pour un musicien, la musique ne saurait avoir une étiquette nationale. Il n'est que la musique tout court, avec ses lois et ses formes élaborées patiemment à travers les siècles. Et cependant, l'on peut prétendre que la musique ainsi considérée aboutit fatalement à une impasse. Du moment que la matière musicale est destitué de tout coloris particulier et offerte à quiconque, l'on devine qu'avec l'énorme concurrence des artisans internationaux, cette matière s'épuise en soi après s'être tarie dans les combinaisons formelles auxquelles elle se trouve soumise […] Au bout de quelques années, la symphonie savante apparaît avec toutes ses rides, irrémédiablement désuète. Ainsi de Beethoven, de Mendelssohn, de Schumann, de Franck. […] En revanche, les poèmes libres pour orchestre et les actions lyriques basées sur l'élément populaire, ont conservé toute leur saveur. Les magnifiques productions de l'école russe, de même que celles de la jeune école espagnole, ont su gagner les suffrages de l'élite musicienne et de la foule, et semblent devoir braver l'épreuve du temps." Ibid., 7. Throughout *L'essor*, Collet expands on this argument, praising those Spanish composers who have quoted, imitated or parodied folklore and, by so doing, have conferred on their compositions an identity that European audiences would mostly agree to identify as "Spanish": "pour pénétrer le sentiment d'une race, non seulement il faut connaître la cristallisation de son idéal artistique dans les œuvres de ses grands génies, mais encore savoir écouter le chant populaire que Herder appelait la voix du peuple" Ibid., 11.

[159] Dahlhaus, *Nineteenth-Century Music*, 36–37.

of other national cultures. By contrast, they predicated French culture upon "universal" values of humankind, which, they thought, found their supreme formulation in the 1789 Revolution.[160]

A politics of marginalization underlies Collet's description of Spanish music. His emphasis on Spanish folklore and popular music reads like an attempt to reduce Spain to subaltern notions of class. In this aspect, even a knowledgeable scholar like Collet wrote under the influence of the mainstream trend among French critics and musicians, who, since the eighteenth century, regarded Spanish music through the sole prism of popular music and, to a lesser extent, Church music.[161] To cite just one example, the prestigious *Revue d'histoire et de critique musicales* (1901–02) founded by Jules Combarieu and edited by Louis Laloy, included reviews of classical "Spanish music" concerts, and performances of Wagner, Beethoven and French music in Spain, under the rubrique "Musique éxotique et populaire."[162] Similarly, the "Debussyste" Jean Marnold declared that, although "Spain possesses a 'national' music—or precisely because it has one—it has been sterile in creative musicians."[163] Critics with a greater knowledge of the Spanish musical scene strongly expressed their disagreement with this idea. Such is the case with Jean-Aubry, who claimed that

> we should not believe that Spain should only represent to us a source of themes which we will manipulate more or less […] For, to the surprise of many, Spanish music does exist, not only popular or dance music, but a music which is conscious and a worthy rival of any national school: the French, Russian and German modern schools.[164]

Roland-Manuel, a composer and musicologist who, though not particularly interested in Spanish music, wrote an influential book on *Manuel de Falla* (1930)

---

[160] Jann Pasler, *Composing the Citizen: Music as Public Utility in Third Republic France* (Berkeley: University of California Press, 2009), 94–134. Fulcher, *French Cultural Politics*, 35–47.

[161] Judith Etzion, "Spanish Music as Perceived in Western Music Historiography: A Case of the Black Legend?" *International Review of the Aesthetics and Sociology of Music* (1998): 94–95, 102–108.

[162] Anon, "Musique éxotique et populaire," *Revue d'histoire et de critique musicales (Revue musicale)* (March 1902). Under that rubric, it included a review of the Concerts Lamoureux in Barcelona, Teatro Novedades, March 11, 12, and 13. The program was Wagner, Beethoven and French music.

[163] "l'Espagne possède une musique 'nationale,'—et même parce qu'elle en possède une et celle-là,—elle resta stérile en musiciens créateurs." Jean Marnold, *Musique d'autrefois et d'aujourd'hui* (Dorbon-Ainée: Paris, 1911), 359.

[164] "N'allons pas croire encore que l'Espagne ne doive être pour nous qu'une fontaine où puiser des thèmes sonores que nous désarticulerons plus ou moins […] Car, dût la plupart s'en étonner, la musique espagnole existe, non pas seulement la musique populaire ou la musique de danse, mais une musique consciente digne de rivaliser avec n'importe quelle des écoles nationales: École française, école russe, ou école allemande modernes." Georges Jean-Aubry, "Le mouvement musical en provence. La musique moderne espagnole," *Le guide du concert* (November 1910).

that clearly shows the influence of Collet's ideas, made a similar claim: "but Spain has refused, for a long time, if not always, to submit to the elemental rule which forbids other peoples to possess at the same time a vivacious popular music and an original classical music."[165]

Like Jean-Aubry and Roland-Manuel, Collet did believe in a Spanish "school" of composers, but he tried to "folklorize" them, that is, to subject them to the politics of difference just described. His stress on "difference" suggests that he tried to emasculate and engender Spain, to cast it through subaltern notions of gender in which the exotic, the erotic and the feminine conflate, as in *Carmen*.[166] Collet relies on the coercive argument that "peripheral" nations ought to "root" their cultural expressions in order to find their place in the international arena; in other words, they ought to build their identity upon the use of cultural elements European audiences perceived as "different." Thus, the "newly born" nations, to use an expression coined by the Romanian ethnomusicologist Constantin Brailoiu, could more easily gain the approval of those that claimed to be "central," such as France and Germany.[167] Not only would the "peripheral" nations attract more attention through the appeal of their "difference" or "exoticism" but, more importantly, they would not be perceived as vying for cultural hegemony.

Collet's distinction not only draws on power differences but contributes to reinforce them in the interest of French hegemony. Collet's fellow *hispaniste* Raoul Laparra—who will be dealt with in Chapter 3—formulated a very similar model of cultural hierarchy in a more blatant way. Laparra argued that "Spain must defend itself rashly and tenaciously from any foreign influences," for, "should it lose the incomparable treasure on which its international prestige is

---

[165] "Mais l'Espagne a refusé longtemps, sinon toujours, de se soumettre à la loi élémentaire qui interdit aux autres peuples la possession simultanée d'une musique populaire vivace et d'une musique savante originale." Roland-Manuel, *Manuel de Falla* (Paris: Éditions "Cahiers d'art," 1930), 10.

[166] Colmeiro, "Exorcising Exoticism, 127–144. Linda Phyllis Austern, "'Forreine Conceites and Wandring Devises': The Exotic, the Erotic, and the Feminine," in *The Exotic in Western Music*, ed. Jonathan Bellman (Boston: Northeastern University Press, 1998). Robert L. A. Clark, "South of North: Carmen and French Nationalisms," in *East of West: Cross-Cultural Performance and the Staging of Difference*, ed. Claire Sponsler and Xiaomei Chen (New York and Basingstoke: Palgrave Macmillan, 2000), 187–216.

[167] The Rumanian ethnomusicologist Constantin Brailoiu gained early awareness of these issues: "Tandis que les compositeurs issus de civilisations citadines anciennes, lesquels n'empruntent à autrui que pour mieux orner un art déjà accompli et nourrir un langage universel, les nouveaux venus se singularisent, au contraire, de propos délibéré et accentuent à plaisir les contrastes, alors même qu'ils aspirent à se faire accueillir dans le concert (notons bien: symphonique) européen. Tributaires du dehors, mais repliés sur eux-mêmes (et par là centrifuges), ils devaient osciller parfois entre deux attitudes contradictoires, tantôt tournant résolument le dos à l'étranger, dont ils attendaient les leçons (Moussorgsky), tantôt s'en assimilant les mœurs au point de s'y fondre (Sibelius)." Constantin Brailoiu, "Les écoles nationales," in *Les musiciens célèbres*, ed. Jean Lacroix (Geneva: L. Mazenod, 1946), 214.

based, it will fall into oblivion due to its geographically remote position."[168] To be sure, Laparra must have thought that Spain suffered from its "territorial marginality" and was only a "small power, situated in a peripheral position"—to paraphrase a more recent diagnosis.[169] He exhorts those nations most at risk of losing cultural and political influence, and those that lay farthest from the centers of political and economic power, to make themselves conspicuous in order not be wiped off the map. Although Laparra most likely wanted to vindicate "Spanish culture," his selective and—one could even say—discriminatory distribution of difference honors a hierarchic model of cultural (re)production and dissemination that is undergirded by a coercive politics of exoticism and marginalization.

The resources for building French hegemony displayed in L'essor go well beyond the subtle manifestations just described. Collet deploys a wide range of strategies in order to argue that the "renaissance" of Spanish music in the twentieth century—reflected in the title—was not only facilitated but also encouraged and guided by French musicians. In other words, "Spanish music" was a nineteenth-century French discovery to which Spanish composers began contributing only in the twentieth century:

> How curious! Spain had always cultivated its popular songs as if hiding, as if hesitating about the imponderable value of such a guarantee of survival.... It was necessary that foreigners reveal to Spaniards the inestimable value of their popular treasures for the latter to end up believing in it.... In this case, it is the French who have the honor of having supported and encouraged the timid attempts of young Spanish composers to found a national school. The latter could not count on any official support in their motherland. All posts in the conservatoires were occupied by masters who had trained in Italy, the taste of which dominates musical theater. As regards the symphony, who could have cultivated it if no orchestral company was there to perform it?[170]

---

[168] "que l'Espagne se défende, et âprement, et tenacement, des influences étrangères. Elles ne peuvent rien lui apporter; elles peuvent tout lui ôter. Et quand l'Espagne n'aura plus rien, c'est-à-dire quand elle aura perdu l'incomparable trésor qui fait son prestige à l'extérieur, elle sera à jamais oubliée, par le fait même de sa position géographique écartée" Raoul Laparra, "Espagne," Le Ménestrel (November 14, 1924).

[169] Jover Zamora, España en la política internacional, 112.

[170] "Chose curieuse! L'Espagne avait toujours cultivé le chant populaire mais comme en se cachant, comme en doutant de la valeur impondérable d'un tel gage se survie... Il a fallu que les étrangers révèlent aux Espagnols l'inestimable valeur de leur trésor populaire pour que ces derniers finissent par y croire"; "En l'occurrence, c'est à des Français que revient l'honneur d'avoir soutenu, encouragé les timides essais des jeunes compositeurs espagnols en vue de fonder une école nationale. Ceux-ci ne pouvaient compter sur aucun appui officiel dans leur propre patrie. Toutes les places conservatoriales étaient occupées par des maîtres formés par l'Italie dominatrice du théâtre... Quant à la symphonie, qui l'eût pu cultiver, alors que nulle compagnie orchestrale n'était là pour l'interpréter?" Collet, L'essor, 8.

Collet construes Spain as a cultural periphery of France. He argues that the Spanish national musical school exists only thanks to the support and encouragement of French musicians, who have instilled a sense of national pride in their Spanish counterparts—a prejudice that spread over other disciplines.[171] In order to nuance the imperialistic overtones of this argument, however, Collet provides a grim description of the state of musical culture in Spain; thus he feels empowered to construe the presence of Spanish composers in Paris as a forced exodus or exile rather than the result of French political and cultural propaganda. As we have seen, there were certain grounds supporting Collet's arguments, such as the dissatisfaction of Spanish composers regarding the lack of official support, the absence of orchestral infrastructure and the pervasiveness of Italian taste, which made it difficult to explore other aesthetic realms. Although Collet's arguments echo the concerns shared by a certain strand of Spanish composers, he arranges them into a narrative of exile that suits an image of France as a cultural Mecca or forum of humankind.

Collet supplements this narrative of exile with a patronizing and dichotomous distinction between nature and civilization that, once again, casts a superior gaze upon Spain:

> The masters Vincent d'Indy, Paul Dukas and Claude Debussy have well merited from Spain and Art, having attracted to them, by their strong personality, the several Spanish artists whom such a miserable situation has condemned into exile. They have known how to discern what those young musicians could contribute that was new and not yet indebted to any clans or parties, to those so appropriately called "chapels." They have limited themselves to giving technical advice, thanks to which the autodidacts from beyond the Pyrenees have learnt to develop their unique gifts harmoniously.[172]
>
> [...]
>
> It is necessary to observe that the Spaniards exiled in France, the motherland of ruthless criticism and of an examination taken

---

[171] The prominent *hispaniste* Alfred Morel-Fatio similarly declared that "everything that is known about the history of Castilian languages is due to the work of foreigners, which Spaniards do not even bother reading." Alfred Morel-Fatio, "Espagne (Bulletin Historique)," *Revue Historique*, vol. 3 (1987) 407. Quoted in Niño Rodríguez, *Cultura y diplomacia*, 504.

[172] "Les Maîtres Vincent d'Indy, Paul Dukas et Claude Debussy, en attirant à eux, par leur forte personnalité, les quelques artistes espagnols qu'une situation aussi misérable condamnait à l'exil, ont bien mérité de l'Espagne et de l'Art. Ils ont su discerner ce que pouvaient apporter d'inouï des musiciens jeunes et non inféodés encore à des clans ou partis, à ces 'chapelles' si bien dénommées. Ils se sont bornés à des conseils techniques grâce auxquels les autodidactes d'au-delà des Pyrénées sauraient développer harmonieusement des dons uniques." Collet, *L'essor*, 9.

to a degree of frenzy and cruelty, will refine their style and will find the audacity that will help them stand out before the admiration of musical élites. The others, those who have remained in Madrid and Barcelona, which always stay out of fashion, will find it more difficult to make themselves known to the world, and will not participate so easily from the glory dispensed to their nomad siblings. But we, who regard them with indifference to partisanisms, we observe them with an equal complaisance, happy to signal out those among their works which, having been conceived for eternity, have endured the test of time and deserve to be listened to in this demanding Paris without it entailing that the audience approaches from the too tyrannical model established by Debussy, Ravel, d'Indy, Fauré, Stravinsky or Schoenberg.[173]

In these two fragments, Collet represents the Spanish musician as an unskilled, unrefined "autodidact" whose cultural singularity and naïve unawareness provide a freshening respite from the political and cultural battles being waged in France. By contrast, he represents his French counterparts as a selection of skilled, refined, "élite," demanding musicians. These and other binaries underpin Collet's understanding of the relation between French and Spanish music. For instance, he identifies French music with "harmonious" civilization and defines Spanish music as a domesticable form of wilderness; he regards French and Spanish identity as norm and difference, Self and Other, culture and nature, universal and vernacular respectively. Ultimately, the arguments that Collet employs to locate "Spanish music" rest upon the longstanding binary of mind and body that has pervaded "Western" thought since Plato. The mind-body dualism encapsulates the coercive strategies at play in Collet's imagination, and connects with other hierarchical binaries, such as male-female. As Judith Butler has argued, "any uncritical reproduction of the mind/body distinction"—as may be found in Collet's writings—"ought to be rethought for the implicit gender hierarchy that the distinction has conventionally produced,

---

[173] "il nous faudra remarquer que les Espagnols exilés en France, patrie de la critique impitoyable et de l'examen poussé jusqu'à la frénésie et à la cruauté, raffineront leur style, et rechercheront l'audace qui les désignera à l'admiration des élites musicales. Les autres, les Madrilènes et les Barcelonais, toujours en retard sur la mode du jour, auront plus de mal à se faire connaître dans le monde, et ne participeront pas aisément à la gloire départie à leur frères nomades. Mais nous, qui allons vers eux, indifférents aux mesquines questions de 'chapelles', nous les observerons avec une égale complaisance, heureux si nous pouvons signaler quelques-uns de leurs œuvres qui, conçues sub specie aeternitatis, demeurent à l'épreuve du temps et méritent d'être écoutées en cet exigeant Paris, sans que la pensée de l'auditeur ait à les rapprocher du type un peu trop tyrannique qu'établirent les Debussy ou les Ravel, les d'Indy ou les Fauré, les Stravinsky ou les Schonberg." Ibid., 30.

maintained and rationalized."[174] Given its capacity to reflect these power differences, "body" seems a more appropriate metaphor to describe the location of "Spanish music" in the modern French imagination than the otherwise highly suggestive "soul."[175]

According to Collet, French composers cautiously restrict themselves to providing technical advice in order not to smother the alleged spontaneity of Spanish musicians. This distinction between technique and nature, again, relies on binaries such as civilization and savagery, or élite and popular, exploited by right- and left-wing populisms of the 1920s and 1930s.[176] Just as Collet assigns French composers a well-defined function, he designates Spanish composers as the sole providers of "ethnic" material, as far as "Spanish music" is concerned. For Collet, national identities are the "natural" expression of a given composer's ethnic background. From this viewpoint, the process through which identities are fabricated is masked, and so is the "French" intervention in negotiating hegemonic formulations of "Spanish music." By applying national labels in a deterministic and imposing manner, Collet nominates the Other and keeps it at a cautionary and safe, but still palpable, distance.

Collet's description of d'Indy helping composers from "different" backgrounds seems consistent with the Schola's reputation as a haven for the so-called regionalist composers. Building on Collet's arguments, both Spanish and French regionalist composers in the Schola appear to have contributed to casting Paris as a forum of cultures to which they flocked in order to sanction and validate their cultural expressions.[177] Spain is thus equated to a French province, reduced to being a cultural periphery of Paris. Collet develops the argument in this fragment:

> Once the isolated Spaniards came over to submit to them [Debussy, d'Indy, Dukas and Fauré] their timid essays, which self-evidently showed the possibility of a Spanish national school that was worthy of comparison with the Russian school, and even presented striking analogies with regard to its songs, rhythm and harmony, our masters responded to the sons of Iberia with encouragement and even praises.... Thereafter,

[174] Judith Butler, *Gender Trouble: Feminism and the Subversion of Identity* (New York and London: Routledge, 1999), 17.
[175] The use of "soul" as a metaphor should be credited to Parakilas in "How Spain Got a Soul."
[176] Tom Brass, *Peasants, Populism, and Postmodernism: The Return of the Agrarian Myth* (London and Portland, OR: F. Cass, 2000).
[177] This is encapsulated in Musk's contention that, throughout the Third Republic, "Paris continued in its status as the centre of French civilization and provided the focal point for political, musical and literary activity directed towards the rejuvenation of the nation. The position of the capital as arbiter of Frenchness was significant." Musk, "Regionalism," 227.

the Spanish school achieved recognition and could measure itself up, in concerts and on the stage, against the illustrious Russian school, which it equaled in compositional "curiosities" and surpassed in color and rhythmic ardor.[178]

Once the Spaniards subjected their compositions to the verdict of French composers, they could measure up against their European counterparts.[179] In other words, Collet construes Paris as Spain's only access to the European cultural arena, and he establishes a relation of dependency.

Russia and Spain in the Latin Union

In the passage above, Collet associates Spain and Russia by way of the alleged similarities between what was understood as their respective folkloric capital. As we will see, the rationale behind Collet's and similar comparisons between these two cultures is the fact that they similarly sought to find a place in Europe by negotiating their distance to what was perceived to be its center and margins. Just how he describes that negotiation reflects Collet's frame of mind, for he subordinates Russia and Spain to France through a relation of cultural dependency. He casts Spain and Russia as cultural peripheries of France, and partakes in the Orientalist discursive practice that lumps together, intermingles and even confuses cultures deemed "peripheral."[180]

To a certain extent, by the end of the nineteenth century Western powers still perceived Russia as a backward and savage country, despite its rapid expansion through Asia during the nineteenth century. They regarded its cultural production as lacking in refinement, and thought its colonial acquisitions to be unworthy of comparison with their own empires.[181] But, like Spanish music, Russian

---

[178] "lorsque des Espagnols isolés vinrent leur soumettre de timides essais qui démontraient de toute évidence la possibilité d'une école espagnole, digne en tous points de l'école russe et présentant même avec elle quant au chant, au rythme et à l'harmonie, des analogies frappantes, nos maîtres n'eurent pour les fils d'Ibérie que des encouragements, voire que des louanges... Dès lors, l'école espagnole se trouvait reconnue et pouvait se mesurer au concert et sur la scène avec l'illustre école russe qu'elle égalait en 'curiosités' d'écriture et surpassait en coloris et en fougue rythmique." Collet, L'essor, 14.

[179] A year before, he put the same idea more blatantly: "Au demeurant l'esprit critique est essentiellement français, et il arrive qu'un créateur étranger vient humblement se soumettre à la férule française, à l'épuration parisienne généralement profitable." Henri Collet, "Critiques et musiciens," Le courrier musical (November 1928).

[180] Derek B. Scott, "Orientalism and Musical Style," Musical Quarterly 82, no. 2 (1998): 309–310; Ralph P. Locke, Musical Exoticism: Images and Reflections (Cambridge: Cambridge University Press, 2009), 177. Parakilas, "How Spain Got a Soul," 138.

[181] Alison Sinclair, "Spain's Love Affair with Russia: The Attraction of Exotic (Br)others," European Review of History 11, no. 2 (June 1, 2004): 207–209, 217–219. Ralph P. Locke, Musical Exoticism, 222–223.

music—or the French concept of it, provided there was one—offered itself as a valuable cultural ally in the rhetorical fight against German music, not the least because the destinies of France and Russia had been united by a military alliance between 1892 and 1917.[182] The Russian revolution, however, imbued perceptions of Russian music and its relation with Spanish and French music with a range of new connotations, which critics were more or less ready to accept, even after France official recognized the Soviet regime in 1924. Some argued that the "real" Russian tradition was continued by the nearly one million Russians who took exile between 1918 and 1921, some of whom believed themselves to be acting as "temporary guardians of their country's interests until the Bolshevik perversion had run its brief, murderous course"[183]—just as the Spaniards who fled the Franco dictatorship (1936–1975) claimed that they represented the "true" legacy and continuation of the Spanish tradition betrayed in the uprising.[184] This was not Collet's case, as he declared that the Russian school could have "overshadowed" the "incomparable brightness" of the Spanish school, only "if, continuing with the glorious popular tradition of The Five, it had avoided the pitfalls of a mechanical Bolshevism, which destroys all sonorous beauty, all poetic dreams, and all lyrical sentiment."[185]

Rather than an imposition, French views of a union of Russian and Spanish music built upon the predisposition of Spanish and Russian musicians to engage in that sort of anti-German propaganda, or, conversely, helped to stimulate it. Collet could have drawn inspiration from Adolfo Salazar's essay on *Boris Godunof*, which was published in 1923 and described a Russo-Hispanic musical bonding established by virtue of common traits such as clarity and balance.[186] By using the terms of French neoclassicism, Salazar departed from the French view of Spain and Russia, as well as the one that prevailed in the latter two countries

---

[182] Collet dedicated an article to the Russian Five, Les Six, and the Spanish Grupo de los Ocho. Collet, "Espagne," *Le ménestrel* (April 17, 1931). Jean-Aubry judged Russian, French, and Spanish music nationalism as full of vitality ("vitalité") and richness ("richesse") and opposed them to German music (*La musique et les nations*, 67–68); he also referred to these three nations as those whose music is essential for Europe, and deemed German music superfluous (*La musique française d'aujourd'hui*, 12).

[183] Robert H. Johnston, *New Mecca, New Babylon: Paris and the Russian Exiles, 1920–1945* (Kingston: McGill-Queen's University Press, 1988), 5. On the arrival of exiled Russian musicians in Paris see Roger Nichols, *The Harlequin Years: Music in Paris, 1917–1929* (Berkeley: University of California Press, 2002), 261–262.

[184] Sebastiaan Faber, *Exile and Cultural Hegemony: Spanish Intellectuals in Mexico, 1939–1975*, 1st ed. (Nashville: Vanderbilt University Press, 2002), 3–7.

[185] "L'école musicale espagnole brille aujourd'hui d'un incomparable éclat. Seule, l'école russe eût pu lui porter ombrage si, continuant la glorieuse tradition populaire de la Koutschka, elle eût évité l'écueil d'un bolchevisme mécanique destructeur de toute beauté sonore, de tout rêve poétique, de tout sentiment lyrique."

[186] Adolfo Salazar, *Modesto Mussorgsky y su Boris Godunof. Boceto histórico artístico* (Madrid: Antonio Matamala, 1923). See Ruth Piquer, *Clasicismo moderno, neoclasicismo y retornos en el pensamiento musical español (1915–1939)* (Sevilla: Doble J, 1910), 121–122.

at the turn of the century, namely, that their cultural similarities were based on their common status as cultural "peripheries." Indeed, Alison Sinclair describes their relationship at that time as a "love affair" between two "exotic (br)Others." Sinclair explains the way "in which one country idealises and projects a series of desires upon the culture and identity of another nation"; for Spanish intellectuals and writers, "the beloved [Russia] moves between being an object of desire and a model of a strong subject offering the possibility of identification."[187] The Spanish writers who traveled to Russia engaged in "an ongoing imaginary relating to masculine desire, in which Russian women were observed and interpreted as emblems of the sensual," to the point that "Russia was conjured up as Spain's mystic and primitive Asiatic Other."[188] In other words, Spanish representations of Russia in the early twentieth century relied on similar strategies and tropes as nineteenth-century representations of Spain used by French travelers.

Although, as we shall see shortly, there were precedents among Spanish musicologists for the formulation of a Franco-Russo-Spanish alliance, Collet could have well considered the work carried out by Diaghilev's Ballets Russes. This company's relations with the Spanish artistic avant-garde took a significant step forward during the First World War, in which neutrality turned Spain and, most particularly Barcelona, into a pole of attraction for European artists and musicians.[189] The Ballets Russes's Spanish tours of 1916 and 1917 acquainted Spaniards with highlights from their repertoire, which mostly consisted of Russian composers from the avant-garde and the nineteenth century but also included works by French composers, such as Chabrier's *España*, Lalo's *Symphonie espagnole*, Ravel's *Pavane pour une infante défunte* and Debussy's *Ibéria* and *Prélude à l'après-midi d'un faune*.[190] Most importantly, the visit of the Ballets Russes elicited passionate reactions that evince the extent to which a "foreign" modernism could raise important questions about the nature and development of the arts in Spain, and even about the path that artistic formulations of Spanish identity should follow.[191] Diaghilev's Spanish experience materialized in several productions,

---

[187] Sinclair, "Spain's Love Affair with Russia," 209.

[188] Ibid., 218.

[189] Carol A. Hess, " 'Un alarde de modernismo y dislocación': Los Ballets Russes en España, 1916–1921," Yvan Nommick and Antonio Álvarez Cañibano, eds. *Los Ballets Russes de Diaghilev y España* (Granada and Madrid: Fundación Archivo Manuel de Falla, INAEM, 2000), 215–227; on Spain's neutrality and the European avant-garde see Robert A. Davidson, *Jazz Age Barcelona* (Toronto: University of Toronto Press, 2009).

[190] For a detailed account of these tours see Yolanda F. Acker, "Los Ballets Russes en España: recepción y guía de sus primeras actuaciones (1916–1918)," in *Los Ballets Russes*, ed. Nommick and Cañibano, 229–252.

[191] Hess, "Un alarde," 216–217; John K. Walsh, "España y los Ballets Russes de Serge Diaghilev. Contexto histórico: España durante la Primera Guerra Mundial," in *Los Ballets Russes*, ed. Nommick and Cañibano, 23–30; for a list of performances in Madrid see, in the same volume, Beatriz Martínez del Fresno and Nuria Menéndez Sánchez, "Una visión de conjunto sobre la escena coreográfica madrileña (1915–1925) y algunas observaciones acerca de la influencia rusa en el desarrollo del *ballet* español," 181–182; see also Hess, *Manuel de Falla*, 95–98; 111–113.

among them *Las Meninas, Cuadro flamenco* and above all *The Three-Cornered Hat*, which premièred at the Alhambra Theatre in London in 1919, and brought together Léonide Massine's choreography, Falla's music and Picasso's costumes and décors. Even after the War, Diaghilev took a trip to Seville in the company of Stravinsky in order to find material for a new project, which would never come to fruition.[192] Picasso would take part in further relevant productions of the Ballets Russes, such as *Parade* (1917) and *Mercure* (1924), while other Spanish painters such as Joan Miró, José María Sert, Juan Gris and Pedro Pruna collaborated in productions such as *La légende de Joseph* (1914), with music by Richard Strauss, choreography by Mikhail Fokine and stage designs by Sert; *Las Meninas* (San Sebastián, 1916), based on music by Gabriel Fauré, with choreography by Massine and settings by Sert; the opera-ballet *Le Astuzie femminili* (1920), which brought Massine and Sert together again and was closely based on the eponymous original by Cimarosa, orchestrated by Respighi; and *Cuadro flamenco* (1921). Gris made the settings for *Cuadro flamenco* (1921) and *Les Tentations de la Bergère* (1924), with Henri Casadesus's arrangements of Montéclair's original music and choreography by Bronislava Nijinska; and Pruna painted for *Les matelots* (1924), with a score by Georges Auric on a libretto by Boris Kochno, and *Pastorale* (1925), which brought together once again Pruna, Auric and Kochno. Miró painted, together with Marx Ernst, the surrealistic backdrops for *Romeo and Juliet* (1925), with music by Constant Lambert; and *Jeux d'enfants* (1932), with music by Bizet.[193]

The Ballets Russes did not just provide a space in which Russian, French and Spanish musicians and artists could collaborate and exchange ideas. Despite the prevalence of adverse reactions, some Spanish critics' comments were empathetic in attempting to find common cultural Russo-Spanish roots in the works presented by the Ballets Russes. In 1922, the critic Juan Gómez Renovales wrote that, although upon "the first arrival in Madrid of the Russian dancers [...] the public perceived them as something exotic" the "sublime dances" of "this people"—meaning the Russians in general—are "only comparable with the Moorish dances, whose legacy may be found in our Meridional dances, full of light and joy."[194] By upholding an alleged commonality between Spanish and

---

[192] Richard Buckle, "La deduda de Diaghilev con España," in *Los Ballets Russes*, ed. Nommick and Cañibano, 31–32.

[193] Francisco Baena, "Breve itinerario de los pintore españoles en los Ballets Russes," in *Los Ballets Russes*, ed. Nommick and Cañibano, 253–275; Guillermo de Osma, "Sert, Gris, Pruna y Miró," in *Los Ballets Russes*, ed. Nommick and Cañibano, 47–56.

[194] "La primera llegada a Madrid de los bailarines rusos"; "el público los veía como algo exótico"; "danzas sublimes, únicamente comparables a las danzas moras, de cuya herencia nos quedan las nuestras meridionales, llenas de luz y alegrías." Juan Gómez Renovales, "Los Bailes Rusos," *Mundo gráfico* (December 6, 1922), 579, quoted in Martínez del Fresno and Menéndez Sánchez, "Una visión de conjunto," 187.

Russian folklore, Gómez Renovales followed a host of late-nineteenth-century French and Spanish critics. Significantly enough, however, on this occasion such a view was prompted by an avant-garde spectacle like the Ballets Russes. A few years before, Joaquín Fesser had expressed an equally empathetic response, which nevertheless shifted from racial discourses and focused on questions of influence. The 1916 season of the Ballets Russes in Spain prompted him to argue that, although "we are another race […] we could maybe hope that the passage of this Russian company leaves some partial and healthy influences in the art of stage and costume designers, dancers and extras, and not a small enthusiasm among choreographers and composers."[195] Thus, Fesser acknowledged the role that the Ballets Russes played in the modernization of musical culture in Spain.

Besides the receptivity of certain Spanish critics to establishing cultural bonds among Russia, Spain and—eventually—France, those bonds also depended on the attitudes shown by the non-Spanish musicians who collaborated with the Ballets Russes. Carol Hess has shown how Stravinsky's visits to Spain in 1916 and 1921 offered themselves as timely opportunities to establish and celebrate Russo-Spanish cultural bondings on the basis of the composer's symbolic stature. If, during his first visit, it was Falla who formulated an anti-German union of Spanish and Russian composers, in 1921 Stravinsky overtly declared to the newspaper *La Voz*, in a sensationalistic tone, "Defend me, Spaniards, from the Germans, who do not understand and have never understood music."[196] One may, therefore, understand the Franco-Russo-Spanish alliance as a discursive trope that, even if—unlike the Latin Union—it did not materialize in a sustained form of propaganda, at least it gave expression to a series of shared concerns.[197]

From the perspective of French and Spanish critics, the cultural bondings with Russia could gain more overtly anti-German connotations if they were re-inscribed in the Latin Union. However, this task proved problematic, as Russia did not possess Roman ruins, a Romance language, or any of the elements that French and Spanish intellectuals would normally identify as "Latin." In the face of this setback, critics and musicologists resorted to their usually far-fetched cultural strategies. Pedrell invented a Latin connection by identifying reminiscences of Byzantine

---

[195] "Somos otra raza"; "Acaso podamos aspirar, sin embargo, a que el paso de la compañia rusa deje algo de influencias parciales y saludables en el arte de la escenografía, de la sastrería, de la danza y comparsería, y no poco de estímulo entre los directores coreográficos y los maestros compositores." Joaquín Fesser, "Los bailes rusos. Epílogo," *Revista musical hispano-americana*, June 30, 1916, 4–5.

[196] P. Victory, "Los grandes compositores: Una conversación con Stravinsky," *La voz* (March 21, 1921). Quoted in Hess, *Manuel de Falla*, 170; 98–104, 161–163, and Hess, "Un alarde," 225. Also see Sinclair, "Spain's Love Affair with Russia," 217–219.

[197] Louis Jambou, "Stravinsky y Falla: Influencias y paralelismos. Parámetros para un estudio," in *Relaciones musicales entre España y Rusia*, ed. Antonio Álvarez Cañibano (Madrid: Centro de Documentación de Música y Danza, 1999), 101–116.

chant in flamenco, which he linked to Russian music via the Eastern Roman Empire.[198] Whether Pedrell conceived of the alliance between Spanish and Russian music in anti-German terms seems dubious in the light of his own Wagnerian penchants. In his most widespread work, the manifesto *Por nuestra música* (1891), he took an ambiguous position with regard to this matter:

> Wagner has created a new German, solid, far-reaching poetics, which is nevertheless extraneous to the character of our Latin spirit....[199] without fully rejecting either the leitmotiv or Wagner's ideas on the musical drama, the modern Russian school, which has emerged suddenly and abruptly and deserves all my sympathy, has somewhat modified Wagner's principles.[200]

It is not fully clear whether Pedrell's celebration of the Russian school is based on his judgment that it preserved some Wagnerian elements, or the fact that it managed to distance itself from Wagner on the basis of the latter's poetics allegedly being extraneous to the "Latin spirit." Whatever elements of anti-German propaganda Pedrell shared, they were not so much based on animosity—unlike in the case of Collet—as on the argument that musical styles are national, ethnic and nontransferable.

If there was any dubious anti-German element in Pedrell's view of the Russian and Spanish musical alliance, it was not passed on to the work of Albert Soubies. The latter was less suspicious of entertaining any anti-German allegiances, since he published widely on Wagner and German music, as well as seemingly incompatible subjects such as Meyerbeer.[201] Soubies was one of Pedrell's closest friends in France, and his most frequent correspondent.[202] Pedrell took part in the corrections of Soubies's *Musique russe et musique espagnole* (1899),[203] and the former's imprint seems patent in this paragraph:

---

[198] Hess, *Manuel de Falla*, 101.

[199] "Wagner ha creado una poética nueva, alemana, convencida, de incalculables alcances, sí, pero distinta del carácter de nuestro genio latino." Felipe Pedrell, *Por nuestra música: Algunas observaciones sobre la magna cuestión de una escuela lírico nacional motivadas por la trilogía (3 cuadros y un prólogo) Los Pirineos, poema de D. Víctor Balaguer, música del que suscribe* (Barcelona: Henrich, 1891), 27.

[200] "Sin desechar del todo el Leitmotiv ni separarse mucho de las ideas de Wagner sobre el drama lírico en general, la moderna escuela rusa, que ha surgido de repente y como por salto y se lleva todas mis simpatías, ha modificado un tanto las tendencias de Wagner." Ibid., 34.

[201] Yvonne Tiénot, "Soubies, Albert," *Grove Music Online*, ed. Deane Root, http://www.oxfordmusiconline.com/subscriber/article/grove/music/26281 (accessed August 2, 2011).

[202] Francesc Cortès, "Les rapports du cercle de F. Pedrell avec la France," in *Echanges musicaux franco-espagnols XVIIe–XIXe siècles: Actes des Rencontres de Villecroze, 15 au 17 octobre 1998*, ed. François Lesure (Paris: Klincksieck, 2000), 299, 308.

[203] Albert Soubies, *Musique russe et musique espagnole* (Paris: Fischbacher, 1894).

in Spain, like in Russia, there is a musical individuality which is marked by salient traits, and which, today, thanks to the endeavor of erudite and ingenious critics and skilful and delicate artists, seeks to become self-conscious, to disengage itself entirely from the imitation of foreign elements, and to assume a national color through and through. In both lands, this movement has emerged as a tendency to seek inspiration in popular songs and rhythms, which are equally rich, varied, flexible and powerful in both races and both countries.[204]

Soubies anticipates Collet by casting Russian and Spanish culture as "low" and premodern, by reducing their music to folklore and popular music and by prescribing a radical cultural protectionism to curb their modernization. Although he tags Russia and Spain as "races," he does not predicate the alliance on an ethnic basis; nor does he imbue it with an anti-German character.

These ideas spread in the ensuing years. Some critics were eager to celebrate the purported "birth" or "renaissance" of Spanish music as a follow-up to the "miracle" of Russian music in the midnineteenth century. After attending a concert of Spanish music in 1910, Jean-Aubry declared, "let us not wait fifty years as we have done with the Russians, to notice that we are witnessing an admirable blossom."[205] Attitudes like this mask the propagandist, anti-German underpinnings of the French "discovery" of "Spanish music" in the early twentieth century. Furthermore, they conceal the fact that the sudden French fondness for Russian music in the late nineteenth century was, to a certain extent, a form of propaganda aimed at forging and legitimizing the Franco-Russian military alliance of 1891.

In *Musiques d'autrefois et d'aujourd'hui* (1911), Jean Marnold engaged in coercive strategies more intentionally than did Jean-Aubry. Marnold described Russian music as one in which "an Oriental influence manifests itself, which is due either to the proximity of Asia or the affinity of peoples such as the Russian and Scandinavians, or, among the Hungarians, to the Gypsies. It is the case, most especially, of Spanish music, which merely consists, in the end, of rhythms and melismas, the most stereotypical rhythms we know, and the most typical

---

[204] "En Espagne, comme en Russie, on rencontre une individualité musicale marquée de traits saillants, et qui, aujourd'hui, par le multiple effort de critiques érudits et ingénieux, et d'artistes habiles et délicats, cherche, pour ainsi dire, à prendre conscience d'elle-même, à se dégager complètement de l'imitation étrangère, à revêtir un coloris absolument national. Dans l'une et l'autre contrée, l'origine du mouvement a été la tendance à s'inspirer du chant et du rythme populaires, également riches, variés, flexibles et puissants chez les deux races et dans les deux pays." Soubies, *Musique russe et musique espagnole*, 6.

[205] "n'attendons pas cinquante ans comme on l'a fait pout les Russes pour nous apercevoir que nous sous trouvons en face d'une floraison admirable." Georges Jean-Aubry, "Le Havre. Un concert espagnol," *S.I.M. Revue musicale mensuelle* 6, no. 12 (December 1910). Collet echoed these arguments almost two decades later: "La Russie et l'Espagne sont sœurs quant au folklore. Et qui n'a l'impression qu'aujourd'hui la renaissance musicale espagnole 'fait suite' à la renaissance russe?" Henri Collet, "Espagne," *Le Ménestrel* (February 1929).

melismas we know."[206] Perhaps no other critic made so explicit the strategies of marginalization and alienation underpinning the French critics' eagerness to associate Spanish and Russian music. Paul Bertrand waxed almost as blatant when, reviewing a performance of Mussorgsky's *Night on a Bald Mountain* and Rimsky-Korsakov's *Capriccio espagnol*, he characterized both works by "the systematic use of popular themes [...] and an orchestral fabric which is blazing, sumptuous, sometimes savage, and reflects the influence of the Orient, even in its evocation of Andalusia."[207] Russian and Spanish music became two interchangeable commodities in the French imaginary, insofar as their marginal status helped to define France as a center. Jean-Pierre Altermann argued that, although "modern music owes a lot to Russia," "what Debussy found there [...] a Spaniard has just to stay at home to grasp it," since "gypsies have sisters in the Caucasus."[208] He added that the "musical bloom" that Spain must "wake up to" and that "Russia had accomplished earlier" "finds, as it is known, in France, its most varied, subtlest and richest center."[209] French critics repeated these and similar arguments for decades.[210]

Collet's view of Russian and Spanish music, therefore, was a reflection of a more general state of mind, and one could argue that, in this particular aspect, he showed less independence than in others. By sharing in this discursive practice, however, Collet complemented his view of "Spanish music" as one that mediates between the categories of Western civilization and the Orient. As we have seen, Collet and other French critics were eager to entertain and reinforce the ontological distinction between those two categories, rather than question their validity, let alone unearth their coercive underpinnings. In their attempts to define and redefine them, critics found the keys to shaping a form of propaganda suited to their needs and anxieties, and ultimately aimed at reinforcing French hegemony, of situating France at the center of Western civilisation. Thanks to his privileged knowledge of Spanish music, Collet was able to locate Spain in the French imaginary in a position that, with more or less fortune, suited those shared interests.

---

[206] Marnold, *Musiciens d'autrefois*, 359.

[207] "l'emploi systématique des thèmes populaires [...] un revêtement orchestral étincelant, somptueux, par instants sauvage, qui reflète l'influence de l'Orient, même dans l'évocation de l'Andalousie." Paul Bertrand, "Concerts-Colonne. Dimanche 16 janvier," *Le ménestrel* (January 1927).

[208] "La musique moderne doit beaucoup à la Russie"; "ce qu'un Debussy devait trouver là-bas [...] un Espagnol n'a qu'à rester chez lui pour l'y saisir"; "Les gitanes ont de sœurs au Caucase." Jean-Pierre Altermann, "Manuel de Falla," *La revue musicale* 8, no. 2 (June 1921).

[209] "épanouissement sonore"; "s'éveiller à"; "qu'avait fait d'abord la Russie"; "trouve, comme on sait, en France, son centre d'expression le plus varié, le plus subtil et le plus riche." Ibid.

[210] "Puis Mlle Colette Cras, pianiste à l'âme vraiment musicale, au jeu souple et expressif nous fit pleinement goûter la beauté des Nuits dans les jardins d'Espagne; après quoi De Falla céda délicatement la place au Capriccio espagnol de Rimsky-Korsakoff, transition naturelle de l'Espagne à la Russie, de la royauté ibérique à l'empire slave…." René Brancour, "Concerts-Lamoureux. Dimanche 20 mars," *Le ménestrel* (March 1932). Also see Bertrand, "Concerts-Colonne."

CHAPTER 2

"Spanish Music" as Catholic Propaganda

Catholic propaganda proved to be the most effective means of emphasizing common cultural links between France and Spain and, in that way, of attracting Spanish intellectuals. As has been discussed, Charles Maurras and other intellectuals close to Action Française put forward a Catholic image of Spain in order to oppose German Protestantism. By contrast, French musicologists and the Hispanists used similar images with the purpose of countering Italian cultural influence. Amidst ambivalent but passionate reactions to Italian culture and verist opera, Collet and some French musicologists found arguments to oppose eighteenth-century Italian opera in the work of Spanish musicologists. The latter concocted and entertained the myth of an Italian musical "invasion" of Spain in the eighteenth century, when the official taste of the Spanish Court veered toward Italian opera. This myth subsequently rubbed off in reviews of the work of Spanish musicologists in French music journals. However, rather than merely echoing Spanish musicologists, the authors of those reviews reinvigorated debates about the viability and independence of French opera from its Italian counterpart. Furthermore, in the work of Collet, Catholic, anti-Italian propaganda was the basis for establishing a hierarchy of regions and cultures in Spain. As we shall see, the confrontation between Castile and Catalonia in Collet's writings intersected with the vivid intellectual debates that had been gaining momentum in Spain since the midnineteenth century.

French Catholic Propaganda in Spain

At the end of the nineteenth century, the *hispanistes* and other French intellectuals started to engage in a form of propaganda aimed at driving Spain away from the Triple Alliance (1882) and attracting it to France. In order to guarantee the pace of French exports in Spain,[1] which was their leading market up to the First World War, and to compete with German propaganda in that country,[2] the French government invested a significant and growing sum of economic, cultural and human capital, to the point that by the early 1920s Spain became the primary target of French propaganda abroad.[3] But French propaganda was far from unitary. Ideological strands of French intellectuals vied with each other for the attention of the Spanish élites, by way of substantially different propagandistic strategies and discourses, which, to a certain extent, reflected the tensions and fractures of French society.[4] French Catholic groups were highly successful in emphasizing religious bondings between France and Spain and targeting the powerful Spanish Catholic sectors, who held strong misgivings about French republicanism and secularism. They advocated a form of spiritualism that, they argued, differed from "German" materialism and Protestantism. Furthermore, they opposed Spanish Catholicism to Italy's alleged paganism, that is, an invention based on the establishment of a spurious connection between modern Rome and the old Roman empire. Their work started to develop in the framework of the Comité Catholique de Propagande Française à l'Etranger (1915), presided over by the bishop—later cardinal—Alfred Baudrillart, a doctor in literature and theology, author of numerous anti-German and pro-Catholic books and, later, a collaborationist of the Vichy regime. The Comité Catholique met the strong opposition of the Comité International de Propagande, which targeted the socialist and left-wing Spanish sectors; it was directed by the literary scholar Ernest Mérimée, co-founder of the most relevant French institution for cultural propaganda in Spain, namely, the Institut Français de Madrid.[5]

The Comité Catholique outdid their rival Comité International thanks to the organization of several missions that took French intellectuals around Spain during the First World War. The missions were aimed at gaining support for France while concealing propaganda under the appearance of an intellectual exchange. The first of these missions took place in 1916, and was organized by the scholar Maurice Legendre, the future director of the Casa Velázquez for cultural exchange,

---

[1] Aubert, "L'influence idéologique, 64.

[2] Luis Álvarez Gutiérrez, "Intentos alemanes para contrarrestar la influencia francesa sobre la opinión pública en los años precedentes a la Primera Guerra Mundial," in *Españoles y franceses en la primera mitad del siglo XX* (Madrid: CSIC, 1986), 1–22. However, Germany held several advantages. German Hispanism was more developed than its French counterpart, and German science exerted an important influence in Spanish liberal sectors through the spreading of Krausism. Hera Martínez, *La política cultural*, 11–34.

[3] Niño Rodríguez, *Cultura y diplomacia*, 441–442.

[4] On the impact of French debates and polemics on French propaganda in Spain see André Bachoud, "L'affaire Ferrer ou la France en question," in *España, Francia y la Comunidad Europea: Actas del Segundo Coloquio Hispano-Francés de Historia Contemporánea, celebrado en Aix-en-Provence los días 16, 17 y 18 de junio de 1986*, ed. Jean-Pierre Etienvre and José Ramón de Urquijo y Goitia (Madrid: Casa de Velázquez, 1989), 103–105.

[5] Niño Rodríguez, *Cultura y diplomacia*, 261–308.

which finally established itself in Madrid in 1928.⁶ It was aimed at overturning the prejudice that France did not know enough about Spain, and to gather information in order to convince the French authorities about the need to carry out propaganda in Spain. Legendre and the participants tried to convince Spaniards that a Catholic "essence" lay behind the appearance of an anti-clerical France promoted by the Republican government.⁷ This mission boasted, among other intellectuals, the philosopher Henri Bergson and the organist and composer Charles-Marie Widor, who, in his capacity as permanent secretary of the Académie des Beaux-Arts, played an instrumental role in convincing king Alfonso XII to found the Casa Velázquez.⁸ Widor gave a conference on the Ateneo de Madrid, in which he argued that Germans no longer held a monopoly on music and that France and Spain had taken over that role. Furthermore, he paid homage to Enrique Granados, killed earlier that year when the ship he was traveling in was torpedoed by a German submarine.⁹ This mission led to the creation of the Comité de Rapprochement Franco-Espagnol in 1917, the best-funded institution for French propaganda abroad, and a telling testimony to the relevance that the French government granted to propaganda in Spain during the War. The creation of the Comité de Rapprochement signified official sanction of Catholicism as the main form of dialogue with Spain during the War, for the Comité brought together the Catholic strands of French and Spanish intellectuals.¹⁰

The success of French Catholic propaganda in Spain not only was due to a greater organizational capability but was also possible thanks to great receptivity on the part of the most influential and hegemonic strand of Spanish intellectuals. French Catholics reached a good level of understanding with a series of Spanish authors, poets and political thinkers who, from their common concerns, have come to be known as the Generations of 1898 and 1914.¹¹ Among them were the

---

⁶ Charles-Marie Widor, "La Villa Velasquez à Madrid," *Le ménestrel* (September 1920). See also Niño Rodríguez, *Cultura y diplomacia,* 117–121. The program of the three-day opening ceremony included performances of works by Ravel (who played the piano), Falla, Rameau, Lully and Chopin. Delaunay, *Des palais en Espagne,* 173.

⁷ Widor summarized the questions from which the members of the mission had to depart: "Que pense-t-on de nous là-bas? Quelle opinion de la guerre, de la continuité de notre effort, de l'endurance du front, de moral de l'arrière? Quelle que soit la propagande acharnée que se fait contre nous, quel que soit le nombre des agents, des journaux achetés par l'Allemagne, leur est-il possible encore de croire à la décadence de notre race, ainsi que s'efforcent de le proclamer les germanophiles?" Widor, "La Villa Velasquez à Madrid."

⁸ Delaunay, *Des palais en Espagne,* 116–121.

⁹ Niño Rodríguez, *Cultura y diplomacia,* 117–120.

¹⁰ On the Comité de Rapprochement see Niño Rodríguez, *Cultura y diplomacia,* 329, 348. On funding, see ibid., 349.

¹¹ Eric Storm, "The Rise of the Intellectual Around 1900: Spain and France," *European History Quarterly* 32, no. 2 (2002): 139–160. Storm explains the birth of the intellectual—who addresses an "anonymous mass" and postulates an idea of the nation—in France and Spain as a consequence of the fin-de-siècle crisis in these two countries, epitomized in the affaire Dreyfus and the *desastre* respectively. Storm argues that the parallelism of situations facilitated an intense exchange between French and Spanish intellectuals.

authors and essayists Miguel de Unamuno, José Martínez Ruiz alias "Azorín," Ramiro de Maeztu and José Ortega y Gasset, the poet Antonio Machado and, to a certain extent, the painter Ignacio Zuloaga.[12] After relinquishing his early anarchism, Azorín embraced a form of authoritarianism inspired by Maurras, whom he met on a trip to Paris, during the First World War, working as a correspondent for the conservative newspaper *ABC*. Azorín was also inspired by Barrès, from whom he assimilated the idea of an "eternal nation" that must be sought in the common ancestors as well as the inner manifestations of a national character, rather than the exotic traits.[13] Somewhat less directly, Ramiro de Maeztu assimilated Maurras's ideas while working as a correspondent in England. During the First World War he abandoned his early socialism and embraced a Maurrasian idea of social order predicated upon a rejection of German culture and Romanticism. After the establishment of the Second Republic in Spain (1931), Maeztu founded Acción Española, a project that was inspired by Action Française—as its name suggests—and aimed at gathering anti-Republican intellectuals and politicians in Spain, but that, in the end, materialized only in the founding of an eponymous journal.[14]

Beyond their numerous differences and particularities, and regardless of the nature of their religious beliefs, most of these intellectuals concurred in diagnosing a national moral crisis and prescribing Catholic faith as the primary remedy.[15] In this aspect, they built upon the work previously done by other Spanish intellectuals, most especially Marcelino Menéndez y Pelayo, who, in his eight-volume, ambitious and influential *Historia de los heterodoxos españoles* (1880–1882), lay down a history of Spain in which Catholicism functions as the unifying narrative across different periods and locales of the national imaginary.[16] At the turn of the century, Spanish intellectuals used this work as the basis on which to build a rhetorical response to recent events, most notably the so-called colonial *desastre* of 1898, which gave name to the eponymous generation.[17] They read the defeat by the United States that year, in which Spain lost Cuba, Guam and the Philippines, as the definitive symptom of gradual moral decay and as the culmination of the gradual loss of colonial and political power, which started in the

---

[12] For a discussion of Zuloaga and its links with the generations of 1898 and 1914 see Fox, *La invención de España,* 167–174; José Martín Martínez, "Painting and Sculpture in Modern Spain," in *The Cambridge Companion to Modern Spanish Culture*, ed. David T. Gies (New York: Cambridge University Press, 1999), 239–242.

[13] Fox, *La invención de España*, 132–138.

[14] Pedro Carlos González Cuevas, *Acción Española: teología política y nacionalismo autoritario en España (1913–1936)* (Madrid: Tecnos, 1998). Cuevas, *El pensamiento político,* 88–93.

[15] Fox, *Invención de España,* 187–202.

[16] Henry Kamen, *Imagining Spain: Historical Myth & National Identity* (New Haven and London: Yale University Press, 2008), 83–84, 132–133.

[17] Christopher Britt-Arredondo, *Quixotism: The Imaginative Denial of Spain's Loss of Empire* (Albany: State University of New York Press, 2005).

seventeenth century. They believed that Catholicism was tied to the imperial fate they assigned to Spain, and argued that this faith constituted the cohesive force holding the old Spanish empire in Latin America together. Furthermore, they claimed that Catholicism had made possible the forging of Spain in the fifteenth century, under the rule of King Ferdinand II of Aragón and Queen Isabella I of Castile, known as the Catholic kings. Ferdinand and Isabella brought about the unification of the kingdoms of Castile and Aragón through their strategic marriage, and defeated the last remaining Moorish government in 1492, thus completing the Reconquista.[18] Furthermore, in a violent attempt to reach a state of ethnic purity and free themselves from a competitive élite that they ultimately regarded as "foreign," they expelled Jews who refused to convert to Catholicism, in 1492; the population of Islamic descent, the Moriscos, would follow suit in 1609.[19] On the basis of these arguments, the 1898 and 1914 intellectual generations explained Spain's purported crisis as a result of a loss of Catholic and imperial values. To a great extent, their work and attitude have helped perpetuate what Kamen termed the "myth of a Christian Spain," which has produced so many deformed visions of the past.[20] There is little wonder that French Catholic propaganda succeeded in Spain, since it touched on sensitive issues and helped to appease prevailing anxieties.

The Italian Menace and Invasion

After the first Spanish musicologists emerged around the midnineteenth century, they narrated the history of Spanish as a centuries-long fight against foreign influences, predicated upon a dichotomous distinction between indigenous and foreign elements.[21] Among them, Mariano Soriano Fuertes and Felipe

---

[18] A term that entails a dubious identification with the inhabitants of the Iberian Peninsula prior to the Muslim invasion of 711, and consequently entails a conceptualization of the Moors as "foreign." José Álvarez Junco, *Mater Dolorosa: La idea de España en el siglo XIX* (Madrid: Taurus, 2001), 217–221.

[19] Henry Kamen, *The Disinherited: The Exiles Who Created Spanish Culture* (London and New York: Allen Lane, 2007), 7–10; 57–61.

[20] Kamen, *Imagining Spain*, 74–95.

[21] Emilio Ros-Fábregas, "Música y músicos 'extranjeros' en la España del siglo XVI," in *La capilla real de los Austrias: Música y ritual de corte en la Europa moderna*, ed. Bernardo J. García and Juan José Carreras (Madrid: Fundación Carlos de Amberes, 2001), 101–126; Etzion, "Spanish Music, 93–120; Juan Jose Carreras, "From Literes to Nebra: Spanish Dramatic Music Between Tradition and Modernity," in *Music in Spain During the Eighteenth Century*, ed. Malcolm Boyd and Juan José Carreras (Cambridge; New York: Cambridge University Press, 1998), 7–16; Emilio Ros-Fábregas, "Musicological Nationalism or How to Market Spanish Olive Oil," *Newsletter of the International Hispanic Music Study Group* 4, no. 2 (1998): 6–15, Pilar Ramos Lopez, "Mysticism as a Key Concept of Spanish Early Music Historiography," in *Early Music: Context and Ideas. II International Conference in Musicology* (Cracovia: University of Cracovia, 2008), 1–14, and "The Construction of the Myth of Spanish Renaissance

Pedrell argued that the presence of Flemish composers in the Spanish Court during the sixteenth century had contributed little or nothing to the style of Spanish composers.[22] Some of their ideas were anticipated in *Discurso sobre la historia universal de la música*, by the clergyman and organist José de Teixidor, in which he presented Spanish polyphonists of the fifteenth and sixteenth centuries as the masters of their European counterparts.[23] However, more than an update of previous publications, the work of these musicologists took the form of a patriotic and heated response to "foreign" views of "Spanish music" that had brought into question the existence of a Spanish national school of polyphony.[24] The Belgian musicologists François-Auguste Gevaert and Edmond van der Straeten had argued that there was no such thing as a Spanish school of music in the sixteenth century, since Spanish polyphonists had contented themselves with emulating their Flemish counterparts.[25] This view spread to other academic and musicological works, to the extent that the 1905 edition of *The Oxford History of Music* included its discussion of Early Modern Spanish polyphony in the entry on the Netherlands, under the controversial heading "The Offshoots of the Flemish Stock."[26]

The music of the "Golden Age" of Spanish polyphony, which included composers Tomás Luis de Victoria, Cristóbal de Morales and Francisco Guerrero, became a matter of primary concern for Spanish musicologists, since it attracted the attention of European musicologists and therefore was freighted with symbolic value. Victoria's stint in Rome between 1565 and 1587 and his hypothesized training under Palestrina became the object of speculations about the independence of a Spanish musical school, just as with Falla's stay in Paris (1907–1914) as we shall see in Chapter 4. The prevailing tendency among European musicologists to classify

---

Music as Golden Age," in *Early Music: Context and Ideas. International Conference in Musicology* (Cracovia: University of Cracovia, 2003), 1–6; Juan José Carreras, "Hijos de Pedrell: La historiografía musical española y sus orígenes nacionalistas (1780–1980)," *Il saggiatore musicale*, no. 1 (2001): 121–169; Emilio Ros-Fábregas, "Historiografía de la música en las catedrales españolas: Positivismo y nacionalismo en la investigación musicológica," *Codex XXI. Revista de la Comunicación Musical*, no. 1 (1998): 68–135.

[22] Ros-Fábregas, "Musicological Nationalism," 7; Ros-Fábregas, "Música y músicos," 102; Ramos López, "The Construction of the Myth," 1–2; Carreras, "Hijos de Pedrell," 136–137.

[23] Carreras, "Hijos de Pedrell," 134–136.

[24] Etzion, "Spanish music," 94; Carreras, "Hijos de Pedrell," 131–132.

[25] Ros-Fábregas, "Musicological Nationalism," 7; Ros-Fábregas, "Historiografía de la música," 70; Emilio Casares Rodicio, "Las relaciones musicales entre los Países Bajos y España vistas a través de los investigadores del siglo XIX," in *Musique des Pays-Bas anciens-musique espagnole ancienne (ca. 1450–ca. 1650)*, ed. Paul Becquart and Henri Vanhulst (Leuwen: Peeters, 1988), 19–68.

[26] Ros-Fábregas, "Musicological Nationalism," 8; Ros-Fábregas, "Música y músicos," 104. For previous negative views of Spain as the country that does not produce any valuable music, or views of Spanish music as Italianate, see Etzion, "Spanish Music."

Victoria in the Roman school of polyphony, and the allegations that Victoria was an epitome of Palestrina, led to heated responses on the part of Spanish musicologists.[27] In order to vindicate Victoria, Pedrell undertook the edition of Victoria's *Opera Omnia* between 1902 and 1913, published by the prestigious Leipzig house Breitkopf und Härtel.[28]

Spanish musicologists such as Pedrell relied on a dubious identification of Palestrina with Italian music in order to create an Other against which to shape the Self. The identification of "Italian music" as the foremost enemy of Spanish music in the eighteenth and early nineteenth centuries extended beyond the field of religious music, for it also underlay views of Italian opera as a deleterious and corrupt influence. Consequently, Pedrell admonished *zarzuela* or Spanish comic opera, which he regarded as being contaminated by the influence of Italian opera. Instead, he conceptualized the *tonadilla escénica* as the historical genre that embodied the qualities of the Spanish "race."[29] Since this theatrical genre, which presented a few sparse musical numbers, displayed popular characters and everyday situations, Pedrell's defense helped support the view, prevalent among European musicologists, that Spain had only produced "popular" music.

These issues gained primary importance because Pedrell, Soriano Fuertes and others believed that the future of the Spanish musical school depended on the successful formulation of a national operatic genre, that is, one European audiences and critics would unanimously regard as distinctive, independent and competitive.[30] That sort of cultural anxiety was the origin of one of the most powerful and enduring myths of Spanish music historiography, namely, the belief that a national tradition existed after having successfully survived a series of foreign cultural invasions, most conspicuously Italian. Pedrell and Soriano Fuertes argued that Phillip V (1683–1746), the first Bourbon king to reign in Spain (1700–1746), had turned his back on Spanish music and musicians and embraced Italian opera. They took issue with Phillip V's decision to establish a royal company in 1708, the *trufaldines,* formed by Italian actors who had trained in the *commedia dell'arte* tradition and would eventually perform opera. Yet, this foundation by no means entailed the end of royal commissions to Spanish composers, singers and opera companies. Meanwhile, the impact of Italian opera was

---

[27] These judgments still pervaded French criticism during the 1920s. Anon., "Kyrie, VITTORIA [sic]," *Le guide du concert* (December 1924): "Vittoria est un disciple de Palestrina. Espagnol de naissance, c'est à Rome qu'il passa la majeure partie de son existence; tout en conservant son caractère original, il est l'un des plus marquants parmi les maîtres de l'école romaine."

[28] Tomás Luis de Victoria, *Opera omnia, ex antiquissimis, iisdemque rarissimis, hactenus cognitis editionibus in unum collecta, atque adnotationibus, tum bibliographicis, tum interpretatoriis,* ed. Felipe Pedrell, 8 vols. (Leipzig: Breitkopf und Härtel, 1913).

[29] Carreras, "Hijos de Pedrell," 151–152.

[30] Ibid., 137–138; 144.

being felt in the works of Spanish composers through the gradual adoption of recitatives and arias; but the "new" elements coexisted with the older formulas. Juan José Carreras has described this phenomenon as a process of "modernisation,"[31] thus bringing into question the dichotomous distinction between the "indigenous" and the "foreign" and the association between Italian music and "decadence" that underpin Pedrell's and others' writings. One could argue, however, that to characterize the Italian elements as "modern" leads to establishment of another essentialist binary, insofar as it reinforces perceptions of Spain as being backward or peripheral. Once the assimilation of elements from "Italian" opera has begun to take place, the limit between "modern" and "premodern"—just like the boundary between "indigenous" and "foreign"—is subject to negotiation; it turns into the contingent object of discursive practices that tend to reveal their ideological foundations as they aim at fixating and defining that limit.

Pedrell's oft-quoted call to ground modern composition in the use of "national" folklore, in his widely discussed manifesto *Por nuestra música* (1891), should be read in the context of the cultural anxieties just described, as it was meant to formulate a more "rooted" expression with which to cleanse what he conceptualized as "foreign," Italianate elements.[32] Likewise, in his *Cancionero musical popular español* (1922), he argued that the history of "Spanish music" has displayed a "constant and almost general technical practice" throughout the centuries. By virtue of this "personal *modus*," Spanish music has become "national, indigenous, *ours*, without exotic alterations, the daughter of *our* blood, *our* race, *our* genius" (pp. 38–40).[33] This essentialist narrative and the anti-Italian historiographical model established by Pedrell and other Spanish musicologists has been the only one available until recently. Its durability testifies to the effectiveness with which creating and identifying a common enemy boosted a sense of national cohesion.

The Response of French Musicologists

The work of French musicologists and *hispanistes* published since the beginning of the twentieth century helped to conceptualize "Italian music" as the second most deleterious influence on Spanish music, after German music. Following their Spanish counterparts, French intellectuals and musicologists, including Collet and the *hispanistes*, construed the history of Spanish music in

---

[31] Carreras, "From Literes to Nebra," 16.
[32] Pedrell, *Por nuestra música*.
[33] "práctica técnica constante y cuasi general"; "modus personal"; "música nacional, indígena, nuestra sin alteraciones exóticas, hija de sangre de nuestra raza y de nuestro genio" Felipe Pedrell, *Cancionero musical popular español*, 4 vols. (Valls: E. Castells, 1922), 38–40.

the eighteenth and nineteenth centuries as an unremitting fight against Italian music. Furthermore, the *hispanistes* who supported Catholic propaganda, and those who were close to Catholic organizations such as Action Française, entertained the myth that Catholic fervor or a sort of "mysticism" conferred on Spanish music its characteristic and superior element. It could be argued that, rather than imitating their Spanish counterparts, French musicologists entered into a dialogue with them, since information circulated in both directions, as we shall see now.

In addition to supporting Catholic propaganda, French musicologists and the *hispanistes* mirrored, once again, their own concerns over the fate of French music. Just like their Spanish counterparts, they could write a chapter of their musical history as a fight against the dominion of Italian opera. As Katharine Ellis has argued, "the idea of a historically defined, and distinct, French 'musical character' had been problematic since the displacement of *la musique française* by the Italian operatic tradition in the late eighteenth century."[34] Even earlier, the Querelle des bouffons (1752–1754) had brought into question the validity of French as a suitable language for opera, and unleashed a passionate debate that, somewhat obliquely, touched on issues of national identity. These issues regained momentum at the end of the nineteenth century, when Debussy and his supporters, in particular Louis Laloy, took over from their nineteenth-century forerunners' endeavors to situate Rameau at the center of "French" musical traditions.[35] Rameau, let us remember, had spearheaded the defense of the French language during the Querelle, confronting Rousseau and the *encyclopédistes*, who instead turned to Italian opera.[36] The successful reinstatement of Rameau depended on how these issues were retrospectively constructed.

Constructions of Spanish music as an anti-Italian artifact reflected broader political and cultural debates that, even though not comparable to anti-German propaganda in extent or significance, brought to bear on perceptions of Italian music as a foreign menace. Italy joined the Triple Alliance in 1882, committing itself to supporting Germany and Austro-Hungary in case they were attacked by Great Britain or France. Ultimately it stayed neutral in 1914, and changed sides to enlist in the Entente in 1916. Furthermore, a few years before the First World War, amidst aesthetic debates over Rameau and French music history, Italian opera became, once again, a menace, since verists made huge economic profits

---

[34] Ellis, *Interpreting the Musical Past*, 116.

[35] Anya Suschitzky, "Debussy's Rameau. French Music and Its Others," *Musical Quarterly* 86, no. 3 (2002). 398–448. Debussy's "Hommage à Rameau," from his *Images* for piano, dates from 1905. See also Ellis, *Interpreting the Musical Past*, 76–78, 140–141.

[36] Rousseau constituted one of the primary targets of Maurras for his liberal ideas and his lack of patriotism. Maurras wrote scathingly about Rousseau and deemed him a representative of "Germanic barbarism" and someone who "nourished on Hebraic revolt." He also called him a "savage" and a "half-man." David Carroll, *French Literary Fascism*, 75.

on the stages of Paris. This situation elicited impassioned attacks and a heated debate in the press, with French composers and critics claiming that Italian verists were opportunists who catered to the masses and debased operatic production.[37] Unlike Wagnerism or nineteenth-century Italian music, however, this phenomenon did not unleash an identity crisis in the form of an introspective and conflictive search for the purported "true" values of French music.

Some of these issues could lie behind Albert Soubies's three-volume *Histoire de la musique. Espagne* (1899), probably the first French musicological work to echo the anti-Italian diatribes of Spanish musicologists. Soubies could have easily assimilated Pedrell's ideas, since he requested the latter's input for his *Musique russe et musique espagnole* and they entertained a lively correspondence, as discussed in Chapter 1.[38] In the first (1899) of the three volumes, Soubiès set the basis for much of the anti-Italian descriptions of Spanish music to come. He presented Spain as the bastion of Christian religion and argued that Italy had remained under the shadow of paganism:

> One is sometimes tempted to believe that the most authentic Christian sentiment in music must be sought among the Spaniards. Much as the efforts carried out by the Romans have certainly been admirable, they can never fully escape to the suspicion of a secret and permanent paganism, from which—some say—Italy has never been able to free itself.[39]

Soubies construes the Roman legacy as "pagan" in order to undermine well-established constructions of Italy as being the cradle and bastion of Catholicism. Significantly, he casts Spain as Christian rather than Catholic, perhaps in order to signify that his concept of Spanish music was not anti-German.[40] In sum, Soubies understands Christian religion as a sign of cultural hegemony and, on that basis, undermines Italian culture. In addition, he helps to conceptualize Spain as

---

[37] Jean-Christophe Branger, "Les compositeurs français et l'opéra italien: La crise de 1910," in *Le naturalisme sur la scène lyrique*, ed. Jean-Christophe Branger and Alban Ramaut (Saint-Etienne: Publications de l'Université de Saint-Etienne, 2004), 314–342.

[38] Albert Soubies, *Musique russe*; Francesc Cortès, "Les rapports," 299, 388.

[39] "Nous sommes parfois tentés de croire que c'est chez les Espagnols qu'il convient de chercher l'expression la plus authentique du sentiment chrétien en musique. Quelque admirables, en effet, qu'aient été, à cet égard, les Romains, ils n'échappent point toujours au soupçon de ce paganisme permanent et secret, dont, au dire de quelques-uns, l'Italie, à aucune époque, n'a pu se débarrasser entièrement." Albert Soubies, *Histoire de la musique. Espagne, I. Des origines au XVIIe siècle* (Paris: Librairie des Bibliophiles, 1899), 57.

[40] His pro-German stance is evident in his several publications on Wagner and the history of German music. Albert Soubies and Charles Malherbe, *L'oeuvre dramatique de Richard Wagner* (Paris: Fischbacher, 1886); Albert Soubies and Charles Malherbe, *Mélanges sur Richard Wagner* (Paris: Fischbacher, 1892); Albert Soubies, *Histoire de la musique allemande* (Paris: May & Motteroz, 1896). See Yvonne Tiénot, "Soubies, Albert.".

a spiritual reserve, which constituted one of the central arguments of Catholic propaganda among Spanish and French intellectuals.[41]

Barrès and Spanish Intellectuals

Maurice Barrès was the first French intellectual to formulate consistently a Catholic and anti-Italian idea of Spain. From his prominent position in the Comité Catholique de Propagande, Barrès played a key role in introducing the ideas of Spanish intellectuals in France.[42] He was in close contact with some members from the Spanish generations of 1898 and 1914, most especially the author, essayist, critic and thinker Miguel de Unamuno, who held a chair at the University of Salamanca, and whose works epitomize, to a great extent, the Catholic essentialism described above.[43] Furthermore, in the wake of the Dreyfus affair, Barrès took over as president of the radical, right-wing League de la Patrie Française and was close to Maurras, with whom he shared a Catholic, Latin, anti-German and anti-Semitic conception of French identity, differing only in his anti-monarchism. He conceived of French culture as a pre-given condition embodied in the "ancestors" and transmitted through tradition, that is, the myth of a collective past and a homogeneous culture. Further in connection with Maurras, he believed that the fall of the Ancien Régime had brought about a crisis of values.[44] As we shall see, Barrès's ideas on Spanish culture, identity and history exerted a notorious influence on the young Henri Collet.

In February 1915, Barrès published a series of three articles about the organization of French propaganda in Spain, which reveal his idea of the latter country and how he conceived of its relations and cultural bonding with France. The articles appeared in various issues of the anti-German revanchist daily newspaper *L'Echo de Paris*. The fact that they were published on the front page indicates the importance that certain media attached to breaking Spain's neutrality during the War. In "Comment faire notre propagande en Espagne" (February 2), Barrès starts by declaring his intention to prevent Spaniards from failing "to recognize

---

[41] Several years before the war, the Catholic Hispanist Maurice Legendre and the journalist and member of the Académie Française Etienne Lamy put forward a Catholic image of Spain, arguing that civilization did not rely on industrial and economic development, but rather on fidelity to spiritual values and tradition. Niño Rodríguez, *Cultura y diplomacia*, 252–253.

[42] Jean Bécarud, "Barrès et l'Espagne dans mes cahiers," in *Barrès, une tradition dans la modernité. Actes du colloque de Mulhouse, Bâle et Fribourg-en-Brisgau des 10, 11 et 12 avril 1989*, ed. André Guyaux, Joseph Jurt and Robert Kopp (Paris: Honoré Champion, 1991), 233–240; Adelaida Porras Medrano, "Toledo o el secreto de Maurice Barrès," *Thélème. Revista complutense de estudios franceses* 14 (1999): 11–22.

[43] Collet's library held a number of volumes by Unamuno and other Spanish intellectuals in the sphere of the latter, who likewise supported Catholic constructions of Spain. Stéphan Etcharry, "Henri Collet," 160.

[44] Carroll, *French Literary Fascism*, 10–35.

France's generous role" shown in "Marne's radiant victory, which saved Latin civilization."[45] Furthermore, he intends to highlight "the spiritual principles that animate both nations," and to raise awareness that "French blood has been shed in order to help survive a certain soul in which Spain participates."[46] Barrès's main aim, however, is to undermine the secular and anticlerical form of propaganda put forward by Ernest Mérimée, whom he introduces as professor at the Université de Toulouse and director of the Institut Français in Madrid; in reality he was the co-director and a year after founded the main French organization for socialist and secular propaganda, namely, the Comité International de Propagande. Barrès quotes several excerpts from an unidentified letter by Mérimée, in which the latter regretted that, for the Spaniards, "the word France is synonymous with impiety, immorality, demagogy and anarchy," whereas "Germany represents to their eyes moral order […] a principle of authority, the purity of familial lifestyle, and religious piety."[47] Barrès takes issue with Mérimée's manifest intention to "dispel bigotry […] without dissimulating our ideas, our democratic faith, our aspirations to progress."[48] He accuses Mérimée of "preaching French radicalism," and quotes from a letter sent to him by "one of [his] correspondents in Spain," which argues that "many Catholic Spaniards […] hold hostility against the French government for its anti-religious politics, but, in the end, they love France."[49] Barrès's purpose, therefore, is to show that Spaniards prefer a Catholic France, and to undermine the secular and anticlerical strands of French propaganda.

In "Les Voix françaises de l'Espagne" (February 9), Barrès turns away from the question of Catholic propaganda in order to focus on the role of Spain during the War.[50] He quotes the testimonies of several Spanish writers and intellectuals giving their support to France and showing their dislike of German culture, in the context of a poll run by *L'Echo de Paris*. Barrès gathers all those testimonies in order to argue that Spanish intellectuals are "the friends of our soldiers" and have become "fraternally united in order to block the route to those savant and

---

[45] "méconnaître le rôle généreux de la France"; "notre victoire éclatante de la Marne qui sauva la civilisation latine." Maurice Barrès, "Comment faire notre propagande en Espagne," *L'echo de Paris* (February 2, 1915).

[46] "principes spirituels qui animent nos deux nations"; "Le sang de la France est versé pour que survive une certaine âme dont participe l'Espagne." Ibid.

[47] "le mot France est synonyme d'impiété, d'immoralité, de démagogie, d'anarchie"; "l'Allemagne représente à leurs yeux l'ordre moral […] le principe d'autorité, la pureté des mœurs familiales, la piété religieuse." Mérimée, "Letter to Barrès," n.d., quoted in Barrès, "Comment faire notre propagande."

[48] "dissiper des préjugés […] sans rien dissimuler de nos idées, de notre foi démocratique, de nos aspirations vers le progrès." Mérimée, "Letter to Barrès," quoted in Barrès, "Comment faire notre propagande."

[49] "prêcher le radicalisme français." Mérimée, "Letter to Barrès" quoted in Barrès, "Comment faire notre propagande"; "un de mes correspondents en Espagne"; "Beaucoup des Catholiques espagnols […] ont de l'hostilité contre le gouvernement français à cause de sa politique religieuse, mais au fond aiment la France." Anon., "Letter to Barrès," n.d., quoted in Barrès, "Comment faire notre propagande."

[50] Maurice Barrès, "Les voix françaises de l'Espagne," *L'echo de Paris* (February 9, 1915).

barbarian forces that would like to crush Latin civilization."[51] Most significantly, Barrès finishes his article by quoting a letter he personally received from Unamuno, in which the latter states that "we, the Basques," are "fundamentally Spanish."[52] As we shall see shortly, this sort of centralist statement, undermining the endeavors and aspirations of Basque, and more generally nonstate nationalisms, constituted one of the key elements in the agenda of the Generations of 1898 and 1914, one in which Unamuno influenced Barrès and, through the latter, Collet. Unamuno devotes the remainder of his letter to placing French Hispanists on top of their German counterparts. He argues that, since German Hispanists "have suffered the yoke of a German soulless technique," "there is more truth about Spain in the books of Dumas or Gautier, despite being replete with contempt, fantasies and small errors"—a statement he extends to Prosper Mérimée and Victor Hugo.[53] At the end of his letter, Unamuno makes a statement that shows its rhetorical proximity to Collet's obituary of Albéniz, discussed in Chapter 1: "I am sure that with an allied triumph, intellectual and moral Spain will free itself from the pedantry of German technique which invaded us and threatened to suffocate us."[54] This striking similarity does not necessarily rely on direct borrowing, but at the least it suggests that the circulation of ideas and rhetorical elements between French and Spanish intellectuals was intense. In his concluding statement, after quoting Unamuno's letter, Barrès says that "French Hispanists," including "the younger ones, such as Henri Collet," "will want to take notice" of this letter.[55]

In "Réchauffons notre propagande" (February 11), Barrès shows his regrets that the Spaniards, "troubled by German propaganda, ignore how to connect with French thought."[56] He believes that the reason behind this disadvantage is that "our enemies have opened workshops of deception" where "they have

---

[51] "les amis de nos soldats"; "unis fraternellement pour barrer la route à des forces savantes et barbares qui voudrait écraser la civilisation latine." Barrès, "Les voix françaises."

[52] "Nous, les Basques"; "foncièrement espagnols." Miguel de Unamuno, "Letter to Barrès," n.d., quoted in Barrès, "Les voix françaises."

[53] "ont souffert le joug du technicisme allemand sans âme"; "Dans les livres de Dumas ou Gautier sur l'Espagne, remplis de méprises, de fantaisies, de petites erreurs, il y a plus de vérité." Unamuno, "Letter to Barrès," quoted in Barrès, "Les voix françaises."

[54] "Je suis sûr qu'avec le triomphe des alliés, l'Espagne intellectuelle et morale se libérera de ce pédantisme de la technique germaine qui nous envahissa et menaçait de nous suffoquer." Ibid. Compare with: "Dans ces milieux germaines si favorables au labeur sérieux et profitable, Albéniz acquit assez de maîtresse pour être en état d'aborder la haute composition, tout en conservant cette liberté d'allure, cette charmante négligence et cette spontanéité par quoi l'Espagne demeure impénétrable au pédantisme teuton." Collet, "Nécrologie."

[55] "hispanisants français"; "les plus jeunes comme Henri Collet"; "voudront la recueillir et la méditer." Barrès, "Les voix françaises."

[56] "troublés par la propagande allemande ne savent pas où se mettre en communication avec notre pensée française." Maurice Barrès, "Réchauffons notre propagande," *L'écho de Paris* (February 11, 1915).

installed their professors," and have "manufactured an extraordinary ideological artillery."[57] In the postscript, he quotes a letter in which Mérimée shows his disagreement with the portrait that Barrès made of him in the aforementioned article. Mérimée argues that he is not a "radical," and defines himself as "a simple republican, very liberal and very French."[58] Furthermore, he confesses that he "cannot admit […] that the role of France finishes with Louis XVI," by which he means to counter the defense of the Ancien Régime by Action Française.[59] However, at the end of his letter, Mérimée makes a considerable endeavor to reconcile himself with Barrès. He declares: "the dream that I caress" is that, "during one of your oncoming trips" around Spain, "you honor us by explaining to the public of the Institut Français [de Madrid] what is France and what are the multiple reasons to love it."[60]

Mérimée's conclusion strikes me as conciliatory, especially after he and Barrès have given substantial evidence of the ideological divides underpinning the making of French propaganda. Indeed, Barrès's articles in *L'Echo de Paris* show that the contribution of French musicologists to defining the Catholic and—as we shall see—centralist concept of "Spanish music" that gained momentum among Spanish musicologists was limited to the conservative strand of French propaganda, and more particularly to the sphere of the Comité Catholique. This phenomenon can be clearly observed in one of Barrès's essays published a year earlier, *Greco ou le secret de Tolède* (1911).[61] The interest of this essay lies in the fact that, just like Soubies and Spanish musicologists, Barrès construes Italian paganism as the primary enemy of Spanish Catholicism, instead of the more expected German Protestantism. Despite its focus on painting, this book arguably provided the nexus between the work of Spanish musicologists and their French counterparts.

As its title indicates, Barrès's *Greco* deals with the Cretan painter Domenicos Theotocopoulos (1541–1614), better known as El Greco, a sobriquet that denotes his Cretan origins, seen through the prism of Greece. El Greco's life and artistic trajectory lent itself to anti-Italian readings of Spanish culture. He had trained in Venice and owned a workshop in Rome since 1570, but resided in

---

[57] "Nos ennemies ont ouvert des ateliers de mensonges"; "Ils y ont installés leurs professeurs"; "Ils y ont fabriqué une extraordinaire artillerie idéologique." Barrès, "Réchauffons notre propagande."

[58] "radical"; "Je ne suis qu'un simple républicain, très liberal et très français." Mérimée, "Letter to Barrès," n.d., quoted in Barrès, "Réchauffons notre propagande."

[59] "nous ne pouvons admettre […] que le rôle de la France finisse avec Louis XVI." Mérimée, "Letter to Barrès," s.d., quoted in Barrès, "Réchauffons notre propagande."

[60] "le rêve que je caresse"; "l'un des vos prochains voyages"; "vous nous fassiez le grand honneur de venir expliquer vous-même à notre public de l'Institut Français de qu'est la France, et pour quelles multiples raisons il faut l'aimer." Barrès, "Réchauffons notre propagande."

[61] Maurice Barrès, *Greco ou le secret de Tolède* (Paris: Émile-Paul, 1912).

the Spanish city of Toledo from 1577 to his death. Toledo was the capital of the Visigothic Kingdom before the Muslim invasion of the Iberian Peninsula in 711, and between 1522 and 1561 it served as one of the three capitals of Spain, together with Valladolid and Madrid. In *Greco*, Barrès describes Toledo as the "soul of Spain," in that it had brought together the Jewish and Muslim peoples before they were official expelled from Spain in 1492 and 1609–10: "the very noble and loyal, the imperial Toledo, on top of its rough hill, amidst its Roman ruins, its Visigothic basilicas, its Arab mosques, its churches and palaces, remains the soul of Spain."[62] Nevertheless, he proclaimed the superiority of Catholicism: "in Toledo, if my heart never gets cold or my eyes bored, it is because I find there, on every step, the most beautiful fight between Catholicism and Semitism, and Arab or Jewish element which persists under the thick Catholic varnish."[63] This endorsement of ethnic and cultural hybridization, which contemplates Jewish and Arab cultures as an integral—although subordinated—part of Spanish identity, clearly departed from the anti-Semitism and xenophobia that pervade his other writings and that presided in the official doctrine of Action Française. More importantly, he seems to have anticipated Américo Castro's oft-quoted, highly controversial definition of Spanish identity as an Arab, Jewish and Christian hybrid, which the latter expounded upon in *España en su historia* (1948), written in exile from the Franco dictatorship.[64] Like Barrès, Castro conceived of Toledo as the cradle of Spanish civilization but not subordinating all cultures to Christianity.

Like Maurras, in *Greco* Barrès construes Catholicism as the "true" legacy of primitive Christianity, but opposes its Spanish variant to Italian paganism rather than German Protestantism. He contends that, in Toledo, El Greco abandoned the use of "warm colors, proper to the opulent Venice and Papal Rome,"[65] and turned his back on "the picturesqueness and paganism so dear to magnificent Venice," thus becoming a "strange convert."[66] Anti-Italian and Catholic propaganda emerges more conspicuously in Barrès's commentary on El Greco's painting *Martyrdom of Saint Maurice and His Legions* (1580–1581), commissioned by Philip II for El Escorial. Barrès argues that, for the first time, this painting shows independence from "the Italian influences which still persist during El

---

[62] "la très noble, la très loyale, l'impériale Tolède, sur son âpre côte, au milieu de ses ruines romaines, de ses basiliques wisigothes, de ses mosquées arabes, de ses églises et de ses palais, demeurait l'âme de l'Espagne." Barrès, *Greco*, 22.

[63] "Et dans Tolède, si je n'ai jamais le coeur froid, ni les yeux ennuyés, c'est que j'y vois à chaque pas la plus belle lutte du romanisme et du sémitisme, un élément arabe ou juif qui persiste sous l'épais vernis catholique." Barrès, *Greco*. 84.

[64] Aidi, "Interference of al-Andalus," 70–71.

[65] "il abandonne les intonations chaudes, familières à l'opulente Venise et à la Rome des papes." Barrès, *Greco*, 118.

[66] "le pittoresque et le paganisme chers à la magnifique Venise!"; "étrange converti." Ibid., 119.

Greco's early life in Toledo," and proves that "Greco discovered his genius once he imagined himself to be painting the noble Castilians."[67] It is significant that Barrès chose this painting as the basis for his discourse on El Greco's alleged anti-Italian and Castilian allegiances, since it represents the episode in which the Emperor Diocletian ordered the Christian Saint Maurice killed as he refused to pay tribute to the pagan gods. Therefore, Barrès must have thought that this painting could be construed as an emblem of Spanish Catholic resistance against Italy's alleged paganism.

The marks of the generations of 1898 and 1914 in Barrès's *Greco* are clear in the mixture of Catholic and Castilian discourses. In addition to construing Spain's identity as Catholic, Unamuno, Azorín, Machado, Ortega and Zuloaga situated an imaginative and even fictional selection of cultural elements from the central region of Castile—which the city of Toledo belongs to—as the basis of their formulation of Spanish identity.[68] In this aspect, they built upon the work of the *regeneracionistas,* a group of midnineteenth-century intellectuals and politicians. Their leader, Joaquín Costa (1846–1911), was a Maurrasian theoretician who similarly diagnosed a national crisis and prescribed the rule of an "iron surgeon," a semidictator who should cure Spain's "national anatomy" from its current ills.[69] More than the "iron surgeon," however, the aforementioned generations were interested in Costa's postulation of an economic and cultural investment in Castile, which he regarded as a neglected region and the basis for Spain's regeneration. They imbued Costa's defense of Castile with centralist connotations, since they partly blamed Spain's moral crisis on the rise of "peripheral" or nonstate nationalisms, particularly Basque and Catalan. Consequently, they construed Castile as the primary repository of national values, and granted it privileged status in the formation of the Spanish literary canon, with they regarded as the historical and traditional projection of the Spanish "soul." They brought to the attention of scholars and readers the so-called mystical school of poetry, formed by Saints Teresa of Avila and John of the Cross, both of whom resided in Castile. Furthermore, they construed Don Quixote, the fictional hero who rides across the plains of Castile, as an embodiment of national values, an idealistic, chivalric character who fights in pursuit of its goals, undeterred by adversity. In some of their writings, these intellectuals even considered Don Quixote the hero of

---

[67] "Les influences italiennes persistent dans ce début du Greco à Tolède"; "Ainsi Greco découvrit son génie dès qu' il imagina de peindre les nobles castillans." Ibid., 24.

[68] Fox, "Spain as Castile"; Fox, *La invención de España,* 119–120, 151–161. Thomas Harrington, "Rapping on the Cast(i)le Gates: Nationalism and Culture-Planning in Contemporary Spain," in *Ideologies of Hispanism,* ed. Mabel Moraña (Nashville, TN: Vanderbilt University Press, 2005), 107–137.

[69] On the influence of Maurras on Costa see Pedro González Cuevas, *El pensamiento político de la derecha española en el siglo XX: De la crisis de la Restauración al Estado de los partidos (1898–2000)* (Madrid: Tecnos, 2005), 36–39.

the moral reconquest of Latin America, which should bring Spain out of its crisis.[70] This rhetorical "Quixotism," which Christopher Britt-Arredondo has described as the "imaginative denial of Spain's loss of empire,"[71] rubbed off on French propaganda. The artificers of French Catholic propaganda in Spain distinguished between a Quixotic and spiritualist Spain, on the one hand, committed to the ideals that, according to them, united it to France and the allies and severed it from Germany; and, on the other hand, the Spain of Sancho Panza, taking advantage of neutrality in order to profit from the War, and embracing German materialism and positivism instead of French spiritualism.[72] Quixotic propaganda also manifested itself in Barrès's *Greco*. Indeed, Barrès described El Greco as "the deepest painter of Castilian souls,"[73] "of that Spanish soul which is entirely encapsulated in a prosaic Sancho Panza and a visionary Quixote."[74] The case of Barrès illustrates how intense the ideological transfer between French and Spanish intellectuals was after the turn of the century.[75]

Collet and Mysticism

Barrès's ideas deeply influenced the young Collet at the time he was working on his doctoral thesis, *Le Mysticisme musical espagnol au XVIe siècle*, which passed examination at the Sorbonne in 1913 and was published that same year.[76] It is hardly surprising that Collet chose this subject, if one considers that he had graduated from the University of Bordeaux, which constituted one of the nuclei of Catholic propaganda. Indeed, the dissertation he presented in that institution in 1908 in was already focused on the subject of mysticism in Spanish music.[77]

---

[70] Fox, "Spain as Castile," 21–36; Carol A. Hess, *Manuel de Falla and Modernism in Spain, 1898–1936* (Chicago: University of Chicago Press, 2001), 218–222; Harrington, "Rapping on the Cast(i)le Gates."

[71] Britt-Arredondo, *Quixotism*.

[72] Niño Rodríguez, *Cultura y diplomacia*, 248. The Catholic *hispaniste* Maurice Legendre was the only one to support neutrality. He argued that Spain needed to safeguard the "spiritual reserve of the West." Ibid., 252–253.

[73] "le peintre le plus profond des âmes castillanes" Barrès, *Greco*, 117.

[74] "de cette âme espagnole tout entière résumée par le prosaïque Sancho et le visionnaire Don Quichotte." Ibid., 119.

[75] It seems hard to establish in what direction ideas traveled, as Menéndez y Pelayo's Catholic nationalism seems to antedate Maurras's equivalent idea, whereas, more clearly, Action Française served as the model for its Spanish equivalent, *Acción Española*. Pedro Carlos González Cuevas, *Acción Española: Teología política y nacionalismo autoritario en España (1913–1936)* (Madrid: Tecnos, 1998).

[76] Collet, *Le mysticisme*. Collet admitted to Barrès that his *Greco* was the main source behind his mystic construction of Spanish polyphony. Collet, "Letter to Maurice Barrès," May 16, 1916, no. 13, Paris, Bibliothèque Nationale de France, Département de manuscrits, fonds Maurice Barrès. Quoted in Etcharry, "Henri Collet," 248. Collet dedicated to Barrès his novel *L'Île de Barataria*, (Paris: Albin Michel, 1929), with which he won the Prix National de Littérature in 1929.

[77] Collet, "La valeur expressive."

In the academic year 1909–10, he was sponsored by the French Ministère de l'Instruction Publique et des Beaux-Arts to carry on postgraduate studies in Madrid, as part of the first promotion of the École des Hautes Études Hispaniques (1909), a recent foundation of the University of Bordeaux, and the origin of the future Casa Velázquez.[78] The École was directed by the archaeologist Pierre Paris, who unearthed one of the key pieces of Iberian archaeology, the Dama de Elche, along with opening the Iberian art gallery in the Louvre, and cofounding the *Bulletin Hispanique* of the University of Bordeaux.[79] Paris was one of the key artificers of Catholic propaganda in Spain, and the foremost rival of the Republican, left-wing scholar Ernest Mérimée, a professor at the University of Toulouse, with whom Paris would uncomfortably share the direction of the Institut Français de Madrid after its foundation in 1913. During his year of studies at the École, Collet carried on with his research on religious Spanish music, which led to the publication of his study on the Cantigas de Santa María in the *Bulletin Hispanique*.[80]

In *Le mysticisme*, Collet presented a history of sixteenth-century Spanish polyphony predicated upon a centralist, Castilian, Catholic and anti-Italian narrative.[81] One could argue that Collet used history as a vicarious experience of the present and a mirror of his own concerns. Conversely, it seems as if his political views were so firmly grounded that they emerged in his writing of history. Collet's division of Spain into modern regions (*régions*), instead of historical kingdoms or dioceses, reveals a deficient historical conscience.[82] This unawareness allowed Collet to bridge his perceptions of the past and the present and thus project his social and political ideals onto the historical imagination.

In his thesis, Collet presents cultural homogenization as the strategy through which powers exercise hegemony over the territories falling under their control or influence. This stance seems not so much manifest in his interest in revealing the cultural variety of Spain, which he ultimately subjects to a Castilian imperative; instead, it emerges in his criticism of the imposing attitude followed by the pope in reforming the Roman Gradual. In the second chapter, Collet endorses Philip II's decision to maintain the liturgical chants from Toledo despite the papal mandate (pp. 56ff.). Collet argues that a diplomatic conflict arose, from which Spanish music emerged triumphant thanks to its alleged mystical power, which convinced the pope to back down. Consequently, he identifies mysticism as the element that confers on Spanish music its distinctive identity (p. 181),

---

[78] Delaunay, *Des palais en Espagne*, 62.

[79] Niño Rodríguez, *Cultura y diplomacia*, 177–178.

[80] Henri Collet, "Contribution à l'étude des 'Cantigas' d'Alphonse le Savant," *Bulletin hispanique* 13, no. 3 (1911): 270–290.

[81] Collet, *Le mysticisme*.

[82] Ros-Fábregas argues that "the circulation of music and musicians […] followed patterns that had nothing to do with the present distribution of the Spanish autonomous communities." "Musicological Nationalism," 9.

and the force that rendered Spanish music impervious to the influence of the Flemish composers hired by the Habsburg Court in Spain and Italian composers (p. 162). Last, he argued that Castile was the primary focus of Spanish musical mysticism—as will be discussed later.

In reality, the first to point out the alleged presence of mystical elements in Spanish music were the Catholic scholars August Wilhelm Ambros and Karl Proske at the middle of the nineteenth century. They identified "mysticism" in the works of the "Golden Age" of Spanish polyphony in the sixteenth and seventeenth centuries, including composers Tomás Luis de Victoria, Cristóbal de Morales and Francisco Guerrero.[83] However, these musicologists did not differentiate the music of Spanish composers working in the Spanish Royal Chapel from the work of their Dutch counterparts employed by the same institution under Philip II.[84] By contrast, Collet identifies mysticism as the quality that severs Spanish music from the work of European composers.

Barrès's ideological and rhetorical imprint manifests itself in the opening statements of Le mysticisme, which already encapsulate most of Collet's views on Spanish "Golden Age" polyphony:

> In sixteenth-century Spain, religious musicians, who were contemporaries of Teresa of Avila and John of the Cross, Greco or Zurbarán, wrote admirable choral works for the lecterns of Gothic churches, in which it is possible to distinguish a racial originality and a rare expressive virtue. That virtue is Catholic mysticism, and we could even say a medieval mysticism....[85]
>
> The musician who studies them only on the basis of their technique will not be able to appreciate the spirit or their mission.[86]

Barrès's import emerges quite clearly in the attribution of mysticism, as well as in the invocation of the Castilian saints and El Greco, to whom Collet adds another painter, Zurbarán, renowned for his religious paintings displaying monks and

---

[83] Ros-Fábregas, "Musicological Nationalism," 7; Ros-Fábregas, "Historiografía de la música," 72; Ros-Fábregas, "Música y músicos," 103; Ramos López, "Mysticism," 7–8.

[84] Luis Robledo Estaire, "Estructura y función de la capilla musical en la corte de Felipe II," in *La Capilla Real de los Austrias: Música y ritual de corte en la Europa moderna*, ed. Juan José Carreras and Bernardo García García (Madrid: Fundación Carlos de Amberes, 2001), 195–206.

[85] "En Espagne, au XVIe siècle, les musiciens religieux, contemporains de Thérèse de Jésus ou de Jean de la Croix, de Greco ou de Zurbaran, destinaient au lutrin des églises gothiques d'admirables oeuvres chorales que distingue une originalité de race, et qui possèdent une rare vertu expressive. Cette vertu, c'est le mysticisme catholique, et nous pourrons bientôt dire le mysticisme du moyen âge." Collet, *Le mysticisme*, 1.

[86] "Le musicien qui ne les étudierait que par la seule technique ne saurait en apprécier l'esprit ou la mission." Ibid., 1, n1.

saints, in a *chiaroscuro* style—which ironically is reminiscent of Caravaggio, an "Italian" painter.[87] The marks of Collet's other works in the fragment above are also prominent in the construction of stylistic traits as racial or ethnic elements, this also leading him to attribute musical mysticism to "the exclusively religious mentality of the Spanish people in the sixteenth century"[88] Yet, as Kamen has argued,

> the apparently "Christian" culture of the people of Spain between the sixteenth and nineteenth centuries left much to be desired, since both clergy and laity were equally ignorant of basic essentials. Religion ended up (as in many other countries) as an extension of social discourse rather than a system of faith; it was, in other words, what you did rather than what you believed.[89]

The aspect in which this passage most resembles—and, indeed, prefigures— *Albéniz et Granados* is the categorical distinction that Collet establishes between "technique" and "mystique," and the ascription of Spain to the latter. Through that dichotomy, Collet, once again, casts the Spanish musician as an unskilled "noble savage." He reinforces this image by declaring that "without overtly fighting against the rules" Spanish musicians "proceeded as if [those rules] did not exist."[90] Furthermore, this dichotomy indirectly reinforces notions of Spain as being culturally marked, and by extension effeminate and subaltern.[91] This attitude manifests itself in the use of the adjective "medieval" to refer to Spanish "mysticism," or in Collet's choice to locate it in Gothic churches rather than Renaissance architecture. In fact, throughout *Le mysticisme*, Collet argues that the alleged mystical quality of Spanish polyphony is due to Spain having remained isolated from European Renaissance, that is, "quite apart, in truth, from the new ideal of humanist society, where paganism is resuscitated."[92] Again, there are evident connections with his other works. *Le mysticisme* anticipates *L'essor* in imposing a radical cultural protectionism on Spanish culture in order

---

[87] For an account of the constructions of Zurbarán as a mystic painter see Fox, *La invención de España*, 162.

[88] "Il nous paraît inutile d'insister sur la mentalité exclusivement religieuse du peuple espagnol au XVIe siècle." Collet, *Le mysticisme*, 108.

[89] Henry Kamen, *Imagining Spain*, 77.

[90] "sans être en lutte ouverte contre les règles, on procédait comme si elles n'existaient pas." Collet, *Le mysticisme*, 162.

[91] For a discussion of gender and "mark," see Butler, *Gender Trouble*, 13–18; Gayatri Chakravorty Spivak, "Can the Subaltern Speak?" in *Marxism and the Interpretation of Culture*, ed. Cary Nelson and Lawrence Grossberg (Urbana: University of Illinois Press, 1988), 271–313.

[92] "Nous somme bien loin, en vérité, de l'idéal nouveau de la société humaniste, où ressuscite le paganisme." Collet, *Le mysticisme*, 34.

to preserve it from modernization and render it peripheral. However, different from *L'essor*, where folklore constitutes the warrant of aesthetic and cultural independence, it is religious fervor, or to be more precise, orthodoxy, that fulfills the function in *Le mysticisme*. Collet describes Spain as "the most orthodox of Catholic nations and the only one, among them, to have forever embraced the disciplinary intransigence of the Holy See through the Council of Trent."[93] Indeed, Collet claims that "Spain has been protected from the invasion of the Renaissance or the Reformation by the barrier lifted by the Council of Trent."[94]

Le mysticisme is indebted to Barrès in yet another aspect, namely, that it inscribes cultural hybridization in the roots of Spanish mysticism and, in that way, of Spanish identity. Collet argues that "Spanish mysticism manifests the effects of a long contact with the Orient, with the Arab and Jewish philosophies."[95] This form of hybridization allows Collet to cast Spain through the trope of difference, a strategy that, more than reinforcing French hegemony, is aimed, like Barrès's *Greco*, at substantiating the hypothesis that Spanish polyphony—or culture, in the case of Barrès—constituted a distinctive expression. However, both Barrès and Collet limited the extent of hybridization. Although Christian belief presided in Barrès's portrayal of El Greco, as we have seen, racial purity reigned over Collet's rendition of mysticism, as he argues that "orthodoxy wants a purely religious music for the people, just as this music demands from that same people a pure blood, preserved from any contact with Jews, Moors or heretics."[96]

In connection with Pedrell and Spanish musicologists, Collet severs Spanish composers from their Italian (and to a lesser extent Flemish) counterparts.[97] A paragon between Victoria and Palestrina extends over a substantial portion of the book. Collet states that "one could say about Victoria what Barrès wrote about El Greco," arguing that his mysticism stems from "life in sixteenth-century Castile, that life of sentimental glorification [and] purely mystical thought."[98] He remarks that "Victoria was born in holy, Avila like Saint Teresa," and ventures the possibility "that they both had met and seen each other frequently [...] breathing together, in their early youth, the bitter

---

[93] "la plus orthodoxe des nations catholiques et, seule entre toutes, de se lier à jamais, par le Concile de Trente, avec l'intransigeance disciplinaire du Saint-Siège." Ibid., 50.

[94] "défendue de l'invasion renaissante ou réformiste par la barrière du Concile de Trente." Ibid., 31.

[95] "Le mysticisme espagnol se ressent d'un long contact avec l'Orient, avec la philosophie arabe ou juive," ibid., 21. He adds: "Aux Arabes espagnols il faut ajoindre les Juifs." Ibid., 23.

[96] "L'orthodoxie veut une musique purement religieuse pour le peuple, comme elle exige de ce même peuple un sang pur de tout contact avec le juif, le maure ou l'hérétique." Ibid., 108.

[97] He quotes extensively from Pedrell in his chapter 9.

[98] "On pourrait dire de Victoria ce que M. Barrès écrivait du Greco"; "la vie castillane du XVIe siècle, de cette vie toute d'exaltation sentimentale, de cette pensée si purement mystique." Collet, *Le mysticisme*, 380.

scents of an aesthetic land, and learning from the same readings, the 'highest method of contemplation.' "[99] One cannot help observing here a reference to carnal ecstasy, which more than one critic has pointed out in Bernini's sculptural representation of the same Saint Teresa.[100] Prefiguring Collet's *Albéniz*, who stayed "impervious to Teutonic pedantry" after living in the "Germanized" atmosphere of Leipzig and during his stay at the Schola, Collet's Victoria "did not stop being Spanish [while] he mingled for a long time abroad, played a considerable role in Italy and Germany, and was officially considered Palestrina's rival."[101] According to Collet,

> Palestrina's work is countless [and] he tackled all genres with equal mastery. But it is difficult to find, among so many perfect beauties, a "mystical expression," that ineffable quality which emanates from the heart, that passionate movement. That music is impersonal: it stays aloof and does not want to move feelings.[102]

Again, Collet construes non-Spanish elements as expressions of a soulless civilization, in order to cast Spanish culture as human and emotional, and most likely subaltern.

Considering the Catholic agenda that underlies Collet's thesis, it is not surprising that he dedicated it, among others, to the greatest exponent of Catholic propaganda in Spain, Pierre Paris, from the Comité Catholique de Propagande. Paris became the foremost rival of Ernest Mérimée, from the secular Comité International, especially in the period when they both directed the Institut Français de Madrid, a foundation of the universities of Bordeaux and Toulouse, which they respectively represented.[103] Other dedicatees in Collet's thesis include his former teachers from the University of Bordeaux, including the first French professor in Hispanic studies, Georges Cirot; the musicologist Romain Rolland, professor at the Sorbonne; and,

---

[99] "Victoria est né dans la sainte Avila, comme Thérèse de Jésus: et il semble bien possible que tous deux se soient connus et fréquentés. On imagine donc ces futurs mystiques respirant ensemble, en leur prime jeunesse, les âpres senteurs d'une terre ascétique, et se formant par les mêmes lectures spirituelles, à la 'plus haute méthode de contemplation.'" Ibid., 19.

[100] Jill L. Matus, "Saint Teresa, Hysteria, and Middlemarch," *Journal of the History of Sexuality* 1, no. 2 (October 1, 1990): 215–240.

[101] "sans cesser d'être Espagnol, il se mêla longtemps à l'étranger, joua un rôle considérable en Italie et en Allemagne, et fut considéré officiellement comme le rival de Palestrina." Collet, *Le mysticisme*, 380.

[102] "L'oeuvre de Palestrina est innombrable: messes, motets, hymnes, litanies, madrigaux, il aborda tous les genres, et avec une égale maîtrise. Mais il est difficile de trouver, au sein de tant de parfaites beautés, l'expression mystique', ce je ne sais quoi d'ineffable qui vient du coeur, le mouvement passionnel. Cette musique est impersonnelle: elle plane au-dessus de nos nécessités, elle ne veut pas émouvoir." Ibid., 83.

[103] On this rivalry see Niño Rodríguez, *Cultura y diplomacia*, 351–364.

most significantly, Felipe Pedrell and Menéndez Pidal, the latter of whom he met during his visit to Madrid in 1907.[104]

Collet would expand on the ideas presented in *Le mysticisme* in his next monograph, *Victoria*, published one year later (1914). In this book, Collet argued against previous assumptions that the Spanish composer Tomás Luis de Victoria had emulated the style of his Italian counterpart. Collet criticized musicologists for tending to classify Victoria in the Roman school of polyphony and comparing him with Palestrina (pp. 2–3). Collet argues that, unlike Palestrina, Victoria never draws on profane songs as the basis for his compositions (p. 166), and subscribes to Pedrell's view that Victoria's music is more mystical when the two use the same text (pp. 166–167). Reminiscences of Barrès's multiethnic nationalism emerge in his description of Victoria as "this sixteenth-century Spaniard in whom Arabic, Celtiberian, Muslim and Christian mysticism seems incarnated,"[105] a description that reminds us of his portrayal of Albéniz, discussed in Chapter 1. Furthermore, Barrès's rhetoric pervades Collet's analysis of Victoria's oeuvre, which the latter describes as being "as rich in lessons as Saint Teresa's *Moradas*, Greco's paintings or the Toledo cathedral."[106]

If *Le mysticisme* was mostly indebted to Barrès, Pedrell seems to loom large over *Victoria*. As has been discussed, the latter exerted a great influence on the young Collet during his stay in Barcelona in the summer of 1907. At that time, Pedrell was working on the edition of Victoria's *Opera Omnia* (1902–1913), under contract with Breitkopf und Härtel. Pedrell undertook the titanic task animated by the same intention to vindicate Victoria's work and claim his independence from Italian music. The eighth and last volume (1913) included a study of Victoria by Pedrell, published in the original Spanish, plus a French and German translation.[107] This study prefigures Collet's *Victoria* in its main ideas. Pedrell argues that "with the same mystical fervor as Teresa of Avila and John of the Cross, Victoria and our great masters are musician-poets, as shown by their mystical polyphony."[108] In a footnote, he timidly introduces an argument to

---

[104] Full list of acknowledgments: Pierre Paris (Directeur de l'École Française d'Espagne); Collet's former masters in the University of Bordeaux: Georges Cirot, Eugène Bouvy and Fortunat Strowski; Romain Rolland, professor at the Sorbonne; Ramón Menéndez Pidal, professor at the Universidad de Madrid; Felipe Pedrell; acquaintances from the Orfeó Català: Frederic Lliurat and Francesc Pujol. Collet, *Le mysticisme*, i–ii.

[105] "cet Espagnol du XVI siècle en qui s'encarnent les mysticismes arabe et celtibère, musulman et chrétien." Collet, *Le mysticisme*, 9.

[106] "aussi riche d'enseignements que les *Moradas* de sanite Thérèse, la peinture du Greco ou la cathédrale de Tolède." Ibid., 9.

[107] Later published as an independent volume. Felipe Pedrell, *Tomás Luis de Victoria, Abulense. Biografía, bibliografía, significado estético de todas sus obras de arte polifónico-religioso* (Valencia: M. Villar, 1918).

[108] "A la manera de Teresa de Jesús y de Juan de la Cruz en misticismo, Victoria y nuestros grandes maestros son músicos-poetas en sus concentos místicos." Pedrell, *Victoria*, 119.

which Collet would grant much more prominence, namely, that "Victoria never draws the themes of his compositions from the motives of a profane song, unlike what Palestrina and his contemporaries did regularly."[109] Different from Collet, however, Pedrell finds a degree of technical perfection in Victoria's style that the former would never recognize in a Spanish composer, whom, no matter how positively, he ultimately regarded through the noble savage trope. Pedrell argued that Victoria "is more correct and fluid than Palestrina, since he avoids, by way of a superior and refined art, the false relations and harmonic clashes which the latter did not consider it necessary to avoid."[110]

One may argue that the eighth volume of Pedrell's *Opera Omnia* (1913), Collet's *Le mysticisme* (1913) and *Victoria* (1914) were published in such a short period of time that it seems hard to establish who influenced whom. Pedrell was surely the first to assert Victoria's independence from Palestrina, and his ideas spread among French musicologists even before they were published.[111] In his review of the first volume of Victoria's *Opera Omnia* (1902) for *La revue musicale*, Louis Laloy declared that, "while this contemporary of Palestrina employed the same musical forms as the Italian master (masses, motets, hymns, responsories), he maintained a particular accent, more emotional, more ardent, more human."[112] Did he also mean more "mystical"? Laloy had reasons to echo or even appropriate Pedrell's ideas, for he could mirror his own endeavors to sever Rameau from Italianate associations.[113] Even before the first volume of Pedrell's *Opera Omnia* appeared, Albert Soubies wrote that, although "it has been often said that [Victoria] profited from the example of Palestrina […] it could be said that he did not borrow anything"; he added that "Victoria's music does not sound Italian, so to speak, but Spanish," since "his mysticism resembles that of Saint Therese and Saint John of the Cross."[114]

---

[109] "Victoria no busca jamás los temas de sus composiciones en los motivos de una canción profana, como hacían, ordinariamente, Palestrina y casi todos sus contemporáneos." Ibid., 120, n1.

[110] "es más correcto y más fluido que Palestrina, porque evita con finezas de arte superior las falsas relaciones y choques armónicos que éste no creía necesario evitar." Ibid., 119. Furthermore, Pedrell grounds the distinction between a Spanish and an Italian musical school on a matter of "race"—to use his own expression. Ibid., 118.

[111] "plusieurs sources françaises montrent la connaissance des archives personnelles chez Pedrell et sa collection de chansons populaires—recueillies de plusieurs chercheurs—bien avant l'apparition de son Cancionero Musical Popular Español." Cortès, "Les rapports," 313.

[112] "on savait que ce contemporain de Palestrina, tout en employant les mêmes formes musicales que le maître italien (messes, motets, hymnes et répons), avait cependant un accent particulier, plus ému, plus ardent, plus humain." Louis Laloy, "Tomás Luis de Victoria (XVIe siècle). Oeuvres éditées par Ph. Pedrell, Tome I. (Leipzig, Breitkopf et Härtel, 1902)," *Revue musicale* (May 1902).

[113] Laloy's was Debussy's closest ally in the revival of Rameau, among other aspects. Suschitzky, "Debussy's Rameau," 398–400.

[114] "On a souvent répété qu'il profita de l'exemple de Palestrina […] Mais on peut dire qu'il n'emprunta rien […] La musique de Victoria ne sonne pas, pour ainsi dire, comme de l'italien, mais comme de l'espagnol […] Son mysticisme est celui de sainte Thérèse et de saint Jean de la Cruz." Albert Soubies, *Histoire de la musique. Espagne, I*, 70.

Another intellectual who assimilated Pedrell's ideas was Charles Lalo, a philosopher and aesthetician who taught at the University of Bordeaux and whom Collet could have met as a student in that institution. Collet quotes extensively from Lalo in the opening pages of *Le mysticisme*, probably in order to undermine the import of Pedrell in his idea of Spanish polyphony—as shall be discussed later. The influence of Pedrell on Lalo seems evident in this passage from *Esquisse d'une esthétique musicale scientifique* (1908),[115] which Collet cites on the second page of *Le mysticisme*:

> during the fifteenth and sixteenth centuries, men are uniformly imbued with the powerful naturalism of the Renaissance […] and not with that mysticism which one would like to reserve to the musicians of that period, and which one hardly finds in such a pure state as in the Spanish monk Victoria; for Palestrina lived like a careful proprietary and a good family father.[116]

The sources behind Collet's *Le mysticisme* and *Victoria*, therefore, range from Barrès, Pedrell and Lalo to the Spanish artificers of Catholic and Castilian propaganda from the generations of 1898 and 1914, and possibly Soubies and Laloy. Alongside them, mention should be made of the organist, composer and champion of Castilian folklore Federico Olmeda (1865–1909). Collet met Olmeda in his home in the Castilian city of Burgos, just after he left Barcelona in the summer of 1907. Among other works, Olmeda authored the collection *Folk-lore de Castilla ó cancionero popular de Burgos* (Seville, 1903), which gathered songs from that region.[117] Furthermore, he took part in the floral games held in Burgos in 1902, which consisted of poetry contests with floral prizes, following the tradition that originated in Occitan culture and was later adopted by Catalan nationalism from the midnineteenth century.[118] In Olmeda's home, Collet met the composer, musicologist and *hispaniste* Raoul Laparra.[119] Olmeda furnished Laparra with folklore that the latter used as an inspiration for his first opera, *La*

---

[115] Charles Lalo, *Esquisse d'une esthétique musicale scientifique*, (Paris: F. Alcan, 1908).

[116] "aux XVe and XVIe siècles, les hommes sont uniformément imbus du puissant naturalisme de la Renaissance […] et non de ce mysticisme qu'on voudrait parfois réserver aux seuls musiciens de cette époque et qu'on ne trouve guère à l'état pur que chez le moin espagnol Vittoria (*sic*): car Palestrina vécut en propriétaire soigneux et en bon père de famille." Lalo, *Esquisse*, 315, quoted in Collet, *Le mysticisme*, 2 n. 3.

[117] Federico Olmeda, *Folk-lore de Castilla ó cancionero popular de Burgos* (Sevilla: Librería Editorial de María Auxiliadora, 1903).

[118] Miguel Ángel Palacios Garoz, *Federico Olmeda, un maestro de capilla atípico* (Burgos: Instituto Municipal de Cultura, 2003), 122–141. Samuel Llano, "Hispanic Traditions in a Cross-Cultural Perspective: Raoul Laparra's 'La habanera' (1908) and French Critics," *Journal of the Royal Musical Association* 136, no. 1 (2011): 104.

[119] Who will be studied in depth in Chapter 3.

habanera (Opéra Comique, 1908). This opera surely constitutes the first large-scale work entirely focused on Castile with the purpose of dislodging, from the popular imaginary, representations of Spain solely based on stereotypes from the southern region of Andalusia.[120]

The preface to Olmeda's collection *Folk-lore de Castilla* reads like a staunch defense of Castilian culture along the lines of Spanish intellectuals. Olmeda defends Castile against alleged accusations that it is lacking in "traditional customs" and "regional love" (p. 8). However, he sometimes takes on a less regionalist and more imperialistic attitude:

> Castile is the center, the heart of Spain; it speaks the national language, that of the motherland and, for that very reason, its songs have spread to every province....[121]

> Let this region be freed from the heavy yoke it has politically borne for the sake of the unity of the motherland. Thus the noble, heroic, legendary and knightly Castile of our ancestors will be reborn, together with all its songs and traditions.[122]

The marks of the Generation of 1898 are prominent in Olmeda's language-based, centralist, pan-Castilian nationalism, as well as in his reliance on symbols of ancestry and knighthood, possibly implying Don Quixote or the other hero of Spanish intellectuals, El Cid. By contrast, Olmeda did not invoke the mystical school of poetry or any other religious signs. Among the works of Barrès and the aforementioned Spanish intellectuals, Olmeda's Castilian imperialism stands out for its secular character.

Mapping Catholicism

Collet's defense of Catholic mysticism and Castilian identity in the works of Spanish "Golden Age" polyphony therefore constitutes a synthesis of what Spanish and French musicologists and intellectuals had previously put forward

---

[120] "Il est vrai que Laparra a un nom espagnol, qu'il a le type espagnol, et qu'il a vécu en profonde communion avec cette Castille extraordinaire dont il semble que les musiciens espagnols modernes: les Catalans Albeniz, Granados et Nin, les Andalous Turina et Falla, les Valenciens Rodrigo et Palau (pour ne parler que des Espagnols vraiment connues en France), ignorent les fortes vertus." Henri Collet, "Espagne," *Le ménestrel* (December 1929). On Laparra and his opera *La habanera*, see Llano, "Hispanic Traditions."

[121] "Castilla como es el centro, el corazón de España, tiene la lengua nacional, la patria, y por lo mismo, sus cantares se han extendido a todas sus provincias." Federico Olmeda, *Folk-lore de Castilla*, 13.

[122] "Alíviese y aligérese esta región de los efectos del yugo penoso que políticamente ha venido soportando en aras de la unidad nacional de la patria, y seguramente renacerá la hidalga, heroica, legendaria y caballeresca Castilla de nuestros antepasados, con todos sus cantos y tradiciones." Olmeda, *Folk-lore de Castilla*, 14.

in a more fragmentary, or in the case of Pedrell consistent, way. There is another way, however, in which *Le mysticisme* represented a more original and polemical work. In an attempt to account for the "radical opposition of regional characters,"[123] and the "ethnic varieties that can be observed in Spain,"[124] Collet divided "Spanish" music into four regional schools of polyphony (Castilian, Andalusian, Valencian and Catalan) to which he awarded decreasing degrees of mysticism.

According to Collet "the closer one gets to Italy, the more the profound sentiment of Spanish Christian faith becomes modified, weakened and foreign."[125] Although, in principle, this phenomenon singles out the Valencian school as the least mystical of all, Collet argues that

> the Valencians preserved that religious fervor which was the legacy of the mystic Middle Ages, and which prevented them from falling into the profane drama in which the Italian 'madrigalists' had got lost.... By contrast, the Catalans do not escape the reproach of secret paganism which I formerly raised against Palestrina....[126]

> The Castilian school undoubtedly gathered the masters who have best known how to express through music their mystical desire of 'intimate union with the divine' [...] we admire in them a perfect moral balance which excludes neither brilliant imagination nor passionate ardor or persuasive force [...] The source of Castilian music in the sixteenth century is the Imperial City of Toledo.[127]

Just as the Spanish school gained its aesthetic independence from its capacity to resist Italian paganism, so is Castile the region that allegedly has managed to stay away from "foreign" influences. This argument matches the view of the *regeneracionistas* and the generations of 1898 and 1914, who regarded Castile as a poor and neglected region, whose economic recovery should facilitate Spain's way out of the crisis. Furthermore, the marks of Barrès are again quite prominent in the opposition

---

[123] "radicale opposition des caractères régionaux." Collet, *Le mysticisme*, 151.

[124] "Il est certain que bien peu de nations présentent les variétés ethniques que l'on observe en Espagne." Ibid., 243.

[125] "Plus nous nous rapprochons de l'Italie, et plus le sentiment profond de la foi chrétienne espagnole semble se modifier et s'affaiblir en devenant extérieur." Ibid., 307.

[126] "Seulement les Valenciens conservaient cette ferveur religieuse qui état le legs du moyen âge mystique et qui les avait empêchés de tomber dans le dramatisme profane où s'étaient égarés les 'madrigaliers' italiens", "Les Catalans, au contraire, n'échappent pas au reproche de secret paganisme que naguère nous adressions à Palestrina." Ibid., 307.

[127] "L'École Castillane réunit sans doute les maîtres qui ont le mieux su exprimer par la musique ce désir mystique de 'l'union intime avec le divin' [...] on admire en elle ce parfait équilibre moral qui n'exclut ni l'imagination brillante, ni l'ardeur passionnée, ni la force persuasive. [...] Le foyer de la musique castillane, au XVIe siècle, est la Ville Impériale de Tolède." Ibid., 237.

of Spanish Catholicism to Italian paganism, as well as in the designation of Toledo as the focus of Spanish mysticism. The idea that Spanish Golden Age polyphony could be divided into regional schools is in itself not entirely new. Gevaert had already put forward a regional classification of popular music in nineteenth-century Spain, in which Andalusia stood out thanks to its stronger connections with "Arab civilization," and such a thing as Catalan popular music did not exist.[128] However, *Le mysticisme* is, perhaps, the first study to distinguish between regional schools of Early Modern polyphony, and to put that classification at the service of a particular state model, which, in this case, was shared by a certain conservative strand of French and Spanish intellectuals. In this aspect, Collet could have also written under the influence of Olmeda's Castilian nationalism, despite its secularism.

In spite of the important role that the geographical and cultural proximity to an alleged Italian paganism plays as a criterion in Collet's mapping of mysticism, it would be wrong to regard *Le mysticisme* through the sole prism offered by a conceptualization of Italy as Spain's primary Other or "foreign" invasion. As in other works by Collet, there were other equally relevant social and political ideals at stake in *Le mysticisme*, as this excerpt shows:

> And we can also insinuate that the Eastern provinces of Spain, which are less attached to Gothic traditions than, for instance, Castile, were more easily opened to new European ideas; and that, ever since, the abyss would incessantly grow deeper between the conservative and free provinces, between the partisans of "blood purity (pureza de sangre)" and those which welcome all creeds, between the exalted sons of an austere traditionalism and the spirits which are open to the generous ideas of the Renaissance. No sixteenth-century religious feast is celebrated in Barcelona or Valencia. The new dogma of the Immaculate Conception of Mary is celebrated in Seville or Salamanca, and it is in Toledo that the canonization of Ignatius of Loyola and Francis Xavier is commemorated with the most splendid feasts, of which Eastern Spain perceives only a distant echo.[129]

---

[128] François Auguste Gevaert, "Rapport à M. le Ministre de l'intérieure sur l'état de la musique en Espagne, par M. Gevaert, lauréat du grand concours de composition musicale," *Bulletins de l'Académie Royale des Sciences, des Lettres et des Beaux-Arts de Belgique* 19, no. 1 (1852): 184–205. Quoted in Etzion, "Spanish Music," 117.

[129] "Et nous pouvons insinuer aussi que les provinces orientales de l'Espagne, moins attachés aux profondes traditions gothiques que la Castille par exemple, étaient plus facilement ouvertes aux nouvelles idées européennes, et que dès lors l'abîme se creuserait chaque jour davantage entre les provinces conservatrices et les provinces libres; entre les partisans de la 'pureté de sang (pureza de sangre)' et ceux qui accueillaient toutes les confessions; entre les fils exaltés d'un traditionalisme austère, et les esprits ouverts aux généreuses idées de la Renaissance. Aucune des grandes fêtes religieuses du XVIe siècle ne se donne à Barcelona ou à Valence. On célèbre le nouveau dogme de l'Immaculée-Conception de la Vierge à Séville ou à Salamanque, et c'est à Tolède qu'Ignace de Loyola ou François Xavier ont pour leur canonisation les fêtes les plus splendides, dont le Levant ne veut percevoir que les lointains échos." Collet, *Le mysticisme*, 151.

This excerpt translates into a regional level the same criteria with which Collet asserted the independence of a Spanish school of polyphony from its European counterparts. The "conservative" provinces that allegedly preserve a greater medieval ("Gothic") legacy, defend racial—or "blood"—purity and remain impervious to "foreign," European humanism are the most mystical, and therefore Spanish, ones. The rejection of modernization and the endorsement of cultural protectionism that underlie Collet's regional mapping of Catholicism in Spain connects very clearly with regionalist thinkers in France, and especially with Charles Maurras—as we shall see shortly. Ironically, however, the supremacy of Castile as the focus of Spanish mysticism gains centralist overtones when regarded in the context of the ideas of the 1898 and 1914. Indeed, Collet's purpose is not so much to reveal and endorse the cultural variety as to undermine "peripheral" expressions, most conspicuously coming from Catalonia.

Catalan Nationalism

As we have seen, Collet situated the focus of Catholic mysticism in Castile, and argued that the Catalan-Valencian school was the least Catholic in the whole Spanish territory thanks to its geographical and cultural proximity to Italian paganism (pp. 151, 307 and 316). This idea was controversial, not just because of the lack of evidence supporting it but mostly because Collet conceived of mysticism as the quality that conferred on Spanish music both its distinctiveness and its superiority in the face of Italian and Flemish music. By implying that Catalonia was less Spanish, he echoed Catalan nationalist discourses, but also, from his viewpoint, subordinated Catalonia to a Castilian imperative. Therefore, in *Le mysticisme* Collet put forward a hierarchical model of state organization that, for sure, would not be to everyone's liking.[130]

This hierarchical model must be read in connection with the Spanish generations of 1898 and 1914, who tried to curb the rise of nonstate nationalism. In this sense, *Le mysticisme* represents an exacerbation of ideas that had been previously developed, a further turn of the screw aimed at connecting Pedrell's ideological legacy with Spanish intellectuals and Barrès, and sever it from Catalan nationalism, to which it could also be related—as we shall soon see. If *Le mysticism* seems like a logical outcome or development of certain intellectual traditions, it is striking how much it differs from Collet's previous work, especially from his publications dating from before Barrès's *Greco*. In his first writings, Collet

---

[130] In his complete edition of the works of the Catalan composer Joan Pau Pujol, the Catalan musicologist Higini Anglès aimed to demonstrate that mysticism was equally present in all regional schools of polyphony. Ros-Fábregas, "Historiografía de la música," 74; Ros-Fábregas, "Musicological Nationalism," 8.

situated Catalonia at the head of Spain's economic and political regeneration, in line with current trends in Catalan nationalism. Furthermore, he stood close to Pedrell's Catalan side, while he dedicated little attention to Olmeda, the staunch Castilian nationalist. Collet's anti-Italian stance, however, remained unaltered during his progression from a Catalan to a Castilian Spanish nationalism.

Collet first expressed his support for Catalan nationalism in "La musique espagnole moderne" (1908).[131] This article reflects Collet's state of mind only a few months after he returned from the trip that took him around Barcelona, Burgos, Madrid and Granada in 1907 and 1908. During that trip, he met Pedrell and Olmeda, and gathered material for his thesis. According to Collet:

> The Catalans feel proud of their capital and they are right to do so. It would seem inappropriate to remind them of their special relations with Madrid. It is true, however, that one may not find in Europe another people who may compare to their genius, energy and enthusiasm. They accomplish prodigious deeds in the name of Catalan nationalism.[132]

Collet most likely wrote this article in response to the Catalan critic Frederic Lluirat, who, addressing Collet, argued that "amidst the almost general indifference, Catalonia works, Catalonia shivers, Catalonia exists."[133] By conceptualizing the Catalans as Europeans, rather than Spanish, Collet questions the authority of the state, rendering its boundaries ineffective as far as his analysis of Catalan culture is concerned. This stance contrasts with his endorsement of Castilian mysticism, which, as with the Generation of 1898, he put at the service of state nationalism.

Collet's view of Catalan nationalism must be understood in the context of the debates on the state model that were developing in Spain and France at that time. In France, political and cultural centralism had been deeply ingrained in the Republican ideology since the 1789 Revolution. After the 1871 Commune, it constituted one of the doctrines underpinning the establishment of a social order. As a political doctrine, regionalism existed in France since at least the mid-nineteenth century. At that moment, a literary group named Félibrige, headed by the Provençal poet Frédéric Mistral,[134] set out to recuperate the Provençal

---

[131] Collet, "La musique espagnole moderne, 1er partie."

[132] "Les Catalans sont fiers de leur capitale et ils ont raison. Nous n'avons pas à rappeler le caractère spécial de leurs relations avec Madrid. Mais il est certain que l'on ne trouve peut-être pas en Europe un peuple qui, par son génie, son énergie et son enthousiasme, leur puisse être comparé. Au nom du catalanisme, ils accomplissent des prodiges." Ibid.

[133] "au milieu de l'indifférence quasi générale, la Catalogne travaille, la Catalogne s'agite, la Catalogne existe." Frederic Lliurat, "Lettre de Barcelone. Orfeo Catala," *Bulletin français de la S.I.M.* 4, no. 5 (May 1908).

[134] Musk, "Regionalism, Latinite, 227–231.

language and oppose the cultural standardization imposed from Paris.[135] In the 1890s, their legacy crystallized into an organized political movement spearheaded by Maurras, Action Française and the intellectuals grouped in the more progressive Fédération Régionaliste Française, such as its director Jean Charles-Brun, as well as Louis-Xavier de Ricard and Charles Longuet.[136] French regionalists entered into a dialogue with the Spanish advocates of nonstate nationalisms, which were comparatively more politically developed. A simple comparison between the northern (French) and southern (Spanish) parts of Catalonia and the Basque Country—which had historically held territories over both sides of the Pyrenees—showed how modernization and the building of road infrastructure had proved an efficient means of control and centralization on the part of the French administration.[137] Maurras felt a special attraction for Catalonia, where, conversely, his ideas spread more easily than in other parts of Spain, followed by the Basque Country.[138] In Spain, centralism reigned only for the short periods in which Enlightened liberals held power, that is, 1812, the liberal government of 1820–1823, and the ensuing decade, following the restoration of Ferdinand VII in 1823.[139] The rest of the time, the liberals' centralist project suffered from the threat of Carlism, a premodern, anticentralist doctrine that sought to increase the local privileges of the nobility in northern Spain—as shall be discussed in Chapter 3. Although defeated in several campaigns, the Carlists left a legacy of anticentralist activism that constituted the basis for Basque nationalism at the end of the nineteenth century.

Catalan nationalism greatly attracted French intellectuals, thanks to its greater development as well as Barcelona's cultural and economic appeal. Before Félibrige started its activity around the middle of the nineteenth century, Catalan writers had already constituted a movement known as *renaixença* or "renaissance" in the 1830s. The *renaixença* was a Herder-oriented literary movement that vindicated the use of the Catalan language, the writing of epic poems based on local heroes and the recovery of the Occitan tradition of *jocs florals* (floral games). The *renaixença* has been often compared to the Félibrige, and there is

---

[135] Mège, *Charles Maurras*, 22–25. Thiesse, *Écrire la France*, 23–32; Wright, *Regionalist Movement in France*, 46–51.

[136] Thiesse, *Écrire la France*, 11. Wright argues that regionalism cannot be ascribed to a particular political doctrine or ideology, and that it covered the whole political spectrum. Wright, *Regionalist Movement in France*, 3–24; Anne-Marie Thiesse, *Ils apprenaient la France: L'exaltation des régions dans le discours patriotique* (Paris: Maison des Sciences de l'Homme, 1997); Jean-François Chanet, *L'école républicaine et les petites patries* (Paris: Aubier, 1996).

[137] Peter Sahlins, *Boundaries: The making of France and Spain in the Pyrenees* (Berkeley: University of California Press, 1989), 291; Álvarez Junco, *Mater Dolorosa*, 596.

[138] Pedro Carlos González Cuevas, "Charles Maurras en Cataluña," *Boletín de la Real Academia de la Historia* 195, no. 2 (1998): 309–362.

[139] Álvarez Junco, *Mater Dolorosa*, 357–360.

some basis, insofar as they both represent reactions to the equation between modernization and state nationalism in the form of Catholic and nostalgic looks at an idealized, premodern past.[140]

The rise of industrialism in Barcelona during the 1880s, earlier than in other cities of Spain, brought about modern social and economic transformations such as the growth of an urban bourgeoisie, the constitution of unionist movements and the rise of anarchist protests that led to a number of bombings during the 1890s and the Setmana Tràgica of 1909. This modernization facilitated development of political regionalism and, associated with it, the birth of a cultural *modernisme*,[141] of which Antonio Gaudí's *art-nouveau* architecture became one of the most conspicuous visual expressions. The organization of the *Exposició Universal* in 1888 represented one of the most notorious and exportable signs that Barcelona's industrialization and modernization were being accomplished. These changes facilitated the growth of musical audiences, the creation of symphonic orchestras and societies, and the constitution of workers' choirs.[142] Tied to the rise of the bourgeoisie, Wagner and Shakespeare became two emblems of Catalan identity after the 1880s.[143] The *desastre* of 1898, however, elicited the rage of Catalan politicians against the central government, for it left the Catalan bourgeoisie without one of its primary economic activities, namely, commerce with Cuba.[144]

It seems easy to imagine how these signs of cultural, social and industrial modernization caused a genuine impact on the young Collet during his 1907 visit to Spain. Moreover, they created a climate of enthusiasm for Catalan culture at the beginning of the twentieth century among French regionalist groups, as evinced, among other instances, by the fact that the Schola Cantorum, which held a reputation for welcoming and supporting regionalist composers, organized a concert

---

[140] Daniele Conversi, *The Basques, the Catalans, and Spain: Alternative Routes to Nationalist Mobilisation* (Reno: University of Nevada Press, 1997), 13–17. On the comparison between *félibrige* and the *renaixença* see González Cuevas, "Charles Maurras en Cataluña."

[141] José-Carlos Mainer, *La edad de plata (1902–1939): Ensayo de interpretación de un proceso cultural* (Madrid: Cátedra, 1981), 96–101. Fox, *La invención de España*, 71–79.

[142] On the impact of Barcelona's economic upturn on musical life and the creation of associations see Aviñoa, "Sociedades musicales y modernidad," 277–286; Francesc Bonastre i Bertrán, "El Asociacionismo musical sinfónico en Barcelona (1910–1936): La Orquestra Simfònica de Barcelona, la Orquestra Pau Casals y la Banda Municipal," *Cuadernos de música iberoamericana* 8–9 (2001): 255–276.

[143] Catherine Macedo, "Between Opera and Reality: The Barcelona 'Parsifal'," *Cambridge Opera Journal* 10, no. 1 (1998): 98–101; Alfonsina Janés i Nadal, *L'obra de Richard Wagner a Barcelona*, vol. 82 (Barcelona: R. Dalmau, 1983); Helena Buffery, *Shakespeare in Catalan: Translating Imperialism* (Cardiff: University of Wales Press, 2007).

[144] Angel Smith, "Sardana, Zarzuela or Cakewalk? Nationalism and Internationalism in the Discourse, Practice and Culture of the Early Twentieth Century Barcelona Labour Movement," in *Nationalism and the Nation in the Iberian Peninsula: Competing and Conflicting Identities*, ed. Clare Mar-Molinero and Angel Smith (Oxford and Washington, DC: Berg, 1996), 171–190.

of Catalan music as early as 1905.[145] The émigré Catalans living in Paris played no small part in eliciting French sympathies for Catalonia. As far as musicians are concerned, the greatest Spanish exponents, with the exception of Falla, came from Catalonia, among them Albéniz, Granados, Ricardo Viñes and Joaquín Nin. Even if their music hardly ever referred to Catalan themes or folklore, it could help to shape perceptions of Barcelona as the cultural capital of Spain.[146] Beyond the presence of Catalan musicians, the expedition, in 1916, of sixty personalities from Catalan culture and politics to Perpignan, in order to support France during the First World War, helped to render a positive image of Catalonia.[147] The attraction that French politicians and intellectuals fostered for Barcelona materialized in the organization of two important wartime events in that city, the French Science Exhibition (1916) and the Salon of French Artists (1917).[148]

But ideas flowed in both directions. There was at least one way in which French regionalists influenced Catalan nationalism: use of the "Latin" and "Mediterranean race" tropes. Such discourses constituted the basis of *noucentisme*, a movement that emerged at the beginning of the twentieth century in Catalonia. *Noucentisme* represented a reaction against *modernisme*'s identification with Wagnerism and German Romanticism. From recent archaeological findings, *noucentistes* upheld a "Mediterranean Classicism" with which they sought to detach Catalan culture from German culture and Spanish nationalism.[149] Different from *modernisme*, *noucentisme* pursued the international expansion of Catalan culture and claimed the "Latin arch" as its natural habitat. The *noucentistes* based this pan-Latin imperialism on claims that Catalonia had inherited the wisdom and knowledge of Greek and Latin antiquity, just like the *translatio studii*. Unsurprisingly, the leader of the *noucentistes*, Eugeni d'Ors, was one of Maurras's greatest champions in Spain and a keen supporter of his "integral nationalism."[150] D'Ors

---

[145] R. C., "Concert de musique Catalane," *Le courrier musical* (May 1905). The program, however, consisted of "Andalusian" piano works by Albéniz and Granados, performed by Viñes and Blanche Selva, apart from Catalan songs harmonized by Pedrell and sung by María Gay. The significant fact is that the concept of "Catalan music" was deemed worthy of an exclusive series. On the Schola and regionalism see Andrea Musk, "Aspects of Regionalism in French Music During the Third Republic: The Schola Cantorum, D'Indy, Severac and Canteloube" (Ph.D. diss., Oxford University, 1999).

[146] Montserrat Bergadà, "Pedrell i els pianistes catalans a Paris," *Recerca musicològica* 11–12 (1991–1992) 243–257.

[147] Elisé Trenc and Edmod Raillard, "Les relations franco-espagnoles pendant la guerre. La question catalane vue à travers les activités culturelles françaises à Barcelone," in *Españoles y franceses en la primera mitad del siglo XX* (Madrid: Consejo Superior de Investigaciones Científicas, Centro de Estudios Históricos, Departamento de Historia Contemporánea, 1986), 131.

[148] Ibid., 138–139. See also Niño Rodríguez, *Cultura y diplomacia*, 313–330 ("La misión francesa de 1916: una ofensiva cultural").

[149] González Calleja, "Noucentisme," 44–51.

[150] For a discussion of d'Ors's indebtedness to Maurras, see González Cuevas, "Charles Maurras en Cataluña," 334–340.

described Barcelona as the modern Athens or Rome, just as Maurras and Collet did with regard to Paris. Furthermore, *noucentisme* represented a reaction against the centralist state model put forward by the intellectual generations of 1898 and 1914, and an alternative response to the sentiment of crisis and decadence that followed the colonial *desastre* of 1898.

Collet's aforementioned conception of the Catalan people as Europeans reads like a variant of d'Ors or Maurras's pan-Latin nationalism. His comments on Pedrell, in the same article, give a slightly different impression:

> We have hailed Pedrell as the leader of the Catalan School [...] He had that rare inspiration of creating the National Drama through the use of popular motives [...] The celebrated book *Por nuestra música*, published in Barcelona in 1891, showed that the national tradition of expression [*expressivisme*] was to be renewed by an authentic Spaniard, an heir of Victoria, just as Verdi wished to be the heir of Palestrina [...] Pedrell's qualities are exactly those of his race, and have wonderfully served his musical theater.[151]

As he would later do in *Le mysticisme*, Collet connects Pedrell with Victoria and the Spanish canon, and severs him from Italian culture. Significantly, Collet omits Pedrell's Wagnerian, *moderniste* penchants, on which the latter predicated his anti-Italian stance and which earned him the sobriquet of "the Wagner of Tortosa" (the village where he was born).[152] Furthermore, Collet describes Pedrell as the "leader of the Catalan school." From the excerpt above, however, one feels that Pedrell's Spanish facet, if it does not outweigh his Catalan side, at least matches the latter in importance. In Spain and France, Pedrell was known as the "father" of Spanish musical nationalism, to the extent that a critic wrote that "Spain has only existed as a country of serious music since Pedrell."[153] In France, his reputation grew through his personal acquaintance with Soubies and Bordes, who were more interested in Pedrell's passion for early music than his

---

[151] "Nous avons salué en Philippe Pedrell le Chef de l'Ecole Catalane. [...] Il eut cette inspiration rare ce créer le Drame National par la mise en œuvre des motifs populaires [...] La brochure fameuse Por nuestra música, parue à Barcelone en 1891, montra que la tradition nationale d'expressivisme allait être renouée par un Espagnol authentique, héritier de Victoria, comme Verdi avait désiré l'être de Palestrina [...] les qualités de Pedrell sont celles mêmes de la race, et elles ont servi merveilleusement son théâtre." Collet, "La musique espagnole moderne."

[152] On Pedrell and Wagnerism see Hess, *Manuel de Falla and Modernism*, 17–20.

[153] "L'Espagne n'existe guère comme pays de musique sérieuse que depuis Pedrell." Anon, "Oeuvres de musique espagnole," *Le guide du concert* (October 1913). Carreras discusses Pedrell's rôle as a father of Spanish nationalism: Carreras, "Hijos de Pedrell," 123. See also Albert Soubies, *Histoire de la musique. Espagne, III. Le XIXe siècle* (Paris: Librairie des Bibliophiles, 1899), 97; Jean-Aubry, *La musique et les nations*, 69; Paul-Marie Masson, "La musique espagnole au congrès de Barcelone," *Revue musicale*, August 1936.

nationalist thinking.[154] One of his staunchest advocates was his disciple, the Catalan diplomat and musicologist Rafael Mitjana. In his book-length essay ¡*Para música vamos!* Mitjana presented *Els Pirineus* as "the archetype of new Spanish music," which marks the fact that "the true Spanish opera is born."[155] Moreover he argued that, "being inspired in highly patriotic ideals," *Els Pirineus* has elicited "certain sensitive reactions from the supporters of Catalan *modernisme*, who, even in the field of art, seek to spread brotherly hatred. However, beauty and goodwill are sources of light, and light helps to drive darkness away."[156] Although these ideas spread only among the Spanish-speaking readers of the volume, Mitjana would make them known to French musicologists in his entry on Spanish music history in the *Encyclopédie du Conservatoire* by Lavignac and La Laurencie.[157] In his entry, Mitjana undermined Pedrell's Catalan side and furthered perceptions that the latter was the father of Spanish nationalism. Despite Collet's remark that Pedrell was the "leader of the Catalan school," Mitjana's and others' work helped to consolidate the former's reputation as the father of Spanish nationalism. In France, Pedrell was less commonly associated with Catalan nationalism, or more generally regionalist thinking, despite the fact that he had dedicated his *Marcha Triunfal* (Triumphal March, 1877) to Frédéric Mistral. By emphasizing Pedrell's Catalan nationalism, Collet not only showed that he held a greater knowledge of Catalan and Spanish music than most of his French compatriots but evinced where his allegiances lay at that moment.

Rather than being a contradiction, the coexistence of Catalan and Spanish nationalism in Collet's article should be understood in the context of early-twentieth-century Catalan politics. Collet's stance seems to run parallel with the program of the Lliga Regionalista, the political party that led Catalan nationalism after its foundation in 1901 until approximately the end of the First World War. To a great extent, the Lliga could be considered the political branch of *noucentisme*, especially as it upheld a Mediterranean classicism and a pan-Latin Catalan imperialism.[158] One of its founders and leader, Enric Prat de la Riba, was a close follower of Maurras's ideas—his "twin soul," as González Cuevas has

---

[154] Cortès, "Les rapports."

[155] "el arquetipo de la nueva música española"; "ha nacido la verdadera ópera española!" Rafael Mitjana, ¡*Para música vamos!: Estudios sobre el arte musical contemporáneo en España* (Valencia: Sempere y Cía., 1909), 16, 41. Also see Mitjana, *La música contemporánea en España y Felipe Pedrell* (Madrid: Librería de Fernando Fé, 1901).

[156] "Inspirada en altos ideales patrióticos"; "ciertas susceptibilidades por parte del elemento modernista catalán, que aún en materia de arte se complace en fomentar el odio entre los hermanos. Pero la belleza y la bondad son fuentes de luz y la luz disipa las tinieblas." Ibid., 74.

[157] Rafael Mitjana, "La musique en Espagne: Art religieux et art profane," in *Encyclopédie de la musique et dictionnaire du Conservatoire*, ed. Albert Lavignac and Lionel de la Laurencie, vol. 4, (Paris: Delagrave, 1920), 1913–2351.

[158] González Calleja, "Noucentisme," 48.

defined him.[159] Prat authored a book, *La Nacionalitat catalana* (1906), which, to a great extent, sums the party's "doctrine," to use his expression:

> A consequence of what has been explained so far is the vindication of a Catalan State, which should stand in federative union with the States of the other Spanish nationalities....
>
> Although we have not yet endowed ourselves with a state, a law and a language, and we have not yet reached a full inner expansion, Catalan nationalism has begun the second phase of all nationalisms, namely, the phase of outer influence, the imperialistic phase.
>
> Catalan art and literature, the juridical conceptions, and the political and economic ideal of Catalonia have begun to accomplish their outer task, namely, their pacific penetration in Spain, its transfusion to all other Spanish nationalities and the Spanish organism that governs them.[160]

Prat de la Riba defines Catalonia as a confederate nation in the Spanish state, one that, following a principle of self-determination, aspires to achieve official recognition as a state with its own legal system and language. In contrast to more recent formulations of Catalan nationalism, Prat de la Riba does not seek to sever Catalan and Hispanic identities. Instead, he advocates the imperialistic expansion of Catalan "influence" to the other Spanish "nationalities." He conceives of that "influence" in racial, rather than in merely linguistic or juridical, terms. This stance can be observed in his use of the "blood" metaphor, which in this case is "transfused" into the State body or "organism."

Like Prat de la Riba, the young Collet situated Catalonia at the head of Spain and defined it as an integral part with a distinctive identity. Yet, by construing Pedrell as the head of the Catalan and Spanish "schools," he entered the ground of a discursive battle, since Catalan and Spanish nationalists sought to appropriate Pedrell to the benefit of their respective causes. This conflict can be most clearly observed in how the media reacted to the première of Pedrell's operatic trilogy *Els Pirineus*.

---

[159] González Cuevas, "Carles Maurras en Cataluña," 330. On Prat de la Riba's "adoption" of Maurras's principles see ibid., 330–333. On Maurras's influence on other members of the *Lliga* see ibid., 340–346.

[160] "Conseqüencia de tota la doctrina aquí exposada és la reivindicació d'un Estat català, en unió federativa ab els Estats de les altres nacionalitats d'Espanya," Enric Prat de la Riba, *La nacionalitat catalana* (Barcelona, Tipografia L'Anuari de l'Exportació, 1906), 114; "no s'ha conquistat l'Estat, el dret y la llengua, no hem conseguit la plenitut d'expansió interior, però ja'l nacionalisme català ha començat la segona funció de tots els nacionalismes, la función d'influencia exterior, la funció imperialista. L'art, la literatura, les concepcions juridiques, l'ideal politich y econòmich de Catalunya han iniciat la obra exterior, la penetració pacífica d'Espanya, la transfusió a les demés nacionalitats espanyoles y al organisme del Estat que les governa." Prat de la Riba, *La nacionalitat catalana*, 126–127.

Els Pirineus

Under Pedrell's request, the politician, journalist and historian Victor Balaguer enhanced his poem *El Comte de Foix* poem in order to complete a trilogy with a prologue.[161] From its Wagnerian and symbolist aesthetics, as well as its subject matter, *Els Pirineus* connects with *modernisme* rather than *noucentisme*; it also shows the influence of the *renaixença*, which numbered Balaguer among its greatest exponents. To judge from the scale of Pedrell's opera and the cultural anxieties that it touched upon, *Els Pirineus* may be deemed Pedrell's most politically and culturally relevant and controversial work.[162] Its subject matter is the Albigensian or Cathar Crusade, the thirteenth-century campaign carried out by the Catholic Church, the Papal Inquisition and the French Court, to extinguish the thriving, polytheist Cathar "heresy" in the Languedoc.

A war for religious authority initially, the Albigensian war turned into an armed attempt to assimilate Occitania to France by undermining its cultural difference and political autonomy. The opera's first part, "El Comte de Foix" (The Count of Foix), takes place in 1218 and represents the House of Foix's rebellion against the papal mandate and the Inquisition. The latter two were intent on taking hold of the Foix Castle and excommunicating the Occitan noblemen who did not convert to Catholicism. The second part, "Raig de Lluna" (The Moonbeam), represents the defeat of Montsegur in 1235, a nine-month siege that allegedly led to the burning of the last Cathars and the capture of the Comte de Foix.[163] The third part is set in the battle of "El Coll de Panissars," the last of the Aragonese Crusades, in which the Spanish kingdom of Aragón, under Peter III, otherwise known as Pere el Grande, defeated Philip III of France after the latter invaded the Pyrenees. This victory ultimately entailed a serious blow for the pope's plans, as he had sponsored the invasion in an attempt to secure Aragón for Philip III of France, following the excommunication of Peter III after he conquered Sicily against papal interests.

In *Els Pirineus*, Pedrell dwells on some of the foundational myths of Catalan nationalism. Nineteenth-century Catalan historians defined the Catalan nation as a territorial and cultural spin-off of Occitania that became assimilated to the Kingdom of Aragón.[164] In the eighth century, Charlemagne supported the rebellion

---

[161] On Balaguer and Catalan nationalism see Conversi, *The Basques, the Catalans and Spain*, 16–17.

[162] Francesc Cortès i Mir, "La música escènica de Felip Pedrell: 'Els Pirineus. La Celestina. El Comte Arnau'," *Recerca musicològica*, no. 11 (1991): 63–97.

[163] In truth, the fall of Quéribus in 1255 constitutes the last episode of the Cathar crusade.

[164] Yet, and although Medieval Catalonia looked North more than to the Iberian Peninsula, it cannot be merely considered an appendix of Languedoc, because of the separate linguistic developments of Catalan and Occitan, Catalonia's distinct relationship with the papacy and its participation in the *Reconquista* since the twelfth century. See Adam J. Kosto, *Making Agreements in Medieval Catalonia: Power, Order, and the Written Word, 1000–1200* (Cambridge, UK; New York: Cambridge University Press, 2001), 4–9.

of the territories east and south of the Pyrenees against Muslim rule, and assimilated them to his Frankish empire. These territories formed the *marca hispánica* or Spanish March, a geographical unit with no administrative and political unity or autonomy but a certain cultural and linguistic differential identity.[165] During the ensuing decadence of the Frankish empire, Charlemagne's successors did not manage to curb the increasing prosperity and independence of those territories. The hegemony of Barcelona was extended through the betrothal of count Ramón Berenguer IV with the heiress to the throne of Aragón, Petronilla (1137), as well as military victories, including Lérida and Tortosa and the Kingdom of Valencia, taken from Islam in the midtwelfth century, and Sicily, taken from the Angevins after the Sicilian Vespers of 1282.[166] Catalan nationalists have consistently construed these events as the birth of the Catalan nation.

Arguably, Balaguer and Pedrell identify the thirteenth-century Kingdom of Aragón, in northeastern Spain, as the budding Catalan nation, and read the Coll de Panissars as the victory of Catalan culture and symbols—including religion—against foreign invasions. In his nearly-nine-hundred-page history of Catalonia and Aragón, Balaguer casts the *albijenses* as the victims of a series of ruthless "massacres" and an attack on their freedom of faith, thus showing where his allegiances lie.[167] Furthermore, in *Els Pirineus*, Balaguer and Pedrell construe the Pyrenees referred to in the title as an emblem of Catalan identity, a site on which to build a repository of values shaped in contradistinction to notions of Spanish identity.[168] The Pyrenees offered a contrast with the arid landscapes of Castile or Andalusia—the latter of which prevailed in European perceptions of Spain. The première of *Parsifal* in Barcelona on January 1, 1914—the sought-after first world première following Bayreuth—had proved that Catalan operatic audiences were happy to identify the Pyrenees with a Wagnerian, tempered, Nordic sophistication, contrasted with "backward" Spain, even if other aspects of German culture were not to everyone's taste.[169] *Parsifal* is set in "Montsalvat," in the "northern mountains of Gothic Spain," a place Catalans identified with Montserrat, a medieval monastery in the Pyrenees that became an emblem of Catalan nationalism. These issues helped Catalans contest European views of the Pyrenees as the southern frontier of civilization.

---

[165] Enrique Rodríguez-Picavea, *La corona de Aragón en la edad media* (Madrid: Ediciones Akal, 1999) 7–8.

[166] Paul Freedman, "Cowardice, Heroism and the Legendary Origins of Catalonia," *Past & Present*, no. 121 (1988): 3–28.

[167] Victor Balaguer, *Historia de Cataluña y de la Corona de Aragón* (Barcelona: Librería de Salvador Manero, 1861), 127–135.

[168] Francesc Cortès has argued that the trilogy offers "a view of the Pyrenees as the incarnation of the ideals of the [Catalan] Motherland, the historical cradle of a Catalan national spirit." ("la visió dels Pirineus com a encarnació dels ideals de la Pàtria, el bressol històric català dels esperits nacionals.") Cortès i Mir, "La música escènica," 78.

[169] Macedo, "Between Opera and Reality," 101–103.

Although a subtext of Catalan superiority and hegemony underpins *Els Pirineus*, the Spaniards do not appear as the enemies of the Catalan nation in this opera; the enemies are the French and the pope. This particularity facilitated most critics in trying to appropriate *Els Pirineus* to the cause of Spanish nationalism, helped by the fact that the première in the Teatre del Liceu, Barcelona (1902), was sung in the Italian language, as was customary in Spanish opera houses. Nationalist publications written in the Catalan language, such as the magazine *La Renaixença* and the daily newspaper *La Veu de Catalunya*, considered Pedrell the head of the Catalan nationalist musical school[170]; meanwhile, Catalan publications in the Spanish language, such as the daily newspapers *La Vanguardia* and *El Correo Catalán*, presented Pedrell as a Spanish nationalist, rather than a Catalan one.[171] The rest of the Spanish and European press deemed Pedrell the father of Spanish nationalism.[172] Among them, a host of articles conceptualized Catalan language as a dialect of Spanish and presented Catalan culture as a local Spanish variety or subculture.[173] Interestingly enough, several critics covering the 1896 performance of the Prelude from *Els Pirineus* in Venice refused to consider this trilogy as "Spanish music" on account of its Wagnerian influences.[174] The uniqueness of this stance suggests that, just like their French counterparts, Italian critics regarded German culture as a rival form of propaganda in Spain and therefore construed it as an anti-Hispanic artifact. Interestingly, allegations

---

[170] "Los Pirineus," La Renaixença, Barcelona, 1 Septiembre 1891; "Por nuestra música," *La veu de Catalunya*, Barcelona, 1891. These articles are reproduced in Anon., *La trilogía* Los Pirineos *y la crítica* (Barcelona: [s.n.], 1902).

[171] J. Roca y Roca, "La semana en Barcelona. Por nuestra música…de Felipe Pedrell," *La vanguardia, Barcelona*, September 6, 1891; Francisco Muns, "Por nuestra música. Folleto del maestro don Felipe Pedrell," *Correo Catalán*, Barcelona, October 14, 1891. Quoted from Anon., *La trilogía* Los Pirineos *y la crítica*; Mitjana, *Para música vamos!* 74.

[172] Spanish press: Eustoquio de Uriarte, "La ópera nacional española," *La Ciudad de Dios* (Madrid-Escorial, 1891); A. Noguera, "Una ópera española," *El isleño* (Palma de Mallorca), April 11, 13 and 15, 1893. European press: Alejandro Moszkowki, "[untitled]," *Berliner Tageblatt*, 192, April 16, 1893; Arnaldo Bonaventura, "Il maestro Pedrell e l'opera spagnola," *L'avvisatore artistico* (Roma), June 17, 1893; Carlos Krebs, "El drama musical en España," *Sonntagsbeilage-Vorsische Zeitung* (Berlin), December 16, 1894. Quoted from Anon., *La trilogía* Los Pirineos *y la crítica*); Jean-Aubry, *La musique et les nations*, 69; Paul-Marie Masson, "La musique espagnole"; Albert Soubies, *Histoire de la musique. Espagne*, III, 97.

[173] Louis de Cassembroot, "Un projet de rénovation de l'art lyrique en Espagne," *L'écho musical* (Brussels), October 11, 1891. Quoted from Anon., *La trilogía* Los Pirineos *y la crítica*. The critic Peña y Goñi hailed Pedrell as the "head of the new Spanish school," but, nevertheless, judged *Els Pirineus* as a Catalan opera based on the fact that the libretto was written in Catalan and had been translated into French and Italian, but not Spanish. Antonio Peña y Goñi, "Cuatro soldados y un cabo," *La época*, May 5, 1895, quoted in Luis G. Iberni, "Felip Pedrell y Ruperto Chapí," *Recerca Musicològica* 11–12 (1991–1992): 338.

[174] Leporello, "Rivista musicale," *L'illustrazione italiana* (Turin), March 21, 1897; Giovanni Tebaldini, "Filippo Pedrell ed il dramma lirico spagnuolo," *Rivista musicale italiana* 4, no. 2–3, Turin, 1897. Tebaldini would eventually change his opinion: "Il prologo della trilogia i Pirinei di Filippo Pedrell, al Liceo Marcello di Venezia," *Gazzeta di Milano*, February 23, 1897. Quoted from Anon., *La trilogía* Los Pirineos *y la crítica*.

that Pedrell's style was Wagnerian elicited attempts to appropriate *Els Pirineus* to Spanish—but not Catalan—nationalism.[175]

Failure to associate *Els Pirineus* with Catalan nationalism in France and other European countries may be partly attributed to a lack of familiarity or empathy with the nature and development of nonstate nationalisms in Spain. In some cases, however, full awareness of the claims raised by Catalan nationalism did not deter critics from ascribing *Els Pirineus* to a Spanish agenda and discrediting those who attempted to do otherwise. One such case is the 1902 booklet that Henri de Curzon wrote in response to the première the same year at the Liceu in Barcelona, where it was sung in Italian. Curzon argued vehemently against "the opinion of nationalist Catalans, who declare that neither France nor Spain has anything to do here; that only the Catalans are concerned, and that, for them, the Pyrenees are not today and were not six centuries ago, a frontier, but a center or even a 'spinal cord.'"[176] The reason for such Spanish, and one could even say anti-Catalanist, readings may be attributed to Pedrell's attitude, given that he contributed to shaping readings of *Els Pirineus* as a Spanish work through the publication of an essay on Spanish music nationalism, *Por nuestra música* (1891), as a preface to the first edition of the score.[177] Unsurprisingly, Curzon and Mitjana quoted at length from *Por nuestra musica*, which, in line with Herder's *volkstümlichkeit*, puts forward the idea that the Spanish national music school ought to be grounded in the use of national folklore.[178] By contrast, no reference is found to Catalan nationalism in *Por nuestra música*.

Collet was probably the only critic to associate *Els Pirineus* and Pedrell with both Catalan and Spanish nationalism. He was one of the few French musicologists with sufficient knowledge of Spanish politics to be able to read the work in the context of both ideological and political frameworks. There is little wonder that Collet felt strongly attracted to *Els Pirineus*, which presented Roman Catholicism from the papal court as a foreign invader, just as he would later do in *Le mysticisme*. Pedrell and Collet predicated their Catalan and Spanish nationalist discourses upon the same dichotomous distinction between the "indigenous"

---

[175] J. M. Esperanza y Sola, "Revista musical," *La ilustración española y americana* (Madrid), April 22, 1897; Mínimo, "Instantáneas: Pedrell," *El globo* (Madrid), May 18, 1897: "A wagnerianas suenan, aun para oídos ineducados en cultura musical, las composiciones de Pedrell… De su españolismo no deja duda el estremecimiento de entusiasmo patriótico que sufre nuestro corazón al oír aquella música sublime." Quoted from Anon., *La trilogía* Los Pirineos *y la crítica*.

[176] "l'avis des Catalans *catalanistes*, qui déclarent que ni la France, ni même l'Espagne n'ont rien à voir ici; que, seuls, les Catalans sont en cause et que, pour eux, aujourd'hui comme il y a six siècles, les Pyrénées sont non une frontière, mais un centre ou, pour mieux dire, une 'épine dorsale.'" Henri de Curzon, *Felipe Pedrell, Les Pyrenees* (Paris: Librairie Fischbacher, 1902), 20; also see 44.

[177] Felipe Pedrell, *Por nuestra música*.

[178] He would dwell on the same idea in a French publication three decades later. Felipe Pedrell, "Les artisans du folklor musical espagnol," *La revue musicale* 2, no. 11 (October 1921).

and the "foreign." The difference lay in whether the "indigenous" was Catalan or Spanish, although perhaps this difference mattered little if the purpose was to undermine Roman Catholicism with the purpose of vindicating, as they both did, the independence of the Spanish "Golden Age" of polyphony from Palestrina's far-reaching shadow.[179]

The Paragon Pedrell-Olmeda

Between the publication of "La musique espagnole moderne" (1908) and *Le mysticisme* (1913), Collet's political ideals shifted from a conception of Spain in which Barcelona constitutes the spearhead of national regeneration to a Catholic and Castilian nationalism. Strictly speaking, one could argue that there is no inherent contradiction between these two stances, insofar as Collet's earlier endorsement of Barcelona is predicated on its cultural cosmopolitanism, internationalism and modernism, as much as his later support of Castile was based on its alleged medieval backwardness and its cultural inwardness and self-imposed protectionism. In sum, he imagines Spain as a nation in which both Catalonia and Castile fulfill different but necessary functions, the former championing modernization and the latter acting as the repository of values in danger of extinction. This explains why, even in Collet's most centralist and Castilian work, he found room to describe Catalonia in a manner that arguably reads like an endorsement, even if it contrasts with his idea of Castile. Collet referred to the Pyrenees as "the barrier lifted by a neo-paganism," and described the Catalans as "the most advanced and civilized race in a sad and decadent Spain […] a people fully familiarized with modern ideas, which detaches itself, selfishly, from a maternal rule that it no longer understands."[180] Collet dwells on the dualism between a progressive Catalonia and a backward Spain exploited by Catalan nationalism—a dualism that, as we have seen, most likely underlies *Els Pirineus*. Like Maurras and the Félibrige, he embraces cultural conservatism and prescribes a premodern state of cultural and economic development; however, rather than supporting a nonstate regionalism, he embraces political centralism, masked under the appearance of a Castilian nationalism he assimilated from Olmeda. Although Collet's arguments for endorsing and, subsequently, undermining Catalan culture may not have changed, his allegiances did, as did the

---

[179] As has been discussed, Germany lay at the center of Collet's constructions of the "foreign" where the "indigenous" was nineteenth- and twentieth-century Spanish music; as far as early Spanish music or Catalan music is concerned, however, Italy came to replace Germany in that function.

[180] "barrière dressée par un néopaganisme"; "la race la plus avancée et la plus civilisée d'une Espagne tristement décadente; d'être le refuge d'un peuple tout acquis aux idées modernes, et se détachant, égoïste, d'une règle qui lui fut maternelle, mais qu'il ne comprends plus." Collet, *Le mysticisme*, 324.

ideological underpinnings of his concept of Spanish music. As I shall argue now, this shift was if not motivated then at least accompanied by a reassessment of the role that Pedrell and Olmeda played in shaping the future of Spanish music. Collet established a paragon in which Pedrell represented Collet's earlier Catalan nationalism and Olmeda his later Castilian centralism. Since both had played a substantial role in shaping Collet's views on Spanish music, while he was visiting Spain in 1907 in preparation for his dissertation, this paragon reflects Collet's changing views on the weight of Pedrell's and Olmeda's ideas in his own intellectual upbringing. Through the paragon, therefore, Collet played up his view of the struggles for cultural hegemony that, according to him, confronted Castile and Catalonia.

Far from a formal competition, the paragon developed along an unconnected series of five publications appearing throughout the 1920s. First, this series includes Collet's entry on Spanish music in Lavignac's and La Laurencie's *Encyclopédie de la musique* (1920); then, the second and third installments of an essay titled "La musique espagnole," published in September 1925 in *Le Ménestrel*; fourth, the book *Albéniz et Granados*, published in 1926; and finally, Collet's last book on Spanish music, *L'essor de la musique espagnole au XVIe siècle* (1929).[181] In his entry in the *Encylopédie*, Collet deemed Pedrell an "initiator" who has "dug piles of archival documents and has extracted the substantive marrow. But, without a doubt, he did not have the time to reach perfection."[182] By construing Pedrell as an "initiator" who has not reached "perfection," Collet seems suspicious of wanting to elevate his own musicological work over the putative father of Spanish nationalism. Collet dwells on the same idea in the second installment of "La musique espagnole" (September 4, 1925), where he describes Pedrell as the "precursor" of Spanish music who has inherited and revived the national tradition "left without heirs."[183] Furthermore, in this article Collet describes the "Catalan master" as a symbol of rebellion against Madrid's alleged backwardness and cultural stagnation, thus reinforcing the view that Spain was lagging behind a progressive Catalonia. He argues that Pedrell's tuition at the Madrid Conservatoire between 1894 and 1904 was brought to an end because Madrid "does not like to be given any lessons by Barcelona."[184] He also argues that Pedrell left

---

[181] Henri Collet, "Espagne/Le XIXe siècle. Deuxième partie: La renaissance musicale," in *Encyclopédie de la musique et dictionnaire du Conservatoire*, ed. Albert Lavignac and Lionel de la Laurencie, vol. 4 (Paris: Delagrave, 1920), 2470–2484; Collet, "La musique espagnole (II)," *Le ménestrel* (September 4, 1925); Collet, "La musique espagnole (III)," *Le ménestrel* (September 11, 1925); Collet, *Albéniz et Granados*; Collet, *L'essor*.

[182] "Pedrell fut, en toutes choses, un initiateur. Il a remué des monceaux d'archives et en a extrait la substantifique moelle. Mais sans doute n'eut-il pas le temps d'atteindre la perfection. Ce n'était pas utile pour lui." Collet, "Espagne/Le XIXe siècle."

[183] "précurseur"; "laisée en déshérence." Collet, "La musique espagnole (II)," *Le ménestrel* (September 4, 1925).

[184] "Madrid n'aime pas beaucoup que Barcelone lui fasse la leçon." Ibid. On the polemics between Pedrell and Chapí that led to the former's resignation see Iberni, "Felip Pedrell," 335–344.

Madrid feeling appalled by the few opportunities that the powerful *zarzuela* business left for other genres. This article reads like a moderate expression of Collet's early Catalan nationalism, expressed in "La musique espagnole moderne" (1908, discussed above). From this article, Collet preserves the idea that Pedrell is the head of Spanish and Catalan music nationalisms. In the third installment (September 11, 1925), however, Collet proposes to "associate" the name of Olmeda with that of Pedrell. He regrets that, not being a Catalan, Olmeda has not been appreciated in Barcelona, even though—Collet agues—he is known and venerated in the whole of France.[185]

In *Albéniz et Granados* (1925), Collet questions Pedrell more overtly. He argues that, although Pedrell "seems to everyone's eyes, to have renewed the music of his country," he "published his manifesto *Por nuestra música* […] in 1891, that is, once Albéniz had already published and performed […] most of his compositions written in a Spanish style."[186] Collet's vilification of Pedrell, however, took on a more acrid tone in *L'essor*, where he argued that "one can deduce the whole Spanish movement of musical renewal from Olmeda's musical output" while "Pedrell's offers a more accurate view of the dead past."[187] Collet argued that Olmeda "is the first to have returned to popular song its adequate harmonic atmosphere" and that a comparison with "Pedrell's academic harmonizations" reveals "the striking musical superiority of the former of these two artists."[188] In addition, Collet took issue with the alleged "inanity of Pedrell's lessons," judging him incapable of teaching Albéniz and denying "the slightest connection between such dissimilar masters" as Falla and Pedrell.[189] Lastly, Collet argued, although "Pedrell rebelled against the facile procedure consisting simply 'in writing a *drame lyrique* based on a subject taken from our history or our legends, in writing it in Castilian language and scattering popular themes all over it' […] that is exactly his procedure."[190]

---

[185] "associer." Collet, "La musique espagnole (III)."

[186] "Pedrell qui passe aux yeux de tous, pour le rénovateur de la musique de son pays, n'a lancé son manifeste *Por nuestra música*, précédant son 'œuvre,' qu'en 1891, c'est-à-dire alors qu'Albéniz avait déjà publié et joué […] la plupart de ses compositions de style espagnol." Collet, *Albéniz et Granados*, 107.

[187] "De l'œuvre musicale d'Olmeda se déduit tout le mouvement de rénovation musicale espagnole. De celle de Pedrell nous rapportons une vue plus exacte sur le passé mort." Ibid., 20.

[188] "il est le premier à avoir restitué au chant populaire son atmosphère harmonique adéquate…Il suffit de comparer les harmonisations scolaires de Pedrell pour juger de la supériorité musicale éclatante du premier de ces deux artistes." Collet, *L'essor*, 18.

[189] "Sur l'inanité des leçons de Pedrell à Albéniz nous avons le témoignage de Pedrell lui-même avouant qu'Albéniz n'était pas 'enseignable.' Quant à De Falla, malgré la vive reconnaissance que ce maître garde à son vieux professeur, qui pourrait vraiment admettre, ayant lu les œuvres de celui-ci et de celui-là, qu'il y ait eu jamais le moindre contact entre deux natures aussi dissemblables?" Ibid., 49.

[190] "Pedrell s'élevait contre le procédé facile qui consiste simplement 'à écrire un drame lyrique sur un tel sujet tiré de notre histoire ou de nos légendes, de l'écrire en castillan, et d'y semer des thèmes populaires.' Mais voilà quue son procédé, à lui, n'est pas d'autre…Rien que de sujets historiques ou légendaires espagnols écrits

In sum, Collet undermines four of the qualities that together made up Pedrell's renown and that the former had praised in his "La musique espagnole moderne" (1908).[191] These aspects are Pedrell's reputation as a renovator of Spanish music, his teaching activity, his status as an established theoretician—here undermined by Collet's allegations that his musical works do not illustrate his theories—and Pedrell's alleged authority as a compiler and harmonizer of folklore. In this latter aspect, Olmeda and Pedrell differed significantly, for, unlike the latter, Olmeda did not harmonize the songs he collected. Collet's contention that Olmeda "is the first to have returned to popular song its adequate harmonic atmosphere" paraphrases the latter's intention to "extract, by way of their own harmony, the essence, the soul" of popular songs, expressed in the preface to *Folk-lore de Castilla*.[192] This and other evidence suggests that Collet knew what sources to quote from in order to undo the arguments through which Pedrell's reputation had been established. More particularly, he seems to have directly addressed the obituary written by Falla after Pedrell's death in 1922:

> the sheer comparison of several songs transcribed and harmonized by Pedrell with the transcription and harmonization of those same songs presented in other collections which have preceded his, proves how a song that we had hardly noticed in the former gains an extraordinary value when presented by our musician.[193]

It is unlikely that Falla referred to *Folk-lore de Castilla* as one of the "other collections which have preceded" Pedrell's, since Olmeda did not use harmonizations. However, Collet found inspiration, in this passage, to mold his critique of Pedrell in contrast to Falla's image of his former master.

Collet's comments and strategies strike me as biased, and probably reflect that his relationship with Pedrell may have deteriorated. In 1918, Pedrell referred to Collet's work in a rather resentful and bitter way. In the preface to the standalone

---

en catalan ou en castillan et semés de thèmes populaires ! Ceux-ci s'enchaînent sans interruption sur d'éternelles pédales et se doublant sans trêve au chant." Ibid., 39.

[191] Collet's critique elicited a reaction from one of Pedrell's supporters: "Federic Lliurat étudie dans la Revista Musical Catalana le livre du signataire de ces lignes sur l'Essor de la Musique espagnole au XXe siècle et lui reproche seulement un jugement sévère à l'égard de Felip Pedrell. Il est évident que Pedrell reste une figure centrale de la renaissance musicale chez nos voisins, comme Glinka le reste chez les Russes. Mais comment nier que Pedrell et Glinka demeurent inférieurs à leurs propres élèves et se trouvent dépassés par ce même mouvement qu'ils ont créé? C'est là toute notre constatation." Henri Collet, "Espagne," *Le ménestrel* (October 1930).

[192] "sacar afuera, por medio de la harmonización propia, la esencia, el alma." Olmeda, *Folk-lore de Castilla*, 28.

[193] "La simple comparaison de quelques chants transcrits et harmonisés par Pedrell, avec la transcription et l'harmonisation que, de ces mêmes chants, présentent d'autres collections qui ont précédé celle-ci, nous prouvera comment un chant que nous avions à peine remarqué dans les premiers, acquiert une rare valeur, présenté par notre musicien." Manuel de Falla, "Felipe Pedrell," *La revue musicale* 4, no. 4 (February 1923).

publication of his study on Victoria, originally included in the eighth volume (1913) of the *Opera omnia*, Pedrell took opportunity to "discredit" a "false study" on Victoria, a "monster" that was published shortly after he announced his eighth tome, stealing all of his ideas but rendering "a fake Victoria," which reveals that its author "hardly knows the rudiments of music."[194] Although Pedrell did not reveal the name of the alleged plagiarist, it most likely was Collet, the only author of a monograph on Victoria that saw light almost at the same time as the eighth volume of the *Opera omnia*. Mitjana's scathing review of *Victoria*, published in 1914, set a precedent for Pedrell's attack on Collet, and this must have further aggravated the latter's relationship with his beloved master. Mitjana argued that in *Victoria* "some things have been mended" that had tarnished *Le mysticisme*, which showed "a great impudence and absolute lack of preparation."[195] Despite the improvements, however, *Victoria* is characterized by "a certain lightness and a great lack of seriousness. More than a critical study, the book at stake seems a *novel* about Victoria."[196] Mitjana takes issue with Collet's contention that Victoria embodies the Arab, Celtiberian, Muslim and Christian mysticisms, and his reference to Victoria's "savage nobleness" (p. 157). In other words, he opposes the Orientalism that pervades Collet's works, as has been discussed, and defends an agenda of racial purity. Of more relevance, Mitjana contests Collet's argument that Victoria "is the mystical composer par excellence."[197] He concedes that Victoria's "music is frankly Christian, Catholic, fervent and devout," but argues that "Victoria was never a contemplative spirit [and] mysticism always requires a certain degree of contemplation."[1] He adds that Palestrina usually expresses himself "with an angelic and truly celestial serenity, to which the master from Avila"—that is, Victoria—"rarely has access."[198] Interestingly, in this regard he contradicted not only Collet but also Pedrell.

Collet must have felt hurt by this comments, as is evinced by his attacks on Mitjana in *L'essor*, where he contended that Mitjana

> was hypnotized by the strong personality of the composer from Tortosa [Pedrell] to the point of not being able to see other than through Pedrell's work and ideas. The result is that Mitjana's judgments on the

---

[194] "desautorizar"; "pretendido *Estudio*"; "engendro"; "un Victoria falso"; "apenas sí conoce el *a b c* de la música." Pedrell, *Tomás Luis de Victoria*, vii–viii.

[195] "algo se ha enmendado", "a más de gran atrevimiento, absoluta falta de preparación." Rafael Mitjana, "Acerca de algunos libros que tratan de música y músicos españoles," *Revista de filología española* 1, no. 1 (1914): 156.

[196] "cierta ligereza y gran falta de seriedad"; "Más que un estudio crítico del libro de que tratamos parece ser la *novela* de Victoria." Ibid., 156.

[197] "Es el compositor místico por excelencia." Ibid., 161.

[198] "con una serenidad angélica verdaderamente celestial, a la que muy contadas veces se eleva el maestro de Avila." Ibid., 162.

contemporary musical scene in Spain are plagued with errors, and that the paean of this young erudite of the music by the "Spanish Wagner" [Pedrell again] surpasses all measure and seems today puerile.[199]

Collet does not reveal the nature of those "puerile" judgments, as, more than articulating an informed criticism, his words probably reflect his resentment.

Although it would be tempting to regard these skirmishes as the encounter between two historiographical models of Spanish music history, both sides indulged in contradictions or ideological shifts that are too significant to allow establishing a clear demarcation between them. In particular it is striking how sharply Mitjana's review contrasts with his own views of Victoria, expressed in his entry in the *Encyclopédie de la musique et dictionnaire du Conservatoire* (1920).[200] In this work, Mitjana associates Victoria with Saint Teresa of Avila, since "they both are the offspring of that mystical village par excellence."[201] He adds that Victoria is

> impulsive by virtue of the force of passion, sometimes gets carried away by the voluptuousness of ecstasy, and, like Saint John of the Cross and Saint Teresa of Avila—his contemporaries—he is at the same time mystical and sensual. The same artist who swoons with love in the admirable motet *Vere languores* [...]—ardent and fiery music, with a profound mysticism that reaches up to the sublime—becomes a powerful realist in order to give expression to the hatred unleashed by the Jews against Christ, in certain passages in his passions.[202]

In sum, Mitjana identifies a profoundly mystical and Jewish element in Victoria's music, thus significantly departing from his review of Collet's work, but also reflecting the opinion expressed by Pedrell before. As far as Collet is concerned, the earlier attacks of Pedrell and Mitjana may have sufficed for him to retaliate years later in *L'essor*. However, not everything boils down to personal conflict,

---

[199] "notre critique fut hypnotisé par la forte personnalité du compositeur de Tortosa, au point de ne plus rien voir qu'à travers l'œuvre et les tendances pédrelliennnes. Il en résulte que les jugements de M. Mitjana sur le mouvement musical contemporain en Espagne sont entachés d'erreurs, et que l'apologie que fait le jeune savant de la musique du 'Wagner espagnol' dépasse la mesure et apparaît aujourd'hui puérile." Collet, *L'essor*, 21.

[200] Mitjana, "La musique en Espagne," 1913–2351.

[201] "tous deux sont fils de cette ville mystique par excellence." Mitjana, "La musique en Espagne," 1998.

[202] "Impulsif dans la force de la passion, il se perd parfois dans la volupté de l'extase et comme Saint Jean de la Croix et Sainte Thérèse de Jésus, ses contemporains, il est en même temps mystique et sensuel. Le même artiste qui se pâme d'amour dans l'admirable motet *Vere languores* (Example XVI), page ardente et enflammée, d'un mysticisme profond qui s'élève jusqu'au sublime, devient un réaliste puissant pour exprimer la haine des juifs déchaînés contre le Christ, dans certains passages de ses *Passions*." Ibid., 2000–2001.

as the content of Collet's compositional output experienced a significant change in the early 1920s, which might explain his progressive departure from Pedrell from the mid-1920s (if not his acrid tone). This shift could be described as a sudden and consistent focus on producing works whose titles, texts, or folkloric sources relate to Castile. These works include three song cycles, *Poema de un día,* op. 48–53 (1921), *Cinco canciones populares castellanas,* op. 69 (1923), *Sept chansons populaires de Burgos,* op. 80 (1926); and three collections of piano pieces, *Chants de Castille,* op. 42–46 (1920), *Cantos de Castilla,* op. 62–66 (1921), *Danzas castellanas,* op. 75 (1923). Significantly, twenty-two of the twenty-seven movements that compose these works stem from Olmeda's *Folk-lore de Castilla.*[203] It surely did not escape Collet that the best-represented areas in Pedrell's *Cancionero* are Catalonia and its adjacent regions (Valencia and the Balearic Islands), all of which sum up to 87 songs of a total 267. The two Castiles, Old and New—respectively north and south—and Madrid seem comparatively underrepresented, with only 16 songs, while Andalusia and Galicia occupy the middle rank.[204]

Collet's compositions of the early 1920s show that, even though his construction of Castile as the essence of Spanish identity had remained invariable since *Le mysticisme* (1913) and *Victoria* (1914), the cultural signs that he used to promote it changed significantly. It seems as if, by the end of the War, when Catholic propaganda waned as before, Collet's interest in Castilian music was not grounded in discourses on mysticism, but rather in the secular approach to Castilian folklore that Olmeda had once taught him.[205] Interestingly, this shift runs parallel to Falla's sudden focus on the composition of works that have been consistently connected with the Castilian agenda of the Generation of 1898, overstating the Castilian nature of their sources—as shall be discussed in Chapter 6. These works include, most conspicuously, *El retablo de Maese Pedro* (1919–1923), whose protagonist is Don Quixote, and the *Harpsichord Concerto* (1923–1926), which uses some Golden Age musical sources whose Castilian

---

[203] On Collet's borrowing of folkloric material see Etcharry, "Henri Collet," 133–138. Collet dedicated op. 80 está to Olmeda. Also see Stéphan Etcharry, "Les mélodies castillanes d'Henri Collet (1885–1951): Une approche originale de l'Espagne dans la musique française," in *La musique entre France et Espagne: Interactions stylistiques. Actes du colloque international tenu à Paris, en Sorbonne-Paris IV et à l'Instituto Cervantes, les 14–16 mai 2001,* ed. Louis Jambou (Paris: Presses de l'Univ. de Paris-Sorbonne, 2003), 129–149.

[204] Pedrell, *Cancionero musical popular español.*

[205] "Et nos avons maintenant un autre incomparable guitariste, castillan cette fois-ci, Sainz de la Maza. Un artiste racé, de la lignée des Sor et des Tarrega. Et, qui plus est, compositeur distingué pour son instrument, dont il connaît à merveille les infinies sources polyphoniques." "La dignité, la noblesse d'hidalgo, l'ardeur concentré, la force persuasive, font de Sainz l'interprète idéal de la musique castillane. Il n'est pas jusqu'à son exécution de la Sarabande et Bourrée de Bach qui ne nous révèle le fond castillan d'une musique nourrie des pures traditions polyphoniques espagnols recueillies par les disciples du Collegium Germanicum où enseigna Victoria." Henri Collet, "Concert Sainz de la Maza," *Le ménestrel* (December 1926).

nature is dubious.[206] Perhaps more important than the nature of Falla's works is the fact that they elicited attempts to connect them with the *castellanismo* of the Generation of 1898, thus testifying to a general state of affairs that could be somewhat anticipated in Collet's *Le mysticisme*. Whether the latter motivated Falla's alleged turn to *castellanismo* in *El retablo* is dubious, however, as it seems that Pedrell's *Cancionero* played a more substantial role in shaping that work.[207] Collet's and Falla's formulation of a "Castilian music," therefore, present two alternatives, one secular and one Catholic.[208]

The dynamics of history turned favorable for Falla. The dictatorship of Miguel Primo de Rivera (1923–1930) enshrined the Catholic and Castilian rhetoric of Spain put forward by the Generations of 1898 and 1914, which Falla then defended and which Collet had somewhat departed from.[209] Furthermore, in his endeavor to establish a radical political centralism, Primo de Rivera banned the use of Catalan and other "regional" languages different from Castilian.[210] Even more than the Primo de Rivera dictatorship, however, the Franco dictatorship (1939–1975), which followed the Second Republic (1931–1936), helped to consolidate Castilian mysticism as the primary ingredient of the nationalist doctrine known as *nacionalcatolicismo*.[211] This phenomenon may explain why, among Collet's varied output, *Le mysticisme* is still regarded as his most significant and polemical work, one that has left an enduring and almost indelible mark on the historiography of Spanish early music, which can still be perceived today.[212]

---

[206] Hess, *Manuel de Falla and Modernism*, 209–210 and 249. Few musical quotations in *El retablo* are from Castilian musicians or are related to Castile in any way. Roland-Manuel elaborated on Falla's mysticism in the *Harpsichord Concerto*: Roland-Manuel, *Manuel de Falla*, 54–58. Also see Paul Bertrand, "Manuel de Falla. (À propos d'un livre et d'un concert récents)," *Le ménestrel* (May 1930).

[207] Michael Christoforidis, "From Folksong to Plainchant: Musical Borrowings and the Transformation of Manuel de Falla's Music Nationalism in the 1920s," in *Manuel de Falla: His Life and Music*, ed. Nancy Lee Harper (Lanham, MD: Scarecrow Press, 2005), 231–215.

[208] Unlike my previous argument in "Dos Españas y una sola música: Henri Collet, entre el federalismo y el centralismo," *Cuadernos de música iberoamericana* 15, no. 1 (2008): 75–97.

[209] Alejandro Quiroga Fernández de Soto, "La idea de España en los ideólogos de la dictadura de Primo de Rivera. El discurso católico-fascista de José Pemartín," *Revista de estudios políticos*, no. 108 (2000): 202–209. On the dictatorship's control of education see Carolyn P. Boyd, *Historia Patria: Politics, History, and National Identity in Spain, 1875–1975* (Princeton, NJ: Princeton University Press, 1997), 154. Also see Shlomo Ben-Ami, *Fascism from Above: The Dictatorship of Primo de Rivera in Spain, 1923–1930* (Oxford and New York: Oxford University Press, 1983), 104–106.

[210] Ben-Ami, *Fascism from Above*, 194–196.

[211] Alfonso Botti, *Cielo y dinero. El nacionalcatolicismo en España (1881–1975)* (Madrid: Alianza Editorial, 1992), 17–30.

[212] On Collet's influence on Spanish musicologists see Ros-Fábregas, "Musicological Nationalism," 9–11; Ros-Fábregas, "Música y músicos," 105–110; Ramos López, "The Construction of the Myth," 3–5; Ramos López, "Mysticism," 10–12. An example of Collet's early impact can be observed in Charles Dyke, "Un coup d'oeil sur l'Espagne Musical de la Renaissance," *Le courrier musical* (May 1924).

PART

NEGOTIATING "FRENCH" AND "SPANISH" MUSIC

CHAPTER 3

Citizens or Savages? The Spaniards in Raoul Laparra's *La jota* (1911)

The opera *La jota* (Opéra Comique, 1911) by the French composer Raoul Laparra offers a compelling case for analyzing how a French artist and intellectual reflected his concerns about French politics and society in a representation of Spanish culture. In his second opera, Laparra represented a fictional episode of the First Carlist War (1833–1835) in Spain, and addressed key issues of Spanish politics and national identity, such as the need for territorial, political and social cohesion. As I will argue, Laparra's view of France as a country divided by political and social cleavages such as the Dreyfus affair, regionalist debates and ideological battles between monarchists and republicans impinged upon his representation of Spain in *La jota*. Furthermore, I will analyze the same phenomenon in his writings, which I will use as the basis for establishing a comparative context. As we shall see, it seems as if Laparra used images and descriptions of Spanish culture in order to mirror the political situation in France, for Spain too suffered its own ideological civil war between the Enlightened liberals and their staunchest opponents, the conservative Carlists. These battles led to military confrontations on at least three occasions during the nineteenth century and, as many have observed, lay the foundation for the Spanish Civil War of 1936.[1]

Laparra was sufficiently acquainted with Spain's history and politics to be able to strike a parallel with the situation in France. However, he made extensive use of violence in *La jota*, thus portraying the Spaniard as a brutal "savage," for which he compensated only in part by resorting to the Enlightenment trope of the "noble savage" in his writings. But how can a "country of savages" serve to reflect on the problems affecting "civilized" France? This question encapsulates one the essential dilemmas underlying the thought of *hispanistes* such as Laparra.

[1] Álvarez Junco, *Mater Dolorosa*, 365; Gerald Brenan, *The Spanish Labyrinth: The Social and Political Background of the Spanish Civil War* (Cambridge: Cambridge University Press, 1943).

Their knowledge and love of Spain led them to regard it as a close, familiar culture, with which to engage on an equal footing, and on which to project and reflect national conflicts. However, the inertia of nineteenth- and twentieth-century narratives of cultural imperialism took them to represent Spain by way of subaltern tropes that helped to reinforce French hegemony at the expense of Spain. This contradiction found expression in multiple ways in the work of the *hispanistes*, as the case of Collet has eloquently shown. In this chapter, I am especially interested in how it was manifested in *La jota*, filtered through Laparra's temperament and applied to his view of Carlism and Spanish politics. As I shall argue, the depth and concern of Laparra's insight is unique among French musicians and critics, and certainly symptomatic of a determination to step beyond widespread stereotypes of Spanish culture, politics and history.

In sum, I propose to regard *La jota* as an essay on the problems that affected French society at the time of its composition, as well as Laparra's personal contribution to the nation-building process in the form of a reflection on France's relations with one of its Others. Furthermore, I approach *La jota* as Laparra's participation in the debates on key issues of Spanish politics and society that had brought together or opposed Spanish intellectuals since at least the nineteenth century. Therefore, I connect Laparra's agenda with the work of certain contemporary Spanish thinkers, particularly with the Generation of 1898. In order to situate *La jota* in context, I analyze it in connection with French naturalist operas, which, I argue, played an important role in shaping Laparra's rendition of the Spaniards as violent people. Then, I proceed to examine the political and ideological discourses and constructions of identity in Laparra's writings on Spanish music and culture published in *Le Ménestrel* after 1919. Although Laparra's ideas could have changed during the eight-year interim between *La jota* and the publication of his first writings, these are consistent enough to provide a solid contextual basis for this study. In the last part of the chapter, I assess how Laparra's ideas on politics and society impinged upon *La jota*, and I argue that Laparra believed in a distinction between one's personal allegiances and a sense of political duty, that is, of determining what is good for the nation.

Laparra

Laparra managed to have *La jota* performed at the Opéra Comique at a time when it was particularly difficult for French composers to see their works premièred in Paris opera houses. This early achievement would be matched by others, indicative of a seemingly successful career. He managed to stage two further Spanish operas: *La habanera* (Opéra Comique 1908, his own libretto) and *L'illustre fregona* (Palais Garnier 1931, his own libretto based on Cervantes).

However, Laparra's career cannot be deemed a success. Apart from the press coverage of his opera premières, his music received scant attention during his lifetime. Even after his death, his work hardly drew the attention of scholars.[2] Laparra himself has fallen into oblivion. It therefore seems appropriate to provide a few biographical details here.

Although of Spanish and Italian ancestry, Laparra was born and brought up in the French city of Bordeaux, which started to receive an important inflow of Spanish immigrants and cultural signs in the 1890s. From his early childhood, his family encouraged him to study music. At the age of eleven he entered the Paris Conservatoire, where he studied piano with Louis Diémer and later composition with Gabriel Fauré. A lover of Spanish culture, Laparra first traveled to Spain in 1897 in the company of his brother, the painter William Laparra (1873–1929). In a further trip, between the years 1900 and 1902, he visited Madrid and the city of Burgos. It was in the latter city that he wrote the libretto and composed most of the music for his first opera, *La habanera*, and where he made the acquaintance of Henri Collet in the home of Federico Olmeda, who would provide Laparra with collections of folklore to draw upon for his opera. In 1903 Laparra won the Prix de Rome with his cantata *Alyssa* and consequently spent the years 1904 to 1907 in Rome, where he would complete the orchestration of *La habanera*.

Laparra composed extensive Spanish music, including four operas, three symphonic poems, seven collections of piano pieces, one piece for the harp, two choral works, one song cycle and several songs. He also wrote on Spanish music for the journals *Le Ménestrel* and *Le Matin* during the 1920s and 1930s. He contributed to the 1920 edition of Lavignac's *Encyclopédie de la musique et dictionnaire du conservatoire* with a fifty-page survey of folklore and popular dance in Spain,[3] and wrote a monograph on the subject of *Bizet et l'Espagne* (Paris, 1935). He lost his life in a Franco-British bombing of Boulogne, not far from Paris, where he was undergoing psychiatric treatment at the hospital of Suresnes.

[2] This is the most comprehensive bibliography I have managed to assemble: Samuel Llano, "Hispanic Traditions, 97–140; Palacios Garoz, *El hispanismo musical*; Dumesnil, *La musique contemporaine en France*; Paul Landormy, *La musique française après Debussy* (Paris: Gallimard, 1943), 132–134; Bertrand Pouradier-Duteil, *Les musiciens et les Hauts-de-Seine* (Paris: Sogemo 1991), 150; Anon., "'La habanera'—A New Opera by a New Composer," *New York Times* (August 9, 1908); José Bruyr, "Un entretien avec…Raoul Laparra," *Le guide du concert*, November 29, 1929; Palacios Garoz, *Federico Olmeda*, 122–141. Richard Langham Smith, "Laparra, Raoul," *Grove Music Online*, http://www.oxfordmusiconline.com/subscriber/article/grove/music/16011 (accessed April 15, 2011); Stéphan Etcharry, "Le Prix de Rome de composition de 1903, Raoul Laparra et la cantate Alyssa," *Musiker*, 16 (2009), 7–33.

[3] Raoul Laparra, "La musique et la danse populaires en Espagne," *Encyclopédie de la musique et dictionnaire du conservatoire. 1e partie. Histoire de la musique. Espagne-Portugal*, ed. Albert Lavignac and Lionel de la Laurencie (Paris: Delagrave, 1920), 2353–2400. As most of the entries in the *Encyclopédie*, this one was written in 1914, but published only after the war.

Carlism and Spanish Politics in *La jota*

A *compte-lyrique* in two acts, *La Jota* premiered April 26, 1911, at the Opéra Comique. Laparra wrote the libretto for this opera, composed the music and got deeply involved in the stage production, working hand in hand with the director Albert Carré—just as he had done during the production of his first opera, *La habanera*. In *La jota*, the action is set in Ansó, a village situated in the eponymous valley, next to the Pyrenees in the Spanish region of Aragón. The first act presents the young Soledad from Ansó, who is in love with the Basque Juan de Zumárraga. This character is very likely inspired by Tomás de Zumalacárregui (1788–1835), the Carlist general who won the Basque Country and Navarre for the Carlists during the First Carlist War (1833–1835). The village priest, Mosén Jago, is in love with Soledad and tries to dissuade her from pursuing a relationship with Zumárraga. At the end of the first act, the characters dance a *jota*—a typical, folkloric dance from the Northern regions of Aragón and Navarre—to bid Zumárraga farewell, as he has been summoned by the Carlist troops. The second act opens with Ansó being invaded by the Carlists, led by Zumárraga. The villagers take refuge in the church and face the invaders, spurred by Mosén Jago and Soledad. However, they yield under the Carlists' greater forces, which break into the church and slaughter the villagers. Zumárraga runs to Soledad and snatches her from Mosén Jago, who has turned "diabolically erotic"—to use Laparra's words—and clasps her in his arms. Both lovers die amidst the crossfire while the Carlists crucify the priest.[4]

La jota presents a fictional episode of the First Carlist War (1833–1835),[5] which confronted supporters of the two contenders for the Spanish throne, namely, the *infante* Don Carlos and Isabella II, the legitimate heir to the Spanish throne after female rights to reign were restored in 1833.[6] Although at first sight a war of succession, the First Carlist War embodied a confrontation between two radically different political and ideological conceptions of Spain. On one side, there fought the advocates of liberalism and the Enlightenment, who supported the Napoleonic occupation in 1808–1814, endorsed the liberal Constitution of

---

[4] For a more detailed description see Raoul Laparra, *La jota. Conte lyrique en 2 actes. Poème et musique de Raoul Laparra. Partition pour piano et chante réduite par l'auteur* (Paris: Enoch & Cie, 1911).

[5] Carré contends that the events presented really took place in 1835. Albert Carré, *Souvenirs de théâtre, reunis, présentés et annotés par Robert Favart* (Paris: Robert Favart, 1976/1950), 337; however, I have not managed to track down this battle in the histories of Carlism, nor in the chronicles of Ramón Cabrera, the general who took the lead of the Carlist troops in Aragón in 1835. Mariano Tomás, *Ramón Cabrera (historia de un hombre)* (Barcelona: Juventud, 1939). At least the events in the church might be invented, for Moreau does not include them in his history of the building: Philippe Moreau, *La Iglesia de San Pedro de Ansó* (Huesca: Instituto de Estudios Altoaragoneses, 1988).

[6] For a survey on Carlism see Jeremy McClancy, *The Decline of Carlism* (Reno and Las Vegas, NV: University of Nevada Press, 2000) 1–14.

1812 and defended a centralist, Jacobin model of the state.[7] On the other side, the Carlists defended Ancien Régime values such as the monarchy, Catholicism and the *fueros*, that is, the privileges enjoyed by the noblemen from Navarre, a region neighboring Aragón. They opposed urbanism and industrialization, atheism, administrative centralism, liberalism and socialism.[8] The Carlists feared that the outgoing king, Ferdinand VII, would establish a pact with the liberals, and therefore waged war a civil war that extended throughout Spain in 1833, and that they lost two years later. Following the First Carlist War, Carlism became associated with a variety of conservative movements and ideologies, including Catholic traditionalism, Basque nationalism at the turn of the twentieth century and *nacionalcatolicismo*, that is, the essentialist construction of Spanish national identity as Catholic, which emerged in the second half of the nineteenth century and became official during the Franco regime.[9] Blinkhorn's remark that by 1931 Carlism "was indisputably the oldest continuously existing popular movement of the extreme right in Europe"[10] pays testimony to its enduring power.

In sum, Carlism represents one of the most convoluted, controversial and therefore fundamental phenomena of nineteenth- and twentieth-century Spanish history and politics, given the breadth of conservative ideologies and sociopolitical issues that it has encompassed. There is little wonder that Carlism had awakened the interest and excited the imagination of European travelers during the nineteenth century.[11] In France, Carlism gained greater attention thanks to the presence of exiled Carlists in the southern regions,[12] and given its close connections with Legitimism,[13] a conservative movement for the defense of the Bourbons against any attempts to prevent their rule, as in the 1789 Revolution,

---

[7] In the interest of political and territorial cohesion, the liberals divided Spain into forty-nine provinces that, following the French Jacobin model, were deliberately meant not to coincide with the historical regions. Xose-Manoel Núñez, "The Region as Essence of the Fatherland: Regionalist Variants of Spanish Nationalism (1840–1936)," *European History Quarterly*, 31, 4 (2001) 488–489 [483–518].

[8] Álvarez Junco, *Mater Dolorosa*, 357–366.

[9] Botti, *Cielo y dinero*, 17–30.

[10] Martin Blinkhorn, *Carlism and Crisis in Spain, 1931–1939* (Cambridge: Cambridge University Press, 1975), 2.

[11] Francisco Javier Capistegui, "Between Repulsion and Attraction: Carlism Seen Through Foreign Eyes," *Revista internacional de estudios vascos*, 2 (2008) 119–143.

[12] Jordi Canal, "La reconversión del carlismo (1876–1931)," in *El carlismo y las guerras carlistas. Hechos, hombres e ideas*, ed. Julio Arostegui, Jordi Canal y Eduardo G. Calleja (Madrid: La Esfera de los Libros, 2003) 87–88.

[13] "Since the 1930s, and even earlier in the form of its immediate precursors, it had embodied the Spanish brand of that Catholic traditionalism most fluently articulated by Frenchmen such as the Vicomte de Bonald, and the best-known organized manifestation of which was probably French legitimism. Carlism, however, also possessed that mass element which had been present during the 1790s in the Vendée and the Chouannerie, but which was already effectively lost to French legitimism by the time its Spanish counterpart came into being." Blinkhorn, *Carlism and Crisis*, 3.

the Orleanist succession of 1830, the Second Empire and the Third Republic. Like Carlism, Legitimism espoused Catholic traditionalism, supported the development of rural economy, endorsed the aristocracy and its privileges and opposed industrialization, urban economy, liberalism, socialism and any other signs of technological or social modernization. Further in connection with Carlism, Legitimism lived its heyday in the 1830s and experienced subsequent decay, during which it accommodated or engaged with a variety of conservative political trends.[14] In this sense, it seems relevant that Laparra focused on the First Carlist War (1833–1835), precisely when Legitimism was in its highest hour.

Given Carlism's currency in France, it comes as little surprise that Laparra wrote *La jota*, or that other authors and composers should precede him in the use of that subject. However, as I will argue, Laparra approached the subject from a deeper political concern and with the intention of transgressing the distant, quasi-exotic manner in which the history of Spain found representation in most European operas. A telling example can be gauged from the intense dialogue that Soledad, Juan Zumárraga and Mosén Jago exchange in the second scene of the first act. The scene begins with Soledad praying to the Pilarica—the diminutive variant of the local Aragonese Virgin saint, Pilar—to help her forget Juan's "bad dreams, there, among the Carlists of his race."[15] Juan gives proof of his commitment by sharing his readiness to do "nothing but [his] duty, without remorse," in case there is a battle between the Carlists and Ansó's inhabitants.[16] Indeed, at Mosén Jago's suggestion that, in case of battle, "[his] only faith will be Soledad,"[17] Juan retorts with a statement revealing the anticentralist and even anti-Hispanic connotations of Carlism:

> Juan: Me? To betray? To allow those from Castile / To burn our white farmhouses / And shoot our supple daughters, […] Aragón is not the universe.[18]

Juan targets Castile and Aragón as embodiments of the centralized state, insofar as these regions stem from the two eponymous kingdoms that, in 1469, following the marriage of the so-called Catholic Monarchs, united to form what

---

[14] On the ideology of Legitimists see Geoffrey Cubitt, "Legitimism and the Cult of the Bourbon Royalty," in *The Right in France: 1789–1997*, ed. Nicholas Atkin and Frank Tallett (London and New York: Tauris, 1999), 51–70; on the dynastic conflict see Robert R. Locke, *French Legitimists and the Politics of Moral Order in the Early Third Republic* (Princeton, NJ: Princeton University Press, 1974), 3–4.

[15] "A ses mauvais rêves, là-bas, Chez les carlistes de sa race." Laparra, *La Jota*, Act II, scene 2.

[16] "Rien que mon devoir, sans remords." Ibid.

[17] "Si l'on se bat, ta seule foit sera la Soledad." Ibid.

[18] "Juan: Moi? Trahir? Pour que ceux des Castilles / Brûlent nos caserios blancs / Et fusillent nos souples filles, […] L'Aragón, ce n'est pas l'univers." Ibid.

most historians agree represents the first historical formulation of Spain.[19] Furthermore, at least since the turn of the twentieth century and partly on account of its geographical centrality, Castile became the target of an intense intellectual investment aimed at overcoming a sense of crisis caused by, among other issues, the rise of nonstate—or "peripheral"—nationalisms.[20] However, Zumárraga's anti-Hispanism, or in other words the separatist connotations that Laparra ascribes to Carlism, become more dramatic later in the same scene:

JUAN: [to Soledad] For your love I am from Ansó / But I have left, there / In a remote corner, my cradle
MOSÉN JAGO: Are you not Spanish?
JUAN: My land is Isaba.
MOSÉN JAGO: What are you then?
JUAN: Basque. Basque.
SOLEDAD: Spanish. Renegade!
JUAN: Me?
SOLEDAD: You: Juan Zumárraga.
MOSÉN JAGO: You love each other!
JUAN: Blasphemous, hell has made you from its womb!
SOLEDAD: It has vomited you from its furnace, liar Basque!
JUAN: Perfidious Aragonese! Damned country![21]

The village where Juan comes from, Isaba, is technically not located in the Basque Country but rather in Navarre, which constitutes the ideological, social and military bulwark of nineteenth-century Carlism. This apparent confusion stems from the cultural similarities that unite both regions, which formed as of the ninth century part of the old Kingdom of Navarre, the southern part of which was conquered by the Kingdom of Castile in 1513. Those similarities, which include the use of the same "Basque" language, have given rise to views of Navarre as a political and cultural periphery of the Basque Country. Such views certainly underpin *La jota*,[22] though most likely enriched by an awareness of the service that Carlism paid to the more radical opposition to the centralized, liberal stated

---

[19] Álvarez Junco, *Mater Dolorosa*, 45.
[20] Fox, "Spain as Castile," 21–36; Britt-Arredondo, *Quixotism*.
[21] "Juan: [to Soledad] Par ton amour je suis d' Anso / Mais j'ai laisse, la-bas / Dans un coin, mon berceau. / Mosén Jago: N'est-ce tu pas espagnol? / J: Ma terre est Isaba / MJ.: Qu'es-tu donc? / J.: Basque. Basque. / Soledad: Espagnol. Renégat! / J: Moi? / S: Toi: Juan Zumarraga. / MJ: Vous vous aimez! / J: Blasphématrice, l'enfer te fit de sa matrice! / S: Il t'a vomi de sa fournaise, Basque menteur! / J: Perfide aragonais! Maudit pays!" Laparra, *La jota*, scene 2.
[22] Although, in the synopsis accompanying the published piano vocal score, Laparra introduces Juan as "un Navarrais d'Isaba." Laparra, *La jota*.

represented by Basque nationalism since its rise at the end of the nineteenth century. To a great extent, and despite several contradictions, the ideology of the then-active Basque nationalism, formulated by Sabino Arana (1865–1903), rested upon Carlist doctrines.[23] The *fueros* set the basis for Arana's defense of a territorial and political independence for the Basque Country, while Carlist Catholicism may be regarded in connection with Arana's religious essentialism, which he coupled with a xenophobic agenda.[24]

In sum, in *La jota*, Laparra offers a critical view of Carlism and Spanish politics based on a dramatized performance of the divisions and cleavages that affected Spain at the turn of the century. However, before drawing any premature conclusions on the nature of Laparra's approach to Carlism, it is necessary to situate *La jota* in the context of French operatic culture, as well as in the agenda underlying Laparra's writings on Spanish music and culture.

Spain in French Naturalist Opera

The emergence of French naturalist opera resulted from the influence of Italian operatic movement known as *verismo*. The ground was well prepared for such an influence to take effect because the Italian literary current that gave birth to its operatic counterpart was based, to a large extent, on the premises of the French *naturaliste* novel, formulated by Émile Zola around the middle of the nineteenth century. If the birth of Italian *verismo* can be traced back to Mascagni's *Cavalleria rusticana* (Rome 1890), by the beginning of the twentieth century the vogue was already dying out in Italy. Its impact in France gave birth to the first naturalist operas in the 1890s, such as Bruneau's *L'Attaque du moulin* (1893) and Massenet's *La Navarraise* (1894), and the genre was still very active at least during the first decade. Verismo and naturalism share a series of aspects, most notably a penchant for love-and-death plots and the harshest elements of life. Most of the time they also coincide in displaying remote settings and the local customs of poor regions.[25]

---

[23] Carlism constituted the most important ideology in Arana's upbringing until 1882. See José Luis de la Granja Sáinz, "El antimaketismo: La visión de Sabino Arana sobre España y los españoles," *Norba. Revista de historia* 19 (2006): 191–203. However, in 1897, he published *El Partido Carlista y los Fueros Vasco-navarros*, "which charged that Carlism had exploited Basque needs in the interest of all-Spanish dynastic politics." Stanley Payne, *Basque Nationalism* (Reno: University of Nevada Press, 1975), 77.

[24] Further into Basque nationalism and Carlism see McClancy, *Decline of Carlism*, 233–242 ("The Legacies of Carlism to Basque Nationalism").

[25] Matteo Sansone, "Verismo," in *Grove Music Online*, http://www.oxfordmusiconline.com/subscriber/article/grove/music/29210 (accessed April 15, 2011). I cannot agree with Sansone that "a marked regional character" is a feature that differentiates verismo from naturalisme. Operas such as Bruneau's *L'attaque du moulin* (1893) and *Messidor* (1897), Massenet's *La Navarraise*, Fernand le Borne's *La Catalane* (1907) and Laparra's *La*

There was very likely a precedent for *La jota* in the aforementioned opera *L'attaque du moulin*, with music by Alfred Bruneau and a libretto by Louis Gallet, which premiered at the Opéra Comique on November 23, 1893.²⁶ This opera may be deemed to represent one of the first specimens of French naturalism, even before Bruneau started his collaborations with Zola, on whose story Gallet based his libretto.²⁷ *L'attaque* presents a fictional episode from the Franco-Prussian War of 1870, the adverse outcome of which Zola interpreted as a sign of the Second Empire's decadence and Germany's moral and scientific superiority. Zola's story is set in the village of Rocreuse in Lorraine, more precisely in Père Merlier's mill, which, according to Huebner "is the soul of the village, the village a microcosm of rural France."²⁸ As we will see in due course, this symbolic potential may have played a role in Laparra's unacknowledged but—I argue—self-evident decision to parody, or at least base on, this opera's plot. The events unfold as follows: the staunch patriot Merlier, who lives in the mill with his daughter Françoise, allows the French troops to take refuge in his property. The Germans capture the mill and sentence to death Dominique, a French soldier and Françoise's fiancé. With the help of Françoise, Dominique manages to escape, but Merlier is taken prisoner in his place. Another French attack on the mill ensues, which "liberates" the mill, but by then Dominique has been recaptured and shot dead, and Merlier has succumbed to an errant bullet.

Laparra was not the only composer to challenge the prevailing collective sense of decorum. Gallet and Bruneau had to divest Zola's story of a few of its grisliest elements in order to make it palatable to Opéra Comique audiences. A developed sense of decorum reigned in that institution, despite the daring attitude that Léon Carvalho, the director of Opéra Comique at that time, had previously shown as director of the Théâtre-Lyrique in the 1860s.²⁹ Librettist and composer reduced fighting scenes or episodes to a minimum, and spared the audience Dominique's death after the opening night, and Merlier's in subsequent performances. In order to avoid any potential controversy or diplomatic conflict, the German army was transformed into an "enemy" army and the action was set in the eighteenth century. Like Micaëla in *Carmen*, a new, upright character, the old housemaid Marcelline, was added to serve as a commentator to the action and thus mediate between the audience and the stage horrors.³⁰

---

habanera (1908) and *La jota* (1911) may arguably be considered specimens of French naturalism set in the poor countryside.

²⁶ On this opera see Steven Huebner, *French Opera at the Fin-de-Siècle: Wagnerism, Naturalism, and Style* (Oxford and New York: Oxford University Press, 1999), 412–425.

²⁷ Published in the collection of naturalist stories entitled *Les soirées de Médan*, 1880.

²⁸ Huebner, *French Opera*, 414.

²⁹ Susan McClary, *Georges Bizet: Carmen* (Cambridge: Cambridge University Press, 1992), 16.

³⁰ Huebner, *French Opera*, 415–418.

Even after this severe remodeling,[31] *L'attaque du moulin* shares striking similarities with *La jota*. Both operas present a marginal locale in the national geography, an emblem of rural life—as we will shortly see in the case of *La jota*—that became the object of a sudden and violent attack. A young couple is broken up as a result of the death of a patriotic or politically committed male. There were differences, such as the allegiance of the male lover, who sided with the invaders in *La jota* and with the local inhabitants in *L'attaque du moulin*. Despite these differences, it is very likely that Laparra drew inspiration from this opera and adapted some of its elements in a way that was coherent with his agenda, as will be later revealed.

La jota's naturalist aesthetics cannot be solely ascribed to Laparra's attraction for certain operas such as *L'attaque du moulin*. Naturalism offered a quite adequate aesthetic framework for representing Spain according to longstanding European views of the country as being tragic or violent. This question has received much less attention, if any, than the extensive presence of Hispanic subject matters in previous nineteenth-century operas.[32] However, this testimony by Laparra illustrates precisely that point:

> To accuse a theater of being *vériste*? Let's not condemn anything on account of the value of a word! *Verismo* contains "truth" [vérité], and truth is the profound essence of poetry. Nowhere does this truth reveal itself as tragically as in Spain.[33]

Laparra responded to allegations that he composed under the influence of *verismo*. His last sentence hints at the potential connection existing between the proliferation of onstage violence in naturalist operas such as *L'attaque* or *La jota* and stereotypes of Spain as a tragic country. Indeed, one of the prevailing, centuries-long tropes in European representations of Spain was the "black legend." This consisted of a series of negatives stereotypes about Spain that emerged during the colonialist rivalry between the European powers in the early modern ages, when Spain assembled a vast empire.[34] The "black legend" focused on repressive and violent practices and codes of behavior, such as the application

---

[31] Since most of these changes completely subverted the problematics posited in Zola's story, and given that Laparra was only seventeen when *L'attaque du moulin* premiered, it is more likely that he had access to the score and the libretto.

[32] Hervé Lacombe, "L'Espagne à l'Opéra Comique avant 'Carmen.' Du 'Guitarrero' de Halévy (1842) à 'Don César de Bazan' de Massenet (1872)," François Lesure (ed.), *Echanges musicaux franco-espagnols XVIIe–XIXe siècles: Actes des Rencontres de Villecroze, 15 au 17 octobre 1998* (Paris: Klinsieck, 2000) 161–194. Some of the abundant bibliography on *Carmen* also covers the previous presence of Spain in French opera.

[33] "Accuser un théâtre d'être vériste? Ne condamnons rien sur la valeur d'un mot! Vérisme contient 'vérité' et la vérité est l'essence profonde de la poésie. Or nulle part cette vérité n'éclate aussi tragiquement qu'en Espagne." Bruyr, "Un entretien."

[34] Etzion, "Spanish Music," 93–120; García Cárcel, *La leyenda negra*.

of torture and the death penalty by the highest religious authority in early modern Spain, namely, the Tribunal of the Holy Inquisition. That Laparra's view of Spain relies on this trope shows the extent to which one of the French musicians most eager to transgress European stereotypes about Spain could not—or did not want to—get away from the collective inertia of the power strategies underlying such representations.

Laparra's testimony also reveals how, interfering with the potential connection between naturalism and "Spanish opera," there lay issues of French nationalism in the tense critical atmosphere of Third Republic France. Significantly, Laparra mentions *verismo* instead of *naturalisme*, as critics took issue with the excess of verist formulas in his operas, particularly in *La habanera*.[35] Indeed, the apparent interchangeability of both terms is tied to the cultural anxieties surrounding their similarity.[36] Given that "nationality" was the foremost value in critical debates, opponents of naturalism such as Debussy exploited the aforementioned Italian connection in their condemnation of the style,[37] while composers of naturalist opera such as Bruneau detached themselves from *verismo*.[38] Meanwhile, most French critics defended the superiority of French naturalist operas over their Italian verist counterparts.[39] Though often overlooked, this situation developed over the background of Italy's membership in the Triple Alliance since 1882, with Germany and Austria-Hungary.[40]

This critical state of affairs, which reached a climax in 1910,[41] had deeply impinged upon the reception of Laparra's first opera, *La habanera*, and it is best epitomized in

---

[35] See Llano, "Hispanic Traditions," 97–140.

[36] Branger and Ramaut approach French naturalism and Italian verismo as two branches of a common trend inspired in Zola's novels. "Préambule," *Le naturalisme sur la scène lyrique*, ed. Jean-Christophe Branger and Alban Ramaut (Saint-Etienne: Publications de l'Université de Saint-Etienne, 2004), 9–14; Manfred Kelkel draws a parallel between the birth of contemporary Italian verismo and of French naturalist opera. Kelkel, *Naturalisme, vérisme et réalisme dans l'opéra: De 1890 à 1930* (Paris: J. Vrin, 1984), 13–15. André Michel Spies groups *verismo* and *naturalisme* under the label *fait-divers*, a contemporary journalistic term referring to tragic and violent events, *Opera, State and Society in the Third Republic, 1875–1914* (New York: Peter Lang, 1998), 95; Adriana Guarnieri Corazzol, "Opera and Verismo: Regressive Points of View and the Artifice of Alienation," *Cambridge Opera Journal*, 5, no. 1 (1993), 39–53. This study provides a list of musical traits for *verismo* that could equally be applied to *naturalisme*.

[37] Fulcher, *French Cultural Politics*, 180.

[38] Huebner, *French Opera*, 402.

[39] Such as in the Paris première (1895) of Massenet's *La Navarraise*, which caused critics to despise *Cavalleria rusticana*. See Clair Rowden, "Paris-Londres: *La Navarraise* face à la presse," in *Le naturalisme*, ed. Branger and Ramaut (Saint-Etienne: Publications de l'Université de Saint-Etienne, 2004), 111.

[40] The question of Italy's potential neutrality in case of war with Germany loomed over French politics. On the one hand, by entering the Alliance, Italy committed itself to support Germany and Austria-Hungary in case of a French attack. On the other, in 1902 Italy signed a secret agreement to remain neutral in case this attack should happen. Leonard V. Smith, Stéphan Adouin-Rouzeau and Annette Becker, *France and the Great War, 1914–1918* (Cambridge: Cambridge University Press, 2003), 12.

[41] Branger, "Les compositeurs français," 315–342.

Willy's (Henry Gauthier-Villars's) comparison of this opera with a "Spanish *Cavalleria rusticana*."[42] However uncomfortable Laparra felt about his work being related to *verismo*,[43] the quotation above shows that he did not deny its influence on his music. Instead, he made a phonetic pun, in order to appropriate one of the words most invested with rhetorical value in Third Republic France, namely, "truth."[44]

Massenet's *La navarraise* and Regionalist Operas

Although perhaps no critic exploited the connection between *verismo* and "tragic" conceptions of Spain as extensively as Laparra, there was a close precedent in Massenet's operas, particularly in *La Navarraise* (London, Covent Garden, 1894; Paris, 1895). This is often referred to as Massenet's first verist opera, composed as a competitive response to Mascagni's *Cavalleria rusticana*.[45] However, Huebner has identified elements in Massenet's previous operas, especially in *Manon*, which may be regarded as an inspiration for verist or naturalist opera.[46] Given Massenet's penchant for Spanish subjects, evident in *Don Quichotte* and *Le Cid*, as well as his close association with naturalist opera, there is little surprise that he should have influenced Laparra.[47] Like *La jota*, *La Navarraise* presents a fictional episode of Carlism, though Massenet sets it in 1874, during the Third Carlist War (1872–1876).[48] From this tight connection, we can say that both operas deserve at least brief comparison. Beyond musical or aesthetic similarities, their sociopolitical underpinnings are relevant in my comparison.

The first act of *La Navarraise* opens with the sounds of a battle in a small town in the Pyrenees near the Basque capital of Bilbao. Anita, the girl from the neighboring region of Navarre, enters the scene in search of her beloved Araquil, a soldier in the troupes fighting against Zuccaraga—again, an obvious reference to

[42] Henry Gauthier-Villars, "La habanera. Ghyslaine." *Comœdia* (February 27, 1908). On the reception of *La habanera* see Llano, "Hispanic Traditions."

[43] The indications in the prologue to the 1907 edition of the piano-vocal score of *La habanera* suggest that Laparra would feel uncomfortable with any Italianate association. In this text, Laparra called for the use of declamation and sober gestures in order to "avoid taking Spain to Naples" (évitant de transporter l'Espagne à Naples). Raoul Laparra, *La habanera. Drame lyrique en trois actes. Partition piano et chant réduite par l'auteur* (Paris: Enoch & Cie, 1907).

[44] Lebovics, *True France*; on "sincerity" and music culture in Third Republic France, see Carlo Caballero, *Fauré and French Musical Aesthetics* (Cambridge: Cambridge University Press, 2001), 11–57.

[45] Rodney Milnes, "Navarraise, La," in *Grove Music Online*, http://www.oxfordmusiconline.com/subscriber/article/grove/music/O008723 (accessed April 15, 2011).

[46] Steven Huebner, "La Navarraise face au verisme," in *Le naturalisme*, ed. Branger and Ramaut, 133.

[47] On Massenet's influence in *La habanera* see Llano, "Hispanic Traditions."

[48] The fact that this is the first known opera to base its subject matter on Carlism—I have not identified any examples by a Spanish composer—further reinforces the suspicion that it exerted a pioneering impact on *La jota*.

Zumalacárregui, and a likely inspiration for Zumárraga in *La jota*. Araquil arrives and meets Anita and Remigio, his father, who, discontented about her low-class origins, sets a dowry of 2,000 *douros* as a condition for marriage. Remigio's subsequent promotion to sergeant, following the death of all the officers in the army, makes it even more difficult for Anita to overcome social barriers. In the second act, General Garrido bemoans the extensive casualties among his army, and expresses his wish for the killing of Zuccaraga, which Anita offers to accomplish for 2,000 *douros*. News that Anita has been seen among the Carlist troops in search of Zuccaraga infuriates the mortally wounded Araquil, who believes that she has sold herself to the Carlist leader. A few moments after publicly scolding Anita, Araquil learns of her deed, but he dies slightly after, causing her to go mad. Following this denouement, the war carries on.

There are several similarities and differences between *La Navarraise* and *La jota*, which reveal the extent of Massenet's influence upon Laparra. To begin with, neither opera is set in Navarre, which was the main scenario of the Carlist wars—even though they spread all over Spain. Instead, they depict the neighboring Basque Country and Aragón, where Carlism first expanded, thus helping to identify the Carlists as the attackers and cast the non-Carlist villagers as mere defenders. However, in *La jota*, the male lover fights on the side of the Carlists, thus attenuating the otherwise sharp demonization of Carlism. As we will see in due course, this difference plays a significant role in defining the political subtext of *La jota*, especially if read in the context of Third Republic politics. The main social issue underlying *La Navarraise*, namely, the class conflict so characteristic of turn-of-the-century operas—as we will see in the case of Falla's *La vie brève*—gives way in *La jota* to a clash of political sides, to a civil war whose fatality is symbolized in the absurdly tragic and all-destructive denouement.

It seems unlikely that Laparra could have remained oblivious to an opera with which *La jota* holds such obvious thematic connections. The music for *La Navarraise*, however, seems much more connected to previous operatic traditions. Massenet's melodic and harmonic structures are more periodic, and his modulations follow cyclical patterns, whereas Laparra avoids phrase and period symmetry and constantly introduces chromatic modulations to remote areas that put in question the hegemony of the main tonality for each number. Furthermore, *La Navarraise* is a number opera, whereas in *La jota* the number structure is subjected to great stylization, to the point where it is almost no longer recognizable. Not only does Laparra avoid symmetrical structures in his numbers, but he connects them by way of gradual transitions between the musical textures that characterize them all. *La Navarraise* is clearly under the influence of Italian *verismo* but incorporates Massenet's previous experience, especially as regards the use of a melody-dictated declamation that Debussy and Ravel would oppose. By contrast, *La jota* shows the influence of Wagner, thus departing from *La habanera*, which rather seemed under the sway of *verismo*/naturalism.

Other likely sources of inspiration behind *La jota* are several contemporary operas that equally served their authors to argue the impossibility of returning home after experiencing a change of personal circumstances. Among other examples, Musk has identified Guy Ropartz's *Le pays* (1908–1910, premièred in 1912), Déodat de Séverac's *Le coeur du moulin* (1909) and Joseph Canteloube's *Le Mas* (1910–1913, premièred in 1929) as operas in which the main characters die or suffer the loss of someone loved after returning to their native land following a prolonged absence.[49] Following from these composers' agendas, Musk situates and analyzes these operas in the context of regionalist intellectual and political debates in France. Moreover, "home" in these operas is the countryside, while the temporary, alternative destination that drives the characters away from "home" is always a city, which embodies corruption and represents a deviation from the main characters' allegedly "true" fate. Since the midnineteenth century, prominent French regionalist thinkers such as Frédéric Mistral, Jean Charles-Brun, Charles Maurras and Maurice Barrès capitalized extensively on the aforementioned urban-rural dichotomy in order to undermine the centralizing power that Paris exerted after the French Revolution of 1789.[50] With the exception of Mistral, their ideas spread with the rise of political regionalism in the 1890s. As in these operas, in *La jota* absence from home leads to moral decadence and self-destruction, with no room left for redemption:

> RODRIGO (to Juan): We had offered you our roof / And our sister, your fiancée, / Love and hospitality! / And all that, you monster, / Was it to see you […] Coming back amongst our butchers / With our blood in your face?[51]

In *La jota*, as in the operas mentioned above, the main character, Zumárraga, experiences the "impossibility" of returning to his adoptive home, Ansó, by experiencing the rejection of its citizens—among them Pilar's brother Rodrigo—as well as by paying with his own life and that of his lover. The violent reputation gained by Carlism, which was partly due to the effect of liberal propaganda, serves as a motif of disruption and, hence, as the basis for the criticism encapsulated in Zumárraga's impossible and thwarted return to his "roots."

---

[49] Andrea Musk, "Regionalism, Latinité," 226–249; Andrea Musk, "Aspects of Regionalism."

[50] The bibliography on the history of regionalism in France is very extensive. See, for instance, Thiesse, *Écrire la France* and *Ils apprenaient la France*; also see the Introduction to Wright, *Regionalist Movement in France*.

[51] "Rodrigo: Nous t'avions donné notre toit, / Et notre soeur, ta fiancée, / L'amour et l'hospitalité! / Et tout cela, monstre, c'était / Pour te voir / […] Parmi nos bouchers revenir / Avec notre sang sur la face?" Laparra, *La jota*, 137.

On the basis of the plot and character similarities between *La jota* and the regionalist operas mentioned, it seems compelling to read Laparra's opera as a regionalist expression, which draws on an episode of Spanish history to mirror issues of French politics and culture. It seems plausible to read an adherence to regionalism behind Laparra's defence of Spain's cultural and regional diversity, evident not so much in his choice of removed locales—which, after all, was a staple of verist and naturalist operas—but also in his recreation of folklore from different Spanish regions.[52] Furthermore, in 1927, Laparra declared that "Spain should not be treated as a soloist. It's an ensemble, like all beautiful spectacles."[53] That same year, he published another article in which he asserted that France was as culturally varied as Spain, and regretted "this spirit of ferocious centralization which will end up rendering us completely amorphous and without traits." This article shows how Laparra's thought connects with Maurras's anti-Republicanism and antimodernism, insofar as Laparra blames the Revolution of 1789 for having caused "the decadence of folklore"—it is the Revolution that split France "administratively" and "disfigured" it—and regrets that the Catalan *cobla* is being replaced by jazz, which thus becomes a symbol of urban decadence.[54] It would be simplistic, however, to tag *La jota* as a regionalist opera, insofar as I shall argue that it encapsulates a whole, complex view of the nation and its citizens. In that sense, *La jota* illustrates Wright's remark that "the study of French regionalism is the study of a struggle between two views of the state."[55]

Critical Reactions to *La jota*

To judge from the critics' reactions, violence in *La jota* rose above even the standards of verismo. An anonymous critic writing for the *Journal Amusant* described "the life of the heroes in *La Jota*" as a "hell," and confessed that he would "prefer to see them

---

[52] In *La habanera*, for instance, he imitated folklore from Castile and the Basque Country.

[53] "il ne faut jamais traiter l'Espagne en soliste. C'est un ensemble, comme tous les beaux spectacles." Raoul Laparra, "Espagne," *Le ménestrel* (October 21, 1927).

[54] "Nous avons un peu d'Espagne en France, ou plutôt quelques-un des éléments si différents que la composent […] Un enfant basque est traité comme un enfant flamand. Et cela ne devrait pas être; et cela ne peut pas être. Nous finirons par obtenir une nation 'grise', sans vie réelle parce qu'elle ne sera plus faite de variétés, comme la nature. Au sud-est, notre petite 'Catalogne' disparaît peu à peu, elle aussi, pour se fondre dans le bloc rivé par la Révolution française […] C'est à partir de la Révolution que commence la décadence du folklore. C'est elle qui découpa la France 'administrativement' et la défigura […] Cet esprit de centralisation féroce et qui finira par nous rendre complètement amorphes et sans traits, est celui qui active l'âme de la petite Catalogne française. La voilà, maintenant, qui perd ses chers instruments rustiques, ses voix ensoleillées; les coblas cigalières s'y meurent ou, comble de détresse, appellant à leur secours…le jazz!" Raoul Laparra, "Espagne," *Le ménestrel* (November 4, 1927).

[55] Wright, *Regionalist Movement in France*, vii.

kill each other from the uppermost circle, where fierce music lovers book a seat for two Francs."⁵⁶ A journalistic caricature found among the program notes displayed the three main characters singing two meters above the ground after being thrust into the air by an onstage explosion, and shows the choir in the background being thrown to the floor by the same force. An appalled Alfred Bruneau thought that

> this somber work, severe at the beginning, excessive in its denouement, never indifferent, audacious for most of the public, would have been applauded more had it not abused so much of the shots, shrieks and massive realist effects which, I think, detonate in the place where the work is set.⁵⁷

Victor Debay deemed the fights "conventional [...] artificial and even ludicrous." By contrast, he praised "the antiques and the classics" for leaving "every accident and cataclysm backstage."⁵⁸ Perhaps the most positive appraisal came from Charles Tenroc, who, in his review for *Comoedia* praised the fact that Laparra has "preserved his entire personality" without "getting attached to any allegedly independent school," and argued that "by virtue of its Meridional flavor, Laparra's music is good, French music."⁵⁹ Thus, Tenroc defended Laparra's music from critiques raised three years before against *La habanera*, whose verist elements brought critics to question Laparra's French credentials.⁶⁰

Notwithstanding Tenroc's endorsement, critical reactions show that, once again, representations of Spain were surrounded by scandal, as at the première of *Carmen*, back in 1875.⁶¹ In order not to "hurt certain susceptibilities"—to

---

⁵⁶ "La vie des héros de *la Jota* es un enfer [...] J'aime mieux les voir s'entre-tuer du 'paradis,' ou les mélomanes farouches prennent place pour deux francs." Anon. "Entre cœur et jardin. Opéra Comique. La Jota." Journal Amusant, April 1911. Quote from a cutting found among the program notes at the Bibliothèque Nationale de France. Raoul Laparra, *La jota. Conte lyrique en deux actes* [program notes], Ro 3650.

⁵⁷ "Cette oeuvre sombre, sévère au début, déréglée, excessive au dénouement, jamais indifférente, audacieuse par la majorité du public On l'aurait applaudie davantage si elle abusait moins de coups de feu, des cris, des gros effets réalistes qui, je crois, détonnent dans le cadre où elle est placée." Alfred Bruneau, "Répétition Générale. À la salle Favart, spectacle groupé et varié: Deux actes philosophiques; deux actes tragiques." *Le matin* (April 25, 1911). As is well known, Bruneau was himself a composer of naturalist operas, which contradicts any suspicions that he might have opposed violence on the basis of a fundamental opposition to the aesthetics of naturalism.

⁵⁸ "Malheureusement, le second acte, malgré la lutte qui l'emplit et même à cause d'elle, a refroidi mon enthousiasme. Un combat au théâtre, si bien réglé soit-il, est toujours une chose conventionnelle, factice et même ridicule. Comme les anciens et les classiques avaient raison lorsqu'ils laissaient dans la coulisse tous les accidents et cataclysmes." Victor Debay "La voile du bonheur, La jota," *Le courrier musical* (May 1, 1911).

⁵⁹ "conserver son entière personnalité, ne s'inféoder à aucune école prétendue indépendante"; "A travers la saveur méridionale, la musique de M. Laparra est de la bonne, de la vraie musique française." Charles Tenroc, "M. Raoul Laparra nous parle de 'La jota,'" *Comoedia*, March 26, 1911.

⁶⁰ See Llano, "Hispanic Traditions."

⁶¹ McClary, *Georges Bizet: Carmen*, 111–113.

paraphrase Laparra—and to avoid having the denouement interpreted as an "attack against the Catholic faith," he agreed to suppress the crucifixion of Mosén Jago at the end, following protests from the audience during the first three performances.[62] Next to showing moral concerns, however, critics took issue with noise and its impact on music. This attitude shows that music constituted the primary target of their critical judgment, more than any elements from the drama. Again, Massenet's *La Navarraise* had set the precedent, for its Paris première (1895) elicited some critical opposition to noise.[63] *La jota* exacerbated this effect, as can be gathered from the critics' reactions. Louis Vuillemin remarked that

> executions, yells, groans of pain, imprecations, explosions do not cease for a moment. Certainly, I cannot figure out the relation between such a hell and any music whatsoever. Is there material even for an opera? Certainly not. If not isolated, Raoul Laparra's attempt will usher in a retrogression of musical theater.[64]

Vuillemin found noise extraneous to any preexistent and valid operatic style. Similarly, Paul Souday—who deemed Laparra's libretto "deplorable, pretentious and flashy"—argued that, although the "first act had produced a very positive impression [...] the second act has spoiled it," since "music is absent from it, or at least it disappears under the dreadful racket produced by the gunfire and the assault."[65] Gabriel Fauré, who had taught Laparra in his composition class in the Conservatoire, argued that music "can be heard—when the gunfire permits it—but it does not lend itself to be listened to; one could even doubt that it is necessary, at least during the second act."[66] Fauré's critique could hardly entail a stronger blow to "the musical poverty that characterizes *La Jota*"—from his point of view.[67]

---

[62] "froissait [...] certaines susceptibilités"; "attaque contre la réligion catholique." Jean Prudhomme, "Opéra Comique," *Le temps*, May 7, 1911.

[63] Rowden, "Paris-Londres," 113.

[64] Louis Vuillemin, " 'Le Voile du Bonheur.' 'La Jota,'" *Comoedia* (April 27, 1911): "Fusillades, hurlements, râles de douleurs, imprécations, explosions, ne cessent pas un instant. En vérité, je ne puis concevoir le rapport existant entre un pareil enfer et une musique quelle qu'elle soit. Y a-t-il là matière même à un opéra? Assurément non. La tentative de M. Raoul Laparra, si elle ne devait pas rester isolée, marquerait une rétrogradation du théâtre lyrique."

[65] "déplorable, prétentieux et clinquant"; "ce premier acte avait produit une très favorable impression"; "Le second acte a gâté les choses"; "La musique en est absente, ou du moins elle disparaît sous l'effroyable vacarme de la fusillade et de l'assaut." Paul Souday, "A l'Opéra Comique," *Le temps*, March 23, 1911.

[66] "Elle s'entend—lorsque la fusillade le permet—elle s'entend mais elle ne se fait guère écouter, on pourrait même douter qu'elle soit nécessaire du moins durant tout le second acte." Gabriel Fauré, "Opéra Comique: *La jota*, conte lyrique en deux actes, de M. Raoul Laparra," *Le Figaro*, March 28, 1911.

[67] "la pauvreté musicale qui caractérise *la Jota*." Fauré, "Opéra Comique."

In light of this traditionalist stance, Vuillemin's contention that *La jota* represents a "retrogression of musical theater" seems contradictory. Indeed, noise could represent a modernist feature, as in Stravinsky's *The Rite of Spring*, which premiered in Paris only two years after *La jota*, in 1913.[68] That same year, Luigi Russolo published his futurist manifesto *The Art of Noise*, whose impact on composers such as Edgar Varèse, John Cage and Pierre Schaeffer prompted Jean-Jacques Nattiez to claim that "all twentieth-century music is in effect characterized by a displacement of the boundary between 'music' and 'noise.'"[69] Stravinsky's understanding of noise may be deemed more organic and less abstract than Russolo's, but both suggest the possibility that *La jota* reflected an emergent state of affairs.

In *La jota*, however, its attachment to the drama removed noise from the avant-garde composer's radical understanding of it. Different from avant-garde circles, the more traditionalist Opéra Comique critics perceived noise as an extramusical element, as can be seen in Adolphe Aderer's review: "In the second act, it seems as if the music had stopped. There was nothing but shrieks, screams, gunshots, strategic movements, against which the composer clashed like the assailants against the church."[70] Aderer conceives of noise and music as competing and irreconcilable elements. Pierre Lalo's review illustrates how ascriptions to the absolute music paradigm contributed to shaping perceptions of noise as an extramusical or even antimusical feature:

> the composer of La jota has turned his back on music: rather than exalting inner and deep emotions which stem from the development of musical thought, and which are one of art's creations and constructions, he has preferred external action, superficial agitation, direct sensation, shrieks, imprecations, gunshots, explosions, the crumbling of walls, the most hideous and deafening uproar of non-musical noises that ever burst on any stage.[71]

---

[68] Referring to *The Rite of Spring*, Nichols contends that "no Parisian had ever before been subjected to this level of noise except on a battlefield." Nichols, *The Harlequin Years*, 32.

[69] Jean-Jacques Nattiez, *Music and Discourse. Toward a Semiology of Music* (Princeton, NJ: Princeton University Press, 1990/1987), 45. For a semiology and history of "noise" see ibid., 45–54.

[70] "Au second acte, on pourrait presque dire que la musique est finie. Ce ne sont plus que cris, hurlements, coups de fusil, mouvements stratégiques, contre lesquels le compositeur se heurte comme les assaillants contre l'église." Adolphe Aderer, "Opéra Comique. Le voile du bonheur. La jota," *Le petit Parisien* (April 17, 1911).

[71] "Le musicien de la Jota s'est détourné de la musique: à l'exaltation et à l'émotion intérieures et profondes qui naissent du développement de la pensée musicale, qui sont une création et une construction de l'art, il a préféré l'action extérieure, l'agitation superficielle, la sensation directe, les cris, les imprécations, les coups de fusil, les explosions, les écoulements de murailles, les plus épouvantable, le plus assourdissant tapage de bruits non musicaux qui ait jamais éclaté sur aucun théâtre." Pierre Lalo, "À l'Opéra Comique: Le voile du bonnheur. La jota." *Le temps* (May 4, 1911).

Lalo played out inner-emotional, outer-unemotional binaries so characteristic of romantic musical aesthetics. These binaries can be connected with Schopenhauer's formulation of the "will" as the ultimate "subject" of music, and music as the most direct manifestation of the "will," and by extension of human emotions—a premise that Nietzsche would later contest.[72] This stance is consistent with Lalo's reputation as "a critic who has attempted for a long time to spread Germanic tendencies in France"[73]—as Ravel would have it—and contrasts sharply with wartime reactions to German music and philosophy, especially Wagner and Schopenhauer.[74] But Lalo championed Italian *verismo*, as evinced by his opposition to the "musical protectionism" elicited by a poll on Italian composers published by *Comœdia*, which recorded a strong anti-verist sentiment among prominent French composers, including Fauré, Debussy, d'Indy, Bruneau, Hahn and Dukas, among others.[75] Lalo gives testimony of how *verismo* could accommodate stage violence but not "sonic" violence.

In light of the nearly unanimous critical condemnation of *La jota*,[76] it seems hard to explain why Laparra and Albert Carré decided to go ahead with this work. Carré's long experience as director of the Opéra Comique since 1898 could have helped him to predict adverse reactions to *La jota*. Furthermore, Laparra's first opera, *La habanera* (1908), had already provoked some scandal, on account of its violent and baleful plot.[77] Reviews had deemed this opera "gloomy and hopeless,"[78] a "bloody horror,"[79] "a bloody and somber drama,"[80] and "harshly realist"

---

[72] For an introduction to Schopenhauer's musical aesthetics see Peter Kivy, *Introduction to a Philosophy of Music* (New York: Oxford University Press, 2002), 20–22. On the impact of Schopenhauer's musical aesthetics and Nietzsche's revocation of the former's emotional conception of music see Dahlhaus, *Between Romanticism and Modernism*, 28–31.

[73] Ravel, quoted in Brian Hart, "The Symphony and National Identity in Early Twentieth-Century France," in *French Music, Culture, and National Identity, 1870–1939*, ed. Barbara Kelly (Rochester, NY: University of Rochester Press, 2008), 135.

[74] Marion Schmid, "À bas Wagner!: The French Press Campaign Against Wagner During World War I," *French Music, Culture*, ed. Kelly, 80.

[75] Branger, "Les compositeurs français," 318–319.

[76] Davin de Champclos's review was the sole exception to a unanimous hostility to *La jota*. According to this critic, "What the audience will remember […] are the picturesque dances, a marvellous staging of the second act and, above all, the admirable, unique performance of Marguerite Carré." Gabriel Davin de Champclos, "Les répétitions générales. 'Le voile du bonheur' et 'La jota' à l'Opéra Comique," *Comœdia* (April 25, 1911).

[77] This opera presents the story of Ramón, who kills his brother Pedro out of jealousy about the latter's betrothal to Pilar. Ramón claims no authorship for the crime and succeeds in marrying Pilar, but Pedro's ghost abducts her as Ramón refuses to confess his crime.

[78] Un Monsieur de l'Orchestre, "La soirée. A l'Opéra Comique," *Le Figaro* (February 27, 1908).

[79] Anon., "Un fait-divers, presque banal, si l'art du musicien n'en transfigurait la sanglante horreur," *Le matin* (February 25, 1908).

[80] "une des œuvres sinon des plus séduisantes, au moins des plus curieuses, tant par sa conception que par sa réalisation, que nous ayons entendues depuis longtemps." Victor Debay, "La habanera. Ghyslaine," *Le courrier musical*, March 1908.

on account of its "excessive verismo."[81] The killing of the main character, Pedro, struck *Le Figaro* as violent, as evident in a half-page caricature.[82]

Perhaps Carré sought to provoke critics and audiences, an attitude that corroborates his reputation as a rebellious character, who fought against outdated and "bourgeois" theatrical conventions[83] and put on verist operas amidst resounding protests.[84] Laparra's stormy personality suited his aims, as suggested by this excerpt in which Carré reminisces about the première of *La jota*:

> It was thought at that time that "those horrors" were gratuitous and exaggerated.... Alas! That civil war tableau has taken on a prophetic character now that all that—and even worse—has really taken place in damned Spain.
>
> Raoul Laparra himself conducted his work the opening night. During the battle, it was not anymore a conductor's baton that he seemed to hold in his feverish hands, but a sword with which, from his position, he spurred the fighters. Standing, his eyes on fire, hair in disarray, tie unknotted, his voice, for a moment, mixed with the choir's vociferation. Taken by the action, the musicians stood up. The audience ended up joining in the action, and the performance was brought to an end by a burst—the only pleasant one—of applause, in the tense atmosphere of a boxing combat.[85]

Hindsight allowed Carré to connect the incidents in *La jota* with the Spanish Civil War of 1936, and thus to portray Laparra as a prophetic character. He reported an enthusiastic, almost fervent reaction from the audience that no critic had registered in 1911, and with which he probably intended to support Laparra. However, Carré also depicted Laparra as a lunatic and a maniac, possibly biased by the fact that he had died in a psychiatric hospital in 1943, that is, seven years before the publication of Carré's memoirs. From this testimony, it would be easy to attribute the extensive use of violence in *La jota* to Carré's experimental

---

[81] René Chalupt, "L'Espagne dans la musique française," *Revue musicale* (February 1931).

[82] Un Monsieur de l'Orchestre, "La soirée."

[83] Hughes Imbert, "Albert Carré," *Médaillons contemporains* (Paris, 1903), 123–130.

[84] Branger, "Les compositeurs français," 324.

[85] "L'on estima à l'époque que 'ces horreurs' étaient gratuites et outrées... Hélas! ce tableau de guerre civile a pris un caractère prophétique aujourd'hui que tout cela—et bien pire—s'est produit réellement dans la malheureuse Espagne./Raoul Laparra dirigeait lui-même son oeuvre le soir de la première. A cet acte de la bataille, ce n'était plus un bâton de chef d'orchestre qu'il semblait tenir dans ses mains fiévreuses, mais une épée avec laquelle, de sa place, il animait les combattants. Debout, les yeux en feu, la chevelure en désordre, la cravate dénouée, sa voix, par moment, se mêlait aux vociférations des choristes. Emportés par l'action, les musiciens eux mêmes s'étaient levés. Le public finit, lui aussi, par se mêler au drame, et la représentation se termina, dans l'atmosphère tendue de certains matches de boxe, par une rafale—la seule qu'on entende avec plaisir—d'applaudissements." Albert Carré, *Souvenirs de Théâtre, réunis, présentés et annotés par Robert Favart* (Paris: Plon, 1950), 338.

character and to Laparra's apparent tumultuousness. However, considered in the context of turn-of-the-century French operatic culture described above on the one hand, and read against Laparra's writings on Spanish music and culture on the other, his portrayal of Spain as a violent country and the extensive use of noise seem to rest upon a more organic and developed ideological background than a mental disorder would suggest.

The "Noble Savage" Trope in Laparra's Writings

Laparra's writings so consistently uphold a particular conception of Spanish music, culture and identity that one feels compelled to examine his musical output in connection with them. In particular, three aspects of his writings demand attention in relation to *La jota*: his use of the "noble savage" trope, his class- and race-oriented constructions of violence and his use of tropes of nostalgia.

Laparra's "noble savages" are the Spanish artist and musician. In an article that appeared in December 1919, Laparra advocated "a popular music filtered through an artistic temperament," since through "that continuous rubbing between the artist and the people," "the truly Spanish painter and musician" become "audacious" and "self-assured to the hilt," to the point that "they openly express the bitter urges in their soul without any disparity between conception and realization."[86] Laparra's vindication of the Spanish musician is grounded upon dichotomies such as natural-artificial, spontaneous-calculated, etc. Further in connection with the noble savage trope, Laparra describes the Spanish musician as endowed with "a certain ignorance" that "preserves" his genius," and a "heart" that "supplants" his intellect," a "child" and an "orphan who does not know anything and who, thanks to his ignorance, climbs up to the summit of Beauty in a single leap."[87] In a later contribution to

---

[86] Raoul Laparra, "La semaine musical," *Le ménestrel*, December 19, 1919: "j'ai constaté qu'en Espagne l'artiste, en général, est très près du peuple […] tout ce qui vient du peuple semble marqué d'une sorte de beauté fatale, même ses cruautés […] Il y a dans ce frottement continuel du peuple et de l'artiste à travers la fête, un grand principe de force pour l'art espagnol […] Les hardiesses des Espagnols ne sont que le résultat inconscient de cette cause. Le peintre et le musicien vraiment espagnols ne s'imaginent pas êtres hardis; ils se sentent simplement convaincus jusqu'aux entrailles, tout comme le plus humble chanteur de flamencos, et, sans ergotage entre la conception et le rendu, expriment directement leurs après élans d'âme."

[87] Ibid. "Une certaine ignorance préservant leur génie, leur cœur supplée au savoir; ils y gagnent cet entrave que rien n'entrave et qui permet d'enlever une œuvre entière avec la spontanéité d'une esquisse […] L'art espagnol, c'est, dans sa sublime désolation, la solitude, la Soledad rencontrée au tournant de la rue et dont ont devine le nom à la tristesse embrasée des yeux […] Tel est l'art d'Espagne: un 'enfant' qui donne tout de lui-même si son cœur doit en éclater, pourvu que le cri sorte; un orphelin qui ne sait rien et qui, dans son ignorance, escalade d'un bond les sommets du Beau./L'artiste qui, en dépit du métier nécessaire, aura conservé ces dons natifs pourra, seul, s'appeler Espagnol."

Le Ménestrel, Laparra dwelt further on the "noble savage" trope, as shown by his contention that in Spain "what stands as coarse among educated people becomes impressive among the naïfs"; furthermore, he declared that "those who have managed to learn when they were simple children are like the direct voices of nature, since they have never been attracted by science."[88]

Though one should not neglect the weight of pre-War primitivism and, most especially, of Stravinsky's *Rite* on Laparra's self-fashioning in the 1920s, his "savage" Spanish musician should be connected with earlier French and European intellectual traditions. On the one hand, it can be set in the context of late-eighteenth-century European (mostly German) debates on the nature of the creative, free genius and his contradictory dependence on exemplary rules, a debate that to a great extent revolved around Kant's thought.[89] On the other hand, Laparra's paean of spontaneity, naturalness and ignorance reminds one of Henri Collet's anti-German construction of Albéniz, discussed in Chapter 1. However, rather than an anti-German and therefore pro-French artifact, Laparra's "savage" Spanish musician serves in his fight against the principles of French "corrupted" civilization, when read in the context of Laparra's other writings. Thus, in his contribution to the March 1923 issue of *Le Ménestrel* he proposed Spain, and by extension Spanish culture, as a "safeguard" against the French "atmosphere of rules and coteries."[90] This critique of "French civilization" is grounded, once again, in views of urban culture as corrupt. This connection is particularly evident in his exhortation to "get lost among the poor guitarists of southern Spain," which echoes Falla's and Lorca's constructions of flamenco as removed from allegedly corrupt urban cultures, and ultimately is reminiscent of Bartók's ideas on Hungarian music.[91] Similarly, in another contribution to *Le Ménestrel*, Laparra regretted "the day when popular songs would stop being sung at the cradle" and in which he blamed the "increasingly overwhelming and mindless invasion of the café-concert song."[92]

---

[88] "J'ai vu souvent, de l'autre côté des Pyrénées, ce que l'on eut considéré comme grossier parmi les savants devenir d'impressionnantes qualités chez les naïfs et constituer de précieuses indications d'art. Du reste, il semble que tous ceux qui ont su vraiment ont cherché à apprendre des simples, des enfants, ils sont les voix vraiment directes de la nature, n'ayant pas été inquiétés par la science." Raoul Laparra, "Espagne," *Le ménestrel* (March 9, 1923).

[89] Martin Gammon, "'Exemplary Originality': Kant on Genius and Imitation," *Journal of the History of Philosophy*, 35, 4 (1997): 563–592.

[90] Raoul Laparra, "Espagne," *Le ménestrel* (March 1923).

[91] On Falla, Lorca and flamenco see Timothy Mitchell, *Flamenco Deep Song* (New Haven and London: Yale University Press), 160–177. On Bartók and gypsy music see, Julie Brown, "Bartók, the Gypsies, and Hybridity in Music," *Western Music and Its Others: Difference, Representation and Appropriation in Music*, ed. Georgina Born and David Hesmondhalgh (Berkeley and Los Angeles: University of California Press, 2000) 119–142.

[92] "Le jour où l'on ne chantera plus d'airs populaires à son berceau verra automatiquement se tarir la production musicale. Malheureusement, ce jour est possible. L'envaissement de plus en plus submergeant de l'abêtissante chanson de café-concert nous en fait entrevoir l'aube lamentable menaçant les peuples à la racine de l'idéal." Raoul Laparra, "Espagne," *Le ménestrel* (August 22, 1924).

In sum, Laparra's Spanish noble savage is a critical concoction partly aimed at reinforcing stereotypes about Spain being savage and backward on the one hand, but also "pure" and untainted by corruption and commercialization on the other. Furthermore, Laparra assigns the Spanish noble savage a fundamental role in his critique of French civilization, which reinforces the aforementioned argument that *La jota* constitutes an essay on French politics and identity. However, the question remains as to why, in *La jota*, the noble savage gives way to the evil one through the extensive use of violence.[93] Behind this apparent contradiction, there lies a class- and race-oriented construction of violence aimed at supporting notions of French hegemony.

Laparra's Class-Oriented Concept of Violence

Laparra's aforementioned espousal of "a popular music filtered through an artistic temperament"[94] reads like a populist construction of Spanish identity undertaken from the artist's "superior" vantage point. On that basis, I feel compelled to connect Laparra's rendition of Spanish identity as "popular" with widespread, time-honored, populist strategies. The invention of the "people" as a hegemonic concept has a long history that harks back to at least the French Enlightenment. During the economic crisis of the 1920s and 1930s, when Laparra published most of his articles, that concept informed a sort of Western European populism aimed at defending besieged capitalism from the rise of socialism. Coupled with a conception of the peasants as a homogeneous and ethnically "pure" category, this form of populism led to the rise of fascism.[95]

Laparra's version of populism differs slightly from the one just described. Far from the idealized peasant who prevailed in 1920s populism, Laparra's concept of the "Spanish people" accommodates violence. This peculiarity becomes evident in his remark that "all that stems from the people is marked by a sort of fatal beauty, even its cruelties."[96] Despite its peculiarities, or, precisely thanks to them, Laparra's conception of the "Spanish people" as violent is fit for his hegemonic conception of France. Selective, class- and race-oriented depictions of violence

[93] This contradiction is far from new in history. Ellingson reports that in Henry McKenzie's novel *The Man of the World* (1787), in which the words "savage" and "nobleness" first appeared associated, there is "a noticeable emphasis on savage violence and cruelty." Ellingson, *Myth of the Noble Savage*, 5. However, I argue that this contradiction holds particular implications in Laparra, as I explain below.

[94] "En se répétant ce nom 'Goya!' on se demande quelle musique pourrait traduire en sonorités ce que le peintre a exprimé en formes. Et, tout de suite, on se dit: 'Une musique populaire;' ou, plutôt, une musique dérivée du peuple à travers un tempérament d'artiste." Laparra, "La semaine musicale" (December 1919).

[95] Brass, *Peasants, Populism and Postmodernism*, 1–61.

[96] "tout ce qui vient du peuple semble marqué d'une sorte de beauté fatale, même ses cruautés." Laparra, "La semaine musical" (December 19, 1919).

constitute another time-honored strategy at the service of hegemony, which dates back at least to the Middle Ages. In *The Civilizing Process*, Norbert Elias has described how, in that period, "it was the structure of society that required and generated a specific standard of emotional control."[97] Furthermore, Elias explains that the nobility was the only class taught to restrain its warring emotions, in order to make the violent instincts and martial duties of a nobleman conform to the established protocol of knighthood.[98] In *Madness and Civilization*, Foucault describes how, following the birth of the age of "confinement" at the end of the eighteenth century, madness was categorized as a mental illness and "men, in an act of sovereign reason, confine their neighbours, and communicate and recognize each other through the merciless language of non-madness."[99] According to Foucault, at that juncture the disruption of the historical dialogue between insanity and madness—one of the most conspicuous symptoms of which is violence—or the radical modification of its language through the establishment and scientific foundation of diagnosis, became the main strategy whereby the idea of a sane civilization was shaped and upheld, at the expense of the alienated madman.[100] Similarly, in his "Thesis on the Philosophy of History," Benjamin states that "there is no document of civilization which is not at the same time a document of barbarism."[101] In sum, these thinkers converge in their argument that civilization always depends on the identification, and hence presence, of subaltern elements, who are often characterized by violent behavior. Still, nowadays class constitutes one of the main parameters, together with gender and race, with which to trace a social demography of violence, and statistics show that "violent crime rates are highest in underclass communities."[102] With particular reference to Spain at the turn of the twentieth century, Joshua Goode has uncovered how a representative number of intellectuals availed themselves of race- and class-oriented theories in order to support a scientific discourse on violence.[103] In light of the all-pervasive and longstanding relationship among violence, race and class, Laparra's agenda resembles the logical outcome and by-product of well-established strategies prevailing in his time.

---

[97] Norbert Elias, *The Civilizing Process* (Oxford: Blackwell, 1994/1939), 169.

[98] Ibid., 171.

[99] Michel Foucault, *Madness and Civilization* (Abingdon: Routledge, 2001/1961), xi.

[100] Ibid., 35–61.

[101] Walter Benjamin, "Theses on the Philosophy of History," in *Illuminations*, ed. Hannah Arendt (London: Pimlico, 1999/1955), 248.

[102] Sally S. Simpson, "Caste, Class and Violent Crime: Explaining Difference in Female Offending," *Criminology* 29 (1991–1992), 119. However, as Simpson argues in this article, class cannot be considered as an isolated factor, and there is not a single, infallible model that explains the different ways in which it interacts with gender and race, or that accounts for the variance produced by the different contexts in which these factors operate.

[103] Joshua Goode, "Corrupting a Good Mix: Race and Crime in Late Nineteenth- and Early Twentieth-century Spain," *European History Quarterly* 35, no. 2 (April 1, 2005): 241–265.

But Laparra's concept of the "Spanish people" still differs from the "peasant" of 1920s populism in another essential aspect: it hardly fits into an agenda of ethnic purity. Indeed, Laparra emphasises "difference" through a defense of the "savage," and at times of the "gypsy." This particularity makes it clearer that his hegemonic strategies are meant not so much as a way of establishing a strictly vertical, social hierarchy as a spatial, horizontal and cultural one, in which Spain comes to represent the low Other. The gypsy never came to inhabit the center of racial constructions of Spanish identity but was always cast as a low Other, with the purpose of upholding notions of racial "normality." Similarly, the invention of the violent or "ignoble savage" is a strategy aimed at presenting colonialism under a civilizing light.[104] That Laparra conceived of French culture as hegemonic can be grasped from his description of Paris as the "City of Light" (Ville-Lumière) where "all the beautiful things in the world should be represented," according to "its true destiny," to "the splendid aim that nature has imposed on it."[105] This description of Paris matches postcolonialist conceptions of representation-as-power.[106] Furthermore, it mirrors narratives of French cultural imperialism that found their ultimate fulfillment in the 1931 colonial exhibition, where most world cultures were represented in order to showcase France's colonial power.[107]

In sum, Laparra's ignoble savage represents, at the same time, a critique and an endorsement of civilization. Some strands in feminist theory, especially where it intersects with postcolonial theory, help to account for this double meaning. The parallel between the Other and the female, or the "exotic" and the "erotic" in *Carmen*, shows how a rebellious, low-class female can shake the foundations of male-dominated Western societies.[108] Even if *Carmen's* final death, however, suggests that Bizet condemned or obliterated her recklessness, she may still perform a subversive role. According to McClary, *Carmen* presented French audiences with the unheard-of message that colonial violence returns to the colonizer, and raised fears about the demise of Western civilization, the bourgeoisie and male domination.[109] James Parakilas has carried out an equally fatalistic and postcolonialist reading of *Carmen*, which, to a certain extent, he understands as a

---

[104] Ellingson, *Myth of the Noble Savage*, 11–20 ("Colonialism, Savages and Terrorism").

[105] "La capitale de France est non seulement la Ville-Lumière, mais encore la Ville-Synthèse; comme telle, tout ce qu'il y a de beaux dans le monde devrait être représenté dans son enceinte. Plus Paris ouvrira ses portes aux idéales étrangères, plus Paris ira vers sa vraie destinée, qui est de réaliser, entre ses murs, le forum moral de l'humanité. C'est pourquoi est si regrettable tout ce qui peut retarder son évolution vers le but splendide que lui a imposé la nature." Raoul Laparra, "Espagne," *Le ménestrel* (November 19, 1920). See Pasler, *Composing the Citizen*, 4–5.

[106] Conceptions of representation as power are more appropriate to classical forms of postcolonial theory. See Edward Said, *Orientalism* (New York: Vintage Books, 1978).

[107] Lebovics, *True France*, 51–98.

[108] Austern, "'Forreine Conceits,'" 26–42; McClary, *Georges Bizet: Carmen*.

[109] McClary, *Georges Bizet: Carmen*, 29–43.

spotlight cast on the dark side of colonization. According to Parakilas, *Carmen* tells a story about the incompatibility between individuals from different social and ethnic backgrounds, such as Don José and Carmen, as well as between the metropolis and the colonial world these characters embody respectively.[110]

More generally, some feminist theorists, among them McClary, help to understand that the contradiction underlying Laparra's ambivalent conception of the Spaniard as a "noble" and "ignoble savage" rests upon the need of most critiques of civilization to be based on a celebration of otherness. This attitude often derives from casting an alienating view on the chosen Other, which thus comes to inhabit the lowest positions in the prevailing social and cultural hierarchy. That violence constitutes one of the privileged means with which to celebrate or reinforce the sense of otherness should come as no surprise, insofar as we have seen above the selective use of social and cultural codes of violence providing a privileged means for the construction of hegemony.

Tropes of Nostalgia: The "Agrarian Myth" and "Eternal Nation"

Laparra's writings exhibit a deep and conspicuous sense of nostalgia, which connects with his purpose of offering an isolated image of Spain in *La jota*, and with the fixating notions of race and class encapsulated in his description of the Spaniard as a "noble savage." Tom Brass's study of the "agrarian myth" in *Peasants, Populism and Postmodernism* presents a great potential for analyzing this aspect of Laparra's thought. Although Brass presents several case studies based on Russia, India and Latin America, the "agrarian myth," I argue, has played a pivotal role in France and Spain, articulating definitions of national identity as fixed or "eternal." According to Brass, the "agrarian myth" endorses rural, small-scale economic activity and culture; conceives of religious, ethnic, national, regional, village and family identities as derived from Nature; and fixes and consequently opposes all forms of urban, large-scale economy as well as their derivatives, such as industrialization, bureaucracy, the state, class formation, revolution, socialism and ultimately the spread of Enlightenment ideas. The "agrarian myth" casts the peasantry as a homogeneous category embodying familial unity, ethnic purity, labor force, soil, and territory; by extension, it conceives of the peasant as the main repository of national identity. Therefore, "the agrarian myth is also associated historically with the emergence of nineteenth century European nationalist movements" through its involvement in the process of "'reinventing' traditional folkloric concepts [and] linking an

---

[110] James Parakilas, "The Soldier and the Exotic: Operatic Variations on a Theme of Racial Encounter. Part I," *Opera Quarterly*, 10, 2 (1993–1994), 33–56.

ethnically-specific homogeneous 'people' to a particular territory."[111] Brass argues that the "agrarian myth" lies at the core of fascist ideologies, and that it became particularly powerful during the economic crisis of the 1890s, 1920s and 1930s, by casting industrialization and urban production as "foreign" impositions and eliciting an anti-Semitic, antiforeign sentiment among peasants and farmers.[112]

Laparra's consistent critique of civilization matches Brass's description of the "agrarian myth," as can be seen in an article dating from 1932. In it Laparra condemned the "too developed critical sense" he sees in France and contended that "Spain is ignorant, but that ignorance should constitute a guide to us" (the French people). More importantly, in this text, Laparra took issue with "originality" and "fashion"—a "torturing concern"—while defending the existence of "a more noble ideal than that: to belong to all times." He added:

> That is what Spain is in its art: of all times, and also a bit from every country. And, nevertheless, there is nothing more diverse than Her in her homogeneity. Snobbery finds it harder to penetrate in her than anywhere else. It will manage to do it, maybe, the old miserable, behind the train that glides treacherously between the mountains, bringing the often unfortunate benefits of "development" to the solitary kingdom.[113]

By way of this attack on fashion, Laparra reinforces Spain's alleged backwardness, thus helping to shape constructions of the Spaniard as a savage.

Laparra's critique of fashion connects with the "eternal nation" trope, a foremost element in the thought of some of the most influential French political thinkers. Such is the case with Maurice Barrès's formulation of French identity as a "unified spiritual totality," which followed his realization that the French people could not be racially defined and therefore ought be referred to an "aestheticized, collective past," a "spiritual" bonding grounded in a sense of tradition

---

[111] Brass, *Peasants, Populism and Postmodernism*, 12.

[112] Ibid., 2, 38.

[113] "L'Espagne mérite mieux que d'être à la mode chez nous; elle devrait y être à jamais chez elle et y retrouver ses belles qualités, allées aux nôtres. Nous possédons la mesure, mais elle a le rythme. Nous jouissons (ou souffrons) d'un sens critique très développé; l'Espagne est ignorante, mais cette ignorance même devrait être pour nous un conseil. Les gens trop savants, trop conscients de ce qu'est l'originalité sont, par un jeu du sort, précisément ceux qui ont le plus de mal à l'acquérir; en fait, ils n'y parviennent que rarement et en surface. Ces gens savent aussi ce qu'est la mode, et elle est un souci torturant (pour eux comme pour l'auditeur) dans leur manière. 'La mode avant tout. Oh ! surtout, n'être pas en retard; être de son temps!' cependant il y a un idéal qui est plus grand que ça: être de tous les temps. C'est ce que l'Espagne dans son art est, cela: de tous les temps, et aussi un peu de tous les pays. Et pourtant rien de plus homogène qu'Elle dans sa diversité. Le snobisme a plus de mal à y pénétrer qu'ailleurs. Il y parviendra, peut-être, le vieux misérable, derrière le chemin de fer qui se glisse traîtreusement entre les montagnes, apportant au royaume solitaire les biens souvent tristes du progrès." Raoul Laparra, "Espagne," *Le ménestrel* (August 10, 1923).

and, with it, of fixed values that united French people and segregated them from "foreign" groups. It is hardly surprising that, in the wake of the Dreyfus affair, Barrès identified these groups with the Jews.[114] In David Carroll's words, Barrès conceived of French culture

> as a collective subject whose voice manifests itself in philosophy, art, and literature and is echoed in and supported by the voices of model ancestors, and by monuments and memorials, local customs, and the land itself as it speaks to and is symbolically cultivated by its "native sons."[115]

Whereas Barrès's earliest formulations of French identity were grounded on the "cult of the Self" and psychological arguments, at the end of the century he shifted his attention toward the notion and role of "collective tradition." Among his many works covering this issue, this shift is best exemplified in is his discourse "La Terre et les Morts," which he read at the anti-Dreyfusard Ligue de la Patrie Française in 1899. In a manner similar to what Laparra would later do in his writings, Barrès contended that "French conscience" (*conscience française*) or, in other words, the nation's "moral unity" (*unité morale*), did not reside in a set of ideas or arguments but in a "state of sensibility" (*état de sensibilité*). Barrès's main thesis can be gauged from his remark that "we are the prolongation of our ancestors" and that those who died fighting for France—against Germany—constitute "that voice of the ancestors, that lesson of the earth, there is nothing more valuable than it to form the conscience of a people."[116]

By way of this "cult of the dead," Barrès, just like the equally influential political thinker Charles Maurras, grounded national identity in territory, tradition and nativeness, at the expense of immigrants and diasporic groups—most conspicuously the Jews.[117] The impact of Barrès "cult of the dead" on *La jota* is notorious, especially in Laparra's description of Ansó, which opens the synopsis in the published vocal and piano score:

> Inside a hollow in the great Pyrenees, there is a village where time seems to have stopped. The people who live there have preserved the spirit and the gestures of bygone times. A proud love attaches them to the traditions

---

[114] On Barrès, nationalism and tradition see Carroll, *French Literary Fascism*, 19–41.

[115] Ibid., 21.

[116] "Cette voix des ancêtres, cette leçon de la terre, rien ne vaut davantage pour former la conscience d'un peuple. La terre nous donne une discipline, et nous sommes le prolongement de nos ancêtres." Maurice Barrès, *La terre et les morts: Sur quelles réalités fonder la conscience française* (Paris: Ligue de la Patrie Française, 1899), 20.

[117] On Barrès, Maurras and anti-Semitism see Carroll, *French Literary Fascism*, 19–41 and 71–96.

of their valley, and the years and centuries strike in vain over the immutable aspect of the hamlet. The people who have died a long time ago would recognize the same serpentine streets and would feel moved at recognizing the silhouette of women, who always tie the right side of their green petticoat, and who clothe themselves in that grace which, while peasant, renders them somehow as queens and fairies....[118]

Although devoid of Barrès's overt type of racism, Laparra's use of the "eternal nation" trope equally functioned as an essentialist device aimed at fixating and appropriating Spanish identity, by way of depriving the collective nation-building process of every performative act and negotiable element. With this same purpose, Laparra upholds a radical form of cultural isolationism aimed at protecting Spain, the "solitary kingdom," from the agency of modernization. He presents the latter under the form of technological progress, internationalism and foreign interference, symbolized by "the train that glides treacherously between the mountains."[119] Similarly, in another contribution to *Le Ménestrel*, Laparra contended that "the future of the Spanish national [musical] school" depended "on the condition that Spain defend itself rashly and tenaciously from every foreign influence."[120]

Besides Barrès, Laparra's adherence to the "eternal nation" trope may be also read in connection with the so-called Spanish intellectual generations of 1898 and 1914, particularly with Miguel de Unamuno, one of its most conspicuous exponents of the former generation. In "The Eternal Tradition," the opening essay to his influential collection *En torno al casticismo* (1895), Unamuno defined Spanish national identity as *intrahistoria*, which he described as a collective sense of identity based on a fixed idea of tradition.[121] Further anticipating Laparra, Unamuno rejected formulations of identity that emphasized transitoriness. He took issue with aesthetic vogues that prioritized originality and novelty, and that, in his view, undermined the existence and continuance of "eternal traditions." In the second essay of the same collection, "The chaste historical Castile," Unamuno departs from the agrarian myth and connects with Barrès by describing the people as "a

---

[118] "Dans un creux des grandes Pyrénées, il est un village où le temps semble s'être arrêté. Les gens qui l'habitent ont gardé l'esprit et les gestes des époques révolues. Un amour fier les attache aux traditions de leur vallée, et les années, les siècles sonnent en vain sur l'immuable aspect du hameau. Les morts les plus anciens reconnaitraient les mêmes sinueuses rues et s'attendriraient à la silhouette reconnue des femmes, toujours prises dans le bloc droit de leur basquine verte et vêtes de cette grâce qui les fait, en même temps que paysannes, un peu reines et un peu fées [...]." Laparra, *La jota*.

[119] See again Laparra, "Espagne" (August 10, 1923).

[120] " 'Rien de pareil n'aura existé,' ai-je osé dire, l'autre jour, en causant du futur de l'école espagnole basée sur le chant flamenco. Cependant, il y a un 'mais,' un immense 'mais...,' car ce sera à la condition que l'Espagne se défende, et âprement, et tenacement, des influences étrangères." Laparra, "Espagne" (November 14, 1924).

[121] Miguel de Unamuno, *En torno al casticismo* (Madrid: Espasa Calpe, 2001/1905), 33–58.

historical product that is independent from racial homogeneity or original community."¹²² Unamuno's connections with Barrès are more ambiguous in his treatment of "foreign" elements, which he does not reject on the basis of a racist agenda but rather judges on the quality of their relationship with the *intrahistoria*.¹²³

Laparra's connections with other members from the Generation of 1898 manifest themselves in his contention that "there is nothing more diverse than [Spain] in her homogeneity."¹²⁴ This statement recalls the call on the part of the '98s for unity in diversity, with which this group of intellectuals opposed regionalism and conveyed their fears of political disintegration.¹²⁵ However, Laparra's adherence to their agenda was a liberal one, as shown by his first opera, *La habanera*. This work presented Parisians with a Spain seen through the prism of the central region of Castile, which the '98s imbued with markedly centralist connotations.¹²⁶ However, despite its Castilian agenda, *La habanera* equally incorporated flamenco and musical elements from the southern region of Andalusia, which the Generation of '98—and Laparra himself, quite contradictorily—opposed on the grounds that they had nourished European Orientalist portrayals of Spain since the nineteenth century.¹²⁷ It seems as if Laparra drew freely on elements from hegemonic nationalist discourses in France and Spain. This attitude perhaps not only evinces the extent to which formulations of national identity in both countries were the result of an exchange and negotiation between French and Spanish intellectuals;¹²⁸ it also indicates the liminal position that Laparra inhabited, in between "inner" and "outer" visions of Spain, thanks to his advanced knowledge of Spanish culture and his rare willingness to transgress Hispanic stereotypes.

Ansó as a Microcosm of Spain

Some of the core ideas in Laparra's thought found application in *La jota*. Setting this opera in Ansó seems fully justified, even if it was not one of the key scenarios of the Carlist wars. Ansó matched Laparra's conception of Spain as a

---

¹²² People "son un producto histórico independiente de homogeneidad de raza física o de comunidad de origen." Ibid., 63.

¹²³ On the influence of Unamuno's intrahistoria in Spanish musical culture, see Hess, *Manuel de Falla and Modernism*, 14–31.

¹²⁴ See again Laparra, "Espagne" (August 10, 1923).

¹²⁵ Fox, "Castile as Spain," 29–32.

¹²⁶ Ibid. The use of Castile in *La habanera* evinced the influence of Federico Olmeda, who befriended Laparra and provided him with collections of Castilian folklore during his stay between 1900 and 1902. Olmeda prefaced his compilation *Folk-lore de Castilla* (1903) with a manifesto that reads like a Castilian, centralist and essentialist conception of Spain along the lines of the '98.

¹²⁷ Llano, "Hispanic Traditions."

¹²⁸ Storm, "The Rise of the Intellectual," 139–160.

country isolated from civilization, tied to an eternal essence, and impervious to any foreign influence. An interview with Henry Malherbe published in *Le Temps* confirms this impression:

> There is, in Aragon, a small village next to the mountains, which has not been subdued by civilization. People there preserve their natural candor. They show the serenity that is proper to primitive hearts. They ignore our ugliness and refinement. They drink from the same sources of life.[129]

Laparra's description of Ansó's villagers as candid and "primitive" people, who live outside of civilization, matches his idea of the noble savage Spaniard. In another interview, published in *Comoedia*, Laparra referred to Ansó as a "country of an unyielding race," where "women have kept the ancient costumes, the collar, the green seventeenth-century basquina which matches the green prairies so bluntly; their customs, their beliefs, are anchored in their hearts."[130] Thus Laparra cast Ansó as an isolated place, removed from the passage of time and the effects of modernization, such as racial miscegenation. Pictures of Ansó taken by Albert Carré in August 1910 were included in the program notes in order to reinforce this impression of removal, and to surround Laparra's project with a halo of "authenticity." They show the villagers in various attitudes, standing on the street, chatting with each other, or posing while Alfred Bailly, the stage designer, draws a sketch. Four pictures correspond to the caption "Women from Ansó in mourning, going to church," and show a group of women wearing the same two-piece garment that covers them from head to toe except for their faces and therefore imposes uniformity on them, obliterating any sense of variety or transience.[131] As had happened with *La habanera*, the villager's attitude, their use of folkloric costumes instead of everyday clothes and the fact that they pose for Bailly all give the impression of a calculated immediacy, as of a feeling that time had frozen, which Laparra shares was, to some extent, the result of his and Carré's deliberate intervention.

In light of these sources and, considered in the context of Laparra's later writings, discussed above, one might argue that in *La jota* Ansó functions like a microcosm of his idea of Spain. Two further testimonies further confirm this impression, insofar as they describe Ansó in ways that match Laparra's conception

---

[129] "Il est, en Aragon, un petit village adossé aux montagnes, et que la civilisation n'a point soumis. Là, les hommes ont gardé leur naturelle candeur d'âme. Ils ont la sérénité des cœurs primitifs. Ils ignorent nos laideurs et nos raffinements. Ils s'abreuvent aux sources mêmes de la vie." Henry Malherbe, "Les confidences de M. Raoul Laparra," *Le temps*, March 28, 1911.

[130] "Dans ce pays d'une race inflexible, les femmes ont gardé le costume antique, la collerette, la verte basquina du dix-septième siècle qui s'harmonise si crûment avec le vert des prairies; leurs coutumes, leurs croyances sont ancrées dans leurs coeurs." Tenroc, "M. Laparra nous parle de 'La jota.'"

[131] "Femmes d'Anso, en deuil, se rendant à la messe." Laparra, *La jota* [program notes], Ro 3650.

of Spanish identity. In a passage from his memoirs, Carré, the manager and stage director of the Opéra Comique, reminisced on his visit to this village on the occasion of the production of *La jota* in 1911. As if echoing Laparra's rhetoric, Carré depicted Ansó as "well protected against any foreign interference by the appalling state of its roads" and "hidden by a mountain fold."[132] Seemingly in connection with Laparra's trope of "eternal Spain," Carré reported how the villagers' costumes transported him "very far back in time" (*très loin en arrière*). He described men dressed in a seventeenth-century manner, and women wearing "heavy, green robes [and] tiaras covered in black draperies [which] harked back to the kingdom of Ferdinand the Catholic" (*lourdes robes vertes [et] tiares recouvertes de draperies noires [qui] remontaient au règne de Ferdinand le Catholique*).

Further in line with the "eternal nation" trope, Carré describes Ansó as if caught by surprise in its daily activity and removed from any external gaze. According to Carré, the villagers "twirled for an hour" at the request of their visitors and performed "that ardent and languid Aragonese Jota, which they accompanied with wooden spoons instead of castanets."[133] This seemingly improvisatory response was probably rather well prepared in advance, as suggested by the fact that "the village inhabitants, who were hardly used to receiving visits, had, in order to welcome [Carré and his troupe], livened up their façades with the most beautiful things that they found."[134] Carré's recount reveals again an ambivalent attitude on the part of the villagers, which alternates between a spontaneous and everyday lifestyle and a prearranged exhibit. This contradiction advises us not to take everything in Carré's recount for truth, and it suggests the extent to which he could have assumed the influence of Laparra.

Another source that, unlike Carré's testimony, was clearly removed from Laparra's influence further suggests the extent to which Ansó matched the latter's conception of Spain. In his book *Behind the Spanish Barricades*, the English leftist activist and journalist John Langdon-Davies (1897–1971) recollected a visit to Ansó in the course of a trip around Spain in 1932.[135] Like Carré, he begins his recount by describing the hard accessibility, across "a limestone gorge so narrow that it is sometimes built out over the stream and sometimes tunnelled through

---

[132] "La petite bourgade d'Anso […] était bien défendue contre toute ingérence étrangère par le déplorable état de ses routes." Carré, *Souvenirs*, 337.

[133] "Sur notre demande, les naturels du pays, pendant une heure tourbillonnèrent, devant nous, nous initiant à cette ardente et langoureuse Jota aragonaise, dansée avec accompagnement de cuillères en bois en guise de castagnettes." Ibid., 337.

[134] "Les habitants du village, peu habitués aux visites, avaient, pour nous souhaiter la bienvenue, pavoisé leurs façades avec ce qu'ils avaient de plus beau, châles, tapisseries, etc." Ibid., 337.

[135] Langdon-Davies was an English leftist activist born in South Africa, who sojourned in Spain at intervals during the 1920s and 30s, working as a freelance writer and occasional correspondent for the *Daily News*. He covered Primo de Rivera's coup d'état in 1923, the proclamation of the Second Republic in 1931 and the outbreak of the Civil War in 1936. Miquel Berga, *John Langdon-Davies (1897–1971): Una biografía anglo-catalana* (Barcelona: Pòrtic, 1991); Lola Huete Machado, "Padrinos de Hollywood," *El país semanal* (June 18, 2006).

the rock," until it "widens into an unexpected fairyland in the center of which is Ansó." Further in connection with Carré, Langdon-Davies dwells on the anachronistic elements that stand before his eyes. He describes women wearing "Elizabethan ruffs" and men with Roman sandals, all of whom live in "houses that defy description save that they are like the illustrations to some German fairy tale. At the butcher's shop"—he continues—"you buy from a lady who might be Queen Elizabeth." Different from Carré, however, Langdon-Davies provides a sociological and political analysis of Ansó, which presents the priest and the doctor as "the Montague and the Capulet of a modern Spanish village," insofar as they lead the two main competing political factions.[136] Anachronistic as it seems, Langdon-Davies's Ansó is not fully removed from the agency of time and man, and is suffused with a down-to-earth secularism, as suggested by several remarks.[137] Furthermore, Langdon-Davies undermines the potential of Ansó's "backwardness" to become an eternal essence by presenting it as a picturesque, event touristic element.[138] Langdon-Davies recreates an Ansó that is more affected by modernization than Laparra would have liked. However, he concurs with Carré in describing Ansó in a way that matched Laparra's Hispanic agenda, as is most clearly manifest in his contention that "the less the outside world interfered the better it was for everyone."[139] The coincidences between Carré's and Langdon-Davies's descriptions of Ansó in aspects that are among the most important in Laparra's agenda suggest that it constituted a most suitable setting for *La jota*, and that Laparra made his choice carefully.

La jota as a Civil War

The arguments so far presented suggest that in *La jota* Ansó constitutes a microcosm of Laparra's ideologically charged image of Spain, and consequently the locus in which to ground his critique of civilization. This may justify Laparra's making extensive and appalling use of violence and noise, which, with some intuition, the audience could identify as signs of that destructive civilization imagined by him—even if they could not have possibly read Laparra's writings in *Le Ménestrel*. The invading Carlist troops could arguably represent the

---

[136] John Langdon-Davies, *Behind the Spanish Barricades* (London: Martin Secker & Warburg, 1936), 68–70.

[137] Remarks that "religion, even so long ago as 1932, had lost its hold," and that "the leading mind in Ansó is, as so often, the doctor." Furthermore, his leftist allegiances manifest in his contention that "if you have a bad reactionary doctor then the village will be entirely in the hands of a vicious cacique [whereas] if the doctor is strong enough to stand out against the vested interests there is hope for the village." Ibid., 68–70.

[138] He deems Ansó "hardly as advanced in social organization as one of our own villages, but from the point of view of tourists all the better for being a bit backward." Ibid., 70.

[139] Ibid., 70.

modernizing and destructive forces of civilization, while the villagers of Ansó constitute the "real" Spaniards. As the dialogue quoted above shows, Soledad and Mosén Jago staunchly claim to be Spaniards by fiercely opposing Zumárraga's equally passionate anti-Spanish stance. Further in support of this reading, *La jota* offers a far-from-sympathetic view of the Carlists by representing them as devoid of any of the values with which Laparra characterizes and dignifies the Aragonese from Ansó, such as religious faith, respect for authority and sense of community and solidarity. To read *La jota* as an anti-Carlist manifesto would, furthermore, match the representation of a Castilian Spain in Laparra's previous opera, *La habanera*, were it not that he aimed this work more at undermining prevailing Andalusian stereotypes rather than opposing nonstate nationalisms, and that he took a rather secular approach to Castilian themes, which departed from the Generation of 1898.

Despite of all this evidence, the identification of Carlism with Laparra's derogatory conception of civilization in *La jota* needs discussion. To begin with, the Carlists who attack Ansó in *La jota* do not come from the city or bear the clear marks of civilization, but instead "descended, like wolves, from the mountains and turned up at the village" (*descendirent comme des loups la montagne et se présentèrent au village*).[140] Second, such a reading contradicts the somehow sympathetic view of Carlism that exudes from Laparra's aforementioned regionalist allegiances and traditionalist conception of collective identity. Third, and, more important, to depict the Carlists as a civilizing force stands in fundamental contradiction with the ideology of the movement, given that it was precisely their enemies, the liberals, who advocated the "civilized" ideals of Enlightenment. Given their religious fervor, the Carlists would more aptly suit the role of defenders than attackers of the church in Ansó. Conversely, the Aragonese people of Ansó are not suitable representatives of the liberals, given their traditionalist advocacy of Catholic values through their invocation of God and the Pilarica Virgin, as shown in this passage from the second-act battle:

MOSÉN JAGO: Aragonese, what drives you?
LES ARAGONAIS: The Virgin, our captain.
MOSÉN JAGO: Aragonese, who is your best friend?
LES ARAGONAIS: The Lord, who is promised to us.
MOSÉN JAGO: Who is your most wicked enemy?
LES ARAGONAIS: Satan.
MOSÉN JAGO: Who incarnates him in this world?
LES ARAGONAIS: A vile, infamous trinity.

[140] See synopsis in Laparra, *La jota*.

MOSÉN JAGO: Cry their names out to the universe.
LES ARAGONAIS: Don Carlos, cannibal; Cabrera, the vampire; the dreadful Villaréal.
MOSÉN JAGO: Do you know who is the worst of all?
LES ARAGONAIS: Zumalacárregui.[141]

This unsuitable swap of roles seems to contradict the complex dynamics of Carlism.[142] The likelihood that Laparra sought to subvert preestablished perceptions of Carlism and liberalism should not be ruled out.[143] Laparra's reluctance to make overtly political statements does not shed any light on these questions, and it might be taken as a deliberate attempt to depoliticize his opera; he confessed to Tenroc, in the course of an interview, that "the subject of *La jota*, just like *La habanera*'s, is not drawn from history. It is the libretto of Aragonese dance that has suggested the poem to me."[144] In light of these uncertainties, I propose to read beyond the binaries encapsulated in the widespread "myth" of "two Spains" that underpins most historical readings of the Carlist Wars, and that predicates the sole existence of a Catholic, backward and rural Spain on the one hand and a secular, progressive and Enlightened Spain on the other, with no intermediate terms.[145] The intellectual Generation of '98, whose thought, as we have seen, influenced Laparra—through Olmeda—coupled a Catholic

---

[141] "Mosén Jago: Aragonais, qui donc vous mène? / Les Aragonais: La Vierge, notre capitaine. / MJ: Aragonais, quel est votre meilleur ami? / LA: Le Seigneur qui nous est promis. / MJ: Votre ennemi le plus pervers? LA: Satan. / MJ: Qu'il incarne en ce monde? / LA: Une trinité vile, immonde. / MJ: Criez les noms à l'univers. / LA: Don Carlos, cannibal; Cabrera, le vampire; L'affreux Villaréal. / MJ: En savez vous qui soit pire? / LA: Zumalacarregui." Ibid., 177.

[142] Already in *La habanera*, Laparra's first opera, there was an equally fundamental contradiction between his stated will to focus on the region of Castile as a way of getting away from the southern, Andalusian, gypsy Spain of Carmen, and the use of Andalusian folkloric inflections that hold no place in Castilian folklore, and that bring to mind the same kind of stereotypes he wanted to oust. See Llano, "Hispanic Traditions." However, while in *La habanera* this attitude may be explained as a strategy aimed at gaining the support of his audiences by meeting French preconceptions of Spain, which were mostly Andalusian, it seems harder to regard the aforementioned contradiction in *La jota* as the result of Laparra's negotiation with his audiences.

[143] As Brass argues, such an attitude is characteristic of most conservative ideologies reliant on the "agrarian myth" that have sought to look apolitical toward the purpose of more effective results. Brass, *Peasants, Populism and Postmodernism*, 19.

[144] "le sujet de *La Jota*, pas plus que celui de *La Habanera*, n'est tiré de l'histoire. C'est le libretto de la danse aragonaise qui m'a suggéré mon poème." Tenroc, "M. Laparra nous parle de 'La Jota.'"

[145] For an in-depth analysis of the myth of the two Spains see Fernando León Solís, *Negotiating Spain and Catalonia: Competing Narratives of National Identity* (Bristol and Portland, OR: Intellect Books, 2003), 18–23. While insightful, this analysis focuses on the twentieth century, when centralizing discourses mostly fell on the side of the political right, much in contrast to the nineteenth century, when the liberal left defended centralism. Therefore, the categories "liberal regenerationist discourse" and "unitarian conservative discourse" that the author uses to describe the two Spains are inaccurate regarding the context in which Carlism was born and gestated.

essentialism with a defense of territorial unity, just like the Aragonese in *La jota*. Their thinking, therefore, presents connections with liberalism and Carlism, even if they can by no means be related with the latter.[146] One could argue that *La jota* represents Carlism from the condemning perspective of the '98s, were it not that the alleged moral superiority of the Aragonese seems smeared by Mosén Jago's wickedness. Perhaps *La jota* cannot be ascribed to any clear-cut political agenda, and may be read as a condemnation of violence and the social and political cleavage that took Carlists and liberals to confront each other. From this perspective, the aforementioned swap of roles becomes less significant.

Considered in a French context, *La jota* arguably represents a call for consensus amidst the social and political cleavage that engulfed the successive governments and citizens of the Third Republic. France also suffered a civil war, one of an ideological nature, whose most conspicuous symptom was the Dreyfus affair at the turn of the century.[147] Behind the confrontation between Captain Dreyfus's supporters and detractors there lay deeper social antagonisms that opposed republicans and monarchists, pro- and anti-Semites, regionalists and Jacobins, adherents of multiculturalism and xenophobia, the Ancien Régime or the Revolution, the aristocracy or the bourgeoisie, etc.[148] Familiar with Carlism or not, Opéra Comique audiences could have read *La jota* against the backdrop of these ideological struggles, helped by some explicitly political dialogues in this opera. *La jota*, therefore, illustrates Pasler's remark that amidst "irreconcilable ideological differences [in Third Republic France] music and concert life helped people to negotiate the gap between political ideals and political realities," as they helped to "articulate contradictions and suggest ways of accommodating differences."[149]

Beyond its political messages, *La jota* illustrates Laparra's role as a mediator between French and Spanish cultures, trying to find points of contact and mutual understanding. From that position, Laparra helped to undermine prevailing stereotypes about Spain, and to shape the discursive field in which the country was thought and represented. Therefore, *La jota* contributed to reshaping perceptions of Spain, together with more celebrated operas such as *La vie brève*. More than Falla's opera, *La jota* presented an alternative to timeworn gypsy and southern stereotypes that, quite contradictorily, most Spanish composers, including Falla, continued to entertain. In this aspect, *La jota* built on the precedent of Laparra's

---

[146] Indeed, the capacity of the '98s to bridge opposed ideologies can be gathered from their position as a historical transition between nineteenth-century Carlism and the ideology of nacionalcatolicismo (National-Catholicism), which underlay dictator Franco's official discourse on Spanish identity. Britt-Arredondo, *Quixotism*, 173–174.

[147] For a comparison of the Spanish and French case see Storm, "The Rise of the Intellectual."

[148] On the Dreyfus affair and its impact on French musical culture see Fulcher, *French Cultural Politics*.

[149] Pasler, *Composing the Citizen*, 32.

first opera, *La habanera,* as well as other less thorough attempts by Massenet. Seen from this light, *La jota* seems much more than a peripheral contribution to a canon of Spanish music; its cultural significance ought to be assessed from the awareness that those formulations of Spanish that became hegemonic at the time were mainly forged in Paris by Spanish and French composers alike. Despite its modest success, *La jota* shows how "Spanish opera" could mirror and give expression to some of the key dilemmas and struggles that concerned French intellectuals and musicians. Therefore, more than most musical works, *La jota* inhabited—while it helped to enhance—some critical meeting points between French and Spanish culture.

CHAPTER 4

Falla's *La vie brève* (1914) and Notions of "Spanish Music"

Following the death of Albéniz in 1909, French musicians and audiences started to regard Manuel de Falla as the greatest living exponent of the Spanish musical "school." From that position, Falla raised high expectations about the greatest achievement of his stint in Paris (1907–1914): performance of his opera *La vie brève* at the Opéra Comique in 1914. The Opéra Comique's prominence as the second most important opera house in France, Paris's status as a national and international arbiter of taste and, related to it, as a privileged site for negotiating different national identities contributed to investing the première of *La vie brève* with great symbolic significance. This situation led French critics to try to appropriate Falla's success, emphasizing the contribution of Paris and French musicians in bringing about the greatest achievement of a living Spanish composer. They presented Falla as an exile neglected by his motherland, who had discovered his true identity and pursued his ultimate fate in France. Yet *La vie brève* was, to a great extent, a work composed in 1905 and submitted for competition to the Academy of Beaux Arts in Madrid under the title *La vida breve*. Falla would rework the structure and orchestration once in Paris, though to what degree is unknown because of the loss of the 1905 orchestral manuscript.

In this chapter, I analyze constructions of "Spanish music" based on perceptions of *La vie brève* and Falla's time in Paris. Cultural anxieties on the part of French and Spanish critics and musicologists have shaped differing narratives used to describe this opera and to assess the role of Paris and French musicians in bringing about the birth of the idea of a "Spanish musical school." Therefore, *La vie brève* has stayed at the center of debate on the validity and aesthetic independence of a Spanish musical "school." The mystification surrounding the amount and aesthetic import of the changes that Falla introduced in the score while in Paris has contributed to situating this opera at the center of those debates. As we shall see, conceptions of Paris as a cultural center and Spain as on the periphery have dominated those discussions.

La vida breve in Madrid

The one-act opera *La vida breve* was the product of collaboration between the poet and librettist Carlos Fernández-Shaw (1865–1911) and the composer Manuel de Falla (1876–1946). This opera has attracted much attention, thanks not only to Falla's fame but also to the cultural anxieties raised by the singularity of the process that led to its premiere. Falla moved to Madrid in 1897 in search for opportunities denied to him in his native city of Cadix. Shortly after his arrival in the Spanish capital, Falla contacted the poet and librettist Fernández-Shaw, who, having been born in Cadix as well, was known to Falla's family. Fernández-Shaw had extensive experience as a *zarzuela* librettist, having worked with the most renowned composers of the genre, such as Ruperto Chapí and Amadeu Vives.[1] Falla's stage works amounted to a few unsuccessful *zarzuelas*, with which he intended to support himself and his family in Madrid.[2] Their lack of experience in opera did not deter them from entering the competition organized by the Madrid-based "San Fernando" Academy of Beaux Arts in 1904—with the submission deadline March 1905.[3] This opportunity offered itself as the compensation that Falla needed for his failure in the field of *zarzuela*. They had nothing to lose, as the opera was already "very advanced" when the competition was advertised.[4]

La vida breve won first prize in the opera category of the Madrid competition. However, by 1907 they still had not managed to secure a performance, even though the competition's regulations stipulated that "the Academia will try to assure that the prize-winning works will be publicly performed, with the appropriate brilliance, in one of Madrid's theatres."[5] This situation was partly due to the Teatro Real's reluctance to produce operas sung other than in Italian,[6]

---

[1] Le Duc, "De la zarzuela à La vida breve," 47–60; Guillermo Fernández-Shaw, *Un poeta de transición: Vida y obra de Carlos Fernández Shaw* (Madrid: Editorial Gredos, 1986).

[2] On Falla's involvement in zarzuela, see Hess, *Sacred Passions*, 24–33.

[3] For details on the competition see Guillermo Fernández-Shaw, *Larga historia de "La vida breve"* (Madrid: Revista de Occidente, 1972), 22–25. Hess does not consider the possibility that Falla and Fernández-Shaw had begun the opera prior to the competition's advertisement, and therefore depicts Falla "working at white heat." She considers a memo that shows Falla starting the orchestration in February 1905, only one month before the deadline. Hess, *Sacred Passions*, 34.

[4] Fernández-Shaw, *Larga historia*, 22.

[5] Fernández-Shaw, *Larga historia*, 24. Translation by Elizabeth A. Seitz, *Manuel de Falla's Years in Paris, 1907–1914* (Ph.D. diss., Boston University, 1986) 332; quoted in Hess, *Sacred Passions*, 33.

[6] Elizabeth Kertesz and Michael Christoforidis, "Confronting *Carmen* Beyond the Pyrenees: Bizet's Opera in Madrid, 1887–1888," *Cambridge Opera Journal*, 20, no. 1 (2008): 82, describes the Teatro Real's policy. However, a few operas with Spanish language librettos managed to make it to this theater's bill (Hess, *Sacred Passions*, 40). Ironically, these included two other works with librettos by Fernández-Shaw, namely, Ruperto Chapí's *Margarita la tornera* (February 24, 1909) and Amadeu Vives's *Colomba* (1910).

or even possibly to their fears that the "foreign princes and diplomats" attending the would-be première would react negatively to the opera's ethnic agenda (as Pedrell put it in a letter to Falla).[7] Gypsy themes had not prevented the Madrid première of *Carmen* back in 1888, but they did help to channel the critics' opposition to French representations of Spanish culture.[8]

The failure of Falla's Madrid projects, including *La vida breve*, prompted his departure. In the summer of 1907 he left for Paris with plans for a short stay, but remained there until forced to return by the outbreak of the war in 1914. While in Paris, Falla tried hard to secure a public performance for *La vida breve*.[9] According to Carlos Fernández-Shaw's son Guillermo, a few days after arriving in Paris he played the opera on the piano in Paul Dukas's home.[10] Dukas showed interest in *La vida breve* and other works by Falla, gave him some advice and subsequently introduced him to Albéniz, Debussy and other musicians. Through the acquaintanceship of Albéniz, Falla got to know Paul Milliet, the librettist of Massenet's *Hérodiade* (1881) and *Werther* (1887), translator of Boito's *Mefistofele* and Mascagni's *Cavalleria rusticana* into French and, therefore, a suitable translator for *La vida breve*.[11] Milliet managed to obtain an audition for the Opéra Comique's director, Albert Carré, which took place in August 1908 but was followed by delayed negotiations. Meanwhile Falla reworked the score[12] and completed his *Quatre pièces espagnoles* for piano (ca. 1906–1908) as well as his *Trois mélodies* (1909–10) on poems by Théophile Gauthier, for voice and piano.[13] In 1911, Falla approached the Italian impresario Ricordi, who rejected the score on the grounds that it was too musical and not dramatic enough.[14] Finally, Falla and Milliet approached the Théâtre de la Monnaie in Brussels, and in December 1912 the Casino Municipal in Nice, where they finally succeeded in securing a performance.[15] Fernández-Shaw would not live to see the work premièred.

---

[7] "Sólo una novedad tienen que los personajes de su ópera por gitanos fuese inoportunos para ser representados á los príncipes y diplomáticos extrangeros, esto tiene la mar de gracia." Felipe Pedrell, "Letter to Manuel de Falla," July 1, 1906, quoted in Begoña Lolo, "Las relaciones Falla-Pedrell a través de *La vida breve*," in *Manuel de Falla: La vida breve*, ed. Yvan Nommick (Granada: Archivo Manuel de Falla, 1997), 130.

[8] Kertesz and Christoforidis, "Confronting *Carmen*," 82.

[9] "Crea Vd. Que no pierdo mis ilusiones con esa obra [*La vida breve*] y cada vez le tengo más cariño." Manuel de Falla, "Letter to Carlos Fernández-Shaw" (Paris: August 16, 1907). Quoted in Yvan Nommick, "La vida breve entre 1905 y 1914: Evolución formal y orquestal," in *Manuel de Falla*, ed. Nommick (Granada: Archivo Manuel de Falla, 1997), 15.

[10] Fernández-Shaw, *Larga historia*, 36.

[11] Manuel de Falla, "Letter to Felipe Pedrell," February 9, 1908. Quoted in Lolo, "Las relaciones," 132.

[12] Nommick, "*La vida breve*," 35, lists the orchestration treatises that Falla studied while reworking the opera in Paris, following Dukas's advice.

[13] For Falla in Paris, see Hess, *Sacred Passions*, 43–69.

[14] Montserrat Bergadà, "La relación de Falla con Italia: crónica de un diálogo," *Manuel de Falla e Italia*, ed. Yvan Nommick (Granada: Publicaciones del Archivo Manuel de Falla), 23–25.

[15] Fernández-Shaw, *Larga historia*, 39–45.

Verismo and Hispanic Traditions in *La vie brève*

La vie brève premièred at the Théâtre du Casino in Nice on April 1, 1913, presenting Milliet's translation of the Spanish libretto and Jacques Miranne's stage direction. In a telegram, Falla deemed the performance a "complete success" and, according to Guillermo Fernández-Shaw, newspapers from Nice, Monte Carlo and Paris highly praised the work, which brought Falla to the limelight in France.[16] Indeed, following this success Albert Carré agreed to stage it at the Opéra Comique, which took place on January 7, 1914,[17] with stage direction by Carré. The Teatro Real in Madrid followed suit on November 14, 1914, recovering the original Spanish libretto.[18]

The Paris reception of *La vie brève* might be called generally positive, and Falla admitted privately that "with a few exceptions criticism has treated me very well."[19] The most visible element across reviews is the general ascription of the libretto and the music to the realm of *verismo*. However, quite unlike the case of Laparra's *La habanera* just a few years earlier, critics did not associate the purported *verismo* traits in *La vie brève* with any negative Italianate connotations. Léon Vallas, for example, did not think that "vériste" subject matter marred an otherwise "perfect musicality."[20] Cerdannes similarly associated the libretto with *verismo* but thought that "as a whole," this opera was removed from the "Italian school," and he praised Falla as a "composer of race"—which should be read as "Spanish" race.[21] The review in *Excelsior* thought the work "belongs to 'verismo' [but that] it is a Spanish *verismo*, rather than an Italian *verismo*."[22] Alfred Bruneau dismissed the subject matter as "a *fait-divers* that might seem detrimental to the music" but praised Fernández-Shaw's and Falla's treatment of it.[23] Only Pierre

---

[16] Fernández-Shaw, *Larga historia*, 46–48.

[17] December 30, 1913, often given as the date of the Paris performance, corresponds to the dress rehearsal. Hess, *Manuel de Falla and Modernism*, 39.

[18] In my analysis of the notions of "Spanish" music and identity underpinning critical reactions to *La vie brève*, I will consider the Paris performance, for it received wider press coverage on account of the Opéra Comique's higher status, and helped by its former success in Nice. Furthermore, this will help to compare conceptions of Spain as a peripheral culture with Paris constructions of the French provinces.

[19] "Con raras excepciones las prensa se ha portado muy bien conmigo." Letter to Felipe Pedrell, January 13, 1914. Quoted in Lolo, "Las relaciones," 136.

[20] Léon Vallas, *Revue française de musique*, January 10, 1914, quoted in Hess, *Manuel de Falla and Modernism*, 38–39.

[21] Cerdannes, "Casino Municipal de Nice. La vie brève," *Le courrier musical* (April 1913).

[22] "La vie brève appartient au 'vérisme'"; "c'est du vérisme espagnol, au lieu d'être du vérisme italien." R. D. "La vie brève," *Excelsior* (January 1, 1914).

[23] "un fait divers qui peut sembler défavorable à la musique." Alfred Bruneau, "Opéra Comique donne un spectacle coupé, d'intérêt inégal," *Le matin* (December 31, 1913). The term *fait-divers* referred to the rubric in which French newspapers and magazines covered deadly crimes. It was also applied deprecatingly to certain operas sharing in the aesthetics of *verismo* or *naturalisme*. For a discussion of these two terms see Chapter 2. Given

Lalo took issue with "that Italian influence which has pervaded Spanish music for a long time," although this did not spoil his impression that "the score is one of the most delightful things that the Opéra Comique has shown for many years."[24]

There are certainly several elements in *La vie brève* that could lie behind the critics' attribution of this opera to *verismo*. Fernández Shaw's libretto presents a formulaic mixture of passion, jealousy and murder typical of *verismo* operas.[25] Salud, a gypsy from the southern Spanish city of Granada, is in love with Paco, a wooer of a higher class who turns out to be formally engaged with Carmela, a woman of his social class. Once Salud discovers the treachery, she shows up in their wedding, scolds Paco and dies in front of the appalled guests.[26] Other aspects of *La vie brève* are similarly associated with *verismo*, such as the presence of "lower" protagonists characterized by popular speeches, and the short format—two short acts amounting to approximately one hour.[27]

Despite these hardly deniable connections with *verismo*, labeling *La vie brève* with this operatic vogue would require some discussion. With the exception of the use of a tragic ending, the aforementioned features are present in most *zarzuelas,* the genre that Fernández-Shaw had mostly cultivated.[28] One might also object that the setting in the city of Granada, which Falla had never visited, does not correspond to the penchant for rural locales at some remove as was typical of *verismo* literature by Verga and Capuana—although Puccini's *La Bohème* is set in Paris. Yet, the impoverished Albaicín neighborhood where Salud lives with her grandmother (La abuela) and uncle (El tío Sarvaor) is physically and culturally removed from Granada, standing in the steep mountain opposite the contrastingly lavish Alhambra palace, which has inspired so many foreign images of Spain.[29] Many nineteenth-century French and British travelers became fascinated by the Albaicín's intricate, narrow, slanted passages leading to hidden

---

that Bruneau was sensitive to the negatively biased Italianate associations that some critics bore upon his music, it tells of his appreciation for *La vie brève* that he cast them away on this occasion.

[24] "cette influence italienne qui si longtemps domina la musique espagnole"; "La partition est une des choses les plus agréables que l'Opéra Comique nous a fait entendre depuis nombreuses années." Pierre Lalo, "À l'Opéra Comique: Francesca da Rimini. La vie brève," *Le temps* (March 6, 1914).

[25] Including the epitome of this genre, namely, Pietro Mascagni's *Cavalleria rusticana* (1890). For a definition and a brief history of literary and operatic *verismo* see Matteo Sansone, "The Critics' Response to "Cavalleria Rusticana," *Music & Letters*, 71, 2 (1990) 198–201. According to Sansone, the formula of "love, jealousy and revenge" is absent from literary *verismo* and is exclusive to the operatic counterpart.

[26] The libretto was published as Carlos Fernández-Shaw, *La vida breve: Drama lírico en dos actos y cuatro cuadros* (Madrid: Imp. Renacimiento, 1914). The libretto is reproduced in Fernández-Shaw, *Larga historia*, 167–214.

[27] In *La vie brève*, low speeches are represented not so much by way of slang as through the imitation of the gypsy and Andalusian manner of pronouncing some Spanish words. As an example, this includes the name of one of the characters, namely, "El tío Sarvaor," being a deformation of "El tío Salvador" (Uncle Salvador).

[28] Le Duc, "De la zarzuela à *La vida breve*," 47–59.

[29] For a brief history of representations of the Alhambra palace in music, literature and art, see Parakilas, "How Spain Got a Soul," 145–147 and 174–184.

caves where gypsies lived and played flamenco. However, by 1880 the Albaicín caves, and those of the neighboring hill, el Sacromonte, "were regarded as a tourist trap," and foreign visitors were greeted in their own language.[30]

La vie brève departs from previous operatic depictions of Granada, given that it does not display its urban side or the Alhambra palace. In this aspect, this opera arguably encapsulates a critique of urban "civilization" that connects with an early-twentieth-century obsession for peasantry and the recovery of values allegedly lost with modernization.[31] In that sense, *La vie brève* connects with verist and naturalist operas[32] and probably uses the gypsy as an embodiment of the peasant—although some intellectuals and musicians would strongly oppose that identification.[33] The gypsies from the Albaicín live apart from Paco's world of "people in a good position, though not rich."[34] This removal of the gypsy from civilization is consistent with Falla's view of flamenco as pure and untainted by urban commercialization, and directly emanating from nature. Falla organized a flamenco competition in Granada in 1922 with the purpose of restoring allegedly pure and lost forms of flamenco singing.[35]

Falla's focus on "uncivilized" gypsies, however, was partly jeopardized by Alexandre Bailly's settings for the Paris production. Bailly's designs for Salud's home in the second tableaux displayed an Arab arch opening onto a vista of Granada, thus reminding spectators of the Alhambra palace rather than a gypsy cave in el Albaicín.[36] Bailly's work seems representative of the Opéra Comique trend prevalent at that time, in its "eclectic mixture of historical, naturalistic, impressionistic and neo-romantic

---

[30] Charnon-Deutsch, *The Spanish Gypsy*, 127.

[31] "The urban-rural distinction underlies many of the power relations that shape the experiences of the people in nearly every culture." Barbara Ching and Gerald W. Creed, "Recognizing Rusticity: Identity and the Power of Place," in *Knowing Your Place: Rural Identity and Cultural Hierarchy*, ed. Ching and Creed (New York and London: Routledge, 1997) 2.

[32] On the use of urban-rural dichotomies in the work of French regionalist composers of the naturalist circle, see Musk, "Regionalism, Latinité" and "Aspects of Regionalism."

[33] See, for instance, the case of Bartók, who consistently argued that gypsies had corrupted Hungarian music, whereas peasants had helped to preserve it in a state of purity. Brown, "Bartók, the Gypsies, and Hybridity in Music," 119–142.

[34] See the annotations that open the second tableaux, act II, *La vie brève*.

[35] On the competition and its rationale see Mitchell, *Flamenco Deep Song*, 160–175. Falla's conception of flamenco has had multiple critics besides Mitchell: William Washabaugh, *Flamenco: Passion, Politics and Popular Culture* (Oxford and Washington, DC: Berg, 1996) 31; Peter Manuel, "Andalusian, Gypsy and Class Identity in the Contemporary Flamenco Complex," *Ethnomusicology* 33, 1 (1989): 56; Gerhard Steingress, *Sociología del cante flamenco* (Sevilla: 1991), 365–381.

[36] The original picture is held at the Bibliothèque Nationale de France (Paris) Départment de la musique. A reproduction appears in José Miguel Castillo, "Consideraciones sobre las primeras escenografías de 'La vida breve,'" *Manuel de Falla: La vida breve*, ed. Yvan Nommick (Granada: Archivo Manuel de Falla, 1997), 214; also see Castillo's description on p. 181. Torres Clemente remarks that Falla first traveled to Granada in 1915, when the opera had already premiered in Monte-Carlo and Paris. Elena Torres Clemente, *Las óperas de Manuel de Falla. De* La vida breve *a* El retablo de Maese Pedro (Madrid: Sociedad Española de Musicología, 2007).

elements" that shows "the little unifying principle behind *verismo* stage designs" in Paris.[37] Associating the score with *verismo* has also been the object of scholarly discussion. In her monograph on Falla, Suzanne Demarquez avoids applying a single stylistic label, but identifies connections with *verismo* in several passages. They include the music to the ringing of bells in scene 1—which she compares with the similar passage in Charpentier's *Louise*—the duo between Salud and the Grandmother and the Grandmother's announcement of Paco's long-awaited arrival.[38] In addition, Demarquez identifies Wagnerian elements in the smith's song in scene 3, which she compares with the forge scene in *Siegfried*.[39] Hess emphasizes the influence of Wagner's music, which Falla studied extensively during his formative years.[40] Similarly, Torres identifies Wagnerism as the main influence, manifest in Falla's preference for continuity instead of separate numbers, the use of *leitmotifs* and the extensive chromaticism.[41] By contrast, Christoforidis argues that Debussy represented the main influence behind *La vie brève*, as it was presented in Nice and Paris, and that the French composer's orientations were "aimed at creating a more continuous musical texture" and raising "Falla's new awareness of the orchestra."[42]

Another possible source of inspiration behind *La vie brève* was the *zarzuela La Tempranica*, with music by Gerónimo Giménez and a libretto by Julián Romea.[43] This work premièred in Madrid in 1900, when Falla was still trying his luck at *zarzuela* in that city. Like *La vie brève*, *La Tempranica* is set in the gypsy margins of Granada, though in the countryside, and it characterizes the gypsies by way of extensive use of dialect. As Parejo Delgado has argued, there are striking similarities between both works, starting with the plot.[44] In *La Tempranica*, the wealthy Luis suffers an accident while hunting near a gypsy camp, and is rescued

---

Furthermore, Torres Clemente points to the different possible sources that Falla used to acquaint himself with images of Granada for the opera (p. 233).

[37] Manfred Boetzkes and Evan Baker, "Stage Design. 5. The 19th Century," *Grove Music Online*, ed. Stanley Sadie, http://www.oxfordmusiconline.com/subscriber/article/grove/music/O904784 (accessed April 15, 2011).

[38] Suzanne Demarquez, *Manuel de Falla* (Paris: Flammarion, 1963), 57–59.

[39] Ibid., 58.

[40] The Wagnerian elements that Hess identifies are: chromatic harmony (in the forge scene, among other passages), speech-based melody, "aversion to symmetrical phrase structure," continuous music, equal footing of voice and orchestra and leitmotivic strategy. Hess, *Sacred Passions*, 35–37. By contrast, the only traces of *verismo* that Hess identifies are the unisons on page 26 of the score. Ibid., 38.

[41] Torres Clemente, *Las óperas*, 470–472.

[42] Michael Christoforidis, "Manuel de Falla, Debussy, and La vida breve," *Musicology Australia*, 18 (1995), 4, 8.

[43] Interestingly, Iberni has situated *La tempranica* under the impact of verismo in late nineteenth-century Spanish zarzuela, on account of the use of dialect and local customs. Luis Iberni, "Tempranica, La," *Diccionario de la zarzuela. España e Hispanoamérica*, ed. Emilio Casares, vol. 2 (Madrid: Instituto Complutense de Ciencias Musicales, 2006), 798. We may add the choice of the countryside, quite unusual in *zarzuelas*, mostly set in the popular quarters of Madrid, such as Lavapiés.

[44] For a list of these connections see José Parejo Delgado, *Gerónimo Giménez: Un precursor de Manuel de Falla* (Sevilla: Padilla Libros, 1997), 97–98.

and cured by María, a gypsy nicknamed La Tempranica. They fall in love, but Luis leaves her in order to marry a woman of his own social position. When María learns about the marriage, she rushes to his home to claim him, but—unlike Salud in *La vie brève*—she feels unfit for Luis after realizing how much darker her skin is than the bride's. She returns to the gypsy camp and marries Miguel, a gypsy whom she describes as her equal.

La vie brève and *La Tempranica* saw light in the long aftermath of the *desastre*, that is, the 1898 war against the United States in which Spain lost the last colonies of its former empire. The *desastre* arguably marked, in many ways, a substantial portion of the Spanish intellectual production up to the Civil War of 1936, eliciting an intellectual response that, according to Britt-Arredondo, took the form of an "imaginative denial of Spain's loss of empire."[45] Lucy D. Harney reads the racial conflict *La Tempranica* in connection with this "imaginative denial," as she contends that this *zarzuela* "would resonate with Spain's post-war theatre-going audience, a class at once disillusioned, bewildered and demoralized by their country's international collapse, yet desperate to maintain those prerogatives presumably afforded by a glorious imperial heritage."[46] One could object that the sentiment of crisis was mostly restricted to an intellectual elite at the time. Harney's reading of *La Tempranica*, however, provides a compelling point of departure for discussing the presence of postcolonialist undertones in *La vie brève*, building on their similarities. Although, in the context of this opera's Paris première, Spain's relations to its former colonies mattered little, France's relations with its colonial empire of the time were relevant, as the example of *Carmen* had demonstrated three decades before. *Carmen*, *La vie brève* and *La Tempranica* explored the conflict between a superior white male and a subaltern female gypsy, as well as the derived race, class and gender problematics. *La vie brève* could arguably be contemplated similarly as to James Parakilas's reading of *Carmen*, as a statement "that racial difference could make individuals incompatible even though they were in love with each other."[47] From this perspective, *La vie brève* offers itself as a suitable basis for discussing the appropriateness or potential of regarding France and Spain as metropolis and colony respectively, which Susan McClary has proposed in her reading of *Carmen*.[48] There is evidence that Falla felt strongly attracted to Bizet's opera. While in Paris, he attempted to

---

[45] The literature on the subject is wide. Its impact on intellectual life is best studied in Britt-Arredondo, *Quixotism*.
[46] Lucy D. Harney, "Zarzuela and the Pastoral," *Modern Language Notes (MLN)*, 123 (2008): 257.
[47] Parakilas, "The Soldier and the Exotic, 34.
[48] McClary, *Georges Bizet: Carmen*, 62–110. We will see in due course that this type of approach, despite its limitations, helps to uncover the cultural strategies and patterns of behavior that have given birth and helped to develop a peripheral conscience in Falla and other Spanish composers. However, as we shall see, Falla's conception of the role that French music and culture ought to play in the construction of a Spanish musical identity was far more complex and contradictory than the "incompatibility" argument would suggest.

compose a one-act sequel named *La muerte de Carmen* (The Death of Carmen) based on his own libretto, but Bizet's widow was opposed to the project.[49] The Paris première of *La vie brève* could therefore furnish audiences and critics with an opportunity to assess the state of France's relations with its others. Indeed, this type of approach manifested itself through the critics' concern with defining "French music" and measuring its distance to "Spanish music."

Questions of Nationality

Critical reactions to *La vie brève* fell in the context of French debates on national identity.[50] With their ambivalent and mixed reactions to Italian *verismo*, French critics could undermine a work by pointing out connections with that aesthetic realm.[51] Unlike the case of Laparra's *La habanera* several years before, however, critical reactions to *verismo* elements in *La vie brève* were either positive or neutral. This difference in treatment most likely evinces the importance that critics attached to a given composer's national background as a criterion for their judgment. Unlike Laparra, Falla did not have to be examined as a "French" composer. Furthermore, verist elements in Falla's opera were not necessarily perceived as "foreign" or Italianate, but could be regarded as the fruit of a cultural exchange between two southern, "Latin" neighbors. These questions permitted critics to focus on other elements that did not make *La vie brève* seem the product of a competing operatic culture such as *verismo*. Thus, in his review for *Comœdia* Linor identified with some aspects of *La vie brève* and, to some extent, tried to appropriate this work:

> The score is extremely melodic—I intend here melody in its highest and noblest form—wonderfully organized, and symphonically developed with an undeniable and very personal ability. With its picturesque rhythms, it displays all the dazzling Spanish sunlight, ornamented with the rich sonorities of modern polyphony.[52]

---

[49] Hess, *Sacred Passions*, 51.

[50] On the debates on "French" musical identity prior to the First World War, see Barbara L. Kelly, "Debussy and the Making of a *musicien français*: *Pelléas*, the Press and World War I," *French Music, Culture and National Identity, 1870–1939*, ed. Barbara L. Kelly (Rochester, NY: University of Rochester Press, 2008) 58–76; James Ross, "*Messidor*: Republican Patriotism and the French Revolutionary Tradition in Third Republic Opera," *French Music*, ed., Kelly, 112–130; Fulcher, *French Cultural Politics*.

[51] Branger, "Les compositeurs français," 315–342.

[52] G. Linor, "M. Manuel de Falla et 'La vie brève,' M. Franco Leoni et 'Francesa da Rimini,'" *Comœdia* (December 31, 1913). "La partition est extrêmement mélodique—j'entends ici mélodie sous sa forme la plus haute et la plus noble—merveilleusement ordonnancée, développée symphoniquement avec une indéniable et très personnelle habileté. Avec ses rythmes pittoresques, elle possède toute l'éblouissante lumière du soleil d'Espagne, tout en étant parée des riches sonorités de la polyphonie moderne."

Linor seems to take for granted the match between the composer's background and the national outlook of his music. Following many other reviews of "Spanish music," Linor used metaphors such as "sunlight" or "picturesque rhythm." His emphasis on melody and order, however, reminds one of the rhetoric of French musical nationalism, which crystallized into the aesthetics of neoclassicism after the War[53] but which, as we have seen, was already gaining currency at the beginning of the twentieth century. Linor's reference to the "sonorities of modern polyphony" helps to mitigate Spanish difference under the appearance of a cultural modernism or universalism. From his appreciation that *La vie brève* successfully combines national elements with universal modernism, Linor feels compelled to regard "Spanish music" as a national school, thus departing from "exotic" views. He even seems to contemplate "Spanish music" as a cultural ally, if we consider the anti-German connotations of his neoclassical rhetoric. This attitude can be observed in his description of "Spanish music" as a fully accomplished musical renaissance standing on top of a longstanding, glorious national tradition:

> It is impossible to deny the musical renaissance that has taken place in Spain for the past quarter of a century. Our Iberian neighbors have managed to reconstruct a Spanish school which harks centuries back to the time of [Tomás Luis de] Victoria.[54]

Linor applies to "Spanish music" the concerns of nineteenth- and twentieth-century French musicians and critics over the need to ground "French music" in the idea of a national tradition, one that should represent a common inheritance and thus help to stimulate a sense of national cohesion.[55] The nineteenth-century recovery of Rameau and the centrality that he and Couperin gained in aesthetic debates at the turn of the twentieth century should be regarded in that sense.[56] As we have seen, a similar phenomenon took place in Spain, focused on composers of the "Golden Age" of Spanish Music, above all Tomás Luis de Victoria (whom Linor mentions), Cristóbal de Morales and Francisco Guerrero. Felipe Pedrell's edition of Victoria's *opera omnia*, published by Breitkopf und Härtel

---

[53] Jane F. Fulcher, "The Composer as Intellectual: Ideological Inscriptions in French Interwar Neoclassicism," *Journal of Musicology*, 17, 2 (1999), 197–230.

[54] "On ne peut nier aujourd'hui la renaissance musicale qui s'est produite en Espagne depuis un quart de siècle. Nos voisins ibériens sont arrivées à reconstituer une école espagnole qui, de toutes les façons se rattache au passé, à travers les siècles, jusqu'à Vittoria [Tomás Luis de Victoria] lui-même." Linor, "M. Manuel de Falla."

[55] Ellis, *Interpreting the Musical Past*; Fulcher, *French Cultural Politics*.

[56] Suschitzky, "Debussy's Rameau," 398–448, on Ravel and Couperin see Barbara L. Kelly, "History and Hommage," *The Cambridge Companion to Ravel*, ed. Deborah Mawer (Cambridge: Cambridge University Press, 2000), 19–22. Also see Kelly, "Debussy and the Making," 67–68; Ellis, *Interpreting the Musical Past*, 76–78, 140–141.

(1902–1913), followed by Higini Anglès's edition of Morales's complete works, completed in 1954,⁵⁷ heralded the revival of these two composers. As in France, this scholarly and ideological investment in the "national" past developed in conjunction with the composers' study and assimilation of "Golden Age" music. Several works of the 1920s, such as Falla's *El retablo de Maese Pedro* (1923) and his *Harpsichord Concerto* (1926), and Ernesto Halffter's *Sinfonietta* (1925), are representative of this mind-set.⁵⁸

In sum, Linor subtly couched *La vie brève* in the rhetoric of French musical nationalism and described "Spanish music" in a way that was congenial for Falla and Spanish nationalists such as Pedrell. Although Linor acknowledges the presence of signs of cultural difference—embodied in the "dazzling Spanish sunlight"—he sees Spanish music through the prism of the concerns shared by French nationalists. Linor was not the only critic to regard *La vie brève* that way. In his review, Émile Vuillermoz equally couched Falla's opera in the neoclassic aesthetics of sobriety, by identifying "a simplicity of means that borders on dryness—which is, in the end, very Spanish."⁵⁹ Like Linor, Vuillermoz helped to domesticate "Spanish difference." However, the modernism that Linor celebrated as proof of the renaissance of "Spanish music" could be perceived by other critics as a lack of "authenticity." The anonymous review published in *Le Journal* argued that

> being the work of a Spaniard tackling a Spanish subject I expected something more... well, more Spanish! I cannot see what Falla contributes that is new or particularly savory to what I would call the musical iconography of Spain; what he suggested yesterday evening, we had already been presented with thanks to Chabrier, or Lalo, or Rimsky, or Debussy, or Ravel, or Laparra, and above all the late Albéniz.⁶⁰

This critic lays bare, rather bluntly, the problematic inherent to seeking the positive sanction of Parisian audiences and critics in an atmosphere in which nationality was the primary criterion for aesthetic judgment. Falla was exposed to being accepted

---

⁵⁷ And published as part of the nationalist-oriented series *Monuments of Spanish Music*, under the auspices of the state-sponsored Spanish Council for Scientific Research (CSIC). On nationalistic uses of Spain's musical history see Carreras, "Hijos de Pedrell," 121–169. Also see Ros-Fábregas, "Musicological Nationalism," 6–15.

⁵⁸ On Falla and neoclassicism, see Hess, *Manuel de Falla and Modernism*, 199–261.

⁵⁹ "une simplicité de moyens qui va presque jusqu'à la sécheresse—ce qui est au fond, très espagnol." Émile Vuillermoz, "Théâtre des Arts—Opéra Comique," *Revue musicale S.I.M.* (December 1913).

⁶⁰ Anon. "La vie brève," *Le journal* (January 3, 1914). "Mais j'attendais d'un Espagnol traitant un sujet espagnol quelque chose de plus... enfin, de plus espagnol! Je ne vois pas ce que M. de Falla apporte de nouveau ou de particulièrement savoureux à ce que j'appellerai l'iconographie musicale de l'Espagne; ce qu'il nous a suggéré hier, nous l'avions déjà perçu grâce à Chabrier, ou à Lalo, ou à Rimsky, ou à Debussy, ou à M. Ravel, ou à M. Laparra, et surtout au regretté Albéniz."

or rejected for either meeting the standards of "Spanish music" set by Chabrier, Lalo, Rimsky-Korsakov, Debussy and Ravel or challenging them, depending on whether critics were expecting something similar to or different from what they already knew. Had Falla wanted to emulate his French or European counterparts, therefore, he would have had no guarantees of earning critical acclaim. As I shall argue now, these complex and interlocked binaries have been overlooked in discussions that have tried to assess whether Falla's music is an emulation of French composers, instead of describing the contradictions and peculiarities that plagued the negotiation of "Spanish music" in early-twentieth-century Paris.

La vie brève and Questions of Authenticity in Spanish Music

The symbolic significance underlying the Paris première of *La vie brève* at the Opéra Comique—as far as perceptions of "Spanish music" are concerned— has imparted to discussions about the nature and extent of its differences with *La vida breve* (1905) a certain feeling of anxiety. To some extent, this feeling is understandable, since these discussions ultimately bring into question the existence and validity of a "Spanish musical school."[61] Once in Paris, Falla introduced alterations to the 1905 score that some critics and scholars regarded as equivocal signs of artistic maturity or submission to the taste of French audiences.[62] The latter suspicion has led a strand of criticism to declare Falla's output of his Paris sojourn (1907–1914), and particularly *La vie brève*, a "Frenchified" or "exotic" rendition of Spain.[63] Implied in this view is the argument that Falla's international success rests upon his readiness to anticipate and meet French or European preconceptions about "Spanish music," thus "betraying" his "true" identity. The implications of the most prominent Spanish composer of the early twentieth century being influenced by the "Spanish" music of French composers such as Debussy and Ravel, and catering to "foreign" audiences, has raised concerns as to the "true" sources—or even the validity—of Spanish musical nationalism. Furthermore, the presence in Paris of some of the most acclaimed composers of Spanish music history, namely Albéniz, Turina and Granados, has made it seem as if Paris played a key role in giving shape to "Spanish music"

---

[61] For details on these differences see Nommick, "*La vida breve*."

[62] According to Christoforidis, "Since the 1905 version of *La vida breve* was basically a number opera in the tradition of the nineteenth-century zarzuela, many of the later modifications, including those suggested by Debussy, were aimed at creating a more continuous musical texture." Christoforidis, "Manuel de Falla, Debussy," 4. It is likely that Falla found the continuous texture more fashionable than the zarzuela-oriented number structure.

[63] Hess, *Manuel de Falla and Modernism*, 58–59, 179–180.

in the early twentieth century. In this section, I will discuss the strengths and weaknesses of some of the arguments supporting the view that Falla's music is a plain product of French exoticism.

The consideration of Falla's music as "exotic" has a staunch advocate in James Parakilas, who, in his article "How Spain Got a Soul," has situated this composer at the end of a European—mostly French and Russian—tradition of "exoticizing" Spain.[64] The contentious character of his arguments means he deserves to be quoted at length:

> Because of his persistent engagement with a foreign view of his own culture, his astoundingly methodical lifelong study of exotic musical Spains, and his equally methodical transformations of the exoticizing ideas he studied, Falla makes an exemplary case of auto-exoticism—as a political plight, as a psychological condition, as an artistic dilemma. We can ask, for instance, why, if it was French culture that expressed the strongest need to exoticize Spain—the strongest need to define Spain by its difference—why Falla should have felt so drawn to France. Did not he feel condescension from the French in their exoticization of Spain, resentment that his country was made the object of their musical ogling? In his published writings, at least, there is no trace of that. The simplest explanation may be that he accepted the premise of French difference from Spain, though on his own terms. It may have suited his own needs to believe in one Catholic, Latin country that, unlike his own, could be as modern as, and artistically and intellectually more advanced than, any of its Protestant, Germanic competitors. Holding that belief about France would have left him room to celebrate the difference of Spain—the beauty and value of its unmodern cultural traditions—in his own music, even as he produced that music by following the most advanced French concepts of exoticism.[65]

Following from Parakilas, it would seem that Falla had no alternatives but to either reject representations of Spain found in the music of French composers—even to feel "condescension" and "resentment" toward them—or to fully embrace and emulate them. Parakilas's radical dualism is indebted to primeval postcolonialist formulations, and particularly to Edward Said's seminal essay *Orientalism*.[66] Like Said, Parakilas conceives of representation as a form of domination, and he casts the represented "Other" as a passive object of cultural imperialism. This stance,

---

[64] Parakilas, "How Spain Got a Soul," 137–193.
[65] Ibid., 189.
[66] Edward W. Said, *Orientalism: Western Conceptions of the Orient* (New York: Vintage Books, 1978).

whose radicalism has earned Said wide criticism,[67] leaves the purportedly "colonized subject" (Falla and Spain, in this case) no margin to engage critically and selectively with the elements that make up "foreign" representations of his culture, or simply to negotiate or tear down the barriers between what constitutes the "foreign" and the "indigenous." Furthermore, this argument sets the basis for deterministic explanations of the relationship among power, identity and marginalization. Thus, in the opening statements of his article, Parakilas argues that Spain "got a soul"—by which he means that it acquired a recognizable, differential and "exotic" identity—throughout the centuries-long dismantling of its sixteenth-century colonial empire, which ended in the 1898 war against the United States, in which Spain lost its last colonies, Cuba among them. According to Parakilas, this erosion of power led to exoticizing of Spain, following from Said's reflections on power, identity and representation.[68] Yet a definition of "exoticism" is conspicuously absent from Parakilas's article. He seems to imply that "exoticism" consists of lack of "authenticity" in representations of (other) cultures. He argues that Falla's "Spanish music" is mostly based on intertextual imitation rather than on first-hand experience of Spain, and on that basis he interprets Falla's works as examples of musical Orientalism.[69] Yet, to deem Falla's knowledge of Spain irrelevant to his musical style seems hard to prove. At this juncture, we need to understand "exoticism" and "authenticity" as historically and culturally contingent categories.

"Authenticity" is a highly problematic concept. Attempts to endow it with content and meaning have been largely disputed by the different and sometimes conflictive parts involved in the act of representation and perception.[70] Because of its contingency, "authenticity" is malleable under the pressure of differing ideologies. A distinction between "authentic" and "inauthentic" cultural expressions leads to the formation of canons and therefore serves as a strategy of marginalization and exclusion. Furthermore, the distinction overlooks the agency

---

[67] Homi K. Bhabha, *The Location of Culture* (New York: Routledge, 1994); Partha Chaterjee, *Nationalist Thought and the Colonial World: A Derivative Discourse?* (London: Zed Books for the United Nations University, 1986); Néstor García Canclini, *Hybrid Cultures: Strategies for Entering and Leaving Modernity* (Minneapolis: University of Minnesota Press, 1995). Robert Young, *Colonial Desire: Hybridity in Theory, Culture and Race* (New York: Routledge, 1995). On hybridity, music and revisions of Said, see Georgina Born and David Hesmondhalgh, "Introduction: On Difference, Representation and Appropriation in Music," in *Western Music and Its Others: Difference, Representation and Appropriation in Music*, ed. Born and Hesmondhalgh (Berkeley and Los Angeles: University of California Press, 2000), 1–58.

[68] Said, *Orientalism*, 2–3.

[69] Locke, *Musical Exoticism*, 9; Scott, "Orientalism and Musical Style," 309–335.

[70] Richard Taruskin, *Text and Act: Essays on Music and Performance* (Oxford and New York: Oxford University Press, 1995). John O'Flynn, "National Identity and Music in Transition: Issues of Authenticity in a Global Setting," in *Music, National Identity and the Politics of Location*, ed. Ian Biddle and Vanessa Knights (Aldershot: Ashgate, 2007), 19–38.

of transcultural processes in the formation of identities. Attempts to define "Spanish music" offer no exception to these shortfalls. During the nineteenth century, the "Spanish music" of Spanish and European composers was mostly based on stereotypes from the Southern region of Andalusia. This characteristic also applies to Falla's early works, including *La vie brève*. However, it would not be any less "exotic" or more "authentic" to avoid Andalusian stereotypes at the risk of wiping that region off the musical map of Spain. Raoul Laparra deliberately tried to offer a more "authentic" rendition of Spain in his opera *La habanera* (Opéra Comique, 1908) by situating the action in Castile, a region he characterized by a "colder temperament" than Andalusia. However, critical reactions showed that, unlike the critic of *Le Journal* who reviewed *La vie brève*, audiences of *La habanera* did not consider "authenticity" to be a primordial criterion of aesthetic enjoyment—probably with good reason.[71] A decade later, Falla started to compose works similarly focused on Castile with the purpose of leaving Andalusian stereotypes behind. They include *El retablo de Maese Pedro* (1919–1923) and the *Harpsichord Concerto* (1923–1926). Although some critics of his time would agree that these works were more authentic than *La vie brève* or *El amor brujo*, on what basis could we, with hindsight, regard them as "authentic" expressions of Spanish music?

All we can do is describe attitudes rather than define results. As Derek Scott has observed, the rule among European composers since the seventeenth century has been to disregard "accurateness" in musical representations of other cultures, often using very similar or even equivalent—therefore interchangeable—musical signifiers to represent different, even mutually distant cultures.[72] For example, in a visit to Morocco in 1935 Ravel claimed that, at the sight of the French Embassy's gardens, "if [he] wrote something Arabian, it would be much more Arabian than all this."[73] Thus Ravel equated identities to the products of his powerful musical imagination.[74] His attitude can therefore be characterized by a lack of concern for "authenticity." To a "Spanish" listener unaware of a given work's authorship, Debussy's *Ibéria* or Ravel's *Rhapsodie* may eventually sound more authentically Spanish than Falla's works, especially *El retablo* and the *Harpsichord Concerto*, where modernisms often elicit a sense of cultural estrangement among Spaniards.

In sum, Parakilas's contention that Falla's music is "exotic" or "inauthentic" seems hard to support in the absence of any authentic Spanish music with which

---

[71] Llano, "Hispanic Traditions."

[72] Scott, "Orientalism."

[73] Cited in Robert Orledge, "Evocations of Exoticism," *The Cambridge Companion to Ravel*, ed. Deborah Mawer (Cambridge: Cambridge University Press, 2000) 33.

[74] Samuel Llano, "España en la vitrina: Maurice Ravel, el mito de la autenticidad y el neoimperialismo español," *Journal of Spanish Cultural Studies*, 11, 1 (2010): 1–15.

to compare it. Furthermore, by calling Falla's music "exotic" he helps to reify the very "difference" that, as he correctly argues, articulated a European politics of marginalization. Parakilas's daring thesis, however, represents a significant step toward understanding that the ontological distinction among the "Spanish music" of Debussy, Ravel and a "native" Spaniard like Falla is equally contingent, and may at times become futile. Despite my objections, therefore, Parakilas's reading of Falla's years in Paris helps to undermine the spurious distinction implied in the use of categories such as "Hispanic music" or "Spanish music" to distinguish between Debussy's *Iberia*—to take one example—and Falla's *Noches en los jardines de España*. These categories are ultimately predicated upon a fixating, and hence coercive, notion of authenticity.

A "Spaniard" in Paris

Falla only "discovered" his identity as a "Spanish musician" once he was exposed to certain aesthetic and social experiences in Paris. Not that his previous music was less "authentic" or less "Spanish," but in Paris he discovered the advantages of selling his background as cultural "difference"—as Parakilas implies. A close look at Falla's musical interests before he left Madrid for Paris in 1907 shows that Spanish music and composers held little room among them.[75] His engagement with *zarzuela* has been explained as the result of his need to maintain his jobless family by trying his luck at the most profitable music genre in those days—although he turned out to fare rather badly in this matter.[76] *La vida breve* (1905) could arguably be regarded as his first major "Spanish" work, one in which audiences would find a recognizable place in the Spanish territory, that is, Granada, and a conspicuous presence of musical styles commonly associated with Spain. Turina argued that he and Falla first gained conscience of the "need" to compose "Spanish music" during a meeting with Albéniz in a café in Paris.[77] Though not neglecting the influence of Albéniz, Falla would contradict Turina in this respect by crediting Felipe Pedrell with having instigated his nationalist feelings.[78] But Pedrell's alleged wisdom did not fully bear fruit until Falla went to Paris, or at least not in a way that was profitable for the latter.

---

[75] Nommick quotes from Falla's *Apuntes de harmonía* (1902), which reveals that the composers he studied and listened to between 1900 and 1902 were Mozart, Mendelssohn and Beethoven. Nommick, "La vida breve," 28–31.

[76] Hess, *Sacred Passions*, 24–33.

[77] Mariano Pérez Gutiérrez, *Falla y Turina a través de su epistolario* (Madrid: Alpuerto, 1982), 28–32.

[78] Pedrell did not supervise the composition of *La vie brève*, but Falla kept him posted about his progress regarding the performance of this work and sent a copy of the score after the Nice premiere (Lolo, "Las relaciones," 128). Pedrell exerted an important influence on Falla's decisions, having recommended him to leave

It may be objected that certain formulations of "Spanish music" did not contemplate the use of folklore, and instead assimilated the influence of the same Austro-German composers that Falla admired in his youth.[79] Falla's awakening to the appeal of his cultural difference exerted a notorious impact in the outlook of his music, but this does not mean his works were intrinsically more "Spanish" after 1907; to believe that it was would equally entail proclaiming that his latest and probably most prestigious works, namely, *El retablo* and the *Concerto,* are not "Spanish music." Falla's musical compositions registered the change that took place in his conscience during his work in Paris, but not in the only possible way. That Falla took certain advantage of the surrounding eagerness to consume his perceived cultural "difference" does not entail that he could not assume an active and critical role in negotiating certain elements of his varying postulation of "Spanish music" with his French audiences and critics. He equally tried to negotiate with his audiences in Spain and arguably failed, but just because in his home country that negotiation was not mediated by perceptions of cultural difference does not mean that his pre-Paris works were more authentic. To argue that Falla went to Paris in search of ways of "celebrating the difference of Spain"—to quote Parakilas—overlooks that one of the main reasons he left his homeland in 1907 lies in his profound dissatisfaction with the little official and private support and musical infrastructure that was available in Spain. Like most émigré musicians and artists from other countries, Falla sought in Paris opportunities that were denied to him in Spain. Spanish musicians frequently voiced their complaints about the lack of official support and public or private initiatives—i.e., orchestras, ensembles and associations—in the pages of Spanish music journals and daily newspapers.[80] They often accompanied their protests with self-deprecating comparisons with the situation in other European countries, most notably France, Germany and Austria.

Falla hardly ever publicly declared his otherwise unremitting distaste for certain strands of the musical life in Spain, and especially the *zarzuela* business in

---

Spain in 1906, after failure to find a performance for the opera (Lolo, "Las relaciones," 130). Writing for a Catalan newspaper, Pedrell credited himself with having "advised" Falla to go to Paris: Pedrell, "La vida breve," *La vanguardia* (May 29, 1913), quoted in Lolo, "Las relaciones," 136. According to Collet, "sense'l mestre gloriós de la Trilogía, no hi ha dubte que *La vida breve* no hauría nascut." Henri Collet, "La vida breve," *Butlletí de l'Orfeó Català* 9, 125 (1914), quoted in Lolo, "Las relaciones," 137.

[79] One such example is Rogelio del Villar, whose repertoire included a strand of German romanticism, next to works using Spanish folklore. Enrique Franco, "Rogelio del Villar," *Diccionario de la música española e hispanoamericana*, ed. Emilio Casares Rodicio, vol. 10 (Madrid: Instituto Complutense de Ciencias Musicales, 2002), 934–938. See also Consuelo Carredano, "Adolfo Salazar en España. Primeras incursiones en la crítica musical: La Revista musical hispano-americana (1914–1918)," *Anales del Instituto de Investigaciones Estéticas*, 16, no. 84 (2004): 134–138.

[80] Casares Rodicio, "La música española," 261–332.

Madrid, which he nevertheless blamed for the failure to secure a performance of *La vida breve*.[81] His biographer, Jaume Pahissa, has recorded an occasion on which Falla, in his political exile in Argentina, reminisced negatively about the music infrastructure in Spain before leaving.[82] Regarding at least this aspect, Falla was more a man of actions than of words. On returning from Paris, he got involved in the founding of the Sociedad Nacional de Música (1915) and the Orquesta Bética de Cámara (1923) in Seville. The Sociedad was a highly innovative but short-lived project in support of Spanish avant-garde composers,[83] and the Orquesta emerged in the need to find an ensemble that was suitable for his most recent works.[84] Therefore, Paris afforded Falla the material conditions with which to test and negotiate his musical ideas.

The myth of Falla's self-exoticism stems in part from the fact that French critics exploited this situation in order to reinforce notions of French hegemony. As has been discussed in Chapter 1, Collet, Jean-Aubry and Laparra described Paris as the "cultural capital of the world" and a "natural" destination for Spaniards and composers of other nationalities. On the one hand, Collet described the Spaniards in Paris as "exiles" neglected by their "motherland," and cast the French capital as their adoptive Mecca. On the other hand, however, he undermined the import of material factors and emphasized the artistic superiority of French musicians, arguing that they guided their Spanish counterparts, limiting themselves to providing technical advice and helping them find their own self. In other words, Collet nourished the needs and concerns of Falla and other Spanish composers in order to cast Spain as a cultural periphery of Paris. This form of propaganda, I argue, led to subsequent constructions of Falla's music and attitude as examples of self-exoticism.

Falla's Aesthetic Positioning

What were Falla's views on the matter? His writings show an ambivalent assessment of the role that the influence of French composers and his experience in Paris played in shaping his musical style. Next to more liberal utterances showing his eagerness to accept the participation of French musicians in formulating notions of "Spanish music," some writings show instead a defensive stance, aimed at restricting the definition of those notions to the views of "native" Spaniards. This contradiction lays bare the liminal position inhabited by Falla,

---

[81] Hess, *Manuel de Falla and Modernism*, 100–101, 168 and 277.
[82] Jaime Pahissa, *Vida y obra de Manuel de Falla* (Buenos Aires: Ricordi Americana, 1956), 43.
[83] Ibid., 51.
[84] Alberto J. Álvarez Calero, "Manuel de Falla y los orígenes de la Orquesta Bética de Cámara," *Música y educación: Revista trimestral de pedagogía musical* 20, no. 70 (2007): 27–36.

who was caught up between conflictive attempts to reify or tear down cultural boundaries and the limits between notions of French and Spanish music.

The first writing under consideration is the article "Claude Debussy et l'Espagne," published in a special issue of *La revue musicale* (1920) dedicated to the memory of Debussy, who had died in 1918.[85] Animated by a commemorative mood, in this article Falla empathized with Debussy's "Spanish persona" to an extent that proved highly compliant with the underpinnings of European "Orientalism," as defined in Said's eponymous essay.[86] It is no wonder that Falla's article has informed Parakilas's thesis of Falla's auto-exoticism. Falla opens his article with the remark that "without knowing Spain, or without having set foot on Spanish ground, Claude Debussy has written Spanish music" (p. 41).[87] This remark acknowledges Falla's readiness to accept the crossing of established cultural boundaries. By emphasizing that Debussy had never visited Spain, Falla proves compliant with attempts to reduce Spain to a figment of the French imagination. His attitude renders Spain as an example of Said's description of the "Orientalized" Other as one that does not speak for itself but rather is spoken for.[88] On this occasion, it is the Spaniard himself who treats Spain as a spoken-for Other.

There are further elements in "Claude Debussy et l'Espagne" that betray an Orientalist conception of Spain. Falla contemplates Debussy's "Spanish music" in connection with the latter's well-known attraction to Javanese gamelan and "other" musics.[89] Falla seems comfortable with the idea of Spain being reduced to a single color in Debussy's "exotic" palette, or one component among "the vast horizons of sound unfolding before him" (p. 41), instead of the sole object of constant research and concern—as it was in Falla's own work. Again, this attitude matches Scott's description of musical Orientalism as being characterized by an equally detached attitude with regard to the different "Orientalized" cultures.[90] Falla mitigates Debussy's apparent detachment by describing him as naturally

---

[85] Manuel de Falla, "Claude Debussy et l'Espagne," *La Revue Musicale* 1, no. 2 (1920): 206–210.

[86] Said, *Orientalism*.

[87] Numbers in brackets refer to pages from the translated edition: Manuel de Falla, *On Music and Musicians* (London: Boyars, 1979). This statement reads like the opposite of Raoul Laparra's contention that Bizet's *Carmen* is "a work of intuition, but not a 'lived' work," on the basis that Bizet had never traveled to Spain ("une œuvre d'intuition, mais non une œuvre vécue"). Raoul Laparra, *Bizet et l'Espagne* (Paris: Delagrave, 1935), 42; "Bizet eut la vision de l'Espagne à travers la documentation populaire qu'il possédait, et ne s'y rendit jamais." Ibid., 5.

[88] Orientalism is "the corporate institution for dealing with the Orient—dealing with it by making statements about it, authorizing views of it, describing it, by teaching it, settling it, ruling over it [...]" Said, *Orientalism*, 3. "There is very little consent to be found, for example, in the fact that Flaubert's encounter with an Egyptian courtesan produced a widely influential model of the Oriental woman; she never spoke of herself, she never represented her emotions, presence, or history. *He* spoke for and represented her." Ibid., 4.

[89] On Debussy and gamelan, see Annegret Fauser, *Musical Encounters at the 1889 Paris World's Fair* (Rochester, NY: University of Rochester Press, 2005), 195–215. Also see the bibliography Fauser cites.

[90] Scott, "Orientalism," 309.

linked to Spain through a Hispanic personality that manifests "spontaneously," even "unconsciously," in works "without any 'Spanish' intention" (pp. 41–42).[91] Further to emphasize the alleged naturalness of Debussy's musical Hispanism, Falla described him as being "led only by a brilliant intuition" and referred to his works as music in which "not a single measure is taken from Spanish folklore"—by which he meant preexistent tunes. Falla expressed his view that Debussy's disinterest in using "real" folklore allowed him to provide "the truth without the authenticity" (p. 42). Thanks to its ambiguous phrasing, this sentence has lent itself to being interpreted as an attempt on the part of Falla to delimit "Spanish music" as an exclusive ground for native Spaniards—and, indeed, Lamas has read it in this way.[92] In sum, in "Claude Debussy et l'Espagne" Falla appropriates Debussy and turns him into a Spanish composer. Falla was most likely seeking to show his compatriots his pro-French allegiances only two years after the end of the First World War. The conception of "Spanish music" that exudes from his reading of Debussy, however, seems compliant with the attempts to cast Spain as a cultural periphery of Paris, which found consistent expression in the writings of French critics.

The second text under consideration takes us back to our point of departure, that is, *La vie brève*. Falla took issue with a previous article by Turina in *The Chesterian* (1920), in a way that shows a radically different attitude from the one that animated his homage to Debussy that same year. Falla argued against Turina's contention that between 1907 and 1914 "the libretto of *La Vida breve* underwent some alterations after composition, two acts being made out of one, and [that] the score was entirely re-orchestrated."[93] Falla's reaction, published as a letter to the editor in the same volume, is indicative of his heightened susceptibility to suggestions that he might have adapted his work to French audiences:

> It would appear from Turina's article, that I have made some important alterations in my opera "La vida breve" before its performance, and after the work had been awarded a prize by the "Academia de Bellas Artes" in Madrid. But the work was performed in the form in which it was presented to the "Academia" and if it was performed in two acts instead of one, this was done solely for the reason that the change of scenery could not otherwise have been effected. I have, it is true, developed the Dance in the last scene and the Interlude

---

[91] It is worth remembering that Laparra resorted to exactly the same rhetorical strategy when he felt that his Spanish credentials were under question.

[92] Rafael Lamas, "On Music and Nation: The Colonized Consciousness of Spanish Musical Nationalism," *Arizona Journal of Hispanic Cultural Studies*, 7 (2003) 80.

[93] Joaquín Turina, "Manuel de Falla," *The Chesterian* (May 1920). Nommick, "*La vida breve*," 11.

that precedes it. This does not, however, constitute a modification, but simply an addition, and I have merely developed themes which already existed in the work. I have not "entirely re-orchestrated" this opera; I only re-scored certain passages, which the short time allowed for presentation of the work to the "Academia" did not permit me to handle as carefully as I wished, but I have scrupulously retained the original orchestral plan, without permitting myself the slightest fundamental modification.[94]

If, as I have argued, what matters are attitudes rather than results, this quotation makes it difficult to contemplate Falla as a case of self-exoticism. Unlike in "Claude Debussy et l'Espagne," in this article Falla does not leave a door open for the negotiation of "Spanish music." Turina's very slight innuendo (if at all) that he could have stepped onto "the French side" made Falla relinquish the liberal attitude shown in "Claude Debussy et l'Espagne," namely, that writing "Spanish music" was not a matter of birth or blood, and that French composers—or at least Debussy—could take equal part in it. Though one should not neglect the possibility that in 1920 Falla wanted to emphasize his departure from his own prewar creations, his reaction to Turina's suggestions may be ultimately regarded as a defensive attempt to establish an ethnic basis for the definition of "Spanish music," that is, as an endeavor to delimit that concept as the exclusive ground of Spanish composers, inaccessible to non-Spaniards. By understating the magnitude of the changes made on the score, Falla strived to present *La vie brève* as a "Spanish" work.[95] Yet, thanks to the research done by Christoforidis and Nommick, it is possible to conclude that the amount of those changes, though uncertain, lies in between what Turina and Falla contended in their contributions to *The Chesterian*.[96] Falla's exaggerations are indicative of the strained

---

[94] Manuel de Falla, "Letter to the editor," *The Chesterian* (July 1920) 49. Nommick quotes the manuscript letter that Falla sent to Jean-Aubry, written in French ("*La vida breve* entre 1905 y 1904," 11).

[95] Moreover, Falla sued Paul Milliet for including himself as adaptor of the libretto instead of mere translator. The Sociedad de Autores supported Falla. However, Milliet decided to split the original single act into two. Fernandez-Shaw, *Larga historia*, 59–60.

[96] "si bien es cierto que las principales modificaciones afectan a la estructura y la orquestación, también experimentaron cambios la melodía, la armonía, la prosodia y la escritura rítmica durante el largo proceso de revisión de *La vida breve*," Nommick, "*La vida breve*," 12; in preparation for the Nice and Paris performances, "Falla amplia el pasaje que precede a la segunda Danza española (final del 1er cuadro del Acto II) y le añade un interludio (los 20 compases de 1913 se convierten, en 1914, en 66), formando el conjunto una magistral síntesis en la que recapitula todos los temas esenciales de la obra.," ibid., 13; the structural modifications are the result of Debussy's and Messager's feedback, ibid., 13–21; "The impact of Debussy and his music in reshaping La vida breve is perhaps most pervasive in Falla's new awareness of the orchestra. Much of the original orchestration of La vida breve was revised, though perhaps not as thoroughly reworked as was claimed by Joaquín Turina" (Christoforidis, "La vida breve," 8). Falla's biographer, Pahissa, de-emphasised the extent of the changes, probably under Falla's guidance: "No es que modificara ni cambiara las ideas generales ni el plan orquestal, pero sí algún detalle, algunas notas

cultural anxieties prevalent in their cultural environment. More particularly, his response evinces to what extent he let his conflictive perception of himself become a relevant issue in others' perceptions of his work. To avoid having his attitude seem the product of narcissism rather than a symptom of broader cultural struggles, however, it seems worth quoting the only review written by a Spanish critic about the Paris première of *La vie brève*:

> Thanks to *La vie brève* it will be possible to acquire a more veridical idea of Spain abroad, than the one provided by Bizet, Lalo, Chabrier, Ravel or Debussy, and, farther from us, Liszt or Glinka; notwithstanding their musicality and their curiosity for Spain, none of them […] has ever attained that local truth that emanates from the symphonic example in which Falla evokes the evening that falls over Granada, or that wedding celebration, in the second act, where the "singer's" accents are interrupted by the attendants' cheers.[97]

This testimony, by Joaquin Nin, gives a vivid impression of how contested notions of "Spanish music" were, especially if one pits it against the anonymous article in *Le Journal* quoted above that presented *La vie brève* as an inferior emulation of the "Spanish music" by French and European composers.[98] Falla's article in *The Chesterian* and Nin's review show that, despite giving clear signs of openness to the input of French musicians in the formulation of "Spanish music," Spanish composers would claim a ground of their own when they felt that it was under threat. "Spanish music" was a contingent and contested concept, subject to reformulations and negotiations in which French and Spanish composers took part. Their testimonies reveal different attitudes and agendas ranging from the French critics' attempts to appropriate Falla's success to variably open or restrictive responses on the part of Falla and other Spanish musicians. As I have shown, *La vie brève* gained center stage in these cultural struggles.

---

añadidas o sustituidas, para completar o refinar la sonoridad hasta aproximarse, en todo lo posible, a la expresión más exacta de lo que quería 'decir' orquestalmente," Pahissa, *Vida y obra*, 62.

[97] "Avec *La vie brève* on pourra avoir, à l'étranger, une idée espagnole plus véridique que celles que nous donnèrent Bizet, Lalo, Chabrier, Ravel ou Debussy, ou, plus loin de nous, Liszt ou Glinka; en dépit de leur musicalité, de leur curiosité pur l'Espagne aucun d'eux—et pur cause—n'a jamais atteint à cette vérité locale qui se dégage de la page symphonique dans laquelle Falla évoque le soir qui tombe sur Grenade, ou de cette fête de noce, au seconde acte, où les accents du 'chanteur' sont coupés des vivats des assistants." Joaquin Nin, "*La vie brève* de Manuel de Falla," *La tribune musicale* (February 1914).

[98] "ce qu'il [Falla] nous a suggeré hier, nous l'avions déjà perçu grâce à Chabrier, ou à Lalo, ou à Rimsky, ou à Debussy, ou à M. Ravel, ou à M. Laparra, et surtout au regretté Albéniz." Anon., "La vie brève."

PART

BUILDING THE POSTWAR ORDER

CHAPTER 5

Domesticating Difference? *Carmen* and the "French" Canon in the 1920s

Building the postwar order in France required assembling an outstanding collection of musical works that could show the world a fully recovered France, one that was even stronger than in 1914. In that context, new works entered the canon, while some of the "old" ones were targeted as the ground on which to negotiate formulations of national identity. Critics and musicologists situated some of these works at the core of debate on national identity, using them as a yardstick to assess the position that other works occupied in the "French" canon. Parallel to the neoclassical movement in musical composition, the rewriting of the past as a chapter of French music history was the basis for grounding the present in a continuing sense of tradition and thus empowering it. Although this phenomenon was already taking place before the Great War,[1] and even in the nineteenth century,[2] I am interested in the peculiarities that it acquired in the postwar context, especially regarding its impact on the representation of Spanish musical identities.

Boosted by the celebration of its fiftieth anniversary in 1925, *Carmen* became one of the favorites of 1920s French debate on music and national identity. *Carmen* was already well established in the canon mainly thanks to its box-office success. However, as I shall argue, in the 1920s it consolidated and improved its place in the "French" canon after becoming the object of an inquiry into the relation of French music with its Others. Although this phenomenon, as a whole, is no different than what happened to other musical works, its implications as regards French perceptions of Spanish identity are relevant. *Carmen*'s longstanding success was to a great extent based on Bizet's ability to represent "difference," but its "new" aesthetic import was, much to the contrary, grounded in its capacity to stimulate consensus over the nature of the collective self. In this chapter,

---

[1] Fulcher, *French Cultural Politics*, 56–63.
[2] Ellis, *Interpreting the Musical Past*, 147–148.

I shall explain how critics and musicologists dealt with that "difference," through attitudes ranging from accommodating it into personal or collective notions of French identity, to dispensing with it altogether.

Carmen's Early History

In order to understand how *Carmen* helped to relocate "Spanish music" in French culture, one must stop regarding the Spanish elements in this opera as being merely exotic. Paraphrasing Timothy Taylor, one must reach "beyond exoticism," understanding the "exotic" as a catchword that ultimately masks a range of functions performed by a cultural signifier in a given context.[3] To deem the Spanish elements in *Carmen* "exotic" does not do justice to the relevant role that representations of gender, race and class, and by extension of Spanish identity, played in this opera's early—though not immediate—and subsequent success. *Carmen* premièred at the Opéra Comique, Paris, in 1875 and ran for forty-eight performances before being removed from the bill.[4] Notwithstanding whether this number constitutes a failure or success—as scholars dispute—it does not reflect the central position that, years later, *Carmen* would occupy in the repertoire of most opera houses in France and around the world. As I shall argue, *Carmen*'s gradual consolidation in the repertoire depended, to a certain extent, on how prevalent constructions of the Spanish gypsy female were played out in various productions, and how that icon was relocated in the French cultural imaginary. Though chronologically distant from the object of this chapter, the early history of *Carmen* illustrates the origin and foundations of some of the critical and social discourses that facilitated postwar constructions of *Carmen* as an essentially French work. Why *Carmen* was withdrawn from the bill in early 1876 is not entirely clear. Wright argues that, although "a few critics were thoroughly vitriolic or dismissive [...] *Carmen* was damned with faint praise," as the majority of critics were "tepid, mixed or disapproving."[5] Most scholars point to moral concerns on the part of critics and the audience, plus the presence of challenging

---

[3] I am particularly appreciative of Taylor's contention that "there is no such thing as 'the musical Other,' that this is an essentialized concept. People in different historical situations have ways of constructing their Others in different ways." Timothy D. Taylor, *Beyond Exoticism: Western Music and the World* (Durham, NC: Duke University Press, 2007), 7.

[4] Lesley Wright, *Georges Bizet, Carmen: Dossier de presse parisienne (1875)* (Weinsberg: Musik-Ed. Galland, 2001), vi; there is certain disagreement about the number of performances. Gaudier counts thirty-seven performances. Charles Gaudier, *Carmen de Bizet. Étude historique et critique. Analyse musicale* (Pairs: P. Mellottée, 1922), 39. Macdonald counts forty-five: Hugh Macdonald, "Carmen (ii)," *The New Grove Dictionary of Opera*, http://www.oxfordmusiconline.com/subscriber/article/grove/music/O008315 (accessed August 17, 2011).

[5] Wright, *Georges Bizet*, vi.

musical modernisms.[6] Wright reports how the most aesthetically conservative critics applied adjectives such as "Wagnerian," "scientific," "dense," "sad," or "gray" to *Carmen*'s orchestral and harmonic complexities; others condemned what they perceived as excessive use of tunes and dance numbers; and others criticized Galli-Marié's overtly sensual performance in the role of *Carmen*.[7] Clark mentions "the newness of the music" and the "scabrous" subject, given that "Bizet's heroine, although a rather tempered version of her counterpart in the Mérimée novella, is a study in transgression."[8] McClary and Parakilas argue that *Carmen*'s brutal story of violence and racial difference shocked Parisian audiences by showing them, for the first time, the dark side of colonialism.[9] Perhaps for the first time, since uprisings in the colonies started around the midnineteenth century, an opera reflected them through the trope of the rebellious gypsy female.[10]

Mérimée's novel had already provoked some scandal when it was published as a weekly *feuilleton* in the *Revue des deux mondes*, starting in October 1845.[11] Fearing critical and public opposition, the librettists Meilhac and Halévy introduced a morally virtuous character, Micaëla, and omitted certain details from Don José's dubious past. Furthermore, they mitigated the extent of Carmen's engagement with the bandits, and reduced the gravity and number of her crimes.[12] Despite these precautions, the otherness surrounding perceptions of the Spanish female gypsy, reinforced by the display of deviant behaviors, most likely elicited a lukewarm critical reaction at its première, and its subsequent withdrawal a few months later.

Although these facts are well known, they bring to light the role that issues of gender, race and class could play during *Carmen*'s subsequent access to the canon. A first testimony of that role may be found in the reception of *Carmen*'s revival at the Opéra Comique in 1883. On that occasion, success came thanks to a production devoid of any controversial aspects, helped by the acclaim that *Carmen* had earned, in the interim, across the French provinces and abroad.[13]

---

[6] Wright, *Georges Bizet*, vi; McClary, *Georges Bizet: Carmen*, 114; Marc Delmas, *Georges Bizet, 1838–1875* (Paris: P. Bossuet, 1930), 39; Mina Curtiss, *Bizet and His World* (New York: Knopf, 1958), 433.

[7] Wright, *Georges Bizet*, iv.

[8] Clark, "South of North," 187–216.

[9] Parakilas, "The Soldier and the Exotic," 33–34. Susan McClary: "Sexual Politics in Classical Music," in *Feminine Endings: Music, Gender, and Sexuality*, ed. McClary (Minneapolis, London: University of Minnesota Press, 2002/1991) 66–67.

[10] Locke, *Musical Exoticism*, 175.

[11] José Bruyr, "Georges Bizet et son mystère," *Le guide musical*, October 7–14, 1938.

[12] McClary, *Georges Bizet*, 19; Curtiss, *Bizet and His World*, 351; Spies, *Opera, State, and Society*, 30–31; Henry Gauthier-Villars [Emile Vuillemoz], *Georges Bizet* (Paris: Renouard, 1928), 110.

[13] February 15, 1876, a week after it was retired from the bill in Paris, it premiered in the Théatre de la Monnaie, Brussels. In 1878 it succeeded in London, Dublin and Saint Petersburg and was performed in Lyon, Marseille and Angers. Curtiss, *Bizet and His World*, 428–429.

The new Opéra Comique directive introduced significant changes in how the opera was staged and performed.[14] To take just one example, the "rogues" and gypsy dancers populating Lillas Pastia's tavern at the opening of the second act gave way to the *corps de ballet* wearing tutus. Instead of the tavern, there stood, in Gaudier's words, "a clear and vast hostel where sixty to ninety noble visitors and ballerinas show up."[15] Perhaps a more substantial decision was to substitute, for the original mezzo Galli-Marié, the soprano Adèle Isaac in the role of Carmen. Isaac's rendition, in a higher vocal register, was perceived as more feminine, delicate and pure, thus meeting prevalent notions of the female. Furthermore, Isaac was convinced that "Carmen is not wicked" and that "despite her lower class origins, she has an indelible distinction which she owes to her race."[16] Interestingly, although her words do not reveal any attempt to erase difference, early chroniclers and scholars concurred in declaring her rendition less racial. According to Gaudier, Isaac turned *Carmen* into an "honest" woman, by virtue of the "distinguished airs" of her performance, and the "clear soprano voice, which, far from darkening in a miserable atmosphere, enameled the role with high-pitched notes judiciously delivered."[17] Tenroc argued that Isaac managed to "invest the gypsy woman with the attire of a relatively bourgeois distinction."[18] Mina Curtiss contends that Isaac's "moderate control" of her performance secured the success of an otherwise troubled, careless and little-rehearsed production, in which she represented the sole exception to a poor cast.[19]

The audience responded favorably to these changes. The December 23, 1883, *Carmen* reached its hundredth performance, which was commemorated with the installation, in the foyer of the Salle Favart, of a replica of Paul Dubois's bust for Bizet's tomb (he had died June 3, 1875, only three months after the première, and was buried in Père Lachaise cemetery). *Carmen* had entered the Opéra Comique's standard repertoire, helped by the progressive demise of some of the one-time favorites, such as Hérold, Boieldieu and Adam.[20] Isaac's performance

---

[14] Huebner, *French Opera at the Fin de Siècle*, 6.

[15] "une vaste et claire auberge où évoluent de 60 à 100 nobles visiteurs et une vingtaine de danseuses." Gaudier, *Carmen de Bizet*, 42.

[16] "Carmen n'est pas méchante"; "en dépit de bas fonds sociaux qui constituent son milieu, elle garde une indélébile distinction qu'elle doit à sa race." Quoted in Gabriel Bernard, "La question de l'interprétation de 'Carmen,'" *Le courrier musical*, March 15, 1925.

[17] "honnête"; "allures distinguées"; "claire voix de soprano, qui ne sombrait pas dans un médium canaille, mais émaillait le rôle de notes aiguës judicieusement pointées." Gaudier, *Carmen de Bizet*, 39.

[18] "revêtir la bohémienne des atours d'une distinction relativement embourgeoisée." Charles Tenroc, "Les cinquante ans de Carmen. Un anniversaire," *Le courrier musical* (March 1, 1925).

[19] Curtiss, *Bizet and His World*, 432. Curtiss narrates the mishaps that happened during the première, such as Don José dropping the dagger three times.

[20] Gaudier, *Carmen de Bizet*, 43.

had contributed to this success perhaps to a greater extent than any other aspect of the production, to judge from the fact that critics turned to blaming Celestine Galli-Marié's daring performance of 1875 for *Carmen*'s initial "failure."[21] Perceptions of Isaac's performance, therefore, foreshadowed the critical framework that facilitated *Carmen*'s access to a canon of Frenchness during the 1920s, insofar as—contradicting her declarations—it helped to mitigate racial difference and complied with hegemonic gender discourses.

The advent of naturalist opera in the 1890s, together with the impact and high box-office success of Italian verist operas in Paris before the First World War, further helped to mitigate perceptions of difference in *Carmen*.[22] Thanks to *verismo* and naturalism, Parisian operatic audiences grew accustomed to onstage death and violence, and therefore did not perceive the crimes and passions displayed in Bizet's opera as adding to the otherness of the female gypsy—or at least, not in a way that defied conventions. Furthermore, the aesthetic updates brought about by *verismo* and naturalism could help in regarding *Carmen* as a work of the past, and thus apt for embodying values regarded as traditional. The lavish celebration of *Carmen*'s thousandth performance at the Opéra Comique in December 1904 was an opportunity to examine how and to what extent the social and aesthetic changes that took place during the three decades that followed the première modified this opera's position in the canon. The two reviews published in *Le Figaro*, by Gustave Charpentier and Gabriel Fauré, coincide in ascribing from the passage of time a redemptory or soothing effect on perceptions of *Carmen*. Interestingly enough, they furnish diametrically opposed answers to the question of this work's alleged "failure" in 1875. According to Charpentier, "if one imagines the type of opéra-comique that the audience then relished," it seems understandable that "such a violent drama, that soaring, all-burning music, plagued with sulfurous bursts of the most boiling passion, that fantasy, those cries and sighs, those poignant effusions [...] must have caused a rather awkward effect."[23] Charpentier situates this reaction far from "the unanimous admiration that thrives around *Carmen* today."[24] By contrast, Fauré, who refers to *Carmen* as "one of the glorious masterworks in which French music takes pride," cannot "explain why Bizet's music, which is all clarity, sincerity, color, sensitivity and charm, has not

---

[21] Clark, "South of North," 204. Curtiss, *Bizet and His World*, 432.

[22] The start of naturalist opera could be arguably situated in Zola's and Bruneau's *Le rêve* (1891). Kelkel, *Naturalisme, vérisme et réalisme*, 13.

[23] "songe-t-on aux opéra-comiques auxquels le public d'alors prenait son plaisir"; "ce drame violent, cette musique ailée, toute brûlante, traverseé des jets sulfureux de la plus brouillante passion, que cette fantaisie, ces cris, ces soupirs, que ces poignantes effusions"; "dut faire un effet bien étrange." Gustave Charpentier, "La millième de 'Carmen'," *Le Figaro*, December 23, 1904.

[24] "l'unanime admiration qui fleurit maintenant autour de *Carmen*." Charpentier, "La millième de 'Carmen'."

conquered the audience right from the start."[25] What Charpentier describes as an outburst of passion, Fauré regards in Apollonian terms. As we shall see in due course, critics converged on the Apollonian interpretation, even if some of them detected the presence of "savage" elements in *Carmen*.

As far as the history of "Spanish opera" in France is concerned, Raoul Laparra's two earliest contributions, *La habanera* (1908) and *La jota* (1911), helped to raise the standards of violence, even if their harshness still met with the opposition of several critics. *La jota* helped in regarding *Carmen* as an escape from the modernisms that some critics pointed out in Laparra's work, and that, most likely, had to do with the use of noise. This phenomenon can be gathered from Davin de Champclos's review of that opera: "What a joy I will experience, after this day of modernisms, when I plunge into the adorable *Carmen* as in a joyful and sunny bath, the first day they play it at Albert Carré's [opera house]!"[26] A few years before the First World War, therefore, *Carmen* could embody notions of "tradition." Rather than a "dead" tradition, *Carmen* represented one that could be maintained or revived, insofar as it sill afforded a "joyful" and "sunny" respite from "harsh" modernisms, as it did for Davin de Champclos. In other words, in the early 1910s *Carmen* was already established as a national masterwork, if by that one understands a work that provides a measure of "good taste" on which to base judgment of newer ones. As I shall argue now, during the postwar years *Carmen* consolidated that position, insofar as it became the target, vehicle and catalyst of discourses on French identity, and helped to articulate multiple forms of representing and engaging with the Other, more particularly with Spain. This variety of discourses conferred on representations of Spain a great diversity of meanings and positions, ranging from a close, cultural ally in the fight against German culture and verist opera to a distant, exotic and even threatening Other. This discursive repositioning played out in the writings of critics and musicologists, most conspicuously in an unconnected series of monographs devoted to *Carmen* or Bizet. Ultimately, this process formed part of a larger one by which national works were examined as potential embodiments of particular formulations of French nationality. Thus, critics and intellectuals ultimately sought to stimulate a sense of social cohesion and self-confidence that would boost France through its postwar recovery.

---

[25] "l'un des glorieux chefs-d'œuvre dont s'enorgueillit la musique française"; "ce qui ne s'explique pas, c'est que la musique de Bizet, toute de clarté, de franchise, de couleur, de sensibilité et de charme, n'ait pas conquis ce public dès la première heure." Gabriel Fauré, "Théâtre National de l'Opéra Comique: Millième représentation de *Carmen*," *Le Figaro*, December 24, 1904.

[26] "Mais quelle joie, après cette journée de modernisme, je vais avoir à me retremper, comme en un bain de joie et de lumière, dans l'adorable Carmen, au premier soir où l'on jouera du Bizet chez M. Albert Carré!" Davin de Champclos, "Les répétitions générales."

Gaudier, Wagner and the Opéra-comique

The first work that deserves our attention is Charles Gaudier's *"Carmen" de Bizet*, published in 1922.[27] Although very little is known of Gaudier that might help assess the meaning and relevance of his work in his time,[28] his monograph on *Carmen* represents the first significant postwar contribution to enshrining this opera in an anti-German concept of the French canon. This passage encapsulates his point of view:

> Although Bizet has judiciously borrowed several motifs that I will indicate, and although he has imitated some others, it is no less certain that he has tried to make his work "human" rather than "picturesque," and that Carmen is, above all, expressive music, French, Latin, Mediterranean music, if you will. One may search in vain for "Wagnerism." In a previous chapter, I have studied Bizet's alleged Wagnerism, or rather, I have searched in vain for it in his works and ideas. If Wagnerian simply means revolutionary, Carmen is not a revolutionary work: its cut does not differ from the traditional Opéra Comique; it consists of a succession of choirs, arias, duos, trios, quintets, etc., sometimes less arbitrarily sorted and more naturally ordered than in those previous works, but neatly loose and easily detachable. There is a great distance to Wagner's *unendliche Melodie*.[29]

Gaudier's rhetoric reminds one of Nietzsche's construction of *Carmen* as a Latin, Mediterranean and anti-German work.[30] In this respect, Nietzsche anticipated the postwar rhetoric of neoclassicism, which exploited a series of binaries

---

[27] Charles Gaudier, *Carmen de Bizet: Étude historique et critique, analyse musicale*, Les chefs-d'oeuvre de la musique (Paris: P. Mellottée, 1922).

[28] Apart from the fact that he authored an edition of the letters from the nineteenth-century actress Marie Dorval to the author Alfred de Vigny. Marie Dorval, *Lettres à Alfred de Vigny: Recueillies et présentées par Charles Gaudier* (Paris and Abbeville: Gallimard, impr. de F. Paillart, 1942).

[29] "si Bizet a judicieusement emprunté quelques motifs que nous indiquerons, s'il en a brillamment pastiché quelques autres, il n'en est pas moins certain qu'il a plutôt tenté de faire 'humain' que de faire 'pittoresque', et que Carmen est avant tout de la musique expressive, de la musique bien française,—latine, méditerranéenne, si l'on veut./Il ne faut pas s'attendre non plus à trouver dans Carmen du 'wagnérisme'. Dans un chapitre précédent, nous avons étudié le prétendu wagnérisme de Bizet, ou plutôt nous l'avons vainement cherché dans ses doctrines et dans ses œuvres. Si 'wagnérien' veut dire tout simplement 'révolutionnaire', Carmen n'est pas une œuvre révolutionnaire: sa coupe ne diffère pas de celle de l'opéra-comique traditionnel; c'est une succession de chœurs, d'airs, de duos, trios, quintettes, etc., parfois moins arbitrairement amenés et plus naturellement placés que dans telles œuvres précédentes, mais nettement détachés et facilement détachables. Il y a loin de là à la 'mélodie continue' de Wagner." Gaudier, *Carmen de Bizet*, 76.

[30] "Cette musique de Bizet me semble parfaite. Elle approche avec une allure légère, souple, polie. Elle est aimable, elle ne met point en sueur." Nietzsche, *Le cas Wagner*, 4.

in order to create an artificially neat distinction between French and German music.[31] It may be argued that Nietzsche's impact on the aesthetics of neoclassicism significantly helped *Carmen* gain currency in the postwar aesthetic debates over the nature of French musical traditions. In order to further disassociate Bizet from Wagner, Gaudier construes the latter as a revolutionary counterexample. This stance conflicts with the reactionary meaning that Wagner's music gained in certain circles, most especially the Schola Cantorum.[32] However, since the midnineteenth century, French conservative critics tended to see Wagner as a revolutionary composer by associating him with antibourgeois figures such as the realist painter Courbet and the philosopher Pierre-Joseph Proudhon.[33]

Beyond establishing its differences from Wagner's operas, Gaudier's construction of *Carmen* as a "French" work relied on an identification of this work with the opéra-comique genre. It seems ironic that *Carmen*, a work accepted only with difficulty at an institution once "devoted to family gatherings and matrimonial interviews," as Albert Carré would describe it, should once have been deemed an archetypical opéra-comique.[34] This identification, however, had already started a few years after the première of *Carmen*. In turn, attempts to define the opéra-comique as a "French" or "national" genre harken back to the early nineteenth century, and, in the wake of the Franco-Prussian War—that is, a few years before the première of *Carmen*—they had become commonplace.[35] The opéra-comique lent itself as the basis for constructions of French musical traditions for various reasons, but above all because, as Annegret Fauser has argued, "the formation of such ties to the past was part of the Opéra Comique's longstanding

---

[31] Nematollahy, "Nietzsche in France," 169–180; on the wartime and postwar rhetoric of neoclassicism, see Fulcher, *The Composer as Intellectual*, 19–23.

[32] Fulcher, *French Cultural Politics and Music*, 33–34. However, it connected with musicians who, like Alfred Bruneau, upheld the revolutionary foundations of the Third Republic and embraced Wagnerism as a salutary influence on French music. (Fulcher, *French Cultural Politics*, 42–44.) Interestingly, critics extended the revolutionary credentials to French composers who had allegedly experienced Wagner's influence, most conspicuously Berlioz. Lesley Wright, "Berlioz's Impact in France," in *The Cambridge Companion to Berlioz*, ed. Peter Bloom, (New York: Cambridge University Press, 2000), 262 [253–268]. Fulcher, *French Cultural Politics*, 107–108.

[33] Gerald D. Turbow, "Art and Politics: Wagnerism in France," in *Wagnerism in European Culture and Politics*, ed. David Large and William Weber (Ithaca: Cornell University Press, 1984), 139.

[34] "voué aux réunions de famille et aux entrevues matrimoniales." Albert Carré, *Souvenirs de théâtre* (Paris: Plon, 1950).

[35] Fauser, *Musical Encounters*, 79. Wright, *Georges Bizet, Carmen*, viii; Clark, "South of North," 187. Interestingly, most nineteenth-century Spanish critics, with the exception of Pedrell, had construed zarzuela, the genre that most clearly manifested the influence of the opéra-comique and equally alternated music and dialogue, as the national genre par excellence. On zarzuela as a national genre see Hess, *Manuel de Falla and Modernism*, 22–27. On the relation between zarzuela and opéra-comique see María Encina Cortizo, "La zarzuela espagnole du XIXe siècle. Relations et divergences avec le théâtre français du XIXe siècle (1832–1866)," in *Echanges musicaux franco-espagnols XVIIe–XIXe siècles: actes des Rencontres de Villecroze, 15 au 17 octobre 1998*, ed. François Lesure, vol. 4, Domaine musicologique. III, Les rencontres de Villecroze (Paris: Klincksieck, 2000), 83–122.

strategy of repertoire-building."³⁶ It seems disputable, however, to regard the opéra-comique as a well-defined genre in subject matter or form. The humorous situations that once characterized it gave way to a broad range of subjects and moods in the nineteenth century.³⁷ Moreover, although Paris performances of *Carmen* still relied on the original dialogues, many opera theaters preferred to include the music that Giraud composed for the dialogues, thus subverting one of the signs of identification of the opéra-comique genre.³⁸

To emphasize the opéra-comique's alleged traditionalism by pitting it against a revolutionary conception of Wagner—as Gaudier does—entailed a significant departure from the way the Republic tried to appropriate this genre in the late nineteenth century. Sparked by the centenary celebration of the French Revolution, the organisers of the 1889 World Exhibition tried to imbue the opéra-comique genre with revolutionary connotations through a series of performances that, most significantly, included *Carmen*.³⁹ Furthermore, Gaudier bases his defense of *Carmen*'s independence from Wagner on its number structure, which Gaudier considers to be a representative feature of the opéra-comique genre—as opposed to Wagner's *unendliche Melodie* and the apparently seamless structural flow of his operas. Nevertheless, Debussy's *Pélleas et Melisande* (1902), which, since the time of its première, several critics hailed as the first French breakaway from Wagner, arguably drew on Wagnerian techniques and strategies of musical continuity.⁴⁰ This contradiction may be explained as a result of the fact that, as Lydia Goehr has pointed out, "some very specific traits associated with Wagner's *Tristan* were reconceived to be associated with Debussy's antithetical *Pelléas*."⁴¹

An anonymous article published on April 9, 1926, in *Le guide du concert* resorted to similar strategies, probably influenced by Gaudier, or more likely drawing on the longstanding views of this work. The author argued that, although "Bizet was one of the first Wagnerians," *Carmen* "is to a much greater extent built on the French Opéra Comique tradition, rather than on the style and aesthetic

---

³⁶ Fauser, *Musical Encounters*, 80.

³⁷ M. Elizabeth C. Bartlet and Richard Langham Smith, "Opéra comique," *Grove Music Online*, ed. Stanley Sadie, http://www.oxfordmusiconline.com/subscriber/article/grove/music/43715 (accessed April 15, 2011).

³⁸ Macdonald, "Carmen (ii)."

³⁹ Fauser, *Musical Encounters*, 79–91.

⁴⁰ The literature on this issue is vast. See especially Roger Nichols and Richard Langham Smith, *Claude Debussy, Pelléas et Mélisande* (Cambridge University Press, 1989), 79–85; Robert Orledge, *Debussy and the Theatre* (Cambridge: Cambridge University Press, 1982), 91–100; Déirdre Donnellon, "Debussy as Musician and Critic," in *The Cambridge Companion to Debussy*, ed. Simon Trezise (Cambridge: Cambridge University Press, 2003), 46–48; Carolyn Abbate, "*Tristan* in the Composition of *Pelléas*," *19th-Century Music* 5, no. 2 (October 1, 1981), 138.

⁴¹ Lydia Goehr, "Radical Modernism and the Failure of Style: Philosophical Reflections on Maeterlinck-Debussy's Pelléas et Mélisande," *Representations* 74, no. 1 (May 1, 2001) 58.

that the master from Bayreuth has introduced in theater."[42] While admitting to Bizet's early Wagnerism, this author construes the opéra-comique as a "French" tradition—just as Gaudier does. More significantly, however, she or he argues that, although

> Bizet has built, to some extent, on the famous leitmotiv system introduced by Wagner […] one can trace the leitmotiv back to much older works than Wagner's, such as the famous theme "Song of Blondel" from Grétry's *Richard Coeur-de-Lion*, to mention, precisely, an opéra-comique.[43]

This author situates French music at the origin of the leitmotiv, and construes the latter as a key discovery in the history of Western music. Thus, she or he casts Wagner's music as a ramification from a French tradition and furthermore construes the tradition as one that encompasses the origin and apex of Western music history, respectively represented by Grétry and Bizet.[44]

Gaudier and Spanish Music

Gaudier granted the German and Spanish elements in *Carmen* radically different status, even if he contemplated both of them as foreign or extraneous. Although he conceived of the German elements as representative of a foreign menace, he regarded "Spanish music" in *Carmen* as extraneous and conforming to notions of the subaltern, and supporting the idea of a higher, French, Self. He remarks that "although Bizet has judiciously borrowed several motifs […] he has tried to

---

[42] "Il est vrai que Bizet fut un des wagnériens de la première heure"; "bien plus nourrie de la tradition de l'Opéra Comique français, que du style et de l'esthétique introduits, au théâtre, par le maître de Bayreuth?" Anon., "Carmen de Bizet," *Le guide du concert* (April 9, 1926).

[43] "Bizet s'est servi, dans une certaine mesure, du fameux système du leit-motiv introduit par Wagner"; "on peut facilement retrouver le leit-motiv dans des oeuvres bien antérieures à Wagner: le fameux thème de la 'Chanson de Blondel' dans Richard Coeur-de-Lion de Grétry, pour citer précisément un opéra-comique." Ibid.

[44] There existed certain grounds to support that argument, for, as Hervé Lacombe has observed, "the Wagnerian leitmotif has had such an impact that we forget its origins and the widely varied forms that preceded it—especially in the French repertory." Hervé Lacombe, *The Keys to French Opera in the Nineteenth Century* (Berkeley: University of California Press, 2001), 137. But even Lacombe, who narrates the evolution of motivic procedures in "French opera" and compares it to the similar evolution in "Western music," concludes that, although motivic recurrence emerges in French opera at the end of the eighteenth century, "for motifs to follow more numerous and to continuously follow the development of the characters and of the drama, we have to wait for Chausson's *Roi Arthus* (Brussels, 1903) and specially Vincent d'Indy's *Fervaal* (Brussels, 1897). Those composers had carefully studied and assimilated Wagner's late scores." Lacombe, *The Keys to French Opera*, 142.

make his work 'human' rather than 'picturesque.'"⁴⁵ The "picturesque" here reads as savage, especially as opposed to "human" or civilized. In order to detach *Carmen* from savage Spanish music, he undermines the authenticity of Bizet's music: "one must not expect to find, in Bizet's score, a specifically Spanish music."⁴⁶ Other passages reveal that, by "specifically Spanish music," he means "raw material" with which Bizet produces a socially and artistically superior form of art. Furthermore, he drew on the widespread chauvinistic and colonialist prejudice that French composers, including Bizet, had been the first and most accomplished exploiters of the "artistic" potential encapsulated in Spanish music.⁴⁷

This prejudice underpins Gaudier's analysis of the Habanera and Gypsy Song.⁴⁸ Although he admits that Yradier's song already "contains the whole habanera of *Carmen*," he deems its accompaniment "vulgar" and marvels at the "difference between the original and the imitation."⁴⁹ Commenting on the 1875 performance of the "Chanson bohème" (Gypsy Song) that opens the second act, Gaudier reports that it

> was received coldly, not just due to its somewhat tumultuous and disheveled aspect, but also because it constitutes an assassination of harmony and consonance: those obstinate and monotone guitars, which tangle, as they can, with unforeseen modulations, that constant chromaticism, those innovations, or rather those harmonic inventions, shocked the purists, the puritans, who would have preferred order and regularity to reign, even in the Gypsy improvisations.⁵⁰

---

⁴⁵ "si Bizet a judicieusement emprunté quelques motifs [...] il n'en est pas moins certain qu'il a plutôt tenté de faire 'humain' que de faire 'pittoresque.'" He refers to the Spanish themes by Manuel García and Sebastián de Yradier, as discussed below. Gaudier, *Carmen de Bizet*, 66.

⁴⁶ "Il ne faut pas s'attendre à trouver dans la partition de Bizet une musique spécifiquement espagnole." Ibid., 54.

⁴⁷ "Le terroir espagnol est riche en musique populaire, vocale ou dansante... Longtemps l'Espagne a laissé perdre ses richesses ou ne les a pas exploitées elle-même." Ibid., 54; however, aware that a similar top-to-bottom and elitist philosophy animated the works of Spanish composers, he admitted that "En ces dernières années seulement Pedrell, Albeniz, Granados, Manuel de Falla ont su et voulu utiliser les idées et rythmes si spéciaux, si curieux, qu'ils trouvaient à profusion autour d'eux." Ibid., 54.

⁴⁸ As it is well known, the Habanera is based on the song "El arreglito" by the Spanish composer Sebastián de Yradier, which Bizet took from the collection *Echos d'Espagne*, held at the library of the Paris Conservatoire. On the sources of Bizet's borrowings see Ralph P. Locke, "Spanish Local Color in Bizet's Carmen: Unexplored Borrowings and Transformations," in *Music, Theatre and Cultural Transfer: Paris, 1830–1914*, ed. Annegret Fauser and Mark Everist (Chicago: University of Chicago Press, 2009), 316–360.

⁴⁹ "prodigieuse niaiserie"; "contient toute la habanera de Carmen"; "quelle différence entre l'original et l'imitation!" Gaudier, *Carmen de Bizet*, 66.

⁵⁰ "il fut fraîchement accueilli, non pas seulement à cause de son allure un peu tumultueuse et débraillé, mais parce qu'il constituait comme un assassinat de l'harmonie, de la consonance: ces guitares obstinées et monotones, qui se frottent comme elles peuvent à des modulations imprévues, ce chromatisme constant, ces audaces, ou plutôt ces trouvailles harmoniques, choquaient les puristes, les puritains, qui eussent voulu de l'ordre et de la régularité, même dans les improvisations tziganes." Ibid., 77.

Gaudier exploits this song's association with gypsies in order to reinforce its subaltern character. In line with the "noble savage" trope, he construes Spain's otherness as the "shock" of the "purists" and "puritans"; but he also implies that only a French composer can make it effective. In contrast with the Spanish "noble savage," Gaudier's Bizet is a hero and a rebel in the fight against conventions; he is not an "exotic" outcast but a "civilized" artist who consciously seeks to push forward the limits of musical civilization with a constructive and enlightening spirit. In other words, Gaudier does not conceive the "Chanson bohème" as another world, but as a window open on it. Though Gaudier conceptualizes German music and culture as a cultural menace, he casts Spanish music as raw material and a racial Other, a subaltern element that helps to reinforce notions of French hegemony. In this sense, Gaudier's *Carmen* illustrates a general tendency found in the work of French critics and musicologists. From this perspective, Spanish music provides a picturesque backdrop for the battle between German and French music. Unlike the *hispanistes*, Gaudier was not sufficiently familiar with and fond of Spanish culture to raise it to the status of "nation," as the construction of the Latin Union required.

Landormy: Racial Purity, Authenticity and Imagination

Nietzsche's *Le cas Wagner* not only left its imprint on the work of anti-German critics and musicologists but also influenced pro-Germanists such as Paul Landormy. Like Gaudier, Landormy was likely to play an important role in shaping views of *Carmen* during the 1920s, thanks to his professional visibility and academic status. Together with the writer and musicologist Romain Rolland, he organized courses on music history at the École des Hautes Études (1904–1907) and served as a secretary for the music section of the Paris International Exhibition of 1937.[51] Landormy's monographs on Brahms, Schumann, Schubert and Gluck disavow any suspicions that he could have gotten carried away with anti-German biases.[52] Indeed, in his monograph *Bizet* (1924) he aimed at

---

[51] John Trevitt, "Landormy, Paul," *Grove Music Online*, http://www.oxfordmusiconline.com/subscriber/article/grove/music/15950 (accessed April 15, 2011); Fulcher describes his last period as "fascist," because he wrote for fascist journals. Jane F. Fulcher, "Musical Style, Meaning, and Politics in France on the Eve of the Second World War," *Journal of Musicology* 13, no. 4 (October 1, 1995): 443. According to Fulcher, Landormy was formerly involved in the Popular Front. Ibid., 445. It is true that Landormy endorses the Christian patriotism in d'Indy's *Fervaal* (1897): Huebner, *French Opera*, 325. However, Landormy thought that Cocteau's *Le coq* was "ultra-protectionist." François de Medicis, "Darius Milhaud and the Debate on Polytonality in the French Press of the 1920s," *Music and Letters* 86, no. 4 (2005): 584.

[52] See Trevitt, "Landormy," for details on this monograph.

disassociating *Carmen* from Italianate music and, most especially *verismo*, rather than from German music—as shown in this excerpt:

> We arrive at the last pages of the score, in which Bizet reaches the limits of musical pathos by way of the smallest and simplest means. It is impossible to be more poignant in a greater, more extraordinary and more profoundly humane way, in fewer notes than Bizet has written. There is a supreme force rendered with the greatest concision; and if that force is violence, it is not brutality. It is not the accumulation of material means that allows it to obtain that effect, but a just declamation and the power of the expressive accent. There is nothing here of the facile procedures employed by Puccini in *Tosca* to shake our nerves without ever talking to our heart. The verists may claim in vain the example of Bizet. They have not understood its signification.[53]

A comparison with the passage below, from *Le Cas Wagner*, allows us to appreciate the extent to which Landormy drew inspiration from Nietzsche:

> Have we ever heard more painful and tragic accents on the stage? See how they are obtained! Without affectation! Without any false effort! Without the lies of the great style![54]

Rather than targeting Wagner—as Nietzsche did—Landormy humanizes the violent elements in *Carmen*, and pits them against the vulgarity and brutality that he, just like many other critics, perceived in *verismo* since its heyday.[55] While

---

[53] "Nous arrivons à ces dernières pages de la partition dans lesquelles Bizet, par les moyens les plus brefs et les plus simples, atteint les limites du pathétique musical. Il est impossible d'être plus poignant, de l'être d'une façon plus large, plus grande, plus profondément humaine, et de l'être en moins de notes que n'en a écrit Bizet. C'est la suprême force dans l'extrême concision. Et si cette force est violence, elle n'est point brutalité. L'effet n'est pas obtenu par l'accumulation des moyens matériels, mais par la justesse de la déclamation et la puissance de l'accent expressif. Il n'y a rien là du procédé facile qu'un Puccini emploiera dans la Tosca pour nos secouer les nerfs sans jamais parler à notre chœur. Les 'véristes' se réclameront en vain de l'exemple de Bizet. Ils n'ont pas su en comprendre la signification." Paul Landormy, *Bizet* (Paris: F. Alcan, 1924), 204.

[54] "A-t-on jamais entendu sur la scène des accents plus douloureux, plus tragiques? Et comment sont-ils obtenus! Sans grimace! Sans faux-monnayage! Sans le mensonge du grand style!" Nietzsche, *Le cas Wagner*, 4. See especially the following two sentences from Landormy's quoted passage: "Bizet reaches the limits of musical pathos by way of the smallest and simplest means"; "it is impossible to be more poignant in a greater, more extraordinary and more profoundly humane way." ("Bizet, par les moyens les plus brefs et les plus simples, atteint les limites du pathétique musical. Il est impossible d'être plus poignant, de l'être d'une façon plus large, plus grande, plus profondément humaine, et de l'être en moins de notes que n'en a écrit Bizet.")

[55] On verismo and vulgarity see Andreas Giger, "Verismo: Origin, Corruption, and Redemption of an Operatic Term," *Journal of the American Musicological Society* 60, no. 2 (2007): 281–283. Furthermore, this article questions the validity and limits of the term verismo.

acknowledging the presence of pathetic and violent elements in *Carmen*, he packages them in the then-current Apollonian rhetoric of neoclassicism, which honored values such as "concision" and "simplicity," to use some of his expressions.

Landormy's *Bizet* is also remarkable for how it undoes or reverses some of Nietzsche's more problematic rhetorical constructions. Landormy understood that, although *Le cas Wagner* represented rich and powerful cultural capital at the service of French music nationalism, some of its passages undermined the very idea of Western or European civilization and hegemony that he and other French critics upheld through the example of Bizet. Landormy seems to have addressed, more particularly, the next passage, from *Le cas Wagner*, in which Nietzsche contradicts his own description of *Carmen* as a French and Mediterranean work, and places it outside of civilization:

> We are here, in all respects, in a different climate, where another sensuality, sensibility and serenity find expression. This music is cheerful, but its cheerfulness is not at all French or German; it is African, since fatality hovers over it and its happiness is short, sudden and merciless. I envy Bizet because he has the courage to show that sensibility, one that had not hitherto found expression in the music of civilized Europe—I mean this meridional, coppery, ardent sensibility....[56]

In what reads like a direct response to this passage, Landormy argued against allegations that Bizet's music was not French or Mediterranean:

> Let us not forget that *Carmen* is not everything for Bizet, and that, in a more moderate, sweet and nuanced tone, he has written another masterwork, *l'Arlésienne*, which is less "African," and only preserves the French climate from its Mediterranean outlook.[57]

Landormy turns to another work, *l'Arlésienne*, in search of signs of racial "purity." In this he was most likely influenced by the writer and musicologist Rolland, with whom he had organized courses on music history at the École des Hautes

---

[56] "Nous voici, à tous les égards, sous un autre climat. Une autre sensualité, une autre sensibilité, une autre sérénité s'expriment ici. Cette musique est gaie; mais ce n'est point d'une gaieté française ou allemande. Sa gaieté est africaine; la fatalité plane au-dessus d'elle, son bonheur est court, soudain, sans merci. J'envie Bizet parce qu'il a eu le courage de cette sensibilité, une sensibilité qui jusqu'à présent n'avait pas trouvé d'expression dans la musique de l'Europe civilisée—je veux dire cette sensibilité méridionale, cuivrée, ardente...." Nietzsche, *Le cas Wagner*, 5.

[57] "N'oublions pas cependant que Carmen n'est pas tout pour Bizet, et que, dans une gamme de couleurs et de sentiments plus modérée, plus douce et peut-être plus nuancée, il a écrit un autre chef-d'œuvre, l'Arlésienne, moins 'africain,' et qui, de la Méditerranée, ne retient que le climat français." Landormy, *Bizet*, 217.

Études between 1904 and 1907. In his monograph *Musiciens d'aujourd'hui* (1908), Romain Rolland argued that

> *Carmen*, and above all *l'Arlésienne*, are the masterworks of the Latin *drame lyrique*. Their style is bright, concise, definite; their design is traced with an incisive accuracy. This music is full of sunshine and action; it draws its aristocratic distinction from popular sources, and contrasts with Wagner's philosophical symphonies.[58]

Landormy may have been inspired by Rolland's choice of *l'Arlésienne*, alongside *Carmen*, as an example of Latin or Mediterranean, anti-Wagnerian music.

One could argue that a denouement of suicide for love hardly matches the "sweet and nuanced tone" that Landormy finds in *l'Arlésienne*; instead, it rather tells of the taste for tragic endings that began working its way to the stage of the Opéra Comique in the early 1870s.[59] However, *l'Arlésienne* problematizes some of the cultural dilemmas that concerned Landormy. To be more precise, they were already encapsulated in Alphonse Daudet eponymous short story from his *Lettres de mon moulin* (1869), which he later adapted into a melodrama for Bizet to add music to.

Set in a *mas* or rural house in Arles, in the region of Provence, *l'Arlésienne* could arguably be regarded as a "regionalist" work. By regionalist work, I mean not so much one that meets an anticentralist agenda, but one that depicts the countryside as a respite from perceptions of urban culture as being corrupt; one that seeks to appease cultural anxieties over cultural miscegenation and hybridization in the cities, raised by pre-fascist intellectuals such as Maurras and Barrès.[60] As in most regionalist operas by Séverac and Canteloube, "corruption" in *l'Arlésienne* comes from outside the rural environment in which the action is set, a place whose anonymity facilitates the abstraction and, hence, sublimation of the ideals at stake. Having formerly loved a man called Estève, l'Arlésienne threatens to obliterate the fantasy of marital purity on which marriage is conceived in the local community depicted by Daudet. Therefore, she embodies the equivalent of a foreign, invasive corruption, represented in other regionalist works. Yet, by

---

[58] "Carmen et surtout L'Arlésienne sont les chefs-d'oeuvre du drame lyrique latin. Le style en est lumineux, concis, définitif; le dessin des figures est tracé avec une justesse incisive. Cette musique, pleine de soleil et d'action, qui retrempe aux sources populaires son aristocratique distinction, fait contraste avec les symphonies philosophiques de Wagner." Romain Rolland, *Musiciens d'aujourd'hui*. (Paris: Hachette et Cie, 1908).

[59] Perhaps as a reminiscence of the mobilization that the Franco-Prussian War and the ensuing Commune had elicited on all areas of musical activity, including the Opéra and Opéra Comique—and of which *Carmen* constitutes another example. Jess Tyre, "Music in Paris During the Franco-Prussian War and the Commune," *Journal of Musicology* 22, no. 2 (April 1, 2005): 175–178.

[60] Wright, *Regionalist Movement in France*, 3–24.

contrast, l'Arlésienne does not come from the city, that is, from Paris, but from Provence, as denoted by her sobriquet. Through a consequent impression of removal and—related to it—aesthetic and social sublimation, *l'Arlésienne* arguably contributed to reinforcing the sharp cultural divide between northern and southern France from the 1870s.[61]

Different from *Carmen*, therefore, *l'Arlésienne* obliterates racial difference, insofar as its geographical and cultural scope remains confined to the Midi. Writing in the late 1920s, Landormy did not perceive the Midi as the cultural Other that it once represented for Parisians. Moreover, he could link constructions of the Midi as being Mediterranean and Latin—put forward by Maurras and Mistral[62]—with the aesthetics of neoclassicism. Unsurprisingly, Landormy couched Bizet's score for *l'Arlésienne* in a neoclassical rhetoric, as if it were a work by Stravinsky or one of Les Six. He described *l'Arlésienne* as displaying the "simplest means," and as a token that "Bizet has the nervous suppleness of a Latin"[63]; in a more anti-German fashion, he characterized *l'Arlésienne* as the expression of an "art without effort and reflection"; an "art which is not proper to a sentimental or an intellectual, but to a sensitive person"; and art that "ignores the long meditations" and is "incapable, also, of the slow affective reaction which, in others, spread in long and infinitely propagated undulations."[64] As a corollary to this passage of anti-German rhetoric, he bluntly added that "Bizet is not a Wagner or a Franck."[65] Interestingly enough, Landormy yielded to anti-German propaganda when it came to enshrining Bizet in the French canon. Coming from a pro-German critic, this stance suggests that he found no available way of defending Bizet's Frenchness other than severing it from—and opposing it to—notions of German music.

Like Nietzsche, Landormy views *Carmen* from the prism of racial otherness. What Nietzsche regarded as alluring expressions of an African sensibility and sensuality, however, Landormy saw with contempt. His approach to Spanish culture strikes one as bigoted and racist, as he calls the Spaniards "pretentious" (*fanfarons*) and "brutes." Moreover, he reinforces notions of the South as being uncivilized by remarking that Don José is less "pretentious" because he comes from the Basque Country, in northern Spain.[66]

---

[61] Theodore Zeldin, *A History of French Passions 1848–1945: Intellect, Taste and Anxiety* (Oxford University Press, 1993), 44.

[62] Musk, "Regionalism, Latinite," 226–249.

[63] "les moyens les plus simples"; "Bizet a la souplesse nerveuse du Latin" Landormy, *Bizet*, 217.

[64] "art sans effort et sans réflexion." Ibid., 217; "Art qui n'est point d'un sentimental ni d'un intellectuel, mais d'un sensitif"; "Bizet ignore les longues méditations"; "incapable aussi de ces lentes réactions affectives qui, chez certains, s'étalent en de larges ondulations indéfiniment propagées." Ibid., 218.

[65] "Bizet n'est ni un Wagner, ni un Franck." Ibid., 218.

[66] "fanfarons" "brutes." Ibid., 139.

But *Carmen* had gained too much popularity for Landormy to simply dismiss it from the French canon. Its "African sensibility" was not necessarily a liability, provided it allowed conceptualizing the "subaltern" Spanish elements as "foreign" to the "purity" of Bizet's "French" music. Just like Gaudier, Landormy directed his analysis of the Habanera at placing Bizet's arrangement above Yradier's "original" song.[67] He remarked that, in the Habanera, "one can observe how, in the hands of the genius, even the dullest invention can become suddenly transfigured."[68] Thus, he echoed the widespread belief—also shared by Gaudier—that French composers had elevated "Spanish music" to a higher form of art. He also argued that Yradier's song presented a "Spain travestied in French garments, in the Parisian vogue of the Second Empire," thus implying that Bizet's arrangement was more "authentic" than the original.[69] This stance becomes even more explicit in Landormy's analysis of the entr'acte that preludes the fourth act, based on the *polo* "Cuerpo bueno alma divina" from Manuel García's opera *El criado fingido* (1804). Landormy contends that "Bizet's page is infinitely more 'Spanish' than García's," and argues that "the dance spectacles by musicians coming from Spain" have "instructed him much better about the particularities of Hispanism than all the so-called Spanish songs, which have spread all around Europe in forged versions."[70]

Landormy's defense of the authenticity of Bizet's arrangements seems consistent with his perception of *Carmen* as an extraneous, "African" work. A defense of authenticity allows him to legitimize the construction of cultural hegemony, as it implies that French composers can outdo Spaniards in composing "Spanish music." This stance matches Said's contention that, in Orientalist cultural practices, the Other is spoken for instead of listened to.[71] Representations of the Other as subaltern constituted one of the main discursive strategies aimed at justifying the colonial enterprise, as it became manifest in the organization of the World Fairs in Paris.[72] Just as Laparra described Paris as the "forum of humankind"—as discussed in Chapter 3—Landormy helped to conceptualize it as a diasporic, metropolitan, ecumenical and cosmopolitan site where all of the world's cultures meet and are represented, sanctioned and, ultimately, legitimized under French scrutiny.[73]

---

[67] He had first broached this in "L'hispanisme de Bizet," *La revue musicale* (August 1923), from which he quotes several passages.

[68] "on s'aperçoit comment, entre les mains du génie, la plus plate des inventions peut tout d'un coup se transfigurer." Landormy, *Bizet*, 161.

[69] "Espagne travestie sous des habits à la française, à la mode parisienne du second Empire." Ibid., 174.

[70] "la page de Bizet est infiniment plus 'espagnole' que celle de Garcia"; "beaucoup mieux instruit des particularités de l'hispanisme que *toutes* les chansons dites d'Espagne dont on promenait alors à travers l'Europe les contrefaçons banalisés." Ibid., 180.

[71] Said, *Orientalism*, 3.

[72] Fauser, *Musical Encounters*, 5–8; Pasler, *Composing the Citizen*, 549–550.

[73] "forum moral de l'humanité." Laparra, "Espagne" (November 19, 1920).

Landormy examined the sources of *Carmen* in order to defend its "authenticity." He started with Mérimée's novel, which he regarded as a proxy for Bizet's reading of Spanish culture, given that the latter had never traveled to Spain. According to Landormy, Mérimée's *Carmen* "did not just hold the value of an artwork, but also that of a document," since its author had "slept in the humblest inns and associated with the common people, peasants, workers and even bandits."[74] Thus, Landormy conceptualizes popular culture as the repository of national identity.[75] In order to place Bizet's music above popular culture, however, he argues that the "lack of precision" affecting Bizet's work constitutes an "indisputable advantage," and exclaims: "how many countries lose their poetry, to our eyes, when regarded from too close, when contemplated other than in a dream, other than through our whimsical fantasy, which becomes hindered, fettered, broken through contact with facts and their dry exactitude!"[76] The tension between documentary authenticity and imagination just shown reflects the contradictions inherent to the necessity of French cultural propaganda to mask its strategies of cultural hegemony in order to make them less suspicious and, hence, more efficient. By defending the accurateness of Bizet's representation of Spain, Landormy differed from most other critics, who, as we shall see, felt that undermining its authenticity was a necessary step toward reasserting its "French" qualities.

Tiersot: Folklore and the "French" Imagination

In 1925, *Le Ménestrel* published Julient Tiersot's "Bizet et la musique espagnole," which became one of the most influential studies of *Carmen*. Two years after, the American journal *The Musical Quarterly* published an English translation, which facilitated its further spreading.[77] Unlike Landormy, Tiersot has been the object of increasing scholarly interest, given that he played a key role in mapping cultural differences in France through his lengthy and substantial studies on French

---

[74] "n'avais pas seulement la valeur d'une œuvre d'art mais aussi celle d'un document"; "couché dans les moindres auberges, fréquenté les gens du peuple, paysans, ouvriers et même bandits." Landormy, *Bizet*, 173.

[75] A view fueled by the rise of populism in 1920s France and Europe. Brass, *Peasants, Populism and Postmodernism*, 2–20. See also Brass, "The Agrarian Myth, the 'New' Populism and the 'New' Right," *Economic and Political Weekly* 32, no. 4 (1997): 27–42; Fauser, *Musical Encounters*, 253.

[76] "défaut de précision"; "incontestable avantage"; "Que de pays perdent à nos yeux de leur poésie pour être considérés de trop près, pour être vus autrement qu'en rêve et à travers le caprice de notre fantaisie, qui se trouve alors empêché, arrêté, brisé par le contact des faits et leur exactitude toute sèche!" Landormy, *Bizet*, 176–177.

[77] Julien Tiersot, "Bizet et la musique espagnole, I," *Le ménestrel*, 87, no. 39 (September 25, 1925): 394–395; Tiersot, "Bizet and Spanish Music," *Musical Quarterly*, no. 4 (1927): 566–581. Quotations in English will be taken from the 1927 translation.

folklore in the provinces.[78] Tiersot's reading of *Carmen* shows an unremitting and far-fetched attempt to construe Bizet's musical sources as folklore, that is, as an anonymous and fixed repertoire transmitted orally. This stance is consistent with Tiersot's folklorist background, and suggests that he could thus seek to reduce music to a category he found more manageable. The cultural implications of this approach, however, are far-reaching and worthy of examination. As I shall argue, his professional competency as a folklorist could not remain impervious to the agency of narratives of cultural hegemony, which underpin his attempts to cast Spanish culture as subaltern.

Throughout his study, Tiersot tries to reinforce notions of French hegemony by debasing the status of his Spanish sources and deliberately confusing them with a class- and race-oriented, hierarchical conception of popular music. Tiersot argues that Bizet composed the Habanera believing that "El arreglito" was an anonymous popular song. He contends that, even before consulting "Échos d'Espagne," Bizet had heard it "sung by a lady" and transcribed it by ear, learning about its authorship only much later—a detail that no other scholar has ever documented.[79] With the same purpose, Tiersot denies that Yradier is a "master," drives him close to popular music and ultimately casts him away from European music:

> Yradier certainly does not deserve to be ranked among the masters; yet this musician of Spanish America had so absorbed the impressions of his environment that he could seize and record intonations and rhythms sufficiently different from those of European music so as to afford a superficial satisfaction to amateurs of exotic sensations. He was intermediary between the anonymous authors of folk-songs and the veritable creators of art.[80]

In order to deny that Bizet borrowed from a Spanish composer, Tiersot depicts Yradier as a popular musician—just as Laparra did. Tiersot's description of

---

[78] Pasler numbers Tiersot among those "republican scholars" who "adopted evolutionist, assimilationist perspectives when attempting to understand diversity within the French population." Jann Pasler, "Race and Nation: Musical Acclimatisation and the Chansons Populaires in Third Republic France," in *Western Music and Race*, ed. Julie Brown (Cambridge: Cambridge University Press, 2007), 154. See also Pasler, "Theorizing Race in Nineteenth-Century France: Music as Emblem of Identity," *Musical Quarterly* 89, no. 4 (December 21, 2006): 459–504. Fauser, *Musical Encounters*, 252–278.

[79] "aurait entendu chanter par une dame." Tiersot, "Bizet et la musique espagnole," 394–395.

[80] "Yradier mérite certainement pas d'être mis au rang des maîtres. Mais ce musicien de l'Amérique espagnole s'était imprégné d'une ambiance grâce à laquelle il avait appris à noter des intonations et des rythmes assez différents de ceux de la musique européenne pour donner une satisfaction superficielle aux amateurs de sensations exotiques. Il était intermédiaire entre les auteurs anonymes des chansons populaires et les véritables créateurs d'art." Julien Tiersot, "Bizet et la musique espagnole (II)," *Le ménestrel*, vol. 87, no. 40 (October 2, 1925), 401.

Yradier as a Latin American musician is striking not just (or not so much) for its inaccuracy—Yradier came from the Basque Country, in northern Spain—but because he takes that as the basis for defending the authenticity of his Spanish music. Thus, Tiersot follows the Orientalist tendency to lump together cultures deemed distant, "foreign," or "exotic." Perhaps Tiersot was mistaken about the Cuban associations of the Habanera, which, despite evoking *mulatas* or mixed-raced women from Havana, was mainly cultivated by Spanish musicians involved in maritime commerce with Cuba. This confusion, plus the alluring and sensual syncopation of the habanera rhythm, may also lie behind Tiersot's description of Yradier's music as "sufficiently different" from "European music," with which he ultimately casts the Spanish elements in *Carmen* as subaltern and extraneous to European civilization. Throughout his article, Tiersot dwells on similar strategies. Commenting on the so-called Seguidilla—in truth, a Tirana—"Près des remparts de Séville,"[81] which opens the second act, he argues that "Bizet knew nothing of these forms"—the seguidillas—"so different from all that was familiar to France at his time"; he contends that "nothing is more remote from the popular tonality than, for example, [Bizet's] Seguidilla, so rich in harmony"; he explains that distance as the product of "the inventive genius of the well-trained musician."[82]

The most remarkable aspect of Tiersot's review, therefore, consists in the extent of his rhetorical investment and the arguments that he employs to support constructions of French cultural hegemony. Nowhere does this show more clearly and compellingly than in his study of the entr'acte that precedes Act IV, which Gaudier had also written about. Tiersot undertakes a lengthy and painstaking analysis aimed at "discover[ing] in the folk-songs the secret of Spanish character of Bizet's music."[83] As in his description of the Habanera, he denies that the entr'acte is based on the music of a Spanish composer and connects it directly with the popular tradition from which García's song allegedly originated. He argues that Bizet had "composed upon it a new variation" and marveled at "how vastly superior" it is. Once again, Tiersot cast Bizet as a creator and his Spanish source, García, as a mere transcriber. He argued that, although "the general aspect is similar in the Spanish songs and in the French number [...] this latter is not a transcription pure and simple."[84] Much as Tiersot was convinced

---

[81] I owe the identification of this song as a Tirana instead of a Seguidilla to Richard Langham Smith.

[82] "Bizet n'a rien su de ces formes, si différentes de tout ce que l'on connaissait en France en son temps"; "rien n'est plus éloigné de la tonalité populaire que, par exemple, la Séguedille, riche en harmonie"; "Le génie inventif du musicien savant." Tiersot, "Bizet et la musique espagnole (II)," 402.

[83] "découvririons dans les chansons populaires le secret du caractère espagnol de la musique de Bizet." Julien Tiersot, "Bizet et la musique espagnole (IV)," *Le ménestrel*, vol. 87, no. 42 (October 16, 1925), 417.

[84] "composé sur elle une nouvelle variation. Combien celle-ci est supérieure!"; "Le mouvement général, l'allure, la cadence, tout cela est paraille"; celui-ci n'est pas une transcription pure et simple." Tiersot, "Bizet et la

that García's *polos* are just a reflection of the popular tradition on which *Carmen* is allegedly based, he used them as the basis for his assertion of the superiority of Bizet's arrangements. Interestingly, rather than focusing on "Cuerpo bueno, alma divina," he turned to "Yo que soy contrabandista," from García's operatic monologue *El poeta calculista* (1805). This apparent mistake may stem from the fact that, as Locke has pointed out, there reigned some confusion regarding the nature of the source behind the version found in *Echos d'Espagne*.[85] However, it may also reflect Tiersot's intention to reinforce the undeniable similarity between the two *polos* with the purpose of defending their allegedly popular origin, so as to argue that García's "part in the invention was infinitesimal." Indeed, he deems the two *polos* an expression of a "highly characteristic physiognomy" that "those popular Spanish songs" derive "from that *je ne sais quoi* that distinguishes the spirit of various races."[86]

Tiersot defines the opera *El poeta calculista* as a *tonadilla*, that is, an eighteenth-century theatrical intermezzo displaying popular characters and situations, which grew into larger forms with sparse musical numbers.[87] Although García had composed some early *tonadillas*, *El poeta calculista* cannot be ascribed to that genre on account of the extent of its musical content, the virtuoso demands of the vocal part and the "elevated" nature of the subject—a poet's conflict with his ambitions and his reality. Indeed, Radomsky describes *El poeta* as the equivalent, in Spanish language, to the French spectacles that sought to satisfy the cosmopolitan anxieties of an "élite Spanish audience."[88] Through a misleading ascription to the *tonadilla*, however, Tiersot tries to present "Cuerpo bueno" as popular material that Bizet reinvents. Indeed, he mistakenly argues that the *tonadillas* "belonged to the domain of popular art" and that "their authors were undoubtedly musicians of only slight cultivation."[89] True, the *tonadillas* displayed popular characters, appealed to popular audiences and,

---

musique espagnole (IV)," 418. Tiersot even questions the testimonial validity of Bizet's signed slip requesting to consult *Echos d'Espagne* at the Conservatoire Library; he also doubts about Fétis's identification of García's *polo* as Bizet's source, on the basis that he did not provide sufficient evidence. Beardsley would contest this view: "Bizet is only the arranger. The composer is Manuel Garcia." Theodore S. Beardsley, "The Spanish Musical Sources of Bizet's Carmen," *Inter-American Music Review*, no. 10 (1989).

[85] However, Locke does not point out Tiersot's mistake in identifying the source. Locke, "Spanish Local Color," 319–336.

[86] "la physionomie si caracterisée"; "ces mélodies populaires espagnoles"; "ce 'je ne sais quoi' qui distingue l'esprit des races diverses." Tiersot, "Bizet et la musique espagnole (IV)," 417.

[87] Roger Alier. "Tonadilla," in *Grove Music Online*. http://www.oxfordmusiconline.com/subscriber/article/grove/music/28100 (accessed April 15, 2011).

[88] James Radomski, *Manuel García: 1775–1832: Chronicle of the Life of a Bel Canto Tenor at the Dawn of Romanticism* (Oxford: Oxford University Press, 2000), 68.

[89] "Ces œuvres était, à proprement parler, du domaine de l'art populaire. Sans doute elles avait pour auteurs des musiciens, de peu de culture d'ailleurs." Ibid., 417.

in García's time, suffered from the criticism of the Spanish supporters of the Enlightenment and the Napoleonic occupation of 1808, the so-called *afrancesados*.[90] Yet, the *tonadillas* are far from anonymous or popular, as they reflect the interests and views of a certain social elite and, many times, were commissioned by the court.[91] Comparisons with the *tonadilla* provided Tiersot with further arguments to "authenticate" Bizet's sources. Spanish musicologists since Pedrell had construed the *tonadilla* as the first genre that embodied resistance to the Italian cultural "invasion."[92] Despite his attempts to undermine García's authorship of "Cuerpo bueno," Tiersot construes him in a way that could possibly suit his interests as a "Spanish" musician—just like he did with Yradier. Tiersot reports García's alleged "obscure birth," and how "it is said that Gypsy blood ran in his veins," thus reinforcing his otherness[93]; he contends that at the time García composed *El poeta calculista*, "he had not yet emerged from the environment to which he was bound by atavistic ties," and that he sought to elicit "the applause of the populace."[94] Recent research has allowed us to establish the falseness of such testimonies. The alleged "atavistic environment" was the city of Cadix, in southern Spain, which, rather unusually in its time, boasted up to three theaters. In 1812, only a few decades after García's birth (1775), Cadix led a liberal, Enlightened revolution against aristocratic privileges in Spain.[95] García left Madrid for Paris shortly after the première of *El poeta* in 1805, as he failed to secure performances for his works and experienced dire economic straits—just as Falla did a century later.[96] By contending that García sought "the applause of the populace," Tiersot echoed the *afrancesados*' view of the *tonadilla* as being "debased" and "vulgar."

The same contradiction that was present in Landormy's *Bizet* underpins Tiersot's study of *Carmen*, namely, that he tried to establish *Carmen's* centrality in the French canon on the basis of the alleged authenticity of its Spanish sources. Their reactions are strikingly similar, as can be gauged from the close of Tiersot's article:

---

[90] Such as Gaspar Melchor de Jovellanos and Leandro Fernández de Moratín, who embraced French Enlightenment culture and despised Spanish popular culture. On this polemic see Rafael Lamas, "Zarzuela and the Anti-Musical Prejudice of the Spanish Enlightenment," *Hispanic Review* 74, no. 1 (2006): 45–49; Alberto Romero Ferrer, "Un ataque a la estética de la razón. La crítica ilustrada frente a la tonadilla escénica: Jovellanos, Iriarte y Leandro Fernández de Moratín," *Cuadernos de ilustración y romanticismo* 1, no. 1 (1991): 105–127.

[91] Lamas, "Zarzuela," discusses zarzuela as a hybrid of high and low.

[92] Carreras, "Hijos de Pedrell," 151–152.

[93] "de naissance incertaine"; "il avait dans les veines, dit-on, du sang de gitana." Tiersot, "Bizet et la musique espagnole (IV)," 417.

[94] "Il n'était pas encore sorti du milieu auquel le rattachait cet atavisme"; "l'applaudissement du peuple." Ibid., 417.

[95] James Radomski, *Manuel García*, 9.

[96] Ibid., 75.

> Though he [Bizet] had never visited Spain, he knew it through keenest intuition—he divined it. This constitutes no mean addition to his merit; and it is thanks to this intimate, though physically remote, emotional experience that Carmen possesses the vitality which has made it the most widely known French work in the world of to-day.[97]

A tension between intuition and documentation leaps from this passage. In order to vindicate Bizet's work, Landormy denies that the value of Spanish music is a matter of birth or blood and claims that "Spanishness" can be conveyed vicariously, by way of "intuition." He undermines "authenticity" by claiming that the value of *Carmen* can be universally sanctioned and recognized so as to make it "the most widely known French work in the world of to-day." This stance, however, stands in contradiction to his attempts to authenticate Bizet's purported sources, discussed above. Tiersot's paean of intuition led him to compare Bizet's depictions of Provence and Spain in *l'Arlésienne* and *Carmen* respectively:

> It is true that Bizet had a particular ability for assimilating the proper features of peoples he had no affinity with. The music in *l'Arlésienne* is deeply Provençal [...] Nevertheless, Bizet has never been to Provence: he has hardly traveled through it by train. As regards Spain, he has not even approached it.
> It is, therefore, by virtue of his imagination, probably stimulated by readings other than Mérimée, that he has temporarily acquired a Spanish soul.[98]

In this excerpt, Spain becomes the equivalent of a French province, that is, a part of the national imaginary that may be evoked in the nation-building process. In Tiersot's view, Spain and the French provinces—represented by Provence—stand as cultural peripheries. They both lie within the reach of the metropolitan imagination enacted in Bizet's oeuvre. By pairing Spain and Provence, Tiersot could domesticate Spanish difference, make it seem less African and more

---

[97] "Sans avoir lui-même connu l'Espagne, il en a eu l'intuition la plus vive: il l'a devinée. Ce ne fut pas de sa part un médiocre mérite, et c'est grâce à cette intime, quoique lointaine pénétration, que Carmen a dû cette vitalité qui a fait d'elle l'œuvre française la plus répandue qui soit aujourd'hui à travers le mon de." Tiersot, "Bizet et la musique espagnole (IV)," 418.

[98] "Il est certain que Bizet avait un génie tout particulier pour s'assimiler les accents propres à des peuples avec lesquels lui-même n'avait aucune affinité. Sa musique de l'Arlésienne est foncièrement provençale [...] Cependant Bizet n'a jamais été en Provence: à peine y a-t-il passé en chemin de fer. Quant à l'Espagne, il n'en a même pas approché. / C'est donc par l'effet de sa seule imagination, probablement échauffée par quelques lectures autres que celle de Prosper Mérimée, qu'il a pu se faire ainsi, pour un temps, une âme espagnole." Tiersot, "Bizet et la musique espagnole (I)," 393.

European or French, and yet peripheral. From that perspective, the gypsy Carmen could be regarded as the Arlésienne, the Provençal peasant woman of Daudet's tales, an Other that was, after all, one of "us," and no longer the "threatening" gypsy.[99] For Tiersot, "Frenchifying" *Carmen* did not mean "de-Hispanizing" it, but "de-gypsyfying it," domesticating García's allegedly "gypsy" sources and its racial difference so as to turn Spain into a close cultural periphery of France. Tiersot's attitude echoes a European conceptualization of the "peasant" as the ultimate repository of national values and racial purity, at the expense of groups tagged as racially Other, most conspicuously the gypsies.[100] Bartók entertained a similar racist view of the role that gypsies had played in the construction of "Hungarian music."[101] The *cante jondo* competition organized by Falla and Lorca in Granada in 1922, in order to cast flamenco as a fixed, ancestral, oral and folkloric tradition, instead of a popular tradition that underwent constant changes, may be regarded similarly.[102]

As I have pointed out above, Tiersot's work shows striking similarities with Landormy's. In order to avoid having *Carmen* seem too extraneous to French identity, they both praised Bizet's capacity to imagine Spain from a cautionary distance. Furthermore, they used *l'Arlésienne* as an antidote or a corrective for *Carmen*'s racial otherness. More relevantly, as we shall see, Tiersot and Landormy were the only critics to defend the authenticity of *Carmen* as a way of upholding French cultural hegemony.

Negotiating "Spanish music" Through *Carmen*: Laparra and Turina

As we have seen, the writings of Landormy and Tiersot can be characterized by a tension between a tendency to reinforce Spanish difference and, opposed to it, attempts to domesticate it. These two opposed attitudes are representative of larger cultural agendas. The example of *La vie brève*, discussed in Chapter 4, shows how similar stances on the part of other French critics underpinned the negotiation of the ontological barrier that, in the critical imagination, mediated

---

[99] During his visit to the 1889 World's Fair, Tiersot perceived Hungarian music to be inferior on account of its gypsy elements. Fauser, *Musical Encounters*, 256.

[100] Brass, *Peasants, Populism and Postmodernism*, 2–20. See also Brass, "The Agrarian Myth," 27–42.

[101] Brown, "Bartók, the Gypsies, and Hybridity in Music," 119–142.

[102] Mitchell, *Flamenco Deep Song*, 160–177. See Manuel de Falla, "Concurso de 'Cante Jondo' (canto primitivo andaluz)," in Falla, *Escritos sobre música y músicos*, ed. Federico Sopeña (Buenos Aires: Espasa-Calpe, 1950), 146: "serán preferidos los concursantes cuyo estilo popular de canto se ajuste a las viejas prácticas de los *cantaores* clásicos, evitando todo floreo abusivo y devolviendo al *cante jondo* aquella admirable sobriedad, desgraciadamente perdida, que constituía una de sus más grandes bellezas."

between shared notions of French and Spanish music, during a period of intense cultural flow across the Pyrenees. To some extent, the process rested upon widespread discourses on ethnicity and nationality, aimed at delimiting French and Spanish identities and defining them as the exclusive ground for native Frenchmen and Spaniards respectively. By contrast, other agents involved in the negotiation aimed at tearing down or crossing those barriers and undermining the sort of cultural protectionism just described. Some of these agents, however, falsely conceived of transcultural flow as circulating only in one direction. Consequently, they predicated it on a coercive conception of influence, which they understood as a form of cultural propaganda. By opening "Spanish music" to the agency of French composers while erecting a fence around "French music" as the exclusive ground of "native" French people, some French critics and musicians sought to reinforce French cultural hegemony and influence. Moreover, some of them upheld the chauvinistic view that such French composers as Ravel, Debussy, Chabrier and—of course—Bizet had outdone their Spanish counterparts in composing "Spanish music." Thanks to its centrality in aesthetic debates, *Carmen* helped to articulate and test the validity of these and similar arguments during the 1920s.

One of the French composers who regarded *Carmen* from this chauvinistic viewpoint was Raoul Laparra. As we have seen in Chapter 3, Laparra upheld the establishment of a radical cultural protectionism in Spain, while he described the Spanish territory as a battlefield in the fight against German music. In other words, he conceived of Spain as a cultural periphery of France and a privileged target for French cultural propaganda. In an article published in *Le Ménestrel* in November 1925, Laparra took issue with a passage from the yet-unpublished *Albéniz et Granados*, in which Collet described *Carmen* as a work whose "contribution to musical Hispanism is reduced to an artificial light such as the one projected by Schumann and, later, Hugo Wolf, Rimsky-Korsakov or Richard Strauss: that is to say, a 'Polonian' light, to use Albéniz's words."[103] Collet did not so much aim at redefining *Carmen*'s position in the French canon as undermining its Hispanism. He sought to defend the notion that "Albéniz is the very first to give the world, without the use of folklore, a Spanish work, conceived by an authentic Spaniard."[104] Laparra's response to Collet's argument, however, indicates how *Carmen* could help to negotiate formulations of "Spanish music" on the basis of personal ambitions on the one hand, and strategies for achieving cultural hegemony on the other:

[103] "n'apporte, sur l'hispanisme en musique, qu'une lumière aussi factice que celle que projetèrent Schumann et, plus tard, Hugo Wolf, Rimsky-Korsakov ou Richard Strauss: c'est-à-dire, une lumière 'polonaise,' pour parler comme Albéniz, connaisseur s'il en fut." Collet, *Albéniz et Granados*, 107.

[104] "Albéniz est bien le premier à donner au monde, sans recourir au folk-lore, une œuvre espagnole, conçue par un authentique Espagnol." Ibid., 107.

But I cannot see why *Carmen's couleur locale* is so artificial. I have always regarded it as a work of a singularly just intuition […] [It is] a French work, infinitely more Spanish, in an artistic sense, than most works being composed on the other side of the Pyrenees, which are altered by foreign concerns.[105]

By situating the Spanish music of French composers above the production of their Spanish counterparts, Laparra sought to legitimate his own position as a composer who strived to inject a sense of authenticity into notions of "Spanish music." Thus, he found a way to oppose racist forms of cultural protectionism such as Falla's attempts to redefine the expression of "authenticity" and "truth" in Spanish music, by delimiting it to those composers whom the latter regarded as native Spaniards—as we have discussed in Chapter 4.

Laparra's motivation becomes more evident in his monograph *Georges Bizet et l'Espagne* (1935), where he tried to elevate his own portrayals of Spain above the work of other French composers.[106] In this book, Laparra described *Carmen* as "a work of intuition, but not a lived work," insofar as "Bizet had viewed Spain through the popular documents that he possessed, but had never traveled there."[107] Thus, Laparra could defend the assertion that his own work was superior to *Carmen* on the basis of his firsthand experience of Spain.

The case of Laparra illustrates how descriptions of the Spanish elements in *Carmen* helped to redefine and mediate between preestablished notions of French and Spanish music, as well as to negotiate the position that individual agents occupied in that process. By undermining the authenticity of Bizet's *Carmen*, in his late monograph Laparra contributed to domesticating the cultural difference represented in that work, casting it in a French light.

In "Les 50 ans de Carmen," published in *Le courrier musical* in 1925, Joaquín Turina showed a similar concern for authenticity to Laparra's.[108] His intention was rather different, however, as he sought to qualify the Spaniard's input on "foreign" representations of the country. As a preliminary caveat, Turina's position may not be considered representative of the Spaniards' response to *Carmen*, which deserves detailed and careful analysis and does not respond to

---

[105] "Mais je ne vois pas ce que le côté couleur locale de Carmen a de si factice. Il m'a toujours semblé d'une intuition singulièrement juste […] [c'est] une œuvre française, infiniment plus espagnole, au sens artistique, qu'une foule d'ouvrages nés de l'autre côté des Pyrénées, mais altérés de préoccupations étrangères." Laparra, "Espagne," *Le ménestrel* (November 1925).

[106] Laparra, *Bizet et l'Espagne*.

[107] "une œuvre d'intuition, mais non une oeuvre vécue." Laparra, *Bizet et l'Espagne*, 42; "Bizet eut la vision de l'Espagne à travers la documentation populaire qu'il possédait, et ne s'y rendit jamais." Ibid., 5.

[108] Joaquín Turina, "Les 50 ans de Carmen," *Le courrier musical* (March 1925).

generalizations; rather it reflects a particular and individual agenda of a composer who, unlike many of his contemporaries—but just like Falla and Albéniz—engaged in a negotiation with French audiences and composers over the nature of the concept of "Spanish music." Furthermore, Turina wrote with hindsight, in a commemorative and empathetic mood sparked by *Carmen*'s fiftieth anniversary.

Turina argues that *Carmen* "does not interest the Spaniards [...] from a national point of view," and that they prefer "the passages which conserve—like Micaëla's—a remainder of Italian taste."[109] True, on the occasion of the Barcelona (1881) and Madrid (1887) premières, certain critics and members of the audience overtly criticized the way in which the Spaniards were depicted in *Carmen*.[110] It would be striking to witness such emotional responses fifty years after, at the time Turina wrote his article.[111] Indeed, through his general comments he seems to conceptualize the audience as an anonymous mass that reflects or echoes his own point of view. His remark suggests that Spaniards do not buy into Bizet's view of Spain and regard it as being "unrealistic" or "inauthentic." The Spaniards' alleged interest in the Micaëla passages clashes with the prevailing opinion among French critics, that she is a "foreign" character whose moral virtuosity, traditional vocal language and disembodied singing convey uprootedness, cultural detachment, or, more simply, "dullness."[112] From Turina's viewpoint, it seems as if the Spaniards turned to the uprooting passages in order not to conflict with *Carmen*'s "forged" Hispanism. He even suggests that Spaniards Italianized *Carmen*, as he argues that performances at the Teatro Real in Madrid have "altered several stage productions [...] so as to adapt them to the Spanish taste," and "have lain bare how much of *bel canto* there is in that work."[113] Turina's idea of the "Spanish taste" is, therefore, *bel canto*—by which

---

[109] "n'intéresse pas les Espagnols, au moins les contemporains, au point de vue national"; "en préférant toujours les endroits qui conservent—comme ceux de Micaëla—un reste de saveur italienne." Turina, "Les 50 ans de Carmen."

[110] Kertesz and Christoforidis, "Confronting Carmen," 89.

[111] Indeed, he admits that "due to the time elapsed, to that French atmosphere, one must admit that *Carmen*'s music is ours, and that the Spanish soul seems to be enclosed in it." ("Précisément, à cause du temps qui s'est écoulé, à cause de cette ambiance française, il faut reconnaître que la musique de Carmen est une des nôtres et que l'âme espagnole paraît y être enfermée"). Turina, "Les 50 ans de Carmen."

[112] With fifty years' hindsight, Tenroc still thought that "Cette Manon de tabagie, jouant du couteau, parut trop distante de la Dame blanche." Tenroc, "Les cinquante ans de Carmen. Un anniversaire." Landormy describes Micaëla as "insignificant, pale and dull," *Bizet*, 141–142; on the invention of Micaëla: "Loin d'en féliciter les inventeurs, il serait peut être plus équitable de leur chercher une excuse, et l'on peut en trouver une en constatant que l'appoint d'une voix de soprano léger était à peu près obligatoire dans l'équilibre des timbres de cette partition." Gauthier-Villars, *Georges Bizet*, 110; see also Gaudier, *Carmen de Bizet*, 34. Torchet described Micaëla as "une Alice aussi fade que rabattue." Julien Torchet, "Opéra Comique. Carmen," *Comœdia* (December 1907).

[113] "modifié diverses mises en scène, par exemple la scène populaire de la Plaza de Toros pour les adapter au goût espagnol"; "ont mis en relief combien il y a de bel canto dans cette œuvre." Turina, "Les 50 ans de Carmen."

he most likely meant Italian opera—which had reigned at the Teatro Real since its opening in 1850.[114]

Turina's own voice emerges at a later stage in his article, when he argues that the entr'acte before Act 4 constitutes the only popular theme in *Carmen*, and that

> in the rest of the work, it is possible to find very beautiful passages that bear Spanish color, forms and reminiscences, but that always present a very French form. As a matter of coincidence, it is precisely in those passages (in the first and fourth acts) that contain those admirable and genial modulations, that one would search in vain today and that no other composer has ever used. We ignore the genesis of those modulations, but it escapes all analysis.[115]

In sum, Turina regards *Carmen* as a "French" work "ornamented" with "inauthentic" and "superficial" Spanish color.[116] Much as that Spanish color may be fake, however, Turina ascribes to it a substantial role. By identifying *Carmen*'s "admirable and genial modulations" with the "Spanish" passages, Turina situates Spanish popular music at the origin of *Carmen*'s musical modernisms. His contention that those modulations "escape all analysis" arguably casts them away from the confines of "civilized" music. Just as the 1889 Exhibition had prompted French composers to use the Other as a source or inspiration for musical modernisms,[117] Turina believed that musical renovation stemmed from contact with "other" cultures. More importantly, Turina's recount of the Spanish audience disagreeing with Bizet's portrayal of Spain in *Carmen* contributes to the general tendency, widespread among French critics, to undermine the work's Hispanism with the purpose of facilitating its consolidation in the French canon, even if this could hardly be his intention.

[114] A royal foundation, the Teatro Real aimed at fulfilling the crown's taste for Italian opera, at the expense of other repertoires. A royal decree limited the number of operas by Spanish composers to be premièred at that institution, and stipulated that their librettos should be written in Italian. Kertesz and Christoforidis, "Confronting *Carmen*," 82; Joaquín Turina Gómez, *Historia del Teatro Real* (Madrid: Alianza, 1997). The Spanish critic Adolfo Salazar complained to the French press about the Italian taste reigning at the Teatro Real: Adolfo Salazar, "Lettre d'Espagne," *Le courier musical* (April 1918).

[115] "Dans le reste de l'œuvre, on rencontre de très beaux passages de couleur, de formes et de réminiscences espagnoles, mais toujours avec une forme très française. Et,—coïncidence étonnante—c'est précisément dans ceux passages (au 1er et 4e actes) que sont ces modulations admirables et géniales qu'on rechercherait en vain aujourd'hui et qui n'ont été employés par aucun autre compositeur. La genèse de ces modulations, nous ne la connaissons pas, mais elle échappent à toute analyse." Turina, "Les 50 ans de Carmen."

[116] Interestingly, no French critic questioned the authenticity of Carmen's Spanishness at the time of its première. Kerry Murphy, "Carmen: Couleur Locale or the Real Thing?" in *Music, Theater, and Cultural Transfer: Paris, 1830–1914*, ed. Annegret Fauser and Mark Everist (Chicago: University of Chicago Press, 2009), 307–314. Curiously enough, Turina identifies the song behind the prelude to act 4 as the anonymous "El Vito," which he locates in Joaquin Nin's collection of twenty popular Spanish songs—perhaps overlooking the fact that this collection saw light later than *Carmen*. Joaquin Nin, *Cantos populares españoles*, for voice and piano, 2 vols. (Paris: Max Eschig, 1923–1924). "El Vito" is number 18, vol. 2.

[117] Fauser, *Musical Encounters*, 200.

Undermining Authenticity: Vuillermoz

Perhaps no other musicologist went at such lengths to contest any presumptions about the Hispanic authenticity of *Carmen* than Émile Vuillermoz. After graduating from the Conservatoire, Vuillermoz became a staunch opponent of its rival institution, the Schola Cantorum.[118] Curiously enough, the First World War mitigated his former anti-German penchant such that by 1930 his concept of tradition encompassed Bach, Beethoven, Wagner and Strauss alongside Debussy and Ravel.[119] His defense of *Carmen*'s Frenchness, therefore, is not predicated on opposition to Wagner. In 1928, he authored the monograph *Georges Bizet*, which was published under the name of another critic, Willy (Henry Gauthier-Villars).[120] In his book, Vuillermoz attributes *Carmen*'s international success to its alleged forgery of Spanish identity:

> this evocation of Spain, so fictitious and arbitrary, has managed to deceive not just the keenest supporters of exactness as far as *couleur locale* is concerned, but even the Spaniards, who cannot conceive of a bullfight without an excerpt of *Carmen* being performed.[121]

Vuillermoz understood that a representation meeting widely shared stereotypes has more chance of spreading and succeeding than one defying them.[122] Moreover, he implies that French cultural representations of the Other, no matter how "fictitious," earn worldwide recognition, and on that basis he casts Spain as a cultural periphery of France. He concludes that, despite its marked Hispanism, *Carmen* is a "French" work:

> without any doubts, [Bizet] scandalized his contemporaries once again by way of delicious, fugitive and elusive harmonic details; he modulated experimentally and recklessly; he conveyed *couleur locale* by way

---

[118] I use the expression "rival institutions," aware that this rivalry has been exaggerated and was not predicated on a clear-cut distinction. It was, perhaps, a political rivalry. Pasler, "Deconstructing d'Indy," 101–139.

[119] Fulcher, *French Cultural Politics*, 147–150 and 155–158; Fulcher, *The Composer as Intellectual*, 162, 182. Hart, "The Symphony and National Identity," 134–135.

[120] Gauthier-Villars, *Georges Bizet*. The monograph was signed by Henry Gauthier-Villars, alias "Willy," but more recently attributed to Émile Vuillermoz. Winton Dean, "Bizet after 100 Years," *Musical Times* 116, no. 1588 (June 1, 1975): 525–527. See also Christian Goubault, *La critique musicale dans la presse française de 1870 à 1914* (Genève: Slatkine, 1984), 122–123.

[121] "cette évocation si factice et si arbitraire de l'Espagne a su tromper non seulement les partisans les plus résolus de l'exactitude en matière de couleur locale, mais les Espagnols eux-mêmes qui ne conçoivent plus une corrida sans une exécution d'un fragment de Carmen." Gauthier Villars, *Georges Bizet*, 103

[122] His recounting of the Spaniards surrendering to *Carmen*'s "fictitious and arbitrary" Hispanism overlooks the opposition that this work met in its early Spanish reception, and suggests that Vuillermoz missed out on Turina's 1925 contribution to *Le courrier musical*—discussed above.

of a Hispanism which, while approximate, was sufficient enough to trouble the ignorant; he made all critics leap off their seats by finishing Don José's aria "La fleur que tu m'avais jetée" in remote tonalities.[123]

Like Turina, Vuillermoz identified the Spanish elements in *Carmen* as its most modernist aspect, thus linking racial otherness with aesthetic challenges. Despite pointing out "reckless" and "experimental" modulations to "remote tonalities," Vuillermoz's cast *Carmen* in a traditional and conservative mold: "Should we really regard *Carmen* other than as a very traditionalist and, above all, perfectly French opéra-comique? That seems quite debatable!"[124]

In 1922, Gaudier had already presented *Carmen* as a traditional opéra-comique, but Vuillermoz introduces a moral dimension through his commentary of the libretto and production. In his analysis, he pits Mérimée's novella against the alleged traditionalism of Bizet's opera. He characterizes librettists Meilhac and Halévy with a "constant will to sweeten, stump and even trivialize the silhouette of that unrestrained gypsy, neatly portrayed by" Mérimée.[125] Furthermore, he argues that "in order not to alarm the bourgeois and familial clientèle of Mr du Locle"—the director of the Opéra Comique—"the dexterous adapters have subjected Mérimée's characters to a careful make-up."[126]

Vuillermoz likely drew inspiration from Charles Tenroc, who in his fiftieth-anniversary contribution to *Le courrier musical* in 1925 characterized the audience as backward, "aristocratic and familial clientèle," with the purpose of presenting Bizet as a messianic and visionary figure, but not a revolutionary.[127] Likewise, Vuillermoz argues that "Bizet was far from an anarchist and has never wanted to modify the lyrical conventions of his time."[128] Furthermore, he blames the audience's Italianate penchant and moral conservatism for the primeval moral scandal, as he argues that they "would only admit stabbings in historical operas and freedom of love in the remorseful and pathological characters of

---

[123] "Sans doute il scandalisa une fois de plus ses contemporains par de délicieux détails harmoniques, fugitifs et insaisissables; il modula avec recherche et témérité; il fit de la couleur locale d'un ibérisme approximatif mais suffisant pour inquiéter les ignorants; il fit bondir tous les critiques sur leurs fauteuils en terminant par des emprunts aux tons éloignés la romance de José 'La fleur que tu m'avais jetée'." Gauthier-Villars, *Georges Bizet*, 112.

[124] "Faut-il voir réellement dans Carmen autre chose qu'un opéra comique très traditionaliste et surtout parfaitement français? Cela paraît bien discutable!" Ibid., 107.

[125] "On y sent la volonté constante d'adoucir, d'estomper et même de banaliser la silhouette de cette libre bohémienne si nettement campée par le conteur." Ibid., 107.

[126] "Pour ne pas effrayer la clientèle bourgeoise et familiale de M. du Locle, les adroits adapteurs ont fait subir aux personnages de Mérimée un prudent maquillage." Ibid., 107. Vuillermoz describes the adaptations in detail. Ibid., 107.

[127] "clientèle aristocratique et familiale." Tenroc, "Les cinquante ans de Carmen."

[128] "Bizet n'avait rien d'un anarchiste et n'a jamais songé à modifier les usages lyriques de son temps." Gauthier-Villars, *Georges Bizet*, 115.

the genre 'Traviata.'"¹²⁹ By 1920, no spectator would regard *Carmen* or Bizet as revolutionary. That musicologists and critics should consider this subject a matter of discussion suggests to what extent *Carmen* had become valuable cultural capital; it also indicates that reviving a work often involved unearthing and solving some of the aesthetic and cultural polemics that had once surrounded it.

The musicological works discussed present a range of individual and collective strategies aimed at relocating *Carmen* in the French canon, bringing it closer to essentialized and fixating notions of French identity. There was a contradiction between, one the one hand, attempts to uphold the alleged authenticity of the Spanish elements in *Carmen*, such as in the writings of Landormy and Tiersot, and on the other hand the opposite attitude, followed by Gaudier, Vuillermoz and Turina. Furthermore, a tension between attempts to reinforce and domesticate the Spanish difference in *Carmen* underpinned the writings of most critics.

Although authenticity was never a primordial criterion of aesthetic judgment as far as Orientalist works are concerned, it did experience a certain degree of revaluation since 1875. By questioning the authenticity of *Carmen*, Landormy and Tiersot showed that this opera consolidated its position in the French canon at the cost of deceiving preestablished conceptions about Spain. As the building of the postwar order led to formulations of more essentialized and xenophobic definitions of French identity, the Spanish elements in *Carmen* could increasingly appear as foreign.

Beyond divergence, the critics and musicologists who wrote about *Carmen* in the 1920s coincided in grounding this opera in their differing notions of French tradition. Like more mainstream intellectuals of their time, such as Barrès, they regarded tradition as the most assured means of stimulating a sense of community. Gaudier, Vuillermoz and others believed French tradition to be embodied in the opéra-comique, but *Carmen* could arguably be relegated only to this genre. Gaudier and Landormy understood tradition as the historical projection of values such as order, clarity and spontaneity. In that sense, they regarded the past as an open space on which to project concerns of the present. Those values regained currency after the Great War, as they helped to shape the aesthetics of neoclassicism, which found expression in a relatively well-defined semantic and rhetorical field.

The centrality of *Carmen* in the French canon provided an opportunity to renegotiate the ontological and epistemological boundary between notions of French and Spanish music. Laparra and Turina played a substantial role in that negotiation through their writings on *Carmen* and their compositions. Their cases, again, show how individual agendas intersected with larger historical and cultural processes. Beyond divergence, they contributed, more or less directly, to negotiating notions of French and Spanish music through their attempts to Frenchify *Carmen*.

---

[129] "Même travesti d'après l'esthétique du genre, les honnêtes fantoches fabriqués par les librettistes soulevèrent la réprobation des spectateurs qui n'admettent les coups de poignard que dans les opéras historiques et la liberté de l'amour que chez les maladives repenties du genre 'Traviata.'" Ibid., 107.

CHAPTER 6

Showcasing Spain at the Opéra Comique: The Homage to Falla (1928)

In the week between March 9 and 16, 1928, the Opéra Comique hosted an homage to Falla, offering a series of performances of three of his most emblematic works, *La vie brève*, *El amor brujo*, and *El retablo de Maese Pedro*.[1] This event could be well regarded as the corollary to Falla's moment of greatest international recognition in his life. Almost one year before, on May 14, 1927, the Salle Pleyel had celebrated Falla's fiftieth birthday with an homage concert offering performances of the *Siete canciones populares españolas*, *Psyché*, the *Fantasía Bética* and the French première of his *Harpsichord concerto*, played twice on a piano and a harpsichord with Falla in the soloist role.[2] That event represented a unique tribute to a Spanish musician in Paris. In 1928, the Opéra Comique brought Falla again into the limelight, followed by the awarding of the Legion d'honneur, in the course of a reception at the Fondation S. de Rothschild organized by the Association Française d'Expansion et d'Echanges Artistiques.[3] These events

---

[1] Several reviews confuse this homage with the one played at the Salle Pleyel March 19 that same year, which received scant press coverage, and which included performances of the *Harpsichord Concerto*, *The Three-Cornered Hat*, *Noches en los jardines de España* and *Siete canciones populares españolas*. Carol Hess dates the Opéra Comique homage "in the spring of 1926." Hess, *Manuel de Falla and Modernism*, 245. The only source to give precise dates for both events is Carol-Bérard, "Le triomphe de Manuel de Falla," *Une semaine à Paris*, no. 302 (March 9, 1928): 43–44. On the event at the Salle Pleyel see Pierre de Lapommeraye, "Festival Falla." *Le ménestrel* (March 1928).

[2] [André] Schaeffner, "Concert Manuel de Falla," *Le ménestrel*, vol. 89, no. 20, (May 20, 1927).

[3] "A l'occasion de la présence à Paris de Manuel de Falla dont l'Opéra Comique vient de représenter dans un même spectacle *La Vie Brève*, *El amor brujo*, *Les Tréteaux de Maître Pierre*, une réception a été donnée, le mercredi 14 mars, dans l'hôtel de la Fondation S. de Rothschild (11, rue Berryer). L'initiative de cette opportune réunion en l'honneur de la musique espagnole ainsi que de l'original et savoureux compositeur du Tricorne, était due à l'Association française d'Expansion et d'Echanges Artistiques qu'on ne saurait trop féliciter en cette circonstance." Anon, "En l'honneur de la musique espagnole," *La renaissance politique, littéraire, artistique* 16, no. 11 (March 18, 1928): 7. "Au cours d'une réunion organisée par les soins de l'Association française d'expansion et d'échanges artistiques, M. Herriot, ministre de l'Instruction publique et des Beaux-Arts, a remis les insignes de l'ordre de la Légion d'honneur au compositeur Manuel de Falla, dont l'Opéra Comique vient de présenter trois des principaux

show how Falla's reputation abroad depended, to a great extent, on Paris—followed by Britain and Italy.[4] As has been discussed, Paris had become a privileged site for the production of Spanish musical and cultural identities thanks to the emigration of Spanish political exiles, artists, writers and musicians since the nineteenth century,[5] the development of a Spanish vogue[6] and the building of a relevant musical and institutional infrastructure that offered Spanish musicians opportunities they could not find in Spain.

The Opéra Comique responded to the high expectations raised by Falla's uplifted status with three lavish productions that brought together some of the most renowned performers and stage producers in their area, including dancer Antonia Mercé ("La Argentina"), who had moved to Paris in the early 1920s; soprano Ninon Vallin, a veteran in the Opéra Comique[7]; and Spanish painter Ignacio Zuloaga, who had worked for the Opéra Comique in the production of *Carmen* and held a longstanding reputation in Paris.[8] The event received wide critical coverage, from daily newspapers to fashion magazines, and specialized culture and music journals.[9]

The public attending the Opéra Comique that night might have been familiar with the first two works. The Paris première of *La vie brève* had taken place on January 7, 1914, in that same institution; *El amor brujo*, which had premièred at the Teatro Lara in Madrid in 1915, with choreography by Pastora Imperio, received a first concert performance at the Concerts Colonne in 1923 and was fully staged at the Trianon Lyrique on May 22, 1925, with choreography by Mercé. *El retablo*,

---

ouvrages." Anon., "Novelles," *Le ménestrel*, vol. 90, no. 12 (March 23, 1928). There has been confusion as to the dates of this award. Stoianova situates the awarding of the Légion d'honneur in the course of Falla's fiftieth anniversary celebration at the Salle Pleyel in 1927: Ivanka Stoianova, "Concerto por clavecin: Tradition et découverte artistique," in *Manuel de Falla, Latinité et Universalité. Actes du Colloque international tenu en Sorbonne, 18–21 novembre 1996*, ed. Louis Jambou (Paris: Presses de l'Université Paris-Sorbonne, 1999), 279.

[4] Collins, "Falla in Europe," 257–258, 247. On Falla's reception in Britain see Chris Collins, "Falla in Britain," *The Musical Times* (2003): 33–48.

[5] On the political exile and other forms of migration of Spanish musicians in Paris since the nineteenth century, see Montserrat Bergadà, "Les musiciens espagnols à Paris entre 1820 et 1868," in *La musique entre France et Espagne: Interactions stylistiques. Actes du colloque international tenu à Paris, en Sorbonne-Paris IV et à l'Instituto Cervantes, les 14–16 mai 2001*, ed. Louis Jambou (Paris: Presses de l'Université de Paris-Sorbonne, 2003), 19–22.

[6] Alisa Luxenberg, "Over the Pyrenees and Through the Looking-Glass: French Culture Reflected in Its Imagery of Spain," in *Spain, Espagne, Spanien: Foreign Artists Discover Spain, 1800–1900*, ed. Suzanne L. Stratton (New York: Equitable Gallery, 1993), 11–32.

[7] Martin Cooper, Elizabeth Forbes, and Alan Blyth, "Vallin, Ninon." In *Grove Music Online*, http://www.oxfordmusiconline.com/subscriber/article/grove/music/28948 (accessed April 15, 2011).

[8] Further details on "La Argentina" and Zuloaga can be found below.

[9] Including newspapers, some literature and culture journals, and most music journals, with the significant exception of *Le ménestrel*, which, under the title "Festival Falla," reviewed the event at the Salle Pleyel.

however, made its first staged public appearance that night, following its world première at the Hôtel Polignac in 1923 before a selection of two hundred musicians, critics, aristocrats and friends. A concert performance conducted by Falla at the Jean Wiener Concerts on November 13, 1923, followed, plus staged performances at the Bristol Operatic Festival (June 1924), Seville, Barcelona, New York (1925), Amsterdam, Zurich (1926) and Paris (1928).[10]

Once again, Falla's prominence among Spanish composers helped most French critics approach the event as a token of Spain's most renowned living avant-garde composer, and as a showcase of his national background. Such a reputation could lead to a self-defensive attitude, such as shown in Henri de Curzon's review for *La nouvelle revue*: "We work hard on our lyric stages, putting on all sorts of works!… And as if the French were not enough, we bring all the foreigners we can."[11] Perhaps for the first time, "Spanish music" was being regarded as a cultural menace. More subtly and ambiguously than Curzon, perhaps even subconsciously, an anonymous reviewer in the cultural magazine *Cyrano* undermined any possible perceptions of Falla's success as being universal by declaring that "Falla's renown has increased after this test, since it is Spanish."[12] Perhaps a similar view animated Henry Malherbe's comment that Falla "is worth such an homage that the Opéra Comique has paid to a foreigner," a remark that both suggests the exceptionality of the event and indirectly marks a cultural distance from Falla.[13] Gheusi waxed enthusiastic about Falla's triumph in Paris, going so far as to propose Falla as an "example for the admirable, uncertain, perplexing, derailing but still very lively school of our French composers."[14] Like Curzon, and unlike most of the critics we have dealt with in the previous chapters, Gheusi offers testimony that "Spanish music" could now be perceived as something more than an "exotic" influence. Apart from remarkable differences in attitude, and with the exception of Gheusi, all the critics concurred in pushing

---

[10] Juliane Dorsch, "Nostalgia and Modernism in Puppet Music of the 1920s," (Ph.D. diss.: Royal Holloway, University of London, 2011), 124; Hess, *Manuel de Falla and Modernism*, 199–201; on the Bristol performance see John Trend, *Manuel de Falla and Spanish music* (New York: Knopf, 1929), 136–139.

[11] "On travaille, sur nos scènes lyriques; on y fait feu de toutes pièces!… Et comme si les françaises ne suffisaient pas, on fait appel à toutes les étrangères qu'on peut." Henri de Curzon. "La Musique. Opéra Comique: La vie brève, L'amour sorcier, Les tréteaux de Maître Pierre, de Manuel de Falla." *La nouvelle revue* 94 (April 1928): 225–228. Interestingly, he presented Falla as a "Catalan" composer, which shows his lack of familiarity with the composer. Perhaps he was driven by the cases of Albéniz and Granados.

[12] "La renommée de M de Falla sort de cette épreuve grandie, car elle est espagnole." Anon., "Au fil de la scène. Ce qui se joue," *Cyrano* 5, no. 196 (March 18, 1928): 29.

[13] "Le musicien est digne d'un tel hommage rendu à un étranger par le théâtre national de l'Opéra Comique." Henri Malherbe. "Chronique musicale: Manuel de Falla." *Le temps* (March 14, 1928).

[14] "en exemple à l'admirable, incertaine, perplexe, déraillarde et tout de même très vivante école de nos compositeurs français." P. B. Gheusi, "La musique au théâtre. A l'Opéra Comique. Trois pièces de Manuel de Falla." *Le Figaro* (March 11, 1928).

Falla's music beyond national boundaries and construing his music as "Spanish" or "foreign"—an attitude that contrasts with concerns, among certain Spanish critics, that Falla had become Frenchified during his Paris years (1907–1914).[15] With the exception of xenophobic or self-defensive attitudes such as Curzon's, this stance shows the prevalence of ethnic discourses in music criticism, which caused styles to be labeled and classified according to a given composer's perceived national background. From that viewpoint, Falla's music was understood as "Spanish," while Debussy's *Ibéria* or Ravel's *Rhapsodie espagnole* (to pick just two examples) are "French" works with a Spanish tinge. Moreover, the prevalence of center-periphery models of interpretation favored cultures that were considered peripheral, such as Spain, validating their cultural expression by stressing their differential and folkloric aspects, as discussed in Chapter 1. Last, Falla's own attitude contributed significantly, if not determinately, to his being regarded as a Spanish composer, principally through his output, which, excluding *Psyché* and the first and second of his *Trois mélodies*, was entirely devoted to Spain. However, if, as I have argued in Chapter 4, Falla discovered his identity as a composer of "Spanish" music once in Paris, his behavior may be considered a response to critical attitudes similar to the ones just described.

In their attempt to construe Falla's music as "Spanish," however, critics attending the Falla homage met with a challenge. They were presented with three very different works, underpinned by multiple conceptions of Spanish identity. Mostly unaware of the sociopolitical context in which those ideas of Spain had emerged or the intellectual debates surrounding them, critics couched their descriptions of Falla's music in a narrative mold that was familiar to them, thus trying to make sense of such a disparity. Most conspicuously, they resorted to an evolutionary narrative that presented Falla's later works as more artistically and technically mature—and one that Spanish critics equally endorsed.[16] Since they wrote under the assumption that Falla's music was "Spanish," they also described Falla's career as a process by which his music became gradually "more Spanish." Interestingly, this stance required that critics reformulate their notions of "Spanish music," especially regarding the last of his works performed, *El retablo de Maese Pedro* (1923), based on an episode from Cervantes's novel *Don Quixote*. This work, which could well be regarded as under the influence of Stravinsky and neoclassicism,[17] presented none of the signs French critics understood as characteristic of "Spanish music," most conspicuously flamenco

---

[15] Hess, *Manuel de Falla and Modernism*, 58–59.

[16] Piquer, *Clasicismo moderno*, 150–152.

[17] Collins argues that "the unusual scorings of *El retablo de Maese Pedro* and the *Concerto* came about after Falla's exposure to *Renard* and *The Soldier's Tale*." Collins, "Falla in Europe," 263. Hess documents how, already in 1923, several Spanish critics established favorable comparisons between *El retablo* and Stravinsky's works, most conspicuously *Pulcinella*. Hess, *Manuel de Falla and Modernism*, 229–231; Hess, *Sacred Passions*, 149–150.

and Andalusian folklore.[18] In the need to rethink "Spanish music," French critics took the opportunity to renegotiate and redraw the line demarcating notions of French and Spanish musical identities.

Falla's Career and Narratives of Evolution

Months after the Paris première of *La vie brève*, the outbreak of the First World War forced Falla to leave the country. He moved back to Madrid, from which he traveled around Spain following the fate of his latest commissions. He soon made the acquaintance of the theater impresario Gregorio Martínez Sierra and his wife María Lejárraga, who wrote a wealth of plays that, alas, were signed by her husband. With Lejárraga, Falla wrote two stage works: the ballet *El amor brujo* (discussed below) and the pantomime *El corregidor y la molinera* (premièred in 1917 and based on Pedro Antonio de Alarcón's novel *El sombrero de tres picos*, 1874). This latter work was the basis for Falla's ballet *The Three-Cornered Hat*, written for Diaghilev and Massine and premièred at the Alhambra Theatre, London, in 1919. Another work that Falla would complete in these years is the "symphonic impressions" for piano and orchestra *Noches en los jardines de España* (1916).

Following the death of his parents, Falla left Madrid for the calmer Granada in 1920. There he would co-organize with Federico García Lorca the celebrated *cante jondo* competition that so much shaped subsequent constructions of flamenco.[19] Furthermore, in Granada Falla produced a series of works that scholars tend to regard as aesthetically influenced by neoclassicism—despite the problematic use of this term.[20] These works include *El retablo de Maese Pedro* (1923); the Harpsichord Concerto, written for Wanda Landowska, first performed in Barcelona in 1926 and later in the aforementioned homage to Falla at the Salle Pleyel; and the cantata *Psyché* (1924), to a poem by Georges Jean-Aubry. With the exception of *Psyché*, in these "neoclassicist" works, Falla not only made varying use of "early Spanish music" but also abandoned, almost completely—though not altogether –the use of folklore, most especially flamencolike music, that is, Phrygian melodic turns as well as musical images of southern Spain and the gypsies. As Christoforidis has argued, "Falla's application of Pedrell's theories [on folklore and nationalism] involved a greater degree of conceptual and stylistic abstraction and was mediated by the aesthetic precepts of neoclassicism."[21]

---

[18] Christoforidis, "From Folksong to Plainchant, 209–213.

[19] Mitchell, *Flamenco Deep Song*, 160–177.

[20] "If the stylistic label 'neo-classicist' implies an uncomfortably wide range of meanings, it is nonetheless the most accurate description of Falla's works of the 1920s." Carol A. Hess, "Falla, Manuel de," in *The New Grove Dictionary of Music and Musicians*, 2nd ed., ed. Stanley Sadie, vol. 8 (London and New York: Macmillan, 2001), 532.

[21] Christoforidis, "From Folksong to Plainchant," 215.

Falla most likely assimilated the principles of French neoclassicism, particularly a penchant for quoting and using early music, through his collaboration with the Ballets Russes.[22] His focus on Castile, however, may have felt the impact of the 1898 and 1914 Spanish intellectual generations, who regarded that region as a source of economic and cultural regeneration for Spain, as with Laparra's opera *La habanera* (1908).[23]

In sum, by the mid-1920s Falla's oeuvre was, if not as vast as other composers' of his age, at least broad in generic and aesthetic scope. Added to Falla's reputation of being a modest and conciliatory character, this variety has surely contributed to consecrating his lifetime reputation, helping to view his output as bridging notions of "tradition" and "modernity," and mediating between Spains perceived as "clichéd" and "authentic." The homage was the chance to discover a yet-unknown work by Falla, and to survey, in a single evening, the broad stylistic scope that his music covered in less than a decade. Critics and the audience could experience and discover a series of varied and even contrasting vignettes of Spain by the hand of the most renowned living member of the "Spanish musical school." As with other "Spanish" works, they could compare those impressions with their preconceptions, or eventually with knowledge acquired through traveling to or reading about Spain, or listening to other "Spanish" musical works and genres. However, in contrast to performances of other works, the homage struck critics and audiences for the variety of "Spanish" impressions and aesthetic agendas presented there. This sentiment can be best gauged from Malherbe's review, as he left the homage "worn out as after a nervous strain," having witnessed the "immense, summary and contradictory images [that] knock against each other as in a quick dream."[24] In a less dramatic way, the review in *L'Illustration* referred to a succession of "passionate and melancholic," "tragic and superstitious" and "ironic and picaresque" Spains, respectively represented in *La vie brève, El amor brujo* and *El retablo*.[25] More perceptively, Jean Poueigh distinguished "three periods of creative activity, each one corresponding to a different style."[26]

---

[22] Ibid., 216–217.

[23] Fox, "Spain as Castile, 21–36. Britt-Arredondo, *Quixotism*. Thus, Falla's works of the 1920s may come to represent an alternative to Raoul Laparra's earlier, somewhat failed—or, at least, contradictory—attempts to overcome clichéd stereotypes of Spain, especially in his operas *La habanera* and *La jota*. At first sight, Falla's formulation of a "new" non-Andalusian Spain may be judged more "authentic," coherent or organic than Laparra's, in view of the latter's reliance on the very southern, flamenco stereotypes that he tried to oust. See Llano, "Hispanic Traditions," 97–140.

[24] "épuisé comme d'un surmenage nerveux"; "Des images immenses, sommaires et contradictoires se heurtent ainsi qu'en un rêve rapide." Malherbe, "Chronique musicale: Manuel de Falla."

[25] "passionnée et mélancolique"; "tragique et superstitieuse"; "ironique et picaresque." V., "Un spectacle lyrique espagnol à Paris," *L'Illustration* (March 17, 1928).

[26] "trois périodes d'activité créatrice, correspondant chacune à un style différent." Jean Poueigh, "Critique musicale: Opéra Comique," *La rampe* 2, no. 472 (March 1, 1928): 12.

More generally, critical descriptions of the three works helped to shape a narrative of aesthetic evolution in which critics could inscribe Falla's works and styles. Thus they could explain and come to terms with the various, and perhaps discomfiting, ways in which "difference" appeared before their eyes and ears on the night of the Falla homage. A teleological narrative informs Malherbe's description of "these three works so characteristic of his successive styles" as "three portraits of Manuel de Falla by himself at three decisive stages of his life: youth, adolescence and maturity."[27] Tenroc structured Falla's career in three stages, "where he searches himself, where he finds himself, and where he surpasses himself."[28] Gheusi resorted to the "noble savage" trope to emphasize backwardness and primitiveness in Falla's early period, which he characterized by "an ingenuous and robust vitality, rhythmically vibrant, colored by shimmering palettes like an Andalusian shawl of the good old times."[29] Gheusi's description of Falla's early works as "primitive" implied that later works were more advanced. In sum, by inscribing Falla's music into a teleological and evolutionary narrative of self-development, critics reviewing the homage could resolve the tension between their fixating notions of national identity and the "contradictory images" that "knock against each other"—to paraphrase Malherbe—presented before their eyes and ears.

The prevalence of evolutionary narratives in critical reactions to Falla's works could be thought to be under the influence of positivism and, related to it, ideological Darwinism, and their impact on the arts, the humanities and the sciences. As Linda L. Clark has argued, "while the French mind was not 'dominated' by social Darwinism, the name of Darwin often figured in the biologistic social theories constructed in France during the late nineteenth century. Especially after 1870 there was a vast amount of discussion of how the theory of biological evolution […] related to human society."[30] If the defeat in the 1870 war against Prussia sparked a staunch anti-German stance among certain strands of French nationalism that persisted throughout the Third Republic, it also helped to articulate criticisms against the Second Empire on the basis that Prussia's victory had lain bare France's moral, scientific and cultural inferiority. This state of affairs facilitated the influence of German positivism in French universities during

---

[27] "Ces trois œuvres si caractéristiques de ses manières successives"; "trois portraits de M. de Falla par lui-même aux trois époques décisives de sa vie: la jeunesse, l'adolescence et la maturité." Malherbe, "Chronique musicale: Manuel de Falla."

[28] "celle où il se cherche, celle où il se trouve, celle où il se dépasse." Charles Tenroc, "Opéra Comique: La vie brève, L'amour sorcier, Les tréteaux de Maître Pierre," Le courrier musical (April 1928).

[29] "vitalité ingénue et robuste, vibrante de rythme, colorée de palettes chatoyantes ainsi qu'un châle andalou de la bonne époque." Gheusi, "La musique au théâtre."

[30] Clark, Linda L. "Social Darwinism in France." The Journal of Modern History 53, no. 1 (March 1, 1981): 1026.

the early years of the Third Republic. According to Martha Hannah, a series of Republican, anticlerical intellectuals and scholars she describes as "academic modernists" embraced German scientific positivism in the wake of the Sedan defeat, convinced as they were that "Prussia's advantage on the battlefield had originated in the classrooms, laboratories, and seminars of schools, *gymnasia*, and universities," and determined to undermine French Catholicism.[31] The conspicuous manifestation of positivism and rationalism in politics, education and the arts led to an opposite strand of idealist thinking, which, above all, the symbolists advocated through their own work and their support of Wagnerism.[32]

La vie brève and *Verismo*

La vie brève gave critics attending the homage an opportunity to look back at the beginnings of Falla's career with the hindsight offered by his subsequent works. Beyond their differences, most critics agreed in describing this opera as a youthful and immature work that prefigured Falla's later, more mature style. For instance, Malherbe referred to "an incipient personality" and described Falla as "not yet a master of his means," and "still attached to old rules" and "indulgent modulations."[33] Critics thought that, at the time he composed *La vie brève*, Falla was still working under an excessive influence of mostly Italian but also French composers. Thus their perceptions of *La vie brève* were the basis for describing Falla's personal evolution as a progressive "liberation" from "foreign" influences. Significantly enough, this viewpoint underlay visions of *La vie brève* as *La vida breve*, that is, as the work Falla presented for competition to the Academy of Beaux Arts in Madrid in 1905. To take just one example, André Coeuroy remarked that *La vie brève* "dates from twenty years ago,"[34] thus emphasizing its perceived obsolescence.

If *La vie brève* had become outdated, the homage imbued the work with new significance. The need to trace this opera's aesthetic genealogy, in order to incorporate it into descriptions of Falla's personal evolution, gave critics an opportunity to negotiate their relationship with a problematic past. That past was historically recent but cultural distant, since perceptions of it were mediated by the trauma of the First World War and its impact on musical aesthetics. Attempts to bridge the sense of disruption brought about by the War situated

---

[31] Hannah, *The Mobilization of Intellect*, 28. For a broader discussion see 26–37.

[32] Pasler, *Composing the Citizen*, 508, 527.

[33] "une personnalité naissante"; "Il n'est pas encore maître de ses moyens"; "encore assujetti aux vieilles règles"; "modulations complaisantes." Malherbe, "Chronique musicale: Manuel de Falla."

[34] "date d'il y a vingt ans." André Coeuroy, "A l'Opéra Comique: La vida breve, L'amour sorcier. Les tréteaux de Maitre Pierre, de Manuel de Falla." *La revue musicale* 9, no. 6 (April 1928).

constructed memories of the prewar past at the heart of building the postwar order—a phenomenon that gained greater visibility through the massive and rapid construction of war memorials and monuments.[35] A new performance of *La vie brève* could help to reenact that past and negotiate relations with it, insofar as this opera—to judge from Coeuroy—"deeply bears the mark of its time, of a time when *Pelléas* was still an exceptional work, whereas [Charpentier's] *Louise* and Italian *verismo* prevailed."[36] Interestingly, this stance entailed that, thanks to its aesthetic obsolescence and its derived function as a marker of time, a formerly "exotic" and "Spanish" work like *La vie brève* gained cultural significance to the extent that it became a *lieu de mémoire*, an artifact with which to organize a past that was historically recent but perceived as culturally distant or problematic.[37] In a more sensationalist way, one could say that time, trauma and aesthetic change turned *La vie brève* into part of the history of French music—to judge from critical reactions. Falla's subsequent "liberation" from Italian influences enacted a similar struggle being perceived, more generally, in the recent history of French music. Furthermore, this sense of revival and unearthing of a "remote" but relevant, and above all "French," musical past was reinforced by the fact that, with the exception of Louis Schneider and Henri de Curzon, no critic attended the 1914 performance.[38]

But critics perceived Falla as a composer of "Spanish music," which meant that their approach to *La vie brève* as a Spanish work with a relatively important historical and cultural significance, and with which the boundaries between notions of "Spanish" and "French" music could be further negotiated, needed to cope with its perceived verist elements. Therefore, they implemented a series of discursive strategies in order to defend the opera's Spanish credentials in the face of what they conceptualized as "foreign" influences. Some critics described it as a work in which Italian and Spanish elements coexisted in a more or less conflictive, or harmonious, relation. For instance, in his review for *Le Ménestrel* Poueigh described "an artistic temperament musically sensitive to the call of the native soil" (that is, Spain) "but whose theatrical conception is troubled by a less fortunate aesthetics," namely, an "Italian influence [that] reveals itself in

---

[35] Daniel J. Sherman, "Art, Commerce, and the Production of Memory in France After World War I," in *Commemorations: The Politics of National Identity*, ed. John R. Gillis (Princeton, NJ: Princeton University Press, 1994), 186–211.

[36] "un drame lyrique qui porte profondément la marque de son temps, d'un temps où Pelléas n'était encore qu'une œuvre d'exception, alors que Louise et le vérisme italien faisaient loi." Coeuroy, "A l'Opéra Comique."

[37] Pierre Nora, "Between Memory and History: Les lieux de mémoire," *Representations* 26 (1989): 7–24.

[38] "Avec quatorze ans de plus, elle a fait, autant que je m'en souvienne, bien plus d'impression que la première fois." Curzon, "La musique," Opéra Comique, 225–228; Louis Schneider, "La mise en scène et les décors," *Comoedia* (December 1913).

the expression of lyricism. In addition, the drama's subject turns to *verismo*."[39] A few lines afterward, Poueigh clarifies that not just the "theatrical conception" but "all the lyrical accent here proves to be stained by an Italian quality, I repeat, which Ninon Vallin's moving voice cannot render any younger."[40] Poueigh conceives of the relation between the Spanish and Italian elements as "troubling." Furthermore, his testimony lays bare the obsolete connotations of *verismo* in interwar France, or perhaps Poueigh's personal impression that the gap with the prewar years could not be bridged through attempts to revive its cultural signifiers. Interestingly, he somehow turned Falla's opera into a testimony of French history. In his review for *La Revue musicale*, André Coeuroy similarly describes a "fierce fight" between "the conventional dramatic forms a la mode and the composer's emerging personality," the latter being manifest in the "ethnic rhythms [and] vibrant sonorities of popular music."[41] That he conceived of Spanish music and by extension identity as "ethnic" and "popular" represents another instance of the politics of representation underpinning hegemonic notions of French culture. Notions of "difference" in race and class helped to articulate representations of Spanish culture as subaltern.

In Charles Tenroc's review for *Le courrier musical*, the conflictive relationship between the Spanish and Italian elements perceived by Poueigh and Coeuroy gives way to a more harmonious one in which the former prevail over the latter. Tenroc describes *La vie brève* as "a youth, enthusiast and spontaneous work, in which the Italian influence sprawled less manifest than today."[42] Thus, he acknowledged how the passage of time had an effect on how the Italian elements were perceived. "But," he added,

> from my point of view that verist nuance which certain censors mark as a stain, is not relevant. What matters is the frenetic nationalism which throws the drama into a bonfire of passion, the rhythm which drags the dramatic action into a whirl of sonorous life.[43]

---

[39] "un tempérament d'artiste musicalement sensible à l'appel du terroir natal, mais troublé en sa conception théâtrale par une esthétique de moins bon aloi. L'influence italienne se décèle ici dans l'expression du lyrisme. Le sujet de ce drame bref tourne, d'ailleurs, au vérisme." Poueigh, "Critique musicale: Opéra Comique."

[40] "Tout l'accent lyrique s'avère ici entaché d'un italianisme, je le répète, que la magnifique voix émouvante de Mme Ninon Vallin ne parvient pas à rajeunir." Ibid.

[41] "La lutte est poignante, dans la musique de cette Vie Brève, entre les formes conventionnelles du drame à la mode et la personnalité naissante du compositeur"; "rythmes ethniques"; "sonorités vibrantes de la musique populaire." Coeuroy, "A l'Opéra Comique."

[42] "une œuvre de jeunesse, enthousiaste, spontanée, dans laquelle une influence italienne s'étalait moins manifeste qu'aujourd'hui." Tenroc, "Opéra Comique: La vie brève."

[43] "Mais peu importe, à mon sens, cette nuance du 'vérisme' que certains aristarques sévères relèvent comme une tache. Ce qui compte, c'est le nationalisme frénétique qui emporte le drame dans une fougue de passion, c'est le rythme qui entraîne l'action dramatique dans un tourbillon de vie sonore." Tenroc, "Opéra Comique: La vie brève."

It seems ironic that he identified the passionate elements as exclusively Spanish, given that they were also perceived as a staple of verist aesthetics. The use of that argument suggests his perception of *La vie brève* as "Spanish music" could blind him to the presence of certain aesthetic elements.

Other critics examined *La vie brève* in terms of its relationship with French music. The intersection of French, Italian and Spanish cultural signifiers constituted favorable ground for construing *La vie brève* as Latin and anti-German. However, this required that these elements be perceived in a harmonious, or at least nonantagonistic, relationship with each other. Gheusi remarked that, "with fourteen years hindsight, it is striking to discover, here and there, Latin connections with Italian music, and, also, in the process, the influence of our Ravel."[44] Unlike other critics, Gheusi thought that if the passage of time had made the Italian elements emerge more conspicuously, by contrast it had also made it easier to contemplate *verismo* as a Latin feature, especially following Italy's realignment with the Entente in 1915.

Louis Schneider was the only critic not to point out any verist or Italianate connections. In his review for *Le Gaulois*, he argued that "the spectacle entirely belongs to Spain," and that, although Falla "has come to Paris [...] to request the consecration of his art [...] he has managed to preserve his personality."[45] This review may be read in several ways. It may indicate a reluctance to identify with a work generally deemed immature. However, it may also betray an attempt to describe Paris as a cultural metropolis, an environment propitious for achievement of the aesthetic and professional goals of foreigners such as Falla.

Not everyone turned influences into a matter of cultural strategies. In his review for *Le Temps*, Malherbe considered *La vie brève* "a verist drama, in the manner of *Cavalleria rusticana* and *La Navarraise*," but he described Falla's score as "still pervaded by diverse influences then current," consisting of Debussy's *Pelléas*, Rimsky-Korsakov's *Capriccio espagnol*, and Wagner's operas—"at turns *Tristan, Die Walküre, Hérodiade*."[46] A description of the work as being so eclectic could hardly result from cultural strategies such as the ones described so far. Indeed, Malherbe's disinterest in appropriating *La vie brève*, of couching it in the discursive mold of an

---

[44] "A quatorze ans de distance, nous nous étonnons d'y découvrir, ça et là, des parentés latines avec la musique italienne et parfois, dans le procédé, l'influence de notre Ravel." Gheusi, "La musique au théâtre."

[45] "Le spectacle tout entier appartient à l'Espagne"; "il est venu demander à Paris, à la Schola cantorum, la consécration de son art. Mais il a su garder sa personnalité." Louis Schneider, "Le 'Gaulois au théâtre.' Les premières," *Le Gaulois* (March 11, 1928).

[46] "M. Manuel de Falla en écrivant la Vie brève était encore imprégné d'influences diverses, alors à la mode"; "Tour à tour, Tristan, la Walkyrie, Hérodiade." Malherbe, "Chronique musicale: Manuel de Falla." In the second installment of his review, published a week later, Malherbe insisted on the same idea: "Dans la Vie brève, le musicien espagnol garde toute sa considération aux talents et aux doctrines d'autrui." Henri Malherbe, "Chronique musicale: Manuel de Falla II," *Le temps* (March 21, 1928).

anti-Italian or anti-German alliance, seems manifest in his description of the homage as "an homage paid to a foreigner by the Opéra Comique."[47]

EL AMOR BRUJO

Reactions to the "ballet-gitanería" *El amor brujo* and *La vie brève* differed significantly. To begin with, *El amor brujo* was the most applauded and critically acclaimed work that night. Gheusi saw the audience "burst into an ovation as had not been heard at the Opéra Comique for years," and proposed that this work "should […] end the evening insofar as it crowns and dominates it with a dazzling success."[48] Perhaps the settings and costumes by the Gibraltar-born painter Gustavo Bacarisas captivated the audience and critics, as suggested by Velletaz's remark that *El amor brujo* "constitutes the liveliest work from a scenic point of view."[49] A resident in Seville, and representative of the "Andalusian school" of painting, Bacarisas could offer Parisian audiences some of the formulas that the Ballets Russes had made so successful.[50] Drawing inspiration from Diaghilev's company, he cofounded, in 1927, the Ballets Espagnols, together with prominent Spanish dancers such as "La Argentina," who performed *El amor brujo* that night; Encarnación López Júlvez, "La Argentinita"; and Vicente Escudero.[51] This company aimed at introducing the European ballet and artistic avant-garde in Spain, following the innovation in stage techniques put forward by Rivas Cherif, one of its founders and greatest champions.[52] The Ballets espagnols opened in the season 1927–28 with a European tour that included performances of *El amor brujo*, with settings by Bacarisas.[53]

---

[47] "hommage rendu à un étranger par le théâtre national de l'Opéra Comique." Ibid.

[48] "éclater en ovations, comme notre vieil Opéra Comique n'en avait pas connues depuis des années"; "Il devrait, d'ailleurs, terminer la soirée tant il la couronne et la domine d'une réussite éblouissante." Gheusi, "La musique au théâtre."

[49] "constitue au point de vue scénique, la partie la plus vivante du spectacle," E.-F. Velletaz, "A l'Opéra Comique: La vie brève, L'amour sorcier, Les tréteaux de Maître Pierre, de M. Manuel de Falla," *Journal des débats* (March 1928).

[50] For a biography of Bacarisas see José Riquelme Sánchez, "El pintor Gustavo Bacarisas. (Gibraltar 1873-Sevilla 1971)," *Almoraima: Revista de estudios campogibraltareños* 1 (1989): 73–76.

[51] Idoia Murga Castro, *Escenografía de la danza en la edad de plata, 1916–1936* (Madrid: CSIC, 2009), 131–138; and "Escenografía y figurinismo de los bailarines españoles de principios del siglo XX," in *Congreso internacional imagen y apariencia* (Murcia: Ediciones de la Universidad de Murcia, 2009), 6; María Palacios. *La renovación musical en Madrid durante la dictadura de Primo de Rivera: El Grupo de los Ocho, 1923–1931* (Madrid: Sociedad Española de Musicología, 2008) 439.

[52] On Rivas Cherif's involvement in the Ballets espagnols, see Juan Aguilera Sastre and Manuel Aznar Soler, *Cipriano de Rivas Cherif y el teatro español de su época (1891–1967)* (Madrid: Asociación de Directores de Escena de España, 1999).

[53] Other works in that season included *El fandango del candil* (Rivas Cherif, Gustavo Durán, Nestor Martín Fernández de la Torre), *El contrabandista* (Rivas Cherif, Esplá, Bartolozzi), *Sonatina, Juerga, Kinekombo* (Cuban dance with music by M. Ponce), *En el corazón de Sevilla* (a collection of Spanish dances with staging by Ricardo Baroja).

Although Bacarisas's contribution to *El amor brujo* has not survived, other instances of his art, and his personal trajectory, illustrate the blend of Andalusian traditions and European or French modernism that most critics perceived in Falla's score, as we will see shortly. Indeed, one could argue that *El amor brujo* presented the same southern, gypsy stereotypes of *La vie brève* in a more updated aesthetic framework. The scenario narrates the story of the young gypsy Candelas, haunted by the ghost of her dead gypsy lover, who interferes in her new relationship with Carmelo, a white, "higher" male. In the celebrated Ritual Fire Dance, Candelas manages to exorcise and bury the haunting ghost of her former lover. The plot gives Falla an occasion for examining and testing his ideas on flamenco, which years later materialized in the *cante jondo* competition of Granada (1922).

Hess finds significant aesthetic and epistemological differences between the ways in which *La vie brève* and *El amor brujo* portray the gypsies. Whereas Salud's death in Falla's opera could symbolize a form of social punishment, as in Bizet's *Carmen*, Hess identifies in *El amor brujo* a "novel and sympathetic treatment of gypsies" insofar as Candelas "achieves personal and moral triumph by standing up to her deceitful lover."[54] One could argue, however, that, in the denouement Candelas embraces a hegemonic lifestyle to the detriment of her gypsy background and identity, a turn symbolized in the burial of the memory of her former gypsy lover and in her following a white, higher suitor. Such a reading gains credibility in the context of the cultural politics that later took center stage under Franco, shown, among other expressions, in musical films in which a gypsy dancer relinquished her career and identity by marrying a white male suitor and emulating his lifestyle.[55]

Contemporaries of Falla, however, compared these two works in terms of their aesthetic validity and currency, rather than their portrayals of "gypsyness." By 1928, *El amor brujo* had fallen behind the aesthetics of neoclassicism upheld by the Spanish avant-garde, even though the Grupo de los Ocho still included it in their concert programs.[56] Since the early 1920s, most of them had advocated a less clichéd idea of Spain, based on musical representations of the colder, central region of Castile, couched in the "dehumanized" aesthetics of neoclassicism.[57]

---

[54] Hess, *Manuel de Falla and Modernism*, 53, 55.

[55] As Labanyi has argued, this representational strategy became a staple of the nation-building process in Francoist Spain. Jo Labanyi, "Musical Battles: Populism and Hegemony in the Early Francoist Folkloric Film Musical," in *Constructing Identity in Contemporary Spain: Theoretical Debates and Cultural Practice*, ed. Jo Labanyi (Oxford: Oxford University Press, 2002), 206–221.

[56] Palacios registers a concert of "New Music" celebrated at the Teatro Calderón, Madrid, in 1930, in which Falla's *El amor brujo* constituted the only "old" work. Palacios, *La renovación musical en Madrid*, 434–435.

[57] Even though some of this group's members continued to use southern stereotypes eventually. Hess, *Manuel de Falla and Modernism*, 270.

To French critics covering the homage, aesthetic currency mattered to the extent that constructions of Falla's music as "universal" rather than "foreign"—meaning Italianate, German, or Spanish as well, according to different critics—could help them appropriate his success to the cause of French nationalism. Indeed, a lack of concern with the influence of *verismo* or music deemed Italianate marked the difference with respect to *La vie brève* that night, more than any other aspect—including the staging. As we have seen, critics covering the Paris première of *La vie brève* in 1914 emphasized the influence of French composers and appropriated Falla's work and achievements, thus giving rise to the ongoing trope of auto-exoticism and helping to shape notions of French cultural hegemony. This stance rested on one of the key arguments supporting notions of French cultural hegemony, namely, that Paris not only attracted artists and musicians from all countries but offered a favorable environment for developing and expressing their artistic personality and nationality in a way that their motherland could not. In such an "uplifting" environment—according to this form of propaganda—French musicians extended inspiration, and eventually guidance, to "visiting" composers such as Falla. In this context, "influence" became a strongly biased and coercive concept. In 1928, however, as most critics found *La vie brève* outdated, *El amor brujo* was the most likely work to replace it in such discourses.

Critics attending the homage understood *El amor brujo* as Falla's musical coming of age, his first major modernist work, in which, for the first time, he showed independence from any "foreign" (i.e., "non-Spanish") youthful models. For instance, Malherbe called *El amor brujo* the work in which Falla "gains consciousness of his own destiny," where "the cloudy veil that concealed the composer's personality is torn down."[58] Poueigh saw this work as "better attuned to the current modes of feeling and seeing."[59] More elaborately and dramatically, Tenroc described *El amor brujo* as the work in which Falla "has divested himself of his penchant for certain dubious affinities, whose influence has been felt in his homeland during the eighteenth and up to the end of the nineteenth century, [and which] still subsists in Spain despite the musical renaissance sounded by Albéniz."[60] Thus, he referred to Italian music, seen through the prism of the "invasion" myth, as discussed in Chapter 2.

Perceptions of Falla as aesthetically mature and independent did not restrain certain critics from emphasizing the role played by Paris in facilitating his

---

[58] "Avec *El amor brujo*, M. de Falla prend conscience de son destin"; "Avec *El amor brujo*, la voile des nuages qui nous cachait la personnalité du compositeur est déchiré." Malherbe, "Chronique musicale (I)."

[59] "mieux accordée au mode actuel de sensation et de vision." Poueigh, "Critique musicale: Opéra Comique."

[60] "il a dépouillé les tendances vers certaines affinités suspectes dont l'influence s'est fait sentir en sa patrie au cours des XVIIIe et jusque vers la fun du XIXe siècle, influence qui subsiste encore en Espagne malgré le Renacimiento musical sonné par Albeniz." Tenroc, "Opéra Comique: La vie brève."

success. In the case of *El amor brujo*, however, critics also noticed the influence of Stravinsky. Although Stravinsky was not a "native" French composer, some critics regarded his contribution to the musical scene of 1920s Paris, and more important his collaborative involvement in some of the most pressing French cultural struggles, as worthy of appropriation. According to Poueigh, in *El amor brujo*, "the pioneering influence of Debussy and Stravinsky has produced its effect."[61] Gheusi thought that, in this work, "Falla, from so high above, nods to Stravinsky's otherwise seducing inventions."[62] Referring to Falla's music, Coeuroy contends that "it has known *Le Sacre du Printemps* and has loved it, and Stravinsky's specter is present in the orchestration of *El amor brujo* (1915). But the Andalusian appeal is so strong that Falla frees himself: the Russian obsession disappears under the thrust of a certain Spain."[63]

In sum, these critics described *El amor brujo* as a work in which Falla "found himself" through the influence of Debussy and Stravinsky. Although they did not present Stravinsky as a French or Latin composer—and indeed, Coeuroy speaks of a "Russian obsession"—others had done it before. As we have seen in Chapter 1, Russia's membership in the Entente since the late nineteenth century and its key role during the First World War elicited sympathetic responses to Russian music and culture on the part of French critics. We have seen how Henri Collet and other critics exploited this political and military bonding in conceiving the idea of a cultural alliance among French, Russian and Spanish musicians. Stravinsky's first visit to Spain, in 1916, elicited Falla's formulation of a Hispano-Russian music bonding as Latin and anti-German, a view Stravinsky supported in his private notebooks shortly after leaving Madrid.[64] In 1921, during his second visit to Madrid, he assumed an overtly anti-German stance, declaring to the newspaper *La Voz* that the Germans "have no sense of music" and "have never understood music."[65] A similar perception of Stravinsky as a Latin and anti-German composer on the part of French critics led to his rhetorical naturalization, aided by the symbolic relevance of his artistic stature and personal trajectory. He was an exile of the Russian revolution who maintained an ambiguous and intermittent but lifelong relation with Catholicism—which could be

---

[61] "On sent que le debussysme et le stravinskisme de la première heure ont produit leur effet." Poueigh, "Critique musicale."

[62] "Falla fait, de si haut, la nique aux inventions, pourtant séduisantes, d'un Stravinsky." Gheusi, "La musique au théâtre."

[63] "la musique de Falla. Elle a connu *Le Sacre du Printemps*, elle l'a aimé, et dans l'orchestre de *El amor brujo* (1915), le spectre de Stravinsky est présent. Mais l'appel andalou est si puissant que Falla se libère: l'obsession russe disparaît sous la poussée d'une certaine Espagne." Ibid.

[64] Hess, *Manuel de Falla and Modernism*, 98–104, 161–163.

[65] P. Victory, "Los grandes compositores: Una conversación con Stravinsky," *La voz*, March 21, 1921. Quoted in Hess, *Manuel de Falla and Modernism*, 170.

read as anti-Protestant and therefore as anti-German—and embraced Paris as a haven for political and aesthetic freedom.[66] More importantly, he advocated values such as "purity" and "objectivity," which critics considered quintessentially French. Although this attitude did not prevent his staunchest supporter, Jean Cocteau, from eventually warning against his influence in French music in the xenophobic and influential pamphlet *Le coq et l'arlequin*,[67] Stravinsky somehow became rhetorically naturalized in the eyes of certain French musicians. In a letter to Stravinsky of October 24, 1915, Debussy treated him as an ally in the fight against German postromanticism.[68] Significantly, Nadia Boulanger defended him as a "paragon of Frenchness" in the early 1920s.[69] The intersection between constructions of *verismo* as a foreign and misleading influence and Debussy and Stravinsky as guiding or favorable influences constituted the basic argument for drawing *El amor brujo* toward notions of Latin music, and appropriating Falla's success with propagandistic ends.

Malherbe and the Noble Savage

Henry Malherbe's review for *Le Temps* deserves more detailed attention insofar as it exposes more clearly than others some of the cultural tensions underlying performances of Falla at the Opéra Comique. His attitude stands out for lacking in the more overt strategies of appropriation that underlay other critics' approaches to Falla's music. Not that his stance may be taken as unique, as some critics felt that Falla's works were too extraneous to their notions of French identity. E.-F. Velletaz, for instance, said *El amor brujo* was "very characteristic of the Spanish soul," as he had done with *La vie brève*.[70] In Malherbe's review, however, one finds some of the marks of an intellectual who was able to read beyond established binaries and prevailing anti-German sentiment. Malherbe was one of the few music critics of his time who fought in the frontlines during the First World War. He became, indeed, the first French combatant to produce a literary account of the War, *La Flamme au poing,* for which he received the prestigious Prix Goncourt in 1917.[71] His aversion to the war and his staunch

---

[66] On Stravinsky and Catholicism see Robert M. Copeland, "The Christian Message of Igor Stravinsky," *Musical Quarterly* 68, no. 4 (October 1, 1982): 563–579.

[67] Cocteau, *Le coq et l'arlequin*, 29. For a discussion of this work in context see Fulcher, *French Cultural Politics*, 162–167.

[68] Fulcher, *The Composer as Intellectual*, 53.

[69] Ibid., 168. Richard Taruskin, "Back to Whom? Neoclassicism as Ideology," *19th-Century Music* 16, no. 3 (1993): 291.

[70] "est bien caractéristique de l'âme espagnole." Velletaz, "A l'Opéra Comique."

[71] Henry Malherbe, *La flamme au poing* (Paris: A. Michel, 1917).

nationalism did not, however, develop into hatred of German culture, as implied by his monographs on Wagner and Schubert.[72] He developed a late interest in Franco-Spanish musical exchanges, which materialized in his monographs on Bizet's *Carmen* and María Malibrán, Manuel García's daughter.[73]

Malherbe's penchant for bridging cultural gaps and contesting established stereotypes manifests itself in his review of *El amor brujo*, where he challenges established notions of "music," although at the expense of casting Falla as a "noble savage":

> [Falla] always follows the movement inspired by nature. He keeps to a sort of rustic, barbarian simplicity. He sets fire to composition and harmony treatises, as if they were knight-errantry novels. He gets carried away by passion, not theory. He disdains foreign musics and only stays loyal to the music of his country, whose full image he renders with an eager and, at the same time, furious zeal.[74]

Malherbe casts the Spanish musician in the mold of the "noble savage," just as Laparra did in his articles throughout the 1920s. Malherbe depicts Falla as living close to nature, in a "rustic" and "barbarian" state, oblivious to technical and theoretical concerns and developments, and describes him as an emotional rather than rational person. His contention that Falla "disdains foreign musics"—understood as non-Spanish—stands in radical opposition to other critics' attempts to identify the influence of Debussy and Stravinsky in *El amor brujo*. In Malherbe's vivid imagination, Falla's alleged disdain for methods evokes what seems to be a parody of the burning of Don Quixote's library in chapter 6 of the eponymous novel. In Cervantes's novel, however, the barber and priest, quite the contrary, burn Don Quixote's knight-errantry books for the purpose of bringing him back to reason. This covert reference to what many Frenchmen would regard as the most Spanish of all literary myths, plus Malherbe's dwelling on the "passion" stereotype—also evident in the reference to a "furious zeal"—add to the discursive strategies by which this critic cast *El amor brujo* away from notions of French music.

---

[72] Henry Malherbe, *Richard Wagner révolutionnaire* (Paris: Albin Michel, 1938); Henry Malherbe, *Franz Schubert, son amour, ses amitiés* (Paris: Albin Michel, 1949).

[73] Henry Malherbe, *La passion de la Malibran* (Paris: Albin Michel, 1937); Henry Malherbe, *Carmen* (Paris: Albin Michel, 1951).

[74] "Il suit toujours le mouvement que la nature lui inspire. Il s'en tient à une sorte de simplicité rustique, barbare. Il met le feux aux traités de composition et d'harmonie, comme s'il s'agissait de romans de chevalerie. La passion l'emporte et non plus la théorie. Il dédaigne les musiques étrangères et ne garde de fidélité qu'à celle de sa patrie, dont il donne enfin sa pleine image, avec un zèle inquiet et furieux à la fois." Malherbe, Henri, "Chronique musicale."

Other passages from Malherbe's lengthy review of *El amor brujo* equally abound in the rhetoric of the "noble savage" trope. For instance, he describes the libretto as a "childlike fable" plagued with "savage graces" that "would make our spirits laugh";[75] he contends that Falla "relinquishes a tonal plan, modulations and conventional harmonies," deems his choice of tonalities "haphazard," points out the presence of "naively obstinate pedals" and describes his musical language as one where "demented notes have no connection with each other" and which "is opposed to our harmonic system."[76] However, Malherbe does not regard Falla's alleged nonchalance as a liability, but rather as an embodiment of a Rousseaunian critique of civilization. This stance can be gathered from his contention that Falla "has a system of his own which he chose under complete freedom and whose novelty strikes the pedants who, later on, it will charm"; or from his assertion that Falla's music helps to "measure the vanity of scientific music criticism"; or even his appreciation that Falla "does not fetter his passionate reverie with a learned and massive language."[77] These passages show a striking similarity to Henri Collet's obituary of Albéniz, published in 1909 (analyzed in Chapter 1).[78] Interestingly, the chronological distance between Malherbe's review of the homage and Collet's obituary suggests that their discursive similarity rested upon a web of widely shared meanings, tropes and prejudices about Spain rather than on direct intertextuality.[79]

Malherbe's most likely source, however, was Laparra's writings in *Le Ménestrel*, published during the 1920s. The imprint of Laparra's peculiar rhetoric manifests itself in Malherbe's description of "the traces of a bitter pride with which Castilian poverty always dresses itself," as well as a "brutal frankness," "tragic simplicity," "frenetic zeal and cruel rigour." These phrases recall Laparra's rendition of Castile through the trope of the "black legend," which informed not only some

---

[75] "fable puérile"; "grâces sauvages"; "donnerait à sourire à nos esprits."
[76] "renonce à un plan tonal, aux modulations, aux harmonies convenues"; "paraît pris au hasard"; "les notes affolées n'ont pas de lien entre elles"; "C'est contraire à tout notre système harmonique."
[77] "Il a un système à lui qu'il élut en toute liberté d'humeur et dont la nouveauté surprend les pédants que, plus tard, elle enchantera"; "la vanité de la critique musicale scientifique"; "n'emprisonne pas sa rêverie passionné dans une langue savante et nombreuse."
[78] Collet, "Nécrologie."
[79] In his second review of the Opéra Comique's homage to Falla, which he mostly dedicated to *El retablo*, Malherbe dwelled on the use of the "noble savage" trope to describe *El amor brujo*: "Avec *El amor brujo*, la voile des nuages qui nous cachait la personnalité du compositeur est déchiré. M de Falla y apparaît en véritable charmeur rustique. Il se défend d'être savant. Il n'emploie qu'un bagage de terroir pour composer son petit traité de magie dansante. Il s'est informé de toutes les vieilles formules de la sorcellerie musicale de son pays. Il les redit en un patois rénové avec une force tranchante, sans règle ni suite. Là plus qu'ailleurs on trouve sa verve de nature, sa vocation, son génie. Il s'est ainsi créé à lui-même un genre sinon un style, un rythme sinon une langue. Celle seconde veine aboutit à un succès décisif et auquel M. de Falla eût pu se tenir. Mais son ardeur de recherche, sa curiosité intellectuelle ne lui laissent guère de repos." Malherbe, "Chronique musicale: Manuel de Falla II."

of his writings but above all his opera *La habanera* (1908).[80] However, it seems striking that Malherbe associated a work plagued with gypsy and Andalusian stereotypes with Castile. Probably he confused the two works when recalling his impressions of that night, which, as we have seen above, left him "worn out as after a nervous strain," having witnessed the "immense, summary and contradictory images [that] knock against each other as in a quick dream." Malherbe's remarks about "Castilian poverty" rather make sense in connection with *El retablo*, as we will see.

Like Collet and Laparra, Malherbe endorses the state of savagery as a condition of aesthetic freedom, and ultimately political independence. He develops this argument, however, at the expense of surrounding Falla with a halo of alterity. Unlike Laparra and Collet, however, Malherbe makes no direct or oblique mention that German or French music constitutes the target of Falla's alleged critique of civilization. Malherbe's interest in driving *El amor brujo* away from notions of French or European music emerges most conspicuously in his reluctance to mention Stravinsky as the most likely source of Falla's use of a reduced ensemble, where "each instrument takes on an intense expressiveness" and produces "the most dazzling effects."[81] In fact, the politics of hegemony and marginalization underlying the use of the "noble savage" trope find rather unashamed expression in Malherbe's description of Falla's "cult" of the popular:

> Falla professes the cult of very simple, ancient popular songs. He even has a weakness for the most vulgar ones. He takes pleasure in their quaint villainess. He assembles them to the miserable and neglected sources of the spirit of his nation.[82]

A possible awareness of the subaltern condition that his engagement in imperialistic cultural strategies imposes on perceptions of Spain may inspire his otherwise striking and contradictory statement that, "despite its apparent improvisational character, *El amor brujo* seems like a complete masterpiece."[83] As in the case of Laparra, this contradiction illustrates how hard it was to endorse the margins of civilization without reifying their perceived alterity and, consequently, reproducing the very mechanics of power that, to some extent, constitute the target of

---

[80] Llano, "Hispanic Traditions," 97–140.

[81] "Chaque instrument prend une valeur expressive intense"; "de plus éclatants effets." Malherbe, "Chronique musicale: Manuel de Falla II." On Falla taking inspiration from Stravinsky's reduced ensembles see Hess, *Manuel de Falla and Modernism*, 101 and 161.

[82] "M. de Falla a le culte des chansons populaires anciennes très simples. Il a même un faible pour les plus vulgaires. Il se complaît à leur canaillerie désuète. Il les ramasse aux sources misérables et oubliés du génie de sa nation." Malherbe, "Chronique musicale: Manuel de Falla II."

[83] "Malgré son apparente improvisation, *El amor brujo* semble une pièce de maîtrise complète." Ibid.

the criticism encapsulated in the "noble savage" trope. This realization resembles what has prompted Gayatri Spivak to question, rather pessimistically, whether the subaltern can speak at all.[84]

Considered in relation to other reviews, Malherbe's shows that critics felt more comfortable subscribing to one pole or the other of the created binaries between notions of self and Other, French and Spanish music. Not every critic, however, submitted to the reassuring power of those binaries, and so they drew on different rhetorical repositories, perhaps with the purpose of bridging cultural divides. For instance, in their reviews Jean Prudhomme and Jean Chantavoine mediate between the strategies of marginalization and appropriation thus far described, as they attempt to bridge notions of French and Spanish music. Their descriptions of Falla's music acknowledge cultural difference, but one that is domesticated through use of the "French" or "civilized" rhetoric of order, revived in the 1920s through the discursive trope of "neoclassicism." Appropriation manifests subtly, at a rhetorical level, in the absence of any overt comparison with Debussy, Stravinsky or other European composers. In Prudhomme's review, for instance, self and Other, difference and sameness, intertwine and collapse:

> the richness of the score is dazzling. Rhythms, sonorities, balance, colorful timbres, elegant instrumentation, gushing invention, logical use of popular motives, all the most beautiful qualities that a musician should desire are assembled in these pages, which are swamped with clarity and do not hesitate to stay tonal.[85]

Prudhomme wavers between the use of phrases typically applied to Spanish music, such as "dazzling," "colorful," "gushing" and expressions of order such as "balance," "elegant," "logical."[86] He mixes both types of expression, without one coming after the other, and unites them at the end through the catchword "clarity," used both to cast French music as meridional and anti-German and to portray Spanish music as "sunny" and cheerful. Prudhomme's realization that Falla "do[es] not hesitate to stay tonal" contrasts with Malherbe's contention that Falla's language "is opposed to all our harmonic system."[87]

In Chantavoine's review, the encounter between the two semantic worlds described becomes even more harmonious:

---

[84] Spivak, "Can the Subaltern Speak?" 75, 78.

[85] "la richesse de la partition est éblouissante. Rythmes, sonorités, équilibre, coloris des timbres, instrumentation élégante, invention jaillissante, utilisation logique des motifs populaires, toutes les plus belles qualités qu'un musicien doit souhaiter sont rassemblées en ces pages inondées de clarté et qui n'hésitent pas à rester tonales." Jean Prudhomme, "Les premières. Théâtre de l'Opéra Comique," *Le matin* (March 1928).

[86] "éblouissant"; "coloris des timbres"; "jaillissante"; "équilibre"; "élégante"; "logique." Ibid.

[87] "C'est contraire à tout notre système harmonique." Henri Malherbe, "Chronique musicale: Manuel de Falla."

> Besides the Spanish color, so natural to Falla, there is, in the music of *El amor brujo*, something unreal and overwhelming at the same time, which escapes analysis, but where an artist's superiority reveals itself.... Falla achieves those powerful and subtle effects by way of the simplest, most spontaneous means, with a striking sobriety and accuracy.[88]

Unlike Malherbe, however, Chantavoine does not attribute what "escapes analysis" to a putative lack of technique or charming "savagery." He compensates his endorsement of (savage) "spontaneity" with the more restrained and neoclassical "simplicity," "sobriety" and "accuracy." Unlike Prudhomme, Chantavoine does not imbue his review with a Mediterranean rhetoric that may hold anti-German overtones. Indeed, his work reveals, as in the case of Malherbe, an equal interest in French music history and "German" music, especially Beethoven, Liszt and Mozart.[89]

Interestingly, the attitude of Prudhomme and Chantavoine shows how bridging notions of self and Other, French and Spanish music, helped to tear down the rhetorical divides French critics found themselves trapped in. This realization invites contemplation of the music of Spanish composers who, like Falla, tried to challenge and redefine preestablished boundaries between notions of French and Spanish music, as music that plays out how the French conceived of their relations with their Others. In that sense, Falla's music parallels Laparra's *La jota*, in which, as we have seen, an episode from Spanish history serves as the basis for tackling some of the sociopolitical conflicts engulfing France most profoundly.

Disciplining Difference: "La Argentina's" Neoclassical Performance

The issues analyzed so far played out in a particularly intense and peculiar way in the critics' comments on the dance performance and choreography. Not only did most critics regard the performance of "La Argentina" (Antonia Mercé)

---

[88] "Il y a, dans la musique de L'amour sorcier, outre la couleur espagnole, naturelle à M. de Falla, un sens frémissant du mystère—tour à tour pressentiment et hallucination –, quelque chose d'irréel et d'impérieux à la fois, qui échappe à l'analyse, mais où se révèle justement la supériorité d'un artiste"; "M. de Falla réalise ces effets, à la fois puissants et subtils par les moyens les plus simples, les plus spontanés, avec une sobriété et une justesse frappantes." Jean Chantavoine, "La semaine musicale: Théâtre de l'Opéra Comique," *Le ménestrel* (March 16, 1928).

[89] His publications include *Correspondance de Beethoven* (Paris: Calmann-Lévy, 1903); *Beethoven* (Paris: Félix Alcan, 1907); *Liszt* (Paris: Félix Alcan, 1910); *Liszt: Pages romantiques* (Paris: Félix Alcan, 1912); *De Couperin à Debussy* (Paris: Félix Alcan, 1921); *Les symphonies de Beethoven* (Paris: Pierre Mellottée, 1932); *Mozart dans Mozart* (Paris: Desclée de Brouwer, 1948); *Mozart* (Paris: Le bon plaisir, 1949).

as the most salient and gripping feature in *El amor brujo*, but also, as their comments reveal, they captured and exploited, in a highly intuitive and shrewd way, the capacity of the body in movement to perform and negotiate—or, as we shall see in this case, obliterate—prevailing notions of identity, including gender, class, ethnicity and nationality.[90] As with the music, plot and the other elements, La Argentina's performance and choreography elicited attempts to appropriate, universalize, or civilize it. Pastora Imperio's original choreography for the Madrid première in 1915 had brought together and enacted in a visually powerful and captivating way subaltern notions of gender, class and ethnicity, through the trope of the low-class female gypsy. In an interview published by the newspaper *La Patria*, Falla essentialized Imperio's gypsy background and construed it as a mark of authenticity. He described *El amor brujo* as an "eminently gypsy work" to which Pastora Imperio had contributed musical ideas, "the authenticity of which no one could deny."[91] Although Imperio's work was mediated to some extent by the Ballets Russes and current genres such as *cuplé* and music hall, it was not as aesthetically "progressive" as La Argentina's and represents an intermediate step between the latter and nineteenth-century exuberant renditions of Spanish dance, some of which were featured as opera or ballet numbers.[92] The 1928 performance, however, departed from that agenda of "gypsy authenticity." Falla deserves part of the credit thanks to his substantial reworking of the score and the drama, which began shortly after the 1915, prompted by adverse criticism. During the early 1920s the number and extent of the changes introduced by Falla increased, as he removed the dialogues, reshuffled several musical numbers and eliminated substantial portions of sung verse.[93] One may regard these changes as aimed at achieving greater concision and therefore as being in line with Falla's new neoclassical penchants. Since most critics focused on the dance performance, however, it seems likely that the aforementioned erosion of difference relied on La Argentina's work. Much of the innovative politics of the body at work in the 1928 production had to do with her purpose of "dignifying," normalizing, universalizing, tempering and, ultimately, disciplining Spanish dance, which earned her the reputation of inventing "Spanish neoclassical dance"—a title she should share with others, most

---

[90] For a theory of how dance and, more generally, the body in movement helps to negotiate social categories of gender, class, race and ethnicity, see Ann Cooper Albright, *Choreographing Difference: The Body and Identity in Contemporary Dance* (Middletown, CT: Wesleyan University Press, 1997), xiii–xv.

[91] "eminentemente gitana"; "a las que no podrá negárseles la 'autenticidad'"; quoted in Hess, *Manuel de Falla and Modernism*, 55–56.

[92] Hervé Lacombe, "L'Espagne à Paris au milieu du XIXe siècle (1847–1857). L'influence d'artistes espagnols sur l'imaginaire parisien et la construction d'une 'hispanicité,'" *La revue musicale* [ReM] 88, no. 2 (2002): 410. Murphy, "Carmen: Couleur Locale or the Real Thing?" 297–299.

[93] Hess, *Sacred Passions*, 152–153.

notably Antonio.⁹⁴ That purpose resulted, to a great extent, from her training and upbringing in Madrid and Paris.

La Argentina was born in Buenos Aires—hence her appellative—to Spanish parents, with whom she trained in classical ballet, before beginning to explore Spanish dancing as a teenager. La Argentina's innovative language consisted of a stylized blend of flamenco with traditions of Spanish dancing, most notably the *escuela bolera*, which, in turn, resulted from another mixture, of several classical Spanish dances, most prominently the eighteenth-century bolero school, and French classical ballet. La Argentina stylized these traditions through her classical training, and above all thanks to the influence of Fokine, Picasso, the Ballets Russes and the European avant-garde, which she assimilated during her several visits to Paris, where she finally settled in 1921. But her reading of Spanish traditions cannot be solely regarded as a disciplining one, for even within the aesthetics of neoclassicism she dynamized the *escuela bolera* by incorporating flamenco footwork and armwork.⁹⁵ Interestingly, as regards our analysis of representations of Spain, she built most of her dance recitals with dances from a number of Spanish regions, including Castile, Aragón, Navarre, Valencia, Galicia, and Andalusia.

Unsurprisingly, critical comments on La Argentina's performance that night did not indulge in the timeworn use of colorful metaphors. Instead, descriptions of her dance approached reviews of classical ballet, as we will see shortly. Besides her neoclassical approach to Spanish dancing, however, her own declarations on *El amor brujo* might have contributed to eliciting that common reaction. In an interview for *Le Gaulois*, she described this work as "a strange thing, a gypsy scene marked by mysterious superstitions which the Spaniards themselves find hard to understand."⁹⁶ Thus, La Argentina severed *El amor brujo* from what she regarded as "native" perceptions of Spanish identity. Furthermore, she felt "compelled to tone it down, to mitigate" the Ritual Fire Dance, which—she thinks—could otherwise strike French audiences.⁹⁷ Considering her neoclassical approach to Spanish dancing, one could read between the lines of her interview, a critique of more unbridled forms of flamenco dancing, represented by Pastora Imperio's primeval choreography of *El amor brujo*, which arguably constitutes the target of La Argentina's criticism here. Furthermore,

---

⁹⁴ Ninotchka Bennahum, *Antonia Mercé, "La Argentina": Flamenco and the Spanish Avant Garde* (Hanover and London: Wesleyan University Press, 2000). On Antonio and neoclassical Spanish dance, see Elsa Brunelleschi, *Antonio and Spanish Dancing* (London: Adam and Charles Black, 1958).

⁹⁵ See Bennahum, *Antonia Mercé*, 7–11, for a description and analysis of her style.

⁹⁶ "*El amor brujo* est une chose étrange, une scène gitane traversée de superstitions mystérieuses que les Espagnols eux-mêmes comprennent difficilement." Philippe Boubée de Grammont, "Le 'Gaulois au théâtre': Argentina à l'Opéra Comique: Ses impressions," *Le Gaulois* (March 11, 1928).

⁹⁷ "obligée de l'atténuer, de l'adoucir." Ibid.

neoclassicism most likely informs her organicist concerns, manifest in her remark that the Ritual Fire Dance "cannot be accepted unless presented in the context of the drama"[98]; or in her contention that "in order to follow the work's progression, one must overlook neither a single measure of the score, nor any of the performer's gestures."[99] Interestingly, her words and attitude suggest an awareness that structural organicism provides the framework in which cultural difference can be partially or totally neutralized, disciplined, appropriated, or ultimately obliterated.[100]

While satisfying modernist anxieties, La Argentina's neoclassic performance enabled her to contest hegemonic notions of the female gender and gypsy "race" as being marked by difference and therefore as subaltern. To judge from critical reactions, one could say that she succeeded, by and large. Most critics emphasized La Argentina's technical prowess and perfection, thus offering a portrait that contrasted with renditions of Falla as the "noble savage," such as we have seen above. Velletaz remarked that "the eye can, without prejudice of the ear, enjoy the picturesque tableaux presented, and admire Mme Argentina's supple and intelligent art without any reserves."[101] This portrait of La Argentina as a dexterous, technically skilled, intelligent and accomplished professional contrasts with Laparra's and Collet's portrayals of the Spanish musician as an "ignorant" and technically deficient though creative artist, which we have dealt with in previous chapters. Furthermore, Velletaz suggests that dance in *El amor brujo* constitutes a freestanding, independent medium that deserves recognition on its own terms. Velletaz's attempt to sever La Argentina's performance from the rest of the elements in *El amor brujo*, however, met with Coeuroy's remark that "no dancing temperament could better match that music, which is far from picturesque."[102]

The review by Pierre-Barthélemy Gheusi, director of the Opéra Comique during the First World War, author of *L'Opéra-Comique pendant la guerre* (Paris: 1919) as well as various book poems and novels, and cousin of Léon Gambetta, constitutes the most effective attempt to erase difference from La Argentina's performance.[103] Gheusi described her dancing as an expression of

---

[98] "Elle ne peut, en effet, être acceptée que lorsqu'elle vient à sa place dans le drame." Ibid.

[99] "Pour suivre la progression de la pièce, il ne faut pas laisser passer une mesure de la musique, un geste des interprètes." Ibid.

[100] Susan McClary argues that framing "excess" constitutes a regular practice in the Western canon. McClary, "Excess and Frame. The Musical Representation of Madwomen," in her *Feminine Endings*, 80–111.

[101] "L'œil peut donc, sans préjudice pour l'oreille, faire son profit des tableaux pittoresques qu'on lui présente, et admirer sans réserve l'art si souple et si intelligent de Mme Argentina." Velletaz, "A l'Opéra Comique."

[102] "Nul tempérament de danseuse ne s'accorde mieux avec cette musique qui ne veut pas être pittoresque." Coeuroy, "A l'Opéra Comique."

[103] Christophe Luraschi, *Biarritz des goelands: Précedé d'une biographie de Pierre-Barthelemy Gheusi* (Biarritz: Atlantica, 2001).

a disembodied and dehumanized experience. Gheusi found her movements "better than human," saying "it is not a woman who dances, but a soul."[104] He described La Argentina's body as dismembered under the pressure of neoclassic constraints, as she watches "her hands palpitate with a life of their own."[105] However, unity, order and perfection prevail, thanks to a performance in which "every gesture, the smallest attitude, the expressions of a face transfigured by a supreme art, collaborate in offering the audience the delicious shiver of perfection, with a harmonious blend of vivid grace and bewitching charm."[106] These words, plus Gheusi's extolling of "the smoothness of her lines" and "precision of her rhythms,"[107] make it hard to believe that he's reviewing a Spanish dance spectacle, given that with only a few exceptions[108] reviews of flamenco and Spanish dancing most often abounded in words such as "passion" and its derivatives.[109]

The rest of the critics similarly associated La Argentina's performance with the aesthetics of neoclassicism, sidelining any images of difference. According to Prudhomme, "Mme Argentina dances this act with a harmonious expression and elegance."[110] Curzon admires the "smoothness," "gravity," and "sobriety" of La Argentina's performance, as well as "the elegance in the smallest gestures, the subtlest facial nuances."[111] These phrases show a striking rhetorical similarity to Gheusi's review. However, Curzon curbs the restraining effect of his neoclassic rhetoric with the remark that "this little work is admirable for its orchestral color and flavor, for its vibrant, expressive motives."[112] His approach to Spanish music

---

[104] "un mouvement mieux qu'humain"; "Ce n'est plus une femme qui danse: c'est une âme." Gheusi, "La musique au théâtre."

[105] "ses mains palpitent d'une vie séparée." Ibid.

[106] "tous les gestes, la moindre attitude, les expressions d'un visage transfiguré par un art suprême concourent, avec une harmonie faite de grâce vivante et de charme ensorcelé, à donner au spectateur le frisson délicieux de la perfection." Ibid.

[107] "la souplesse de ses lignes"; "la précision de ses rythmes." Ibid.

[108] See, for instance, Stravinsky's description of *Cuadro flamenco* (1921) in terms of "logic," "precision" and "cold calculation." Igor Stravinsky, "Les espagnols aux ballets russes," *Comoedia*, May 15, 1921. Quoted in Ruth Piquer Sanclemente and Michael Christoforidis, "Modernist Representations of the Guitar and the Instrument's Classical Revival in the 1920s," *Proceedings of the First Conference on Interdisciplinary Musicology* (Paris, 2009), http://cim09.lam.jussieu.fr/CIM09-fr/Actes.html (accessed January 31, 2012).

[109] There is also passion, "flame" and "genius [génie]"—a word that reminds one of the catchword *duende*, central in the aesthetics of flamenco. However, she seems in control of the supernatural powers ("ses yeux commandent aux sortilèges"). On the duende and the centrality of the aesthetics of passion in flamenco see Washabaugh, *Flamenco*, vii.

[110] "Mme Argentina danse cet acte avec une expression et une grâce harmonieuses." Prudhomme, "Les premières. Théâtre de l'Opéra Comique."

[111] "souplesse"; "gravité"; "sobriété"; "grâce dans les moindres gestes, les plus subtiles nuances du visage." Curzon, "La musique. Opéra-Comique."

[112] "Ce petit ouvrage est admirable de couleur et de saveur orchestrales, de motifs vibrants, expressifs." Ibid.

is less likely to be tainted by anti-German biases given the interest for Wagner, Schumann and Mozart shown in his writings.[113]

In Schneider's review, the balance between notions of restraint and liberation finds subtler expression. Although the use of adjectives such as "beautiful" and "perfect" arguably cast La Argentina's performance under a neoclassic light, his remark that "her dance displays an unprecedented lightness and boldness" seems more ambiguous.[114] "Lightness" constitutes one of the staples of the aesthetics of classical ballet, especially since *La Sylphide*, but "boldness" rather expresses absence of restraint. Both semantic universes conflate in the phrase "delicate voluptuousness," with which Schneider ultimately characterizes La Argentina's style.[115]

A similar ambiguity finds expression in Chantavoine's review, which attributes to La Argentina's performance "a smoothness of movements and an intense physical movement which are common in the Salpêtrière and Sainte-Anne Hospitals, but which, taken to the theatre, reveal a first-rank artist."[116] By naming two of the most renowned psychiatric hospitals in Paris, Chantavoine evokes female images of madness, which constituted an integral part of male constructions of the female as subaltern from at least the nineteenth century.[117] Chantavoine's comment must have been equally elicited by Candelas's several acts of witchcraft. In the chapter titled "The Sorceress as Hysteric" from their co-written essay *The Newly Born Woman*, Cixous and Clément describe this "feminine role" as a "hysteric," "antiestablishment" character, who "introduces disorder into the well-regulated unfolding of everyday life"; they also characterize the sorceress as a "conservative character," insofar as "every sorceress ends up being destroyed, and nothing is registered of her but mythical traces."[118] From this viewpoint, the sorceress comes to embody a contradiction similar to Carmen's, insofar as her ultimate death obliterates her critical potential. Notwithstanding the obvious correspondences between Candelas and the "hysteric sorceress" of Cixous and Clément, what strikes me as relevant in Chantavoine's

---

[113] Henri de Curzon, ed., *Schumann: écrits sur la musique et les musiciens* (Paris: Fischbacher, 1898); *Les Lieder de Franz Schubert* (Paris: Fischbacher 1899); *Les Lieder et airs détachés de Beethoven* (Paris: Fischbacher, 1905); *Mozart* (Paris: Fischbacher, 1914). See Malcolm Turner and Jean Gribenski, "Curzon, (Emmanuel) Henri (Parent) de," in *Grove Music Online. Oxford Music Online*, http://www.oxfordmusiconline.com/subscriber/article/grove/music/06977 (accessed January 31, 2012).

[114] "sa danse est d'une légèreté et d'une hardiesse inouïes" Schneider, "Le 'Gaulois au Théâtre.'"

[115] "volupté délicate." Ibid.

[116] "une souplesse de mouvements et une intense mobilité de physionomie qui sont chose commune dans les services de la Salpêtrière ou de Sainte-Anne mais qui, au théâtre, révèlent une artiste de premier ordre." Chantavoine, "La semaine musicale."

[117] McClary, "Excess and Frame."

[118] Hélène Cixous and Catherine Clément, *The Newly Born Woman* (Minneapolis: University of Minnesota Press, 1996/1975), 5.

review is the absence or the taming of what Anne Cooper Albright describes as the "frightening representation of woman's sexuality" through dance.[119] Chantavoine renders La Argentina as a "first-rank artist" rather than a mad woman or female other. His review constitutes a telling example of how reactions to La Argentina's performance in the context of the Falla homage were predicated on an attempt to erase or tame all forms of difference. As a result of La Argentina's disciplining of the female gypsy body by way of an avant-garde, neoclassic approach to Spanish dancing, critics registered an otherworldly, disembodied otherness in her performance, rather than a cultural, colonial otherness. The effect of her performance on perceptions of Spanish culture and identity were equally empowering and legitimizing, thanks to the universalizing connotations of the aesthetics of neoclassicism in that context. One could argue, however, that the price of cultural legitimization is the obliteration of difference.

A French Quixote? Cultural Translation and Textual Adaptation in *El retablo de Maese Pedro*

The performance of *El retablo de Maese Pedro* constituted the last vignette through which Spain was showcased at the Opéra Comique on the occasion of the Falla homage. Rather than presenting a fictional story with gypsy characters and issues of racial otherness, this work portrayed Spain through the literary myth that French audiences most associated with Spain: Don Quixote. Thanks to the numerous French translations of the novel—which date back to as early as the seventeenth century[120]—as well as its manifold theatrical and musical adaptations, French audiences were well acquainted with some of its episodes. Different from most other adaptations, however, Falla's is set in a modernist and detached framework, which simultaneously demanded and denied engagement and which, as we will see, confused and challenged the understanding of several critics.[121]

The 1928 performance of *El retablo* raised complex questions of textual adaptation, which mostly had to do with this work's composite nature. Falla composed a musical score and wrote the libretto based on chapters 25 and 26 from Cervantes's *Don Quixote*, subsequently based on the French epic poem *Chanson de Roland*. Furthermore, the Opéra Comique presented a French translation of

---

[119] Albright, *Choreographing Difference*, 104.
[120] For a compelling recount of Don Quixote's translations into French and their readability see Marc Charron, "De la question de la lisibilité des traductions françaises de Don Quijote," in *Doubts and Directions in Translation Studies: Selected Contributions from the EST Congress, Lisbon 2004*, ed. Yves Gambier, Miriam Shlesinger, and Radegundis Stolze (John Benjamins, 2007), 311–322.
[121] See Dorsch, "Nostalgia and Modernism in Puppet Music."

Falla's libretto by his friend Jean-Aubry, instead of the Spanish libretto presented at the world première in the Salon Polignac (1923). As we shall see, Jean-Aubry's translation introduced further layers of semantic complexity.

The 1928 performance of *El retablo*, therefore, offers an opportunity to explore the "ethics of translation" that mediated in French perceptions and representations of "Spanish culture."[122] As Katherine M. Faull has argued, "the treatment of the foreign in the task of translation is inextricably linked to an ethics of the word."[123] Following from this assumption, I propose to regard the "word" as a loose concept that encompasses a variety of cultural codes and practices, and to understand "translation" as the process by which those codes and practices lose part of their "original" meaning as they are reinterpreted in a "new" context. Yet, the "foreign" is, in itself, a contingent and contentious concept on which cultural anxieties are projected and enacted. As my analysis shall show, ethical approaches to "Spanish difference" during the Falla homage ranged from attempts to obliterate it, as in reviews of La Argentina's performance of *El amor brujo*, to more empathetic and engaging attitudes.

In the present study, the concept of "translation" applies to all the aspects of the production, from the libretto to the stage directions. As I shall argue, issues of representation and identity in Falla's textual adaptation gained further layers of semantic structure and complexity in the transcultural and panoptical context of the Falla homage at the Opéra Comique, where various images of Spain were violently juxtaposed and collided with one another. Furthermore, I shall explain how the multilayered structure of meaning production just described complicated itself thanks to the experimentation with avant-garde, metatheatrical devices. But first, it is relevant to understand the symbolic meaning of the Quixote myth in Spanish intellectual debate.

The Don Quixote Myth in Spain

Falla took the subject matter from chapters 25 and 26 of Cervantes's novel *Don Quixote*, which he adapted for the stage. With the help of the production team, he cut away a few passages and altered the framing dialogues in which the otherwise unaltered puppet story unfolds[124]: having stopped at Master Peter's inn,

---

[122] On the concept "ethics of translation" see Sandra Bermann, "Introduction," in *Nation, Language, and the Ethics of Translation*, ed. Sandra Bermann and Michael Wood (Princeton, NJ: Princeton University Press, 2005), 4–7; Jacques Derrida, "What Is a "Relevant" Translation?" *Critical Inquiry* 27, no. 2 (2001): 180–181.

[123] Katherine M. Faull, "Translation and Culture," in *Translation and Culture*, ed. Katherine M. Faull (Cranbury NJ: Associated University Presses, 2004), 13.

[124] Falla substituted Don Quixote's final negotiations with Maese Pedro about the price to be reimbursed for the destroyed puppet theatre, present in the novel, for a love ode to his idealized beloved Dulcinea del Toboso.

Don Quixote witnesses a puppet play based on the *Chanson de Roland*, in which the nobleman Don Gayferos rescues his wife Melisendra, held captive by the Moors. During the puppet performance, Don Quixote scolds the Trujamán or storyteller boy for introducing novelties in the story and not standing by the original source—a feature that adds a further layer of semantic complexity. At the end, driven by the action, Don Quixote takes the play for real and destroys the puppet theater in his attempt to rescue Melisendra.

Falla's musical adaptation of Don Quixote may be read in connection with the work of various prominent Spanish intellectuals, such as Miguel de Unamuno's *La vida de Don Quijote y Sancho* (1905) and Ortega y Gasset's *Meditaciones del Quijote* (1914).[125] Interestingly, Arredondo has described these intellectuals' attitude as "Quixotism" and analyzed how they turned Don Quixote into a national hero.[126] They read Don Quixote as a myth of the regeneration that, they thought, would help Spain recover from the economic recession and moral crisis they believed had engulfed Spanish society. They understood this situation as the result of a centuries-long process of colonial losses, culminating in the 1898 war against the United States in which Spain lost Cuba, the Philippines and Guam. They expected that the example of Don Quixote would instill in the Spaniards a longed-for sense of heroism. Consequently, they portrayed him as the madman and idealistic hero who carried out his deeds unabatedly, overcoming all sorts of adversities. Furthermore, these intellectuals turned the setting of Don Quixote's adventures, the central region of Castile, into the object of an intense intellectual investment. They imbued the region with national symbolic value by emphasizing its links with the Golden Age of Spanish literature, through the "mystic" school of poetry that included Saints Teresa of Avila and John of the Cross. Furthermore, they endowed Castile with centralist connotations, in order to curb the rise of nonstate nationalisms in Spain, most conspicuously Basque and Catalan.

The public and critics who attended the 1928 performance of *El retablo* were not familiar with the meanings that Quixote had acquired in contemporary Spain. To present *El retablo* as part of a showcase of Spanish identities did not help to bridge this cultural gap, especially as *La vie brève* and *El amor brujo* displayed the Andalusian and gypsy stereotypes that *El retablo* was shaped against. Furthermore, Falla read *Don Quixote* from a rather personal point of view, which showed a loose connection with the work of the "Quixotists." His focus on Castile was not so much aimed at fostering Spain's economic and moral recovery as at dislodging time-worn southern stereotypes, such as the gypsies, bullfighters and flamenco dancers.[127] This is the sense in which he declared, in an interview

---

[125] Christoforidis, "From Folksong to Plainchant," 212–213; Hess, *Manuel de Falla and Modernism*, 218–223.
[126] Britt-Arredondo, *Quixotism*.
[127] Christoforidis, "From Folksong to Plainchant," 212–213; Hess, *Manuel de Falla and Modernism*, 210.

with Jean-Aubry held in 1923, that in "*El Retablo* there is nothing southern: everything is Castilian, excepting the first part of the finale, which is based on a Catalonian theme. It is as completely Castilian in character as the *Three-Cornered Hat* is Andalusian."[128] As Christoforidis has documented and Hess has observed, "relatively few of the work's musical materials derive from Castilian sources."[129] This apparent incoherence might possibly testify to the freedom with which Falla subscribed to the thought of the Generation of 1898. Furthermore, one could argue that, if the musical sources of *El retablo* cannot be strictly considered Castilian, they belong to a time, that is, the early modern period, when regional musical schools had not yet been developed. Although it was not necessary to understand the meaning of the Quixote myth in Spain in order to enjoy *El retablo*, failure to appreciate it certainly contributed to a sense of cultural distance that, as we shall see, led several critics to condemn the work.

Staging and Production

Beyond Spanish intellectual debates, *El retablo* may be regarded in connection with avant-garde experiments with puppet theater carried out since the end of the nineteenth century by stage directors Gordon Craig, Adolphe Appia and Vsevolod Meyerhold.[130] Craig's formulation of the "Super-marionettes" most likely informed Falla's decision to represent two of the nonpuppet characters, Don Quixote and Sancho Panza, as marionettes. Falla must have assimilated the Super-marionettes from Gregorio Martínez Sierra and his then-wife María Lejárraga. The Sierra-Lejárraga matrimony played a key role in introducing new staging techniques in Spanish theater during the 1910s and 1920s, precisely under the influence of Appia, Meyerhold and above all Craig.[131] Falla collaborated with them in several productions, most notably *El amor brujo* and *El corregidor y la molinera*, the latter of which was the basis for *The Three-Cornered Hat*. By the 1920s, however, the use of puppets had become a relatively common practice among the Spanish avant-garde. As José Antonio Sánchez has argued, experiments with puppets and marionettes were inextricably linked to the birth

---

[128] "De Falla Talks of his New Work Based on a Don Quijote Theme," *Christian Science Monitor*, September 1, 1923, 23. Quoted in Dorsch, "Nostalgia and Modernism," 150.

[129] Michael Christoforidis, "Manuel de Falla, Early Music and the Harpsichord in 'El Retablo de Maese Pedro,'" in *Five Centuries of Spanish Keyboard Music: Proceedings of FIMTE Symposia 2002–2004*, ed. Luisa Morales (Barcelona: LEAL, 2007), 343–356. Hess, *Manuel de Falla and Modernism*, 210–211.

[130] Eckhard Weber, "Falla y Lorca: Entre la tradición y la vanguardia," in *Falla y Lorca: Entre la tradición y la vanguardia*, ed. Susana Zapke (Kassel: Reichenberger, 1999), 117–154; Hess, *Manuel de Falla and Modernism*, 201; Dorsch, "Nostalgia and Modernism," 157.

[131] José Antonio Sánchez, "'The Impossible Theatre': The Spanish Stage at the Time of the Avant-Garde," *Contemporary Theatre Review* 7, no. 2 (1998): 9–10.

of the figure of the stage director in Spain in those years.[132] The impresario, stage director and playwright Cipriano Rivas Cherif played a key role in introducing the marionettes. He likely influenced Falla for, besides working for the theater, he helped to found the Ballets Espagnols and wrote several choreographies for La Argentina.[133]

Besides the European avant-garde, *El retablo* should also be connected with the traditional Andalusian popular theater known as *cristobicas*, which started to be revived in Falla's natal Cadix in the 1920s. Falla contributed to this revival by carrying out, together with García Lorca, research trips and fieldwork around the Andalusian villages. This work was the basis for Lorca's collection of puppet-theater plays entitled *Los Títeres de Cachiporra*.[134] Falla's *El retablo* likely influenced Lorca's puppet farce *El retablillo de Don Cristóbal*, written in 1923 and first performed in 1935. Like Falla, Lorca toyed with the setting of a theater within a theater, and, as in *El retablo*, the nonpuppet characters—Poet and Director—constantly conflict with the puppet story. The Andalusian origin of the *cristobicas* testifies, once again, to the flexibility of Falla's approach to *castellanismo*, which, as argued above, the 1898 intellectuals had modeled against *andalucismo*.

Besides Falla's staging decisions, Ignacio Zuloaga's settings and the stage direction of Georges Ricou[135] characterized the 1928 production of *El retablo*.[136] The choice of Zuloaga is telling of the care put into the production, as perhaps no other painter met the ideals of the 1898 and 1914 intellectual generations so closely.[137] Through his paintings of the 1920s, Zuloaga contributed to creating a national imaginary based on elements from Castile and references to a Catholic mysticism. He painted a portrait of Barrès in 1913, and, like the latter and Spanish intellectuals, he was a passionate admirer of El Greco's paintings.[138] Zuloaga's close relationship with his old friend and, later, brother-in-law,

---

[132] Sánchez, "The Impossible Theatre," 10.

[133] Sánchez, "The Impossible Theatre," 10–12; Aguilera Sastre and Aznar Soler, *Cipriano de Rivas Cherif*.

[134] Weber, "Los Títeres, Falla y Lorca" 117–120; Dorsch, "Nostalgia and Modernism," 131.

[135] Georges Ricou directed the Opéra Comique between 1925 and 1931, together with Louis Masson as co-director and Albert Carré as honorary director. Nichols, *The Harlequin Years*, 82. There is very little information on Georges Ricou. The Grove Dictionary does not include an entry or any reference in other entries. Ricou was the manager of the Opéra Comique at the time when Debussy's *Pelléas et Mélisande* premiered there. Orledge, *Debussy and the Theatre*, 50.

[136] Zuloaga's settings are conspicuously absent from the scholarly work and biographies on Zuloaga. Significantly, Lafuente Ferrari's extensive and well-documented biography of Zuloaga does not include any reference for the 1928 production of *El retablo* in the appended catalogue of works. Enrique Lafuente Ferrari, *La vida y el arte de Ignacio Zuloaga* (Madrid: Revista de Occidente, 1972).

[137] Fox, *La invención de España*, 167–174; Martín Martínez, "Painting and Sculpture in Modern Spain," 239–242.

[138] Jesús Rodríguez del Castillo, *Ignacio Zuloaga el hombre* (Zarauz: Icharopena, 1970), 138. Ghislaine Plessier, *Étude critique de la correspondance de Zuloaga et Rodin de 1903 a 1917* (Paris: Éditions Hispaniques, 1983), 23. Barrès, *Greco*.

the painter Maxime Delthomas, might have contributed to his being hired. Delthomas, who designed the marionettes for *El retablo*, formed part of the Opéra Comique's directive.[139] Zuloaga also enjoyed a longstanding friendship with Falla, who figured among the many artists and intellectual personalities visiting the former's home in Zumaya;[140] Falla was one of the musicians who stayed closest to Zuloaga, along with Albéniz, Satie, Ravel, Pau Casals, Miguel Llobet, Ángel Barrios and others.[141] Perhaps one of the most telling testimonies of their friendship is the portrait of Falla by Zuloaga, which is set before a Castilian landscape and shows El Greco's influence rather conspicuously.[142] Zuloaga shared with Falla the same predisposition for negotiating "Spain" with his French counterparts. Indeed, they met in Paris, where both earned their first recognition.[143] Like Falla, Zuloaga evolved from an early *andalucismo* toward an embrace of *castellanismo*.[144] They collaborated on several ventures, including the *cante jondo* competition organized by Falla and Lorca in Granada in 1922. Zuloaga exhibited some of his paintings there, and played an instrumental role in bringing several personalities to the competition, notably the Polignac princess. Other collaborations between Falla and Zuloaga included the production of *El retablo* in San Sebastian (1932) and a ballet plotted by Zuloaga, based on Gregorio el Botero, an acquaintance from the Castilian village of Sepúlveda, who equally inspired his eponymous painting. Diaghilev's Ballets Russes were to perform this ballet, which ultimately never came to fruition.[145] The relationship between Falla and Zuloaga waned with time. From his exile in Argentina, Falla attributed this decline to his health issues, which left him with limited capacity to write letters.[146] Despite Falla's reluctance to base his friendships on political grounds, these should not be altogether discarded, for Zuloaga was awarded the Mussolini Prize at the Venice Biennial and received several homages from the Franco

---

[139] Plessier, *Étude critique*, 22. On Falla's relationship with Delthomas see Rodriguez del Castillo, *Ignacio Zuloaga*, 176–184.

[140] Lafuente Ferrari, *La vida y el arte*, 114. Jesus María de Arozamena, *Ignacio Zuloaga: El pintor, el hombre* (San Sebastián: Sociedad Guipuzcoana de Ediciones y Publicaciones, 1970), 220. Falla and Zuloaga also met in the opening of the Goya museum in the latter's natal village, Fuendetodos. Lafuente Ferrari, *La vida y el arte*, 115. On this opening see also Arozamena, *Ignacio Zuloaga*, 204–205.

[141] Lafuente Ferrari, *La vida y el arte*, 104.

[142] Arozamena, *Ignacio Zuloaga*, 171.

[143] Zuloaga traveled extensively to Paris and even lived there at different moments of his life, since the early twentieth century. For a full account of Zuloaga's stays in Paris see Rodríguez del Castillo, *Ignacio Zuloaga*, 110, 129, 138, 176–184, 196.

[144] The subject of "Vispera de toros," which he submitted—unsuccessfully—to the 1900 Paris International Exhibition, differs significantly from his later Castilian paintings. Rodriguez del Castillo, *Ignacio Zuloaga*, 196.

[145] Arozamena, *Ignacio Zuloaga*, 228, 14, 124.

[146] The 1950 edition of Lafuente Ferrari's monograph quotes the "Carta de Manuel de Falla a la Familia Zuloaga, 7 de Noviembre de 1945, Alta Gracia, Provincia de Córdoba, Argentina." Lafuente Ferrari, *La vida y el arte*, 295.

regime.[147] Meanwhile Falla went into exile and rejected Franco's seductive offers, which were aimed at turning the composer into cultural capital in support of the dictatorship.[148] Although these events may not have provoked a rupture, they could have contributed to a cooling of their relationship.

The 1928 performance of *El retablo* was for Falla and Zuloaga an opportunity to bring together their individual experiences and put into practice several avant-garde, distancing effects. Their project, however, fell into an adverse, if not hostile, interpretive context. To begin with, *El retablo* met with the opposition of certain critics who were unable or reluctant to regard the puppet theater as "art."[149] In his review for *Le Ménestrel*, Jean Chantavoine stated that *El retablo* "is only an entertainment" (*divertissement*) "and not a very accomplished one"; according to Chantavoine, "Falla seems to have experienced the influence of certain works which, during or after the war, have taken the puppet show procedures to the greatest and most serious stages."[150] Chantavoine seems to regard the use of puppets as inappropriate of a "serious stage." Though his remark mostly exudes a concern for artistic stature, it deserves analysis in the context of the anti-German connotations of "seriousness," analyzed in Chapter 1. Jean-Aubry, who translated the libretto of *El retablo* into French, construed French identity as comic in order to oppose Germany's alleged seriousness. This stance can be gathered from his anti-German wartime pamphlet *La musique française d'aujourd'hui*, and especially from his comments on Ravel's humorous opera *L'heure espagnole*:

> [*L'heure espagnole*] invites us to consider the engaging question of "the comic in music"; engaging, at least, for those whom the religion of seriousness at any price, has not deprived of the virtues that, for a long time, constituted the advantage and attraction of our race. For too long a time, a foreign sense of gravity has influenced French music.[151]

---

[147] Arozamena, *Ignacio Zuloaga*, 305–305.

[148] Hess, *Sacred Passions*, 256, 228–241.

[149] Dorsch's remark that an obituary of Appia, including a reference to Craig, appeared in the cover of the *Comoedia* issue in which the review of the Falla homage was published, suggests that the critical opposition to the use of puppets in *El retablo* was not so much based on unawareness as on aesthetic incompatibilities. Dorsch, "Production Problems and Depersonalised Puppets," 27. See Jacques Copeau, "L'art et l'oeuvre d'Adolphe Appia," *Comoedia*, (March 12, 1928), 1.

[150] "Les Tréteaux ne sont qu'un divertissement et ce divertissement n'est pas très réussi"; "M. de Falla, dans cette parade, semble avoir subi l'influence de quelques ouvrages qui, pendant ou depuis la guerre, ont transporté sur les scènes les plus vastes et les plus sérieuses, les procédés de Guignol"; Chantavoine, "La semaine musicale Opéra Comique."

[151] "Elle est le lieu de considérer la question attachante du 'comique musical,' attachante, du moins pour ceux que la religion du sérieux à tout prix n'a pas par trop démunis de quelques vertus qui firent de tout temps l'avantage et l'agrément de notre race. Assez longtemps le sens d'une gravité étrangère influença la musique en France." Jean-Aubry, *La musique française d'aujourd'hui*, 116.

Jean-Aubry interprets the comic in *L'heure* as irrefutable proof of its Frenchness, and he considers seriousness as a foreign—surely meaning German—element. It is hardly striking that Chantavoine defended seriousness, since his aesthetic allegiances were rather pro-German, without it necessarily meaning anti-French. Chantavoine trained at the University of Berlin with the German musicologist Max Friedländer in 1898 and between 1901 and 1903. He wrote monographs on Beethoven, Liszt and Mozart, and translated librettos of operas by Wagner, Strauss and Mozart. He was also concerned with defining French tradition, as evinced in *De Couperin à Debussy* (1921).[152] In sum, Chantavoine condemned *El retablo*'s lack of artistic stature but, by so doing, most likely helped to sever that work from notions of German music.

The critics' understanding of *El retablo* was also hindered by the prevalence of the absolute music paradigm. This kind of approach had already manifested itself through the general endorsement of La Argentina's neoclassic and disembodied performance of *El amor brujo*. As far as *El retablo* is concerned, it emerged most ostensibly in Curzon's review, especially in his remark that "the subject-matter has given [the musical composition] a rambling character, with a disconcerting slowness. One could almost even speak of gaps."[153] His contention that the Trujamán's "fast but long" recitations "constantly break the unity of the musical fabric" suggests that his critique rests on a general prejudice against music composed for the stage.[154] Unlike most symphonic music, stage music cannot rely on strictly musical means to achieve unity or structural coherence, as other factors come into play. By mentioning the Trujamán's recitations, Curzon acknowledges that the requirements of dramatic verisimilitude may conflict with the continuity of musical discourse, which constitutes his primary concern. One should not neglect, however, the possibility that Curzon had trouble with the difficulties of translating and singing the *trujamán*'s recitations, which were based on a rather idiosyncratic Spanish tradition—as shall be discussed later. Furthermore, in his review Curzon takes issue with some aspects of the staging, which "somehow prevent [him] from following [*El retablo*] well."[155] He feels uncomfortable with the presence of "cardboard figures *greater than the human scale*"—his emphasis— and the smallness of the puppets;[156] "one would better understand, therefore,

---

[152] Malcolm Turner, "Chantavoine, Jean," in *Grove Music Online*, ed. Stanley Sadie, http://www.oxfordmusiconline.com:80/subscriber/article/grove/music/05417 (accessed April 15, 2011); J.-G. Prod'homme, "Jean Chantavoine. Nécrologie," *Revue de musicologie* 34, no. 103–104 (December 1952): 166–167.

[153] "le sujet lui a donné un caractère décousu, avec des lenteurs, on dirait presque des trous, qui déconcertent." Curzon, "La musique: Opéra Comique."

[154] "Ses boniments, rapides et pourtant longs, et sur la même note, autant que des épisodes variés, rompent constamment l'unité de la trame musicale." Ibid.

[155] "empêche un peu de la bien suivre." Ibid.

[156] Arozamena justifies the marionettes by saying that Falla could avoid the journalists from inside. "Falla, podía huir de los periodistas metiéndose en la cabeza de Sancho y temblaba ante aquel derroche de limpias locuras." Arozamena, *Ignacio Zuloaga*, 184.

that [they] were...real characters on human scale," given that, although "it is true that, in Cervantes, they are articulated puppets [...] one cannot conceive of Don Quixote being hypnotized by plain figures in painted cardboard!"[157] Curzon has trouble with the multiplicity of dramatic levels in *El retablo*, and wishes for a plain dramatic structure in which the puppets are represented by humans. His testimony is remarkable for its concern for verisimilitude, which finds expression in his manifest—but thwarted—desire to engage with Don Quixote's own engagement with the puppets. In this particular aspect, at least, Curzon sympathized with Falla's intentions, for, as Juliane Dorsch has argued, several indications in the score were aimed at making the audience identify with Don Quixote.[158] One feels tempted to tag Curzon's stance as conservative; it seems he could have raised a similar objection to any other puppet theater play. His reaction lays bare *El retablo*'s complex politics of engagement, characterized by a tension between, on the one hand, a focus on a linear narrative being told by the Trujamán's comments on the action and, on the other hand, distancing and distorting effects such as the aforementioned multilayered dramatic structure and discordant puppet sizes. One could add musical effects such as what Hess describes as "abrupt splashes of modal color" in the opening sinfonia.[159]

Other critics similarly took issue with certain aspects of the staging and performance. Writing for *Le Gaulois*, Schneider complained that "one cannot understand the story presented under the form of a recitative," for which he blamed Olga Kamienska, the soprano in the role of the Trujamán.[160] Possibly, the use of a "pierced gag of a grotesque cardboard mask," as described by another critic, further smudged the singer's articulation.[161] In his review for *La Liberté*, Dezarnaux was even more explicit in labeling as "disastrous" the effect produced by representing Don Quixote and Sancho "by cardboard figures larger than human scale, inside of which the unfortunate singers are lodged."[162] Dezarnaux must have voiced a general impression, to judge from the fact that the singers were brought down to the orchestra pit after the first performance and were replaced by miming actors on the stage.[163]

---

[157] "cartonnages *plus grands que nature*"; "on comprendrait mieux, dès lors, que les marionnettes fussent,...des vrais personnages de taille normale"; "Il est certain que dans Cervantès ce sont des poupées articulées"; "On ne conçoit pas Don Quichotte s'hypnotisant sur des figurines plates de carton peint!" Curzon, "La musique: Opéra Comique."

[158] Dorsch, "Nostalgia and Modernism," 140–141.

[159] Hess, *Manuel de Falla and Modernism*, 213.

[160] "Malheureusement, on ne comprend pas le boniment explicatif, sous forme de récitatif." Schneider, "Le Gaulois au théâtre."

[161] "le bâillon percé d'un cartonnage caricatural." Gheusi, "La musique au théâtre."

[162] "désastreux"; "par des cartonnages plus grands que nature, dans lesquels se logent les malheureux chanteurs." Robert Dezarnaux, "La Musique," *La Liberté* (March 12, 1928): 1–2.

[163] "Depuis la première représentation, ils déploient leur maîtrise habituelle dans la fosse de l'orchestre. D'autres interprètes, non préoccupées du texte, miment, sur la scène, les rôles de don Quichotte et de Sancho." Malherbe, "Chronique musicale: Manuel de Falla II."

Appropriating *El retablo*

Had critics not grappled with the issues of staging described above, they would have most likely found *El retablo*'s avant-garde credentials to be a suitable basis for their discursive strategies. In other words, the use of cardboard figures and masks not only hindered the understanding of the text but ultimately interfered with the critics' intention to appropriate Falla's symbolic status. Precisely the most supportive critics were the most willing or prepared to understand *El retablo*'s modernisms. Coeuroy, for instance, situated *El retablo* "in the antipodes of *La vie brève*'s grandiloquences," calling it "a spectacle of poetry and allusion which takes part in the current movement of scenic liberty."[164] He described the production as "an original spectacle," deemed Falla "a fertile master of unexpected transformations" and contended that *El retablo* "sets a precedent recommendable to explorers of new symbols"[165]; he also remarked that the latter work "addresses a literate audience [and] arouses their sophisticated curiosities."[166] Last of all, he remarked that Falla's musical "comments" on Cervantes's novel "will recall those keen on searching for analogies, certain paraphrases—more ornamented—in recent mime dramas produced by Diaghilev"—by which he was probably referring to Stravinsky's *Apollon musagète*.[167] Once again, associations with Stravinsky provided a source of legitimacy.

Charles Tenroc similarly identified an "attraction for Stravinsky" in *Le Courrier musical*. Whether he conceived of Stravinsky's music as a Frenchifying influence, however, is dubious in light of his ambiguously xenophobic stance. Although his holding the post of president of the Ligue Nationale pour la Défense de la Musique Française since its founding in 1916 tells us about his anti-German principles, he gave pride of place to xenophobic and anti-Russian expressions by other musicologists in the pages of *Le Courrier musical*, where he acted as chief editor. In 1923, this journal published Louis Vuillemin's attacks on Jean Wiéner in 1923, whom he accused of honoring an eclectic and Semitic aesthetics by programming Stravinsky and Les Six.[168] Tenroc's intentions of Frenchifying *El retablo* seem less ambiguous when he points out the presence of "post-Debussyan ferments" in the score,[169] and they become gradually

---

[164] "Aux antipodes des grandiloquences de la Vie Brève"; "C'est un spectacle de poésie et d'allusion qui participe au mouvement actuel de liberté scénique." Coeuroy, "À l'Opéra Comique."

[165] "C'est un spectacle original"; "un maître fécond en avatars inattendus"; "crée un précèdent recommandable aux explorateurs de nouveaux symboles." Ibid.

[166] "Il s'adresse à un public lettré, émoustille ses curiosités blasées." Ibid.

[167] "commentaires"; "rappelleraient, à ceux qui veulent absolument chercher des analogies, certaines paraphrases, plus tarabiscotées il est vrai, des récents mimodrames montés par M. de Diaghilev." Ibid.

[168] Fulcher, *The Composer as Intellectual*, 31, 144.

[169] "l'attirance stravinskiste"; "les ferments post-debussystes." Tenroc, "Opéra Comique: La vie brève."

clearer as one progresses through his review. Tenroc argues that *El retablo* "is no longer descriptive Spanish music with indigenous, primitive [*primaires*] rhythms, deathblows and foot stamping. It has become the Hispanizing translation of impressions caused by Spain, passed through a Debussyan filter."[170] This argument encloses a politics of cultural hegemony and a coercive conception of "influence," which Tenroc understands as a taming force. He tries to dissimulate the propagandistic underpinnings by denying that "those concessions to internationalism [...] diminish the specific value of Falla's art" and calling them "needs of universal evolution"[171]; he acknowledges that "the music stays away even more [than *El amor brujo*] from *La vie brève*, by way of a will to expunge every trace of Italianism."[172] However, his review is deeply suffused with colonialist narratives:

> Shaking off the yoke of an ordinary Italianism, not blushing about his juvenile impetus or the Arabian blood [*sève*] that circulates in *El amor brujo*, he ornaments his leafy and thorny bouquet with a flower grown in the greenhouse, and tempers the strong flavor of his Mediterranean flowers.[173]

This passage presents French influence as a civilizing and domesticating force, which tames the "thorny" and "uncultivated" aspects of Italian, Mediterranean and, by extension, Spanish cultures. The greenhouse stands as a symbol of human, rational and civilized control over wild nature, here represented by the lack of refinement that allegedly affects southern cultures. Seen in the light of these arguments, Tenroc's reference to a "Debussyan filter" reads like an artifact used to support the building of French cultural hegemony. Tenroc puts the noble savage trope at the service of cultural imperialism, which other critics concealed under the appearance of a Rousseaunian critique of civilization. However, Tenroc's review of *El retablo* stands out for his capacity to read through that work's sharp modernisms, cultural idiosyncrasies and staging mishaps, which other critics clashed with.

---

[170] "Ce n'est plus la musique espagnole descriptive aux rythmes autochtones primaires, estocades et patadas. Elle est devenue l'hispanisante traduction d'impressions éveillés par l'Espagne, passées au filtre debussyste." Ibid.

[171] "Est-ce à dire que ces concessions à l'internationalisme, ou plutôt ces nécessités d'évolution universelle, diminuent la valeur spécifique de l'art de M. de Falla? Non, certes." Ibid.

[172] "la musique s'éloigne encore davantage de celle de La Vie brève dans la volonté d'expurger toute trace d'italianisme." Ibid.

[173] "Secouant le joug d'un italianisme sans qualité, sans rougir ni de ses élans juvéniles ni de la sève arabe qui circule dans El amor brujo, il orne son bouquet de feuillages et d'épines d'une flore cultivée en serre, tempère la saveur forte de ses fleurs méditerranéens." Ibid.

Malherbe: Quixotism and the Latin Union

Different from the way in which he approached *La vie brève* and *El amor brujo*, in his review of *El retablo* Malherbe tried to appropriate this work by way of rhetorical strategies and calculated stylistic associations such as those employed by Tenroc. Unlike the latter, however, Malherbe did not try so much to represent French music and musicians as guides to Falla's personal success or his artistic "self-discovery." Despite his fondness for Austro-German composers, Malherbe rather aimed at bringing *El retablo* closer to notions of a Franco-Spanish ("Latin"?) bonding in order to drive it away from "German music." In this aspect, Malherbe showed more anti-German determination than Falla, whose relation with German culture and music was ambiguous and variable. Falla had signed the wartime "Manifesto of Solidarity of the Allied Nations" published by the journal *España* on July 9, 1915, and contributed to Adolfo Salazar's markedly anti-German *Revista Musical Hispano-americana* with a highly propagandistic obituary of Granados, who was killed in 1916 by a German submarine. To the *Revista*, he also contributed a prologue to the would-be Spanish edition of Jean-Aubry's anti-German pamphlet *La musique française d'aujourd'hui*, which never saw light. Falla's staunch Catholicism and rejection of Protestantism elicited further misgivings about German culture.[174] However, Falla held great respect and even admiration for the music of Wagner and Beethoven, and despite his aversion for atonality he was able to appreciate certain contrapuntal and dramatic procedures in Schoenberg's *Pierrot Lunaire*.[175] Like Pedrell, he valued the "German tradition" on its own grounds, but rejected its spreading over other cultures, particularly Spain.

Malherbe's delving into issues of identity relied on his ability to understand, assimilate and read beyond *El retablo*'s modernisms. Like other critics, Malherbe struggled with some staging decisions, such as the use of "giant cardboard figures" to "render real characters in the scale of magnified marionettes." According to Malherbe, the singers Dufranne and Salignac—in the roles of Don Quixote and Sancho—were "squeezed into those cardboard figures," as a result of which they "moved and sang with visible difficulty."[176] However, these setbacks did not prevent Malherbe from appreciating *El retablo* as "a lyric confession" in which Falla "has revealed himself in his essence."[177] He judged "the score" to be "of too great an importance for today's

---

[174] Hess, *Manuel de Falla and Modernism*, 59–78.

[175] Collins, "Falla in Europe," 265–266.

[176] "artistes éminents tels que MM. Zuloaga et Delthomas"; "cartonnages géants"; "mettre les personnages vivants à l'échelle des marionnettes grandies"; "engoncés dans ces cartonnages, se déplaçaient et chantaient avec une difficulté visible." Malherbe, "Chronique musicale: Manuel de Falla."

[177] "confession lyrique"; "il s'est révélé dans son vif." Ibid.

music to be studied cursorily" and, therefore, entirely devoted a second, lengthy musical *feuilleton* in *Le Temps* to fully explore *El retablo*.[178]

The cultural strategies underpinning Malherbe's reading of *El retablo* took the appearance of a formalistic, textual and philological approach. This attitude, however, differed significantly from the formalistic stance taken by Curzon and Chantavoine, discussed above. Uniquely, Malherbe did not "exoticise" *El retablo* in order to defend its Spanish qualities. Instead, he emphasized its connections with Cervantes's novel, thus inscribing Falla's work in national traditions and—as we shall see—"race," which were also the two staples of prevailing discourses in French nationalism. Malherbe stated that Falla "has fully assimilated Cervantes's text" to the point that "his music presents the most vivid links with the literary masterpiece" and is indeed "run through with the same sap"—a metaphor of blood and race.[179] Malherbe's concern for textual fidelity showed in his discussion of Falla's score: "in order to bow to the games of Cervantes's great satire [Falla] stands by the precise nuances displayed by the famous writer [and] applies himself to interpret the ironic subtleties and the vast perspectives."[180] Furthermore, Malherbe censored Falla's decision to alter the beginning and ending of Cervantes's episodes, by remarking that "an artist so pure as Falla should have completely respected Cervantes's brilliant text."[181] Malherbe regards textual fidelity as the essential criterion underlying *El retablo's* access to the Spanish musical canon.

Malherbe's approach to textual adaptation strikes me as stifling, insofar as Falla's alterations to Cervantes's text were minimal. By denying that a sixteenth-century Spanish literary work may require certain adaptations when presented to a twentieth-century French musical audience, he denies the agency of time, space and genre in an act of interpretation. Even more striking is the fact that this attitude did not stop him from trying to "Frenchify" or appropriate *El retablo*. More particularly, he implied that French musicians had guided Falla toward the artistic and national achievement represented by *El retablo*. He found in the music for scene 1, "Charlemagne's Court," "a fine and noble nostalgia that resembles [Maurice Ravel's] *Le Tombeau de Couperin*."[182] Commenting on scene 2, in which

---

[178] "La partition des *Tréteaux de Maître Pierre* est d'une trop grande importance, dans la musique présente, pour qu'on l'étudie légèrement." Ibid.

[179] "Il s'est si bien pénétré du texte de Cervantès"; "sa musique se présente dans les plus vivants rapports avec le chef-d'œuvre littéraire"; "parcourue par le même suc et la même sève." Malherbe, "Chronique musicale: Manuel de Falla II."

[180] "Pour se plier aux jeux de la grande satire de Cervantès […] Il se tient toujours dans les nuances précises du célèbre écrivant. Il s'applique à en interpréter les subtilités ironiques et les vastes perspectives." Ibid.

[181] "Un artiste aussi pur que M. de Falla eût dû respecter intégralement, semble-t-il, le texte génial de Cervantès." Ibid.

[182] "une fine et noble nostalgie et qui s'apparente au *Tombeau de Couperin*." Ibid.

the captive Melisendra moans over the absence of her husband Don Gayferos, he remarked that "this lament naturally has a Debussyan aspect, but it recalls the [piano] prelude *Des pas sur la neige* rather than *Pelléas* [et Mélisande]."[183] Although Debussy and Ravel were Falla's main aesthetic inspirations at the time he composed *El retablo*,[184] Malherbe uses those comparisons in order to appropriate Falla's work. This intention becomes more evident in light of Malherbe's far-fetched and spurious anti-German arguments. Commenting on Falla's music for scene 4, in which Don Gayferos rides to the rescue of Melisendra, Malherbe states that "his ride through the Pyrenees has nothing in common with the ride of the Valkyries" in Wagner's opera.[185] Why mention it, then, if not to establish a suspicious and spurious distance from Wagner or German music? Here, critical judgment seems to be based on mere word similarities and therefore reduced to sheer rhetorical playfulness. Malherbe's comments on the music for the end of scene 6, in which Don Quixote believes the puppet action to be real and destroys the theater, take on a similar rhetorical character. In contrast with his previous judgment, Malherbe admits that "the composer has become serious" and that "the last measures of the score […] take on a Wagnerian aspect."[186] In order to justify what he regards as stylistic deviance, Malherbe asks: "Is Don Quixote not Lohengrin's or Tristan's cousin? Is he not Parsifal's true brother who, like him, accomplished his deeds and lived in Spain?"[187] Malherbe draws on the fact that Parsifal is set in Montserrat, in the Catalan Pyrenees, in order to justify Falla's Wagnerist excursion.

Malherbe's endeavors to connect *El retablo* with the Spanish literary and artistic canon reach beyond the issues of textual fidelity discussed above, and rely on the type of rhetorical artifice just described. For instance, he compared *El retablo*'s reduced instrumental ensemble with the "tiny, stumpy and hairy" dwarfs painted by Velázquez,[188] rather than with its more evident source, that is, Stravinsky's recent works.[189] In a similar vein, Malherbe stated that, although

---

[183] "Cette plainte est naturellement d'allure debussyste, mais elle rappelle plus précisément le prélude *Des pas sur la neige* que *Pelléas*." Ibid.

[184] For, as Collins has documented, Falla played music by Debussy, Ravel and Stravinsky as incidental music during a domestic performance of Lorca's puppet plays back in 1923, the year he finished *El retablo*. Collins, "Falla in Europe," 261.

[185] "Sa chevauchée dans les Pyrénées n'a rien de commun avec la chevauchée des Valkyries." Malherbe, "Chronique musicale: Manuel de Falla II."

[186] "Le compositeur est devenu sérieux." "Les dernières mesures de la partition […] prennent l'allure wagnérienne." Ibid.

[187] "Don Quichotte, n'est-il pas le cousin de Lohengrin, de Tristan? N'est-il pas véritablement le frère de Parsifal qui, comme lui, accomplit ses exploits et vécut en Espagne?" Ibid. Malherbe refers to the fact that *Parsifal* is set in Montserrat, in the Catalan Pyrenees.

[188] "menus, trapus, velus." Ibid.

[189] Hess, *Manuel de Falla and Modernism*, 101 and 161.

"the distant color of the past is achieved by way of the harpsichord […] Falla uses [it] less for its quaint grace than its guitar sonority."[190] Malherbe imbues the harpsichord with national symbolic significance by way of a far-fetched comparison with the instrument that became an icon of Spanish identity, the guitar. Although Falla drew some of the musical sources for *El retablo* from Gaspar Sanz's treatise *Instrucción de música sobre la guitarra española* (1674), there is no evidence that he sought to evoke the guitar's sonority, and he drew inspiration equally from harpsichord music of the French Baroque, prompted by the publication of works by Couperin and Chambonnières in *La Revue musicale* (October 15, 1920).[191] Malherbe's comment seems to empathize with the Spanish avant-garde's ideological construction of the harpsichord as an embodiment of Spanish traditions. They looked back at the Italian composer and harpsichordist Domenico Scarlatti, resident in the Spanish Court (1733–1757) in a way that resembled the revival of Rameau and Couperin by Debussy, Ravel and others.[192]

Although Spanish neoclassicism may arguably be regarded as a French import, Falla pioneered the use of the harpsichord. *El retablo* and his *Harpsichord Concerto* (1923–1926) antedated Poulenc's *Concert champêtre* (1926–27), also written for Wanda Landowska.[193] Malherbe most likely learned about the modernist, neoclassical connotations of the harpsichord in Spain through the article "Les Musiciens Espagnols anciens et le clavecin" published a few years before in *Le courrier musical* by the Spanish musician Joaquin Nin, residing in Paris. In line with Falla and Salazar, Nin associated Scarlatti with Spanish musical traditions and argued that "a number of his works can be considered part of the Spanish musical domain."[194] In contrast to the Spanish avant-garde, however, he anticipated Malherbe more closely by finding "the guitar's musical expression" more appropriate to the Spanish temperament, on the basis that "the strings, directly plucked by the fingers in manifold ways, do not cease responding to the performer's

---

[190] "La couleur lointaine du passé est obtenue grâce au clavecin." "Falla emploie encore moins le clavecin pour sa grâce désuète que pour sa sonorité de guitare." Malherbe, "Chronique musicale: Manuel de Falla."

[191] Christoforidis, "Manuel de Falla, Early Music and the Harpsichord," 343–356.

[192] Interestingly, in 1929, only one year after the homage, Falla referred to Scarlatti as "ours." Letter from Falla to Raffaele Calzini, October 20, 1929 (AMF 6812), quoted in Nancy Lee Harper, *Manuel de Falla: His Life and Music* (Lanham, MD: Scarecrow Press, 2005), 184. On the harpsichord and the Spanish avant-garde, see Christoforidis, "Falla, Early Music and the Harpsichord"; Christoforidis, "From Folklore to Plain Chant," 216–217; Elena Torres Clemente, "La presencia de Scarlatti en la trayectoria musical de Manuel de Falla," in *Manuel de Falla e Italia: Estudios*, ed. Montserrat Bergadà et al. (Granada: Archivo Manuel de Falla, 2000), 63–122. On the revival of French baroque see Suschitzky, "Debussy's Rameau"; Fulcher, *French Cultural Politics and Music*. On Ravel and Couperin see Fulcher, *The Composer as Intellectual*, 68–69.

[193] Interestingly, French works that paid homage to baroque harpsichordists and their music, such as Ravel's *Le tombeau de Couperin* (1914–1917), were written for the piano.

[194] "bon nombre de ses pièces peuvent être considérés comme faisant partie du domaine musical espagnol." Joaquín Nin, "Les musiciens espagnols anciens et le clavecin (II)," *Le courrier musical* (December 1925).

will."[195] The impact of Nin's articles can be traced to Jean-Aubry's influential *La musique et les nations,* which expands on the question just described.[196]

Malherbe's strict observance of textual fidelity reaches a climax toward the end of his review, where it conflicts with—but ultimately outdoes—his attempts to construe *El retablo* as an anti-German work. Malherbe argues that Falla chose the subject matter in order "to provide an explanation of his art by way of an illustrious writer."[197] He illustrates his point by referring to the passage in which, following Don Quixote's rebukes to the Trujamán's lack of accuracy, Master Peter adds: "Leave off those flourishes…let your plain song carry on without mingling any vacuous ornaments, any smearing counterpoints that smudge all the music."[198] Recently, Dorsch has keenly connected Maese Pedro's rebuke with Falla's indication in the piano vocal score that "the three singers should make a point of avoiding every kind of theatrical mannerism."[199] In light of Malherbe's attempts to construe *El retablo* as an anti-German work, and considering the German associations that counterpoint gained in certain circles, however, it seems as if this critic was trying to use Maese Pedro's rejection of rhetorical "counterpoint" as a way of describing Falla's alleged stylistic preferences.[200] More intentionally, he argues that "further contributing to the cause" of Falla's attempt to provide an explanation of his art, "Jean Aubry's version is lightly arranged." Instead of standing by the original text, Jean-Aubry adds "vacuous ornaments" and "smearing counterpoints," which, in Malherbe's view, "are totally out of the question."[201] Jean-Aubry, let us remember, authored one of the most vitriolic anti-German manifestos during the war,[202] and although he contributes to

---

[195] "L'expressivité musicale de la guitare"; "les cordes, attaquées directement par les doigts de cent manières différentes, ne se lassent pas de répondre aux appels du joueur." Joaquín Nin, "Les musiciens espagnols anciens et le clavecin," *Le courrier musical* (November 1925).

[196] Jean-Aubry, *La musique et les nations,* 67–68.

[197] "pour nous fournir l'explication de son art par un écrivain illustre." Malherbe, "Chronique musicale: Manuel de Falla II."

[198] "Laisse-toi ces fioritures… que ton plain-chant se suive sans que s'y mêlent ornements vides, contrepoints qui ne font que tout brouiller." Ibid.

[199] Manuel de Falla, *El retablo de Maese Pedro,* piano reduction (London, 1924), unpaginated. Quoted in Dorsch, "Nostalgia and Modernism," 140.

[200] He surely was aware of the anti-German connotations that some French musicians ascribed to counterpoint. Categorical and unfounded descriptions of Austro-German music as "la grande musique," one that is based on contrapuntal techniques, served to contrast its alleged complexity and elaborateness with notions of French music as "simple" and "pure," especially during the height of neoclassicism in the 1920s. Fulcher, *The Composer as Intellectual,* 34–41, 53–55.

[201] "D'ailleurs, pour les besoins de la cause, la version de M. G.-J. Aubry est légèrement arrangée. La traduction exacte de la réplique de maître Pierre este celle-ci: 'Continue de chanter en plain-chant sans te mettre dans le contrepoint car le fil casse par le menu.' Il n'est question nulle part 'd'ornements vides, de contrepoints qui ne font que tout brouiller." Malherbe, "Chronique musicale: Manuel de Falla."

[202] Jean-Aubry, *La musique française d'aujourd'hui.* See also Hess, *Manuel de Falla and Modernism,* 65–68.

the cause of anti-German propaganda Malherbe scolds his inventions, just as Don Quixote rebukes the Trujamán. It seems as if Malherbe's heightened and Quixotic sense of philological rigor conflicted with his attempts to appropriate Spanish culture and Falla's achievements to the cause of an anti-German form of French nationalism.[203]

Despite of all his attempts to Hispanize and, ultimately, Latinize *El retablo*, Malherbe was not blind to the disadvantages of cultural estrangement. He complained that, in the translation, "the recitative, which is almost composed by only two modes, C and G, becomes incomprehensible to our audience."[204] This remark could possibly explain why several critics, including Chantavoine and Curzon, had trouble with the Trujamán's recitations. That Malherbe read the Trujamán's recitation as "Spanish" suggests a capacity that was unique among French critics, to recognize "Spanish music" beyond flamenco. The Trujamán's recitation draws on the *pregón*, a Spanish tradition of spreading news, telling stories and articulating political speeches in the public squares.[205] The *pregón* found its way to the Spanish musical stage through *zarzuelas* such as Bretón's highly-celebrated *La verbena de la Paloma*. Although it is unlikely that Malherbe was familiar with the *pregón* tradition, his delving into issues of cultural translation contributed to explaining the overall impression that *El retablo* left in the audience; to judge from the anonymous review in Cyrano, they thought it was "a bit long and comically laborious."[206] The difficulties in translating and performing *pregones*, even in Spanish, might have played a part in this impression.

The critical reception of *El retablo*'s 1928 performance illustrates how the literary character who had become a myth of Spanish regeneration subsequently turned into the focus of an inquiry into the nature of Spanish and French music and identity, once taken to the stage of the Opera Comique. This functional transformation became possible only after Cervantes's novel underwent an adaptation that affected all aspects of the production. Jean-Aubry's translation played out notions of French and German music, thus inscribing Cervantes's novel in a new interpretive context. The staging by Falla, Zuloaga, Ricou and

---

[203] Indeed, he subjected Jean-Aubry's translation to a rigorous examination, deeming the prosody "faulty," and criticizing that "the accents, correct in Spanish, fall on the wrong syllables in the French adaptation," since they "have truly been too much neglected. "défectueuse"; "Les temps, justes en espagnol, tombent à faux dans l'adaptation française"; "les accents y ont été vraiment par trop négligés." Malherbe, "Chronique musicale: Manuel de Falla II."

[204] "La psalmodie du récitatif, faite à peu près uniquement sur deux modes, *do* et *sol*, devient incompréhensible à nos auditeurs." Ibid.

[205] For a description and history of the *pregón* see Antoni Rossell, "Le pregón: Survivance du système de transmission oral et musical de l'épopée espagnole," *Cahiers de littérature orale*, 32 (1992): 165–175. Also see Laura Santana Burgos, "La traducción de un pregón callejero: La ópera El retablo de maese Pedro de Manuel de Falla," *El genio maligno. Revista de humanidades y ciencias sociales*, no. 3 (2008): 130–137.

[206] "a paru un peu longuet et d'un comic assez laborieux" Anon., "Au fil de la scène," 29.

Delthomas explored the connotative possibilities of a multilayered dramatic structure that developed the idea of creating a theater within a theater, and questioned the nature of human identity by blurring the limits between man and marionette. Falla looked back at his country's musical history with the purpose of disassociating "Spanish music" from flamenco and popular culture and grounding it in a sense of tradition. French critics read *El retablo* in the context of their own cultural struggles, and by so doing they made their own contribution to the complex process of textual adaptation and cultural translation underpinning this homage to Falla. Beyond their own individual agendas, critics reflected the strained critical atmosphere of Third Republic France, in which the tension between the "foreign" and the "indigenous," the Other and the self, prevailed, and found conflicting forms of expression.

A comparison between reviews of *El retablo* and *El amor brujo* shows that, despite their perceived otherness, Spanish folklore and the female gypsy flamenco dancer could offer themselves as a more suitable basis for the critics' strategies of appropriation than the "normative" male hero Don Quixote, when the latter was presented within a modernist, detached and challenging aesthetic framework. However, reactions to La Argentina's neoclassic choreography and performance show that a more moderate form of modernism than the one presented in *El retablo* could, quite the contrary, help to assimilate the Spanish elements to the aesthetics of "French" neoclassicism. Furthermore, the absence of folklore in *El retablo* challenged the critics' preestablished notions of "Spanish music"—with the exception Henry Malherbe, who was the only critic able to read Spain beyond flamenco.

Next to these two works, *La vie brève* showed French audiences in 1928 how distant their recent past felt, but it also offered them an opportunity to negotiate their relationship with it, and help them bridge the gap opened by the trauma of war. In that sense, a "Spanish" work like *La vie brève* could be taken as part of the history of French music, especially since it gave critics the opportunity to analyze and reassess their notions of the "indigenous" and the "foreign," when these two categories were mapped onto two "southern" countries, Spain and Italy. Unlike German or Italian music, Spanish music did not represent a cultural menace, and it gained enough discursive transparency for French critics to identify with it and measure their distance to other national styles. Despite its discursive transparency, however, that *couleur locale* could not be dispensed with; it had to be present in order for the work of a Spanish composer to match preestablished notions of "Spanish music" and therefore remain confined and restricted to a place that was traceable, close at hand, but distant enough to avoid the Other mingling too much with the self.

CONCLUSIONS

The wide array of experiences shared or revealed in the writings and works of Collet, Laparra, Falla, Albéniz and other musicians who lived in France in the early twentieth century shows that the meanings of "Spanish music" in that context largely surpassed in range and scope the ones that we generally ascribe to it in publications and in academic or everyday conversation. Whether they sought intellectual or sensual pleasure in composing, producing, performing and writing about "Spanish music," whether they strove to express or fulfill a patriotic sentiment, or whether they pursued economic profit and professional recognition, those musicians and critics helped to conceptualize "Spanish music" as a complex web of experiences and meanings that foreclose any restrictive or categorical definition of the concept. Rather than as a fixed repertoire, let alone "the work of Spanish composers," therefore, we should try to think of "Spanish music" as a dynamic historical and cultural process that precisely encompasses a set of individual and collective experiences, as well as the personal and institutional agents engaged in their practice—and, of course, the repertoire at stake.

By emphasizing the richness and complexity of the processes that underlie historical formulations of "Spanish music," I have not intended to complicate the task of writing history. Instead, I propose to use our increasing knowledge of the concept—or the results of our endeavors to fill it with content—as a privileged prism through which to gain deeper insights into a particular historical context with the purpose of learning lessons that apply to our current experiences. To be more precise, the historical enquiry carried out in this volume has sought to help to undermine and leave behind our fear of understanding one of the key chapters in the historical formation of "Spanish music"—namely, its production in early twentieth-century Paris—as a cultural enterprise in which emotional, intellectual and material interests met with varying degrees of harmony and conflict. In other words, one should contemplate the possibility that the individual and collective agents involved in the historical production of "our" national heritages and legacies did not take a disinterested part in that cultural endeavor, and some of the their most relevant decisions were informed by criteria differing from the ones we tend to imagine as fittest for the purpose.

Composing and writing about "Spanish music" today, or in early-twentieth-century Paris, therefore, may not necessarily rely on individual or collective agendas that result from conscious and willing acts of choice. Falla's, Albéniz's and Turina's decision to become "Spanish composers" or composers of "Spanish music," and to follow particular formal procedures or subscribe more or less consciously and flexibly to ideological agendas, shows their individual responses to cultural, ideological and material needs or anxieties that they shared among themselves and with other musicians, artists, intellectuals and audiences at large. This realization should not necessarily lead to undermining the power of individual will, but rather to emphasizing the role that the underlying and visible tensions of French musical culture played in the process whereby the ideas of "Spanish music" that would become so influential for many decades to come gained shape during the period concerned.

Similarly, the writings of French musicologists and critics about "Spanish music" reveal the extent to which prevailing concerns that should, in principle, remain extraneous to their subject bear on their narrative strategies with or without their conscious will. To think of a "French" idea of "Spanish music" as the unworthy and contaminated by-product of French nationalism, however, fails to account for the willingness of Spanish musicians such as Falla, Albéniz, Turina and Granados—to mention only a few—to engage with their French counterparts in the formulation of their own ideas of "Spanish music." To distinguish between "Spanish" and "French" ideas of "Spanish music" in the period concerned, moreover, ignores the sustained historical presence of French and European borrowings in the construction of Spanish nationalist doctrines.

The aforementioned similarity between the processes underlying the formation of "Spanish music" and other forms of collective identity invites consideration that performances of "Spanish music" in early-twentieth-century Paris provided a venue in which the negotiation of "larger" questions of national identity gained enhanced possibilities. Thanks to the greater public visibility granted by widely attended events, such as the 1928 homage to Falla at the Opéra-Comique, performances of *La jota* and Falla's stage works such as *La vie brève*, *El amor brujo* and *El retablo*, afforded critics a privileged occasion to deal with "Spanish" difference and show the extent to which they felt compelled to measure and redefine the distance separating their notions of "French" and "Spanish" music. A detailed analysis of French critics' reactions to these works should have served to warn against the use of generalizations. Behind terms such as "representation," "appropriation" and "accommodation," there lay a wide array of approaches to "Spanish difference." Beyond disparities, however, and despite some French critics' willingness to accept the lessons that Falla allegedly had to offer to the younger French generations, a general sentiment prevailed that "Spanish music" was something "different." Just as Falla, Albéniz and others entered into a negotiation with their French counterparts over the nature and meaning of "Spanish music," French critics and musicians felt compelled by the presence of a "foreign" culture to redefine the ways in which their own culture found expression.

The negotiation of "Spanish music" in early-twentieth-century Paris offers one of the many examples that transcultural borrowings date from further back than the relatively recent focus on the study of music and globalization would suggest. Doubtless, economic and cultural globalization has exacerbated the process through which cultural borrowings make up the fabric of nationalist discourses, and in which their status as "borrowings" or "legitimate" constituents is negotiated. Furthermore, globalization has sparked wide opposition to those processes in the form of deeply rooted—and often xenophobic—nationalism, in which the limit between the "foreign" and the "indigenous" is often traced with little or no historical enquiry. A historical account of those processes—to which I hope to have contributed—offers a somewhat more complete map in which recent transcultural phenomena gain more relief. Thus, one grows increasingly weary of those nationalist discourses that suspiciously claim to be uniform and self-contained. Although the appellative "Spanish music" will not be able to capture the phenomena described in their whole complexity, awareness of the latter should at least help in choosing more consciously and selectively between the inherited politics of identity that become reproduced with it in our usage of the term, whether in academic environments or everyday situations.

BIBLIOGRAPHY

Abbate, Carolyn, "*Tristan* in the Composition of *Pelléas*," *19th-Century Music* 5, no. 2 (October 1, 1981): 117–141.
Acker, Yolanda F., "Los Ballets Russes en España: Recepción y guía de sus primeras actuaciones (1916–1918)," in *Los Ballets Russes de Diaghilev y España*, ed. Yvan Nommick and Antonio Álvarez Cañibano (Granada and Madrid: Fundación Archivo Manuel de Falla, INAEM, 2000), 229–252.
Aderer, Adolphe, "Opéra-Comique. Le voile du bonheur. La jota," *Le petit Parisien* (April 17, 1911).
Aguilera Sastre, Juan, and Manuel Aznar Soler, *Cipriano de Rivas Cherif y el teatro español de su época (1891–1967)* (Madrid: Asociación de Directores de Escena de España, 1999).
Aidi, Hishaam D., "The Interference of al-Andalus: Spain, Islam, and the West," *Social Text* 24, no. 2 (June 2006): 67–88.
Albright, Ann Cooper, *Choreographing Difference: The Body and Identity in Contemporary Dance* (Middletown, CT: Wesleyan University Press, 1997).
Alier, Roger, "Tonadilla," *Grove Music Online,* http://www.oxfordmusiconline.com/subscriber/article/grove/music/28100 (accessed April 15, 2011).
Alonso, Celsa, "La réception de la chanson espagnole dans la musique française du XIXe siècle," in *Échanges musicaux franco-espagnols XVIIe–XVIIIe siècles: Actes des Rencontres de Villecroze, 15 au 17 octobre 1998*, ed. François Lesure (Paris: Académie Musicale de Villecroze, 2000), 123–160.
Altermann, Jean-Pierre, "Manuel de Falla," *La revue musicale* 8, no. 2 (June 1921).
Álvarez Calero, Alberto J., "Manuel de Falla y los orígenes de la Orquesta Bética de Cámara," *Música y educación: Revista trimestral de pedagogía musical* 20, no. 70 (2007): 27–36.
Álvarez Gutiérrez, Luis, "Intentos alemanes para contrarrestar la influencia francesa sobre la opinión pública en los años precedentes a la Primera Guerra Mundial," in *Españoles y franceses en la primera mitad del siglo XX* (Madrid: CSIC, 1986), 1–22.
Álvarez Junco, José, *Mater Dolorosa: La idea de España en el siglo XIX* (Madrid: Taurus, 2001).
Anon., "Au fil de la scène. Ce qui se joue," *Cyrano* 5, no. 196 (March 18, 1928): 29.
———, "Carmen de Bizet," *Le guide du concert* (April 9, 1926).
———, "Chants de Castille, Henri Collet," *Le guide du concert* (May 1925).
———, "En l'honneur de la musique espagnole," *La rénaissance politique, littéraire, artistique* 16, no. 11 (March 18, 1928): 7.
———. "Entre cœur et jardin. Opéra-Comique. La Jota." *Journal Amusant*, April 1911.
———, "Un fait-divers, presque banal, si l'art du musicien n'en transfigurait la sanglante horreur," *Le matin* (February 25, 1908).
———, "'La habanera'—A New Opera by a New Composer," *The New York Times* (August 9, 1908).

———, "La habanera à l'Opéra-Comique? Un fait-divers, presque banal, si l'art du musicien n'en transfigurait la sanglante horreur," *Le matin* (February 1908).

———, "Henri Collet, 'L'essor de la musique espagnole au XXe siècle'," *Le guide musical et théâtral* (December 1929).

———, "Jean-Aubry, Georges," in *Dictionnaire de biographie française*, vol. 18 (Paris: Librairie Letouzey et Ané, 1994), 584–585.

———, "Kyrie, VITTORIA [sic]," *Le guide du concert* (December 1924).

———, "Musique éxotique et populaire," *Revue d'histoire et de critique musicales (Revue musicale)* (March 1902).

———, "Novelles," *Le ménestrel*, vol. 90, no. 12 (March 23, 1928).

———, "Notre enquête sur la crise et la forme du théâtre lyrique," *Le courrier musical* (January 1923).

———, "Oeuvres de musique espagnole," *Le guide du concert* (October 1913).

———, "Rhapsodie espagnole, Albeniz," *Le guide du concert* (February 1926).

———, "Théâtre. Raoul Laparra: Définition du musicien de théâtre," *Le guide musical et théâtral* (December 1929).

———, "Les théâtres lyriques. Carmen," *Le guide du concert* (June 1925).

———, *La trilogía* Los Pirineos *y la crítica* (Barcelona, 1902).

———, "Trio espagnol. E. de Zubeldia," *Le ménestrel* (May 1925).

———, "La vie brève," *Le journal* (January 3, 1914).

———, "Vingt chants populaires espagnols. Joaquin Nin," *Le guide du concert* (June 1925).

Arozamena, Jesus María de, *Ignacio Zuloaga: El pintor, el hombre* (San Sebastián: Sociedad Guipuzcoana de Ediciones y Publicaciones, 1970).

Aubert, Paul, "L'influence idéologique et politique de la France dans l'Espagne de la fin du XIXe siècle à la Première Guerre Mondiale (1875–1918)," in *España y Francia en la Comunidad Europea*, ed. Jean-Pierre Étienvre and José Ramón Urquijo Goitia (Madrid: CSIC, 1989), 57–102.

———, "La propagande étrangère en Espagne dans le premier tiers du XXe siècle," *Mélanges de la Casa de Velázquez* 31, no. 3 (1995): 103–176.

———, "La propagande étrangère en Espagne pendant la première guerre mondiale," in *Españoles y franceses en la primera mitad del siglo XX* (Madrid: CSIC, 1986).

Austern, Linda Phyllis, "'Forreine Conceits and Wandring Devices': The Exotic, the Erotic and the Femenin," in *The Exotic in Western Music*, ed. Jonathan Bellman (Boston: Northeastern University Press, 1998), 26–42.

Aviñoa, Xosé, "Sociedades musicales y modernidad en Cataluña en el primer tercio del siglo XX," *Cuadernos de música iberoamericana* 8–9 (2001): 277–286.

Ayache, Germain, "Les rélations franco-espagnoles pendant la guerre du Rif," in *Españoles y franceses en la primera mitad del siglo XX* (Madrid: CSIC, 1986), 287–293.

Aymes, Jean-René, *L'Espagne romantique (temoignages de voyageurs français)* (Paris: Editions A. M. Metailie, 1983).

Bachoud, André, "L'affaire Ferrer ou la France en question," in *España, Francia y la Comunidad Europea: Actas del Segundo Coloquio Hispano-Francés de Historia Contemporánea, celebrado en Aix-en-Provence los días 16, 17 y 18 de junio de 1986*, ed. Jean-Pierre Etienvre and José Ramón de Urquijo y Goitia (Madrid: Casa de Velázquez, 1989), 103–114.

Baena, Francisco, "Breve itinerario de los pintore españoles en los Ballets Russes," in *Los Ballets Russes de Diaghilev y España*, ed. Yvan Nommick and Antonio Álvarez Cañibano (Granada and Madrid: Fundación Archivo Manuel de Falla, INAEM, 2000), 253–275.

Balaguer, Victor, *Historia de Cataluña y de la Corona de Aragón* (Barcelona: Librería de Salvador Manero, 1861).

Bancroft, David, "Two Pleas for a French, French Music," *Music and Letters*, no. 48 (July 1967): 251–258.

Barrès, Maurice, "Comment faire notre propagande en Espagne," *L'echo de Paris* (February 2, 1915).

———, *Greco ou le secret de Tolède* (Paris: Émile-Paul, 1912).

———, "Réchauffons notre propagande," *L'echo de Paris* (February 11, 1915).
———, *La terre et les morts: Sur quelles réalités fonder la conscience française* (Paris: Ligue de la Patrie Française, 1899).
———, "Les voix françaises de l'Espagne," *L'echo de Paris* (February 9, 1915).
Bartlet, M. Elizabeth C., and Richard Langham Smith, "Opéra comique," *Grove Music Online*, ed. Stanley Sadie, http://www.oxfordmusiconline.com/subscriber/article/grove/music/43715 (accessed April 15, 2011).
Baruzi, Joseph, "Recital E. del Pueyo," *Le ménestrel* (April 1923).
———, "Récitals E. del Pueyo," *Le ménestrel* (December 1923).
Baudin, G., "Le Trio de Barcelone," *Le ménestrel* (February 1928).
Beardsley, Theodore S., "The Spanish Musical Sources of Bizet's Carmen," *Inter-American Music Review*, no. 10 (1989).
Bécarud, Jean, "Barrès et l'Espagne dans mes cahiers," in *Barrès, une tradition dans la modernité: Actes du colloque de Mulhouse, Bâle et Fribourg-en-Brisgau des 10, 11 et 12 avril 1989*, ed. André Guyaux, Joseph Jurt, and Robert Kopp (Paris: Honoré Champion, 1991), 233–240.
Ben-Ami, Shlomo, *Fascism from Above: The Dictatorship of Primo de Rivera in Spain, 1923–1930* (Oxford and New York: Oxford University Press, 1983).
Benjamin, Walter, "Theses on the Philosophy of History," in *Illuminations*, ed. Hannah Arendt (London: Pimlico, 1999/1955).
Bennahum, Ninotchka, *Antonia Mercé "La Argentina": Flamenco and the Spanish Avant Garde* (Hanover and London: Wesleyan University Press, 2000).
Berga, Miquel, *John Langdon-Davies (1897–1971): Una biografía anglo-catalana* (Barcelona: Pòrtic, 1991).
Bergadà, Montserrat, "Les musiciens espagnols à Paris entre 1820 et 1868," in *La musique entre France et Espagne: Interactions stylistiques. Actes du colloque international tenu à Paris, en Sorbonne-Paris IV et à l'Instituto Cervantes, les 14–16 mai 2001*, ed. Louis Jambou (Paris: Presses de l'Université de Paris-Sorbonne, 2003), 17–40.
———, "Pedrell i els pianistes catalans a Paris," *Recerca musicològica* 11–12 (1991–1992): 243–257.
———, "La relación de Falla con Italia: Crónica de un diálogo," in *Manuel de Falla e Italia*, ed. Yvan Nommick (Granada: Publicaciones del Archivo Manuel de Falla).
Bermann, Sandra, "Introduction," in *Nation, Language, and the Ethics of Translation*, ed. Sandra Bermann and Michael Wood (Princeton, NJ: Princeton University Press, 2005), 1–11.
Bernard, Gabriel, "La question de l'interprétation de 'Carmen'," *Le courrier musical* (March 15, 1925).
Bertelin, Alb., "Aptitudes musicales comparées des races latine et germanique," *Le courrier musical* (November 1918).
Bertrand, Paul, "Concerts-Colonne. Dimanche 16 janvier," *Le ménestrel* (January 1927).
———, "Manuel de Falla. (À propos d'un livre et d'un concert récents)," *Le ménestrel* (May 1930).
———, "Société Nationale de Musique (14 mars)," *Le ménestrel* (March 1925).
Bhabha, Homi K., *The Location of Culture* (New York: Routledge, 1994).
Blinkhorn, Martin, *Carlism and Crisis in Spain, 1931–1939* (Cambridge: Cambridge University Press, 1975).
Boetzkes, Manfred, and Evan Baker, "Stage Design. 5: The 19th Century," *Grove Music Online*, ed. Stanley Sadie, http://www.oxfordmusiconline.com/subscriber/article/grove/music/O904784 (accessed April 15, 2011).
Bonastre i Bertrán, Francesc, "El Asociacionismo musical sinfónico en Barcelona (1910–1936). La Orquestra Simfònica de Barcelona, la Orquestra Pau Casals y la Banda Municipal," *Cuadernos de música iberoamericana* 8–9 (2001): 255–276.
Born, Georgina, and David Hesmondhalgh, "Introduction: On Difference, Representation and Appropriation in Music," in *Western Music and Its Others: Difference, Representation and Appropriation in Music*, ed. Georgina Born and David Hesmondhalgh (Berkeley and Los Angeles: University of California Press, 2000), 1–58.

Botti, Alfonso, *Cielo y dinero. El nacionalcatolicismo en España* (1881–1975) (Madrid: Alianza Editorial, 1992).
Boubée de Grammont, Philippe, "Le 'Gaulois au théâtre': Argentina à l'Opéra-Comique: Ses impressions," *Le Gaulois* (March 11, 1928).
Boucher, Maurice, "Joaquín Turina: 'Le quartier de Santa Cruz' (El barrio de Santa Cruz). Rouart, Lerolle et Cie.," *La revue musicale [ReM]* 8, no. 1 (November 1926).
Boyd, Carolyn P., *Historia Patria: Politics, History, and National Identity in Spain, 1875–1975* (Princeton, NJ: Princeton University Press, 1997).
Brailoiu, Constantin, " Les écoles nationales," in *Les musiciens célèbres*, ed. Jean Lacroix (Geneva: L. Mazenod, 1946), 214–217.
Brancour, René, "Concerts-Lamoureux. Dimanche 20 mars," *Le ménestrel* (March 1932).
Branger, Jean-Christophe, "Les compositeurs français et l'opéra italien: La crise de 1910," in *Le naturalisme sur la scène lyrique*, ed. Jean-Christophe Branger and Alban Ramaut (Saint-Etienne: Publications de l'Université de Saint-Etienne, 2004), 314–342.
———, and Alban Ramaut, eds., *Le naturalisme sur la scène lyrique* (Saint-Etienne: Publications de l'Université de Saint-Etienne, 2004).
Brass, Tom, "The Agrarian Myth, the 'New' Populism and the 'New' Right," *Economic and Political Weekly* 32, no. 4 (1997): 27–42.
———, *Peasants, Populism and Postmodernism: The Return of the Agrarian Myth* (London and Portland, OR: Frank Cass, 2000).
Brenan, Gerald, *The Spanish Labyrinth: The Social and Political Background of the Spanish Civil War* (Cambridge: Cambridge University Press, 1943).
Britt-Arredondo, Christopher, *Quixotism: The Imaginative Denial of Spain's Loss of Empire* (Albany: State University of New York Press, 2005).
Brooks, Jeanice, "Italy, the Ancient World and the French Musical Inheritance in the Sixteenth Century: Arcadelt and Clereau in the Service of the Guises," *Journal of the Royal Musical Association* 121, no. 2 (1996): 147–190.
Brown, Julie, "Bartók, the Gypsies, and Hybridity in Music," in *Western Music and Its Others: Difference, Representation and Appropriation in Music*, ed. Georgina Born and David Hesmondhalgh (Berkeley: California University Press, 2000), 119–142.
Bruneau, Alfred, "Opéra-Comique donne un spectacle coupé, d'intérêt inégal," *Le matin* (December 31, 1913).
———, "Répétition générale. À la salle Favart, spectacle groupé et varié: Deux actes philosophiques; deux actes tragiques," *Le matin* (April 25, 1911).
Brunelleschi, Elsa, *Antonio and Spanish Dancing* (London: Adam and Charles Black, 1958).
Bruyr, José, "Un entretien avec…Raoul Laparra," *Le guide du concert* (November 29, 1929).
———, "Georges Bizet et son mystère," *Le guide musical* (October 7–14, 1938).
Buckle, Richard, "La deduda de Diaghilev con España," in *Los Ballets Russes de Diaghilev y España*, ed. Yvan Nommick and Antonio Álvarez Cañibano (Granada and Madrid: Fundación Archivo Manuel de Falla, INAEM, 2000), 31–32.
Buffery, Helena, *Shakespeare in Catalan: Translating Imperialism* (Cardiff: University of Wales Press, 2007).
Butler, Judith, *Gender Trouble: Feminism and the Subversion of Identity*, 1st ed. (New York and London: Routledge, 1999).
Caballero, Carlo, *Fauré and French Musical Aesthetics* (Cambridge: Cambridge University Press, 2001).
Calvocoressi, Michel-Dimitri, "Concerts Ricardo Viñes," *Le courrier musical* (May 1905).
Canal, Jordi, "La reconversión del carlismo (1876–1931)," in *El carlismo y las guerras carlistas. Hechos, hombres e ideas*, ed. Julio Aróstegui, Jordi Canal y Eduardo G. Calleja (Madrid: La Esfera de los Libros, 2003), 87–104.
Canteloube, Joseph, "La musique populaire, les 'coblas' et les instruments catalans," *Le courrier musical* (November 1929).
Capistegui, Francisco Javier, "Between Repulsion and Attraction: Carlism Seen Through Foreign Eyes," *Revista internacional de estudios vascos* 2 (2008): 119–143.

Carol-Bérard, "Le triomphe de Manuel de Falla," *Une semaine à Paris*, no. 302 (March 9, 1928): 43–44.
Carré, Albert, *Souvenirs de théâtre, réunis, présentés et annotés par Robert Favart* (Paris: Robert Favart, 1976/1950).
Carredano, Consuelo, "Adolfo Salazar en España. Primeras incursiones en la crítica musical: *La revista musical hispano-americana* (1914–1918)," *Anales del Instituto de Investigaciones Estéticas* 16, no. 84 (2004): 134–138.
Carreira, Xoan Manuel, "La musicologia spagnola: Un'illusione autarchica?" *Il saggiatore musicale* 2, no. 1 (1995): 105–142.
Carreras, Juan José, "From Literes to Nebra: Spanish Dramatic Music Between Tradition and Modernity," in *Music in Spain During the Eighteenth Century*, ed. Malcolm Boyd and Juan José Carreras (Cambridge; New York: Cambridge University Press, 1998), 7–16.
———, "Hijos de Pedrell: La historiografía musical española y sus orígenes nacionalistas (1780–1980)," *Il saggiatore musicale*, no. 1 (2001): 121–169.
Carroll, David, *French Literary Fascism: Nationalism, Anti-Semitism, and the Ideology of Culture* (Princeton, NJ: Princeton University Press, 1995).
Casares Rodicio, Emilio, "La música española hasta 1939 o la restauración musical," in *España en la Música de Occidente: Actas del congreso internacional celebrado en Salamanca, 29 de octubre-5 de noviembre de 1985,* ed. José López Calo, Ismael Fernández de la Cuesta, and Emilio Casares Rodicio, vol. 2 (Madrid: Instituto Nacional de las Artes Escénicas y de la Música, 1987), 261–332.
———, "Las relaciones musicales entre los Países Bajos y España vistas a través de los investigadores del siglo XIX," in *Musique des Pays-Bas anciens-musique espagnole ancienne (ca. 1450–ca. 1650)*, ed. Paul Becquart and Henri Vanhulst (Leuwen: Peeters, 1988), 19–68.
Cascardi, Antonio, "Beyond Castro and Maravall: Interpellation, Mimesis, and the Hegemony of Spanish Culture," in *Ideologies of Hispanism*, ed. Mabel Moraña, vol. 30 (Nashville, TN: Vanderbilt University Press, 2005), 138–159.
Castillo, José Miguel, "Consideraciones sobre las primeras escenografías de 'La vida breve'," *Manuel de Falla: La vida breve*, ed. Yvan Nommick (Granada: Archivo Manuel de Falla, 1997), 169–221.
Cerdannes, "Casino Municipal de Nice. La vie brève," *Le courrier musical* (April 1913).
Chalupt, René, "L'Espagne dans la musique française," *La revue musicale* 13, no. 123 (February 1932).
Chanet, Jean-François, *L'école républicaine et les petites patries* (Paris: Aubier, 1996).
Chantavoine, Jean, "La semaine musicale: Théâtre de l'Opéra-Comique," *Le ménestrel* (March 16, 1928).
Charnon-Deutsch, Lou, *The Spanish Gypsy: The History of a European Obsession* (University Park: Pennsylvania State University Press, 2004).
———, "Travels of the Imaginary Spanish Gypsy," in *Constructing Identity in Contemporary Spain: Theoretical Debates and Cultural Practice*, ed. Jo Labanyi (Oxford: Oxford University Press, 2002), 22–40.
Charpentier, Gustave, "La millième de 'Carmen'," *Le Figaro*, December 23, 1904.
Charron, Marc, "De la question de la lisibilité des traductions françaises de Don Quijote," in *Doubts and Directions in Translation Studies: Selected Contributions from the EST Congress, Lisbon 2004*, ed. Yves Gambier, Miriam Shlesinger, and Radegundis Stolze (John Benjamins, 2007), 311–322.
Chaterjee, Partha, *Nationalist Thought and the Colonial World: A Derivative Discourse?* (London: Zed Books for the United Nations University, 1986).
Chimènes, Myriam, *Mécènes et musiciens: Du salon au concert à Paris sous la IIIe République* (Fayard, 2004).
Ching, Barbara, and Gerald W. Creed, "Recognizing Rusticity: Identity and the Power of Place," in *Knowing Your Place: Rural Identity and Cultural Hierarchy*, ed. Ching and Creed (New York and London: Routledge, 1997) 1–38.

Christoforidis, Michael, "From Folksong to Plainchant: Musical Borrowings and the Transformation of Manuel de Falla's Music Nationalism in the 1920s," in *Manuel de Falla: His Life and Music*, ed. Nancy Lee Harper (Lanham, MD: Scarecrow Press, 2005), 209–246.

———, "Manuel de Falla, Debussy, and La vida breve," *Musicology Australia*, 18 (1995): 1–10.

———, "Manuel de Falla, Early Music and the Harpsichord in 'El Retablo de Maese Pedro,'" in *Cinco siglos de música de tecla española: Actas de los Symposia FIMTE 2002–2004*, ed. Luisa Morales (Barcelona: LEAL, 2007), 343–356.

———, "Manuel de Falla, Flamenco and Spanish Identity," in *Western Music and Race*, ed. Julie Brown (Cambridge: Cambridge University Press, 2007).

Cixous, Hélène, and Catherine Clément, *The Newly Born Woman* (Minneapolis: University of Minnesota Press, 1996/1975).

Claeys, Gregory, "The 'Survival of the Fittest' and the Origins of Social Darwinism," *Journal of the History of Ideas* 61, no. 2 (2000): 223–240.

Clark, Linda L., "Social Darwinism in France," *Journal of Modern History* 53, no. 1 (March 1, 1981): 1025–1044.

Clark, Robert L. A., "South of North: Carmen and French Nationalisms," in *East of West: Cross-Cultural Performance and the Staging of Difference*, ed. Claire Sponsler and Xiaomei Chen (New York and Basingstoke: Palgrave Macmillan, 2000), 187–216.

Clark, Walter, *Isaac Albéniz: Portrait of a Romantic* (Oxford and New York: Oxford University Press, 1999).

Cocteau, Jean, *Le coq et l'arlequin: Notes autour de la musique* (Paris: Ed. de la Sirène, 1918).

Coeuroy, André, "A l'Opéra-Comique: La vida breve, L'amour sorcier. Les tréteaux de Maitre Pierre, de Manuel de Falla." *La revue musicale* 9, no. 6 (April 1928).

Coindreau, Maurice, "Cante jondo," *La revue musicale [ReM]* 4, no. 3 (January 1923).

Collet, Henri, *Albéniz et Granados* (Paris: Felix Alcan, 1926).

———, "Concert Sainz de la Maza," *Le ménestrel* (December 1926).

———, "Contribution à l'étude des 'Cantigas' d'Alphonse le Savant," *Bulletin hispanique* 13, no. 3 (1911): 270–290.

———, "Critiques et musiciens," *Le courrier musical* (November 1928).

———, "Espagne," *Le ménestrel* (February 1929).

———, "Espagne," *Le ménestrel* (December 1929).

———, "Espagne," *Le ménestrel* (October 1930).

———, "Espagne (I)," *Le ménestrel* (February 1929).

———, "Espagne (I)," *Le ménestrel* (June 1929).

———, "Espagne (II)," *Le ménestrel* (February 1929).

———, "Espagne (II)," *Le ménestrel* (June 1929).

———, "Espagne (III)," *Le ménestrel* (February 1929).

———, "Espagne/Le XIXe siècle. Deuxième partie: La renaissance musicale," in *Encyclopédie de la musique et dictionnaire du Conservatoire*, ed. Albert Lavignac and Lionel de la Laurencie, vol. 4 (Paris: Delagrave, 1920), 2470–2484.

———, *L'essor de la musique espagnole au XXe siècle* (Paris: Félix Alcan, 1929).

———, "L'internationalisme musical," *Le courrier musical* (December 1919).

———, "Madrid," *L'actualité musicale (supp. S.I.M. Revue musicale mensuelle)* (July 1910).

———, "La musique au Chili," *Comœdia* (September 10, 1920).

———, "La musique espagnole (I)," *Le ménestrel* (August 1925).

———, "La musique espagnole (II)," *Le ménestrel* (September 4, 1925).

———, "La musique espagnole (III)," *Le ménestrel* (September 11, 1925).

———, "La musique espagnole moderne," *Le courrier musical* (May 1918).

———, "La musique espagnole moderne, 1er partie," *Bulletin français de la S.I.M.* 4, no. 9 (September 1908).

———, "Musique et expression," *Le courrier musical* (December 1922).

———, *Le mysticisme musical espagnol au XVIe siècle* (Paris: Felix Alcan, 1913).

———, "Nécrologie," *Revue musicale et bulletin de la S.I.M.* 5, no. 7 (July 15, 1909).

———, "El porvenir de la música española," *La gaceta musical* (May 1, 1928): 18–19.
———, "La valeur expressive de la musique religieuse espagnole au XVIe siècle" (Bordeaux: Université de Bordeaux, 1908).
———, *Victoria* (Paris: Felix Alcan, 1914).
Collins, Chris, "Falla in Britain," *Musical Times* (2003): 33–48.
———, "Falla in Europe: Relations with His Contemporaries," in *Manuel de Falla: His Life and Music*, ed. Nancy Lee Harper (Lanham, MD: Scarecrow Press, 2005), 247–284.
Colmeiro, José F., "Exorcising Exoticism: 'Carmen' and the Construction of Oriental Spain," *Comparative Literature* 54, no. 2 (April 1, 2002): 127–144.
Conversi, Daniele, *The Basques, the Catalans, and Spain: Alternative Routes to Nationalist Mobilisation* (Reno: University of Nevada Press, 1997).
Copeau, Jacques, "L'art et l'oeuvre d'Adolphe Appia," *Comœdia* (March 12, 1928), 1.
Copeland, Robert M., "The Christian Message of Igor Stravinsky," *Musical Quarterly* 68, no. 4 (October 1, 1982): 563–579.
Cortès i Mir, Francesc, "La música escènica de Felip Pedrell: 'Els Pirineus. La Celestina. El Comte Arnau'," *Recerca musicològica*, no. 11 (1991): 63–97.
———. "Les rapports du cercle de F. Pedrell avec la France," in *Échanges musicaux franco-espagnols XVIIe–XIXe siècles: Actes des Rencontres de Villecroze, 15 au 17 octobre 1998*, ed. François Lesure (Paris: Klincksieck, 2000), 297–318.
Cortizo, María Encina, "La zarzuela espagnole du XIXe siècle. Relations et divergences avec le théâtre français du XIXe siècle (1832–1866)," in *Échanges musicaux franco-espagnols XVIIe–XIXe siècles: Actes des Rencontres de Villecroze, 15 au 17 octobre 1998*, ed. François Lesure, vol. 4, *Domaine musicologique. III, Les rencontres de Villecroze* (Paris: Klincksieck, 2000), 83–122.
———, and Ramón Sobrino Sánchez, "Asociacionismo musical en España," *Cuadernos de música iberoamericana* 8–9 (2001): 11–16.
Cubitt, Geoffrey, "Legitimism and the Cult of the Bourbon Royalty," in *The Right in France: 1789–1997*, ed. Nicholas Atkin and Frank Tallett (London and New York: Tauris, 1999), 51–70.
Curtiss, Mina, *Bizet and His World* (New York: Knopf, 1958).
Curzon, Henri de, *Felipe Pedrell, Les Pyrenees* (Paris: Librairie Fischbacher, 1902).
———, "La musique. Opéra-Comique: La vie brève, L'amour sorcier, Les tréteaux de Maître Pierre, de Manuel de Falla," *La nouvelle revue* 94 (April 1928): 225–228.
———, "Opéra-Comique.—Représentation de Mme Argentina et de sa troupe de ballets espagnols: Sonatina, ballet en un acte de Halffter;—Triana, fantaisie sévillane tirée d'Ibéria d'Albeniz et orchestrée par F.—F. Arbós;—Suite de danses," *Le ménestrel* (May 1929).
Cuvardic García, Dorde, "El trapero: El otro marginal en la historia de la literatura y de la cultura popular," *Káñina. Revista de artes y letras de la Universidad de Costa Rica* 31, no. 1 (2006): 217–227.
Dahlhaus, Carl, *Between Romanticism and Modernism: Four Studies in the Music of the Later Nineteenth Century* (Berkeley: University of California Press, 1980).
———, *Nineteenth-Century Music* (Berkeley: University of California Press, 1989).
Davidson, Robert A., *Jazz Age Barcelona* (Toronto: University of Toronto Press, 2009).
Davin de Champclos, Gabriel, "Les répétitions générales. 'Le voile du bonheur' et 'La jota' à l'Opéra-Comique." *Comœdia* (April 25, 1911).
Dean, Winton, "Bizet after 100 Years," *The Musical Times* 116, no. 1588 (June 1, 1975): 525–527.
Debay, Victor, "La habanera. Ghyslaine," *Le courrier musical* (March 1908).
———, "La voile du bonheur, La jota," *Le courrier musical* (May 1, 1911).
Delaunay, Jean-Marc, *Des palais en Espagne: L'ecole des hautes études hispaniques et la Casa de Velázquez au coeur des relations franco-espagnoles du XXe siècle (1898–1979)* (Madrid: Casa de Velázquez, 1994).
DeLeonibus, Gaetano, *Charles Maurras's Classicising Aesthetics: An Aestheticization of Politics* (New York: P. Lang, 2000).
Delmas, Marc, *Georges Bizet, 1838–1875* (Paris: P. Bossuet, 1930).
Demarquez, Suzanne, *Manuel de Falla* (Paris: Flammarion, 1963).

Derrida, Jacques, "What Is a 'Relevant' Translation?" *Critical Inquiry* 27, no. 2 (2001): 174–200.
Dezarnaux, Robert, "La musique," *La liberté* (March 12, 1928): 1–2.
Donnellon, Déirdre, "Debussy as Musician and Critic," in *The Cambridge Companion to Debussy*, ed. Simon Trezise (Cambridge: Cambridge University Press, 2003), 43–60.
Dorsch, Juliane, "Nostalgia and Modernism in Puppet Music of the 1920s," (Ph.D. diss., Royal Holloway, University of London, 2011).
———, "Production Problems and Depersonalised Puppets: 'Distancing Effects' of Falla's El retablo de Maese Pedro (1923) as Perceived by the Parisian Press," master's diss., Royal Holloway, University of London (2005).
Dorval, Marie, *Lettres à Alfred de Vigny: Recueillies et présentées par Charles Gaudier* (Paris and Abbeville: Gallimard, impr. de F. Paillart, 1942).
Duchesneau, Michel, *L'avant-garde musicale et ses sociétés à Paris de 1871 à 1939* (Liège: Mardaga, 1997).
Dumesnil, René, *La musique contemporaine en France*, 2 vols. (Paris: Armand Colin, 1930).
Dyke, Charles, "Un coup d'oeil sur l'Espagne Musical de la Renaissance," *Le courrier musical* (May 1924).
E. B., and Pierre Paris, "Chronique," *Bulletin hispanique* 11, no. 2 (1909): 227–228.
Elias, Norbert, *The Civilizing Process* (Oxford: Blackwell, 1994/1939).
Ellingson, Terry Jay, *The Myth of the Noble Savage* (Berkeley: University of California Press, 2001).
Ellis, Katharine, *Interpreting the Musical Past: Early Music in Nineteenth-Century France* (New York, Oxford: Oxford University Press, 2005).
Estrée, Paul d', "'Bizet' par H. Gauthier-Villars," *Le guide du concert* (December 1911).
Etcharry, Stéphan, "Henri Collet (1885–1951), compositeur: Un itinéraire singulier dans l'hispanisme musical français" (Ph.D. diss., Université de Paris-Sorbonne, 2004).
———, "Les mélodies castillanes d'Henri Collet (1885–1951): Une approche originale de l'Espagne dans la musique française," in *La musique entre France et Espagne: Interactions stylistiques. Actes du colloque international tenu à Paris, en Sorbonne-Paris IV et à l'Instituto Cervantes, les 14–16 mai 2001*, ed. Louis Jambou (Paris: Presses de l'Univ. de Paris-Sorbonne, 2003), 129–149.
———, "Le Prix de Rome de composition de 1903: Raoul Laparra et la cantate Alyssa," *Musiker*, no. 16 (February 2009): 7–33.
Etienvre, Jean-Pierre, and José Ramón de Urquijo y Goitia, eds., *España, Francia y la Comunidad Europea: Actas del Segundo Coloquio Hispano-Francés de Historia Contemporánea, celebrado en Aix-en-Provence los días 16, 17 y 18 de junio de 1986* (Madrid: Casa de Velázquez, 1989).
Etzion, Judith, "Spanish Music as Perceived in Western Music Historiography: A Case of the Black Legend?" *International Review of the Aesthetics and Sociology of Music* 29, no. 2 (1998): 93–120.
Faber, Sebastiaan, *Exile and Cultural Hegemony: Spanish Intellectuals in Mexico, 1939–1975*, 1st ed. (Nashville: Vanderbilt University Press, 2002).
Falla, Manuel de, "Claude Debussy et l'Espagne," *La revue musicale* 1, no. 2 (1920): 206–210.
———, *Escritos sobre música y músicos: Debussy, Wagner, El cante jondo*, 3rd ed. (Madrid: Espasa-Calpe, 1972).
———, "Concurso de 'Cante Jondo' (canto primitivo andaluz)," Falla, *Escritos sobre música y músicos*, ed. Federico Sopeña (Buenos Aires: Espasa-Calpe, 1950), 140–147.
———, "L'Espagne et Claude Debussy," *Le courrier musical* (October 1918).
———, "Felipe Pedrell," *La revue musicale* 4, no. 4 (February 1923).
———, "Letter to the editor," *The Chesterian* (July 1920), 49.
———, *On Music and Musicians* (London: Boyars, 1979).
Faull, Katherine M., "Translation and Culture," in *Translation and Culture*, ed. Katherine M. Faull (Cranbury, NJ: Associated University Presses, 2004), 13–24.
Fauré, Gabriel, "Opéra-Comique: *La jota*, conte lyrique en deux actes, de M. Raoul Laparra," *Le Figaro* (March 28, 1911).
———, "Théâtre National de l'Opéra-Comique: Millième représentation de *Carmen*," *Le Figaro* (December 24, 1904).

Fauser, Annegret, *Musical Encounters at the 1889 Paris World's Fair* (Rochester, NY: University of Rochester Press, 2005).
Fernández-Shaw, Guillermo, *Larga historia de "La vida breve"* (Madrid: Revista de Occidente, 1972).
———, Guillermo, *Un poeta de transición: Vida y obra de Carlos Fernández Shaw* (Madrid: Editorial Gredos, 1986).
Fesser, Joaquín, "Los Bailes Rusos. Epílogo," *Revista musical hispano-americana* (June 30, 1916): 4–5.
Foucault, Michel, *Madness and Civilization* (Abingdon: Routledge, 2001/1961).
Fox, Edward Inman, *La invención de España: Nacionalismo liberal e identidad nacional* (Madrid: Cátedra, 1997).
———, "Spain as Castile: Nationalism and National Identity," in *The Cambridge Companion to Modern Spanish Culture*, ed. David T. Gies (Cambridge: Cambridge University Press, 1999), 21–36.
Franco, Enrique, "Rogelio del Villar," *Diccionario de la música española e hispanoamericana*, ed. Emilio Casares Rodicio, vol. 10 (Madrid: Instituto Complutense de Ciencias Musicales, 2002), 934–938.
Freedman, Paul, "Cowardice, Heroism and the Legendary Origins of Catalonia," *Past & Present*, no. 121 (1988): 3–28.
Fulcher, Jane F., "The Composer as Intellectual: Ideological Inscriptions in French Interwar Neoclassicism," *Journal of Musicology* 17, no. 2 (1999): 197–230.
———, *The Composer as Intellectual: Music and Ideology in France 1914–1940* (New York: Oxford University Press, 2005).
———, *French Cultural Politics & Music: From the Dreyfus Affair to the First World War* (New York: Oxford University Press, 1999).
———, "Musical Style, Meaning, and Politics in France on the Eve of the Second World War," *Journal of Musicology* 13, no. 4 (October 1, 1995): 425–453.
Gallois, Jean, *Henri Collet ou l'Espagne impérieuse* (Geneva: Editions Papillon, 2001).
Gammon, Martin, "'Exemplary Originality': Kant on Genius and Imitation," *Journal of the History of Philosophy* 35, no. 4 (1997): 563–592.
García Canclini, Néstor, *Hybrid Cultures: Strategies for Entering and Leaving Modernity* (Minneapolis: University of Minnesota Press, 1995).
García Cárcel, Ricardo, *La leyenda negra: Historia y opinión* (Madrid: Alianza Editorial, 1992).
Gaudier, Charles, *Carmen de Bizet. Étude historique et critique. Analyse musicale,* Les chefs-d'oeuvre de la musique (Paris: P. Mellottée, 1922).
Gauthier-Villars, Henry, *Georges Bizet* (Paris: Renouard, 1928).
———, [Emile Vuillemoz], *Georges Bizet* (Paris: Renouard, 1928).
———, "La habanera. Ghyslaine," *Comœdia* (February 27, 1908).
Gautier, Théophile, "Shakespeare aux Funambules," in *L'art moderne* (Paris: Charpentier, 1856), 167–179.
Gheusi, P. B., "La musique au théâtre. A l'Opéra-Comique. Trois pièces de Manuel de Falla," *Le Figaro* (March 11, 1928).
Gies, David T., ed., *The Cambridge Companion to Modern Spanish Culture* (New York: Cambridge University Press, 1999).
Giger, Andreas, "Verismo: Origin, Corruption, and Redemption of an Operatic Term," *Journal of the American Musicological Society* 60, no. 2 (2007): 271–315.
Gilman, Sander L., "Nietzsche, Bizet, and Wagner: Illness, Health, and Race in the Nineteenth Century," *Opera Quarterly* 23, no. 2–3 (March 31, 2007): 247–264.
Goehr, Lydia, "Radical Modernism and the Failure of Style: Philosophical Reflections on Maeterlinck-Debussy's Pelléas et Mélisande," *Representations* 74, no. 1 (May 1, 2001): 55–82.
González Calleja, Eduardo, "Noucentisme, Catalanisme et arc latin," *La pensée de midi*, no. 1 (2000): 44–51.
González Cuevas, Pedro Carlos. "La recepción del pensamiento maurrasiano en España (1914–1930)," *Espacio, tiempo y forma* 3 (1990): 343–356.

———. *Acción Española: Teología política y nacionalismo autoritario en España (1913–1936)* (Madrid: Tecnos, 1998).

———, "Charles Maurras en Cataluña," *Boletín de la Real Academia de la Historia* 195, no. 2 (1998): 309–362.

———, *El pensamiento político de la derecha española en el siglo XX: De la crisis de la Restauración al Estado de los partidos (1898–2000)* (Madrid: Tecnos, 2005).

González Peña, María Luz, "Fernández Shaw, Carlos," *Diccionario de la zarzuela. España e Hispanoamérica*, vol. 1 (Madrid: Instituto Complutense de Ciencias Musicales, 2006).

Goode, Joshua, "Corrupting a Good Mix: Race and Crime in Late Nineteenth- and Early Twentieth-Century Spain," *European History Quarterly* 35, no. 2 (April 1, 2005): 241–265.

Goubault, Christian, *La critique musicale dans la presse française de 1870 à 1914* (Genève: Slatkine, 1984).

Granja Sáinz, José Luis de la, "El antimaketismo: La visión de Sabino Arana sobre España y los españoles," *Norba. Revista de historia* 19 (2006): 191–203.

Greenfeld, Liah, *Nationalism: Five Roads to Modernity* (Cambridge, MA: Harvard University Press, 1992).

Guarnieri Corazzol, Adriana, "Opera and Verismo: Regressive Points of View and the Artifice of Alienation," *Cambridge Opera Journal* 5, no. 1 (2008): 39–53.

Guillot, Pierre, "Déodat de Séverac: Quelle 'méditerranéisation' de la musique?" in *La musique dans le Midi de la France: XIXe siècle. Actes des rencontres de Villecroze, 16 au 18 mai 1996*, ed. François Lesure, vol. 2 (Paris: Klincksieck, 1996), 309–324.

Hannah, Martha, *The Mobilization of Intellect: French Scholars and Writers During the Great War* (Cambridge, MA: Harvard University Press, 1996).

Harney, Lucy D., "Zarzuela and the Pastoral," *Modern Language Notes (MLN)* 123 (2008): 252–273.

Harper, Nancy Lee, ed., *Manuel de Falla: His Life and Music* (Lanham, MD: Scarecrow Press, 2005).

Harrington, Thomas, "Rapping on the Cast(i)le Gates: Nationalism and Culture-Planning in Contemporary Spain," in *Ideologies of Hispanism*, ed. Mabel Moraña (Nashville, TN: Vanderbilt University Press, 2005), 107–137.

Hart, Brian, "The Symphony and National Identity in Early Twentieth-Century France," in *French Music, Culture, and National Identity, 1870–1939*, ed. Barbara Kelly (Rochester, NY: University of Rochester Press, 2008), 131–148.

Hera Martínez, Jesús de la, *La política cultural de Alemania en España en el período de entreguerras* (Madrid: CSIC, 2002).

Hess, Carol A., "'Un alarde de modernismo y dislocación': Los Ballets Russe en España, 1916–1921," in *Los Ballets Russes de Diaghilev y España*, ed. Yvan Nommick and Antonio Álvarez Cañibano (Granada and Madrid: Fundación Archivo Manuel de Falla, INAEM, 2000), 215–227.

———, "Falla, Manuel de," in *The New Grove Dictionary of Music and Musicians*, 2nd ed., ed. Stanley Sadie, vol. 8 (London and New York: Macmillan, 2001), 529–535.

———, *Manuel de Falla and Modernism in Spain, 1898–1936* (Chicago: University of Chicago Press, 2001).

———, *Sacred Passions: The Life and Music of Manuel de Falla* (Oxford: Oxford University Press, 2005).

Hoffman, Léon-François, *Romantique Espagne. L'image de l'Espagne en France entre 1800 et 1850* (Paris: Presses Universitaires de France, 1961).

Huebner, Steven, *French Opera at the Fin-de-Siècle: Wagnerism, Naturalism, and Style* (Oxford and New York: Oxford University Press, 1999).

———, "Naturalism and Supernaturalism in Alfred Bruneau's Le Rêve," *Cambridge Opera Journal* 11, no. 1 (2008): 77–101.

———, "La Navarraise face au verisme," in *Le naturalisme sur la scène lyrique*, ed. Jean-Christophe Branger and Alban Ramaut (Saint-Etienne: Publications de l'Université de Saint-Etienne, 2004), 129–150.

Huete Machado, Lola, "Padrinos de Hollywood," *El país semanal* (June 18, 2006).
Iberni, Luis G., "Felip Pedrell y Ruperto Chapí," *Recerca musicològica* 11–12 (1991–1992): 335–344.
———, "Tempranica, La," *Diccionario de la zarzuela. España e Hispanoamérica*, ed. Emilio Casares, vol. 2 (Madrid: Instituto Complutense de Ciencias Musicales, 2006), 798.
Imbert, Hughes, "Albert Carré," *Médaillons contemporains* (Paris, 1903), 123–130.
Jackson, Jeffrey H., *Making Jazz French: Music and Modern Life in Interwar Paris* (Durham: Duke University Press, 2003).
Jambou, Louis, ed., *Manuel de Falla, latinité et universalité. Actes du colloque international tenu en Sorbonne, 18–21 novembre 1996* (Paris: Presses de l'Université de Paris-Sorbonne, 1999).
———, ed., *La musique entre France et Espagne: Interactions stylistiques. Actes du colloque international tenu à Paris, en Sorbonne-Paris IV et à l'Instituto Cervantes, les 14–16 mai 2001* (Paris: Presses de l'Univ. de Paris-Sorbonne, 2003).
———, "Stravinsky y Falla: Influencias y paralelismos. Parámetros para un estudio," in *Relaciones musicales entre España y Rusia*, ed. Antonio Álvarez Cañibano (Madrid: Centro de Documentación de Música y Danza, 1999), 101–116.
Janés i Nadal, Alfonsina, *L'obra de Richard Wagner a Barcelona*, vol. 82 (Barcelona: R. Dalmau, 1983).
Jankélévitch, Vladimir, *La présence lointaine: Albeniz, Séverac, Mompou* (Paris: Editions du Seuil, 1983).
Jean-Aubry, Georges, *French Music of Today*, Library of Music and Musicians, ed. A. Eaglefield Hull (London: K. Paul, Trench, Trubner, 1919).
———, "Le Havre. Un concert espagnol," *S.I.M. Revue musicale mensuelle* 6, no. 12 (December 15, 1910).
———, "Le mouvement musical en Provence. La musique moderne espagnole," *Le guide du concert* (November 1910).
———, *La musique et les nations* (Paris: Éditions de la Sirène, 1922).
———, *La musique française d'aujourd'hui* (Paris: Perrin et Cie, 1916).
J. N. (Joaquin Nin?), "M. J. Turina," *Le courrier musical* (June 1907).
Johnston, Robert H., *New Mecca, New Babylon: Paris and the Russian Exiles, 1920–1945* (Kingston: McGill-Queen's University Press, 1988).
Jover Zamora, José María, *España en la política internacional: Siglos XVIII–XX* (Madrid: Marcial Pons Historia, 1999).
Kalfa, Jacqueline, "Isaac Albéniz à Paris: Une patrie retrouvée (1893–1909)," *Revue Internationale de Musique Française* 26 (June 1988): 19–36.
Kamen, Henry, *The Disinherited: The Exiles Who Created Spanish Culture* (London and New York: Allen Lane, 2007).
———, *Imagining Spain: Historical Myth & National Identity* (New Haven and London: Yale University Press, 2008).
Kelkel, Manfred, *Naturalisme, vérisme et réalisme dans l'opéra: De 1890 à 1930* (Paris: Libr. Philosophique J. Vrin, 1984).
Kelly, Barbara L., "Debussy and the Making of a *musicien français: Pelléas*, the Press and World War I," in *French Music, Culture and National Identity, 1870–1939*, ed. Barbara L. Kelly (Rochester, NY: University of Rochester Press, 2008), 58–76.
———, ed., *French Music, Culture and National Identity, 1870–1939* (Rochester, NY: University of Rochester Press, 2008).
———, "History and Hommage," in *The Cambridge Companion to Ravel*, ed. Deborah Mawer (Cambridge: Cambridge University Press, 2000), 7–26.
Kertesz, Elizabeth, and Michael Christoforidis, "Confronting *Carmen* Beyond the Pyrenees: Bizet's Opera in Madrid, 1887–1888," *Cambridge Opera Journal* 20 (2008): 79–110.
Kivy, Peter, *Introduction to a Philosophy of Music* (New York: Oxford University Press, 2002).
Kosto, Adam J., *Making Agreements in Medieval Catalonia: Power, Order, and the Written Word, 1000–1200* (Cambridge, UK; New York: Cambridge University Press, 2001).

Krause, Beate Angelica, "Henri Collet et Comœdia. Le feuilleton musical dans une époque de bouleversements artistiques," *Revue internationale de musique française* 10, no. 29 (June 1989): 29–38.

Labanyi, Jo, "Musical Battles: Populism and Hegemony in the Early Francoist Folkloric Film Musical," in *Constructing Identity in Contemporary Spain: Theoretical Debates and Cultural Practice*, ed. Jo Labanyi (Oxford: Oxford University Press, 2002), 206–221.

Lacombe, Hervé, "L'Espagne à l'Opéra-Comique avant 'Carmen.' Du 'Guitarrero' de Halévy (1842) à 'Don César de Bazan' de Massenet (1872)," in *Échanges musicaux franco-espagnols XVIIe–XIXe siècles: Actes des Rencontres de Villecroze, 15 au 17 octobre 1998*, ed. François Lesure (Paris: Klincksieck, 2000), 161–194.

———, "L'Espagne à Paris au milieu du XIXe siècle (1847–1857). L'influence d'artistes espagnols sur l'imaginaire parisien et la construction d'une 'hispanicité'," *La revue musicale [ReM]* 88, no. 2 (2002): 289–431.

———, *The Keys to French Opera in the Nineteenth Century* (Berkeley: University of California Press, 2001).

Lafuente Ferrari, Enrique, *La vida y el arte de Ignacio Zuloaga* (Madrid: Revista de Occidente, 1972).

Lalo, Charles, *Esquisse d'une esthétique musicale scientifique* (Paris: F. Alcan, 1908).

Lalo, Pierre, "À l'Opéra-Comique: Francesca da Rimini. La vie brève," *Le temps*, no. 6 (March 1914).

———, "À l'Opéra-Comique: Le voile du bonheur. La jota." *Le temps* (May 4, 1911).

Laloy, Louis, "Francesca da Rimini. La vie brève," *Comœdia* (December 1913).

———, "Tomás Luis de Victoria (XVIe siècle). Oeuvres éditées par Ph. Pedrell, Tome I. (Leipzig, Breitkopf et Härtel, 1902)," *Revue musicale* (May 1902).

Lamas, Rafael, "On Music and Nation: The Colonized Consciousness of Spanish Musical Nationalism," *Arizona Journal of Hispanic Cultural Studies*, 7 (2003): 75–82.

———, "Zarzuela and the Anti-Musical Prejudice of the Spanish Enlightenment," *Hispanic Review* 74, no. 1 (2006): 39–58.

Landormy, Paul, *Bizet* (Paris: F. Alcan, 1924).

———, "L'hispanisme de Bizet," *La revue musicale* 4, no. 10 (August 1923).

———, *La musique française après Debussy* (París: Gallimard, 1943).

Langdon-Davies, John, *Behind the Spanish Barricades* (London: Martin Secker & Warburg, 1936).

Laparra, Raoul, *Bizet et l'Espagne* (Paris: Librairie Delagrave, 1935).

———, "Espagne," *Le ménestrel* (November 19, 1920).

———, "Espagne," *Le ménestrel* (March 9, 1923).

———, "Espagne," *Le ménestrel* (August 10, 1923).

———, "Espagne," *Le ménestrel* (August 22, 1924).

———, "Espagne," *Le ménestrel* (November 14, 1924).

———, "Espagne," *Le ménestrel* (November 1925).

———, "Espagne." *Le ménestrel* (October 21, 1927).

———, "Espagne," *Le ménestrel* (November 4, 1927).

———, *La habanera. Drame lyrique en trois actes. Partition piano et chant réduite par l'auteur* (Paris: Enoch & Cie, 1907).

———, *La jota. Conte lyrique en 2 actes. Poème et musique de Raoul Laparra. Partition pour piano et chante réduite par l'auteur* (Paris: Enoch & Cie, 1911).

———, "La musique et la danse populaires en Espagne," in *Encyclopédie de la musique et dictionnaire du Conservatoire. 1e partie. Histoire de la musique. Espagne-Portugal*, ed. Albert Lavignac and Lionel de la Laurencie (Paris: Delagrave, 1920), 2353–2400.

———, "La semaine musical," *Le ménestrel* (December 19, 1919).

Lapommeraye, Pierre de, "Festival Falla," *Le ménestrel* (March 1928).

Le Bordays, Christiane, "Henri Collet (1885–1951): Le compositeur," *Revue internationale de musique française*, no. 26 (June 1988): 99–110.

Le Duc, Antoine, "De la zarzuela à La vida breve: Continuité/rupture," in *Manuel de Falla, latinité et universalité. Actes du colloque international tenu en Sorbonne, 18–21 novembre 1996,* ed. Louis Jambou (Paris: Presses de l'Université de Paris-Sorbonne, 1999), 47–60.
Lebovics, Herman, *True France: The Wars over Cultural Identity, 1900–1945* (Ithaca: Cornell University Press, 1994).
León Solís, Fernando, *Negotiating Spain and Catalonia: Competing Narratives of National Identity* (Bristol and Portland, OR: Intellect Books, 2003).
Lesure, François, ed., *Échanges musicaux franco-espagnols XVIIe–XIXe siècles: Actes des Rencontres de Villecroze, 15 au 17 octobre 1998* (Paris: Klincksieck, 2000).
Linor, G., "M. Manuel de Falla et 'La vie brève,' M. Franco Leoni et 'Francesca da Rimini,' *Comœdia* (December 31, 1913).
Llano, Samuel, "Dos Españas y una sola música: Henri Collet, entre el federalismo y el centralismo," *Cuadernos de música iberoamericana* 15, no. 1 (2008): 75–97.
———, "España en la vitrina: Maurice Ravel, el mito de la autenticidad y el neoimperialismo español," *Journal of Spanish Cultural Studies* 11, no. 1 (2010): 1–15.
———, "Hispanic Traditions in a Cross-Cultural Perspective: Raoul Laparra's 'La habanera' (1908) and French Critics," *Journal of the Royal Musical Association* 136, no. 1 (2011): 97–140.
Lliurat, Frederic, "Lettre de Barcelone. Orfeo Catala," *Bulletin français de la S.I.M.* 4, no. 5 (May 1908).
Locke, Ralph P., "Cutthroats and Casbah Dancers, Muezzins and Timeless Sands: Musical Images of the Middle East," in *The Exotic in Western Music,* ed. Jonathan Bellman (Boston: Northeastern University Press, 1988), 104–136.
———, *Musical Exoticism: Images and Reflections* (Cambridge: Cambridge University Press, 2009).
———, "Spanish Local Color in Bizet's Carmen: Unexplored Borrowings and Transformations," in *Music, Theatre and Cultural Transfer: Paris, 1830–1914,* ed. Annegret Fauser and Mark Everist (Chicago: University of Chicago Press, 2009), 316–360.
Locke, Robert R., *French Legitimists and the Politics of Moral Order in the Early Third Republic* (Princeton, NJ: Princeton University Press, 1974).
Lolo, Begoña, "Las relaciones Falla-Pedrell a través de *La vida breve,*" in *Manuel de Falla: La vida breve,* ed. Yvan Nommick (Granada: Archivo Manuel de Falla, 1997), 121–146.
López-Cordón Cortezo, María Victoria, "Pacte de famille ou intérêts d'état? La monarchie française et la diplomatie espagnole du XVIIIe siècle," in *La présence des Bourbons en Europe: XVIe–XXIe siècle,* ed. Lucien Bély (Paris: Presses Univ. de France, 2003), 185–206.
Luraschi, Christophe, *Biarritz des goelands: Précedé d'une biographie de Pierre-Barthelemy Gheusi* (Biarritz: Atlantica, 2001).
Luxenberg, Alisa, "Over the Pyrenees and Through the Looking-Glass: French Culture Reflected in Its Imagery of Spain," in *Spain, Espagne, Spanien: Foreign Artists Discover Spain, 1800–1900,* ed. Suzanne L. Stratton (New York: The Equitable Gallery, 1993), 11–32.
Macdonald, Hugh, "Carmen (ii)," *The New Grove Dictionary of Opera,* http://www.oxfordmusiconline.com/subscriber/article/grove/music/O008315 (accessed August 17, 2011).
Macedo, Catherine, "Between Opera and Reality: The Barcelona 'Parsifal,'" *Cambridge Opera Journal* 10, no. 1 (1998): 97–109.
Madrid, Alejandro, *Sounds of the Modern Nation: Music, Culture, and Ideas in Post-Revolutionary Mexico* (Philadelphia: Temple University Press, 2008).
Mainer, José-Carlos, *La edad de plata (1902–1939): Ensayo de interpretación de un proceso cultural* (Madrid: Cátedra, 1981).
Malherbe. Henri, "Chronique musicale: Manuel de Falla," *Le temps* (March 14, 1928).
———, "Chronique musicale: Manuel de Falla II," *Le temps* (March 21, 1928).
———, "Les confidences de M. Raoul Laparra," *Le temps* (March 28, 1911).
Manuel, Peter, "Andalusian, Gypsy and Class Identity in the Contemporary Flamenco Complex," *Ethnomusicology* 33, 1 (1989): 47–65.
Marnold, Jean, *Musique d'autrefois et d'aujourd'hui* (Paris: Dorbon-Ainée, 1911).

Martín Martínez, José, "Painting and Sculpture in Modern Spain," in *The Cambridge Companion to Modern Spanish Culture*, ed. David T. Gies (New York: Cambridge University Press, 1999), 239–247.

Martínez del Fresno, Beatriz, and Nuria Menéndez Sánchez, "Una visión de conjunto sobre la escena coreográfica madrileña (1915–1925) y algunas observaciones acerca de la influencia rusa en el desarrollo del *ballet* español," in *Los Ballets Russes de Diaghilev y España*, ed. Yvan Nommick and Antonio Álvarez Cañibano (Granada and Madrid: Fundación Archivo Manuel de Falla, INAEM, 2000), 149–213.

Mason, A. L., "Enrique Granados (1867–1916)," *Music & Letters* 14, no. 3 (July 1, 1933): 231–238.

Masson, Paul-Marie, "La musique espagnole au congrès de Barcelone," *Revue musicale*, August 1936.

Matus, Jill L., "Saint Teresa, Hysteria, and Middlemarch," *Journal of the History of Sexuality* 1, no. 2 (October 1, 1990): 215–240.

Maurras, Charles, "Les forces latines," in Marius André, *La fin de l'empire espagnol d'Amérique Latine* (Paris: Nouvelle librairie nationale, 1922), 1–16.

McClancy, Jeremy, *The Decline of Carlism* (Reno and Las Vegas, NV: University of Nevada Press, 2000).

McClary, Susan, *Feminine Endings: Music, Gender, and Sexuality* (Minneapolis, London: University of Minnesota Press, 2002/1991).

———, *Georges Bizet: Carmen* (Cambridge: Cambridge University Press, 1992).

Medicis, François de, "Darius Milhaud and the Debate on Polytonality in the French Press of the 1920s," *Music and Letters* 86, no. 4 (2005): 573–591.

Mège, Philippe, *Charles Maurras et le germanisme* (Paris: L'Æncre, 2003).

Mendès, Catulle, *Richard Wagner* (Paris: Bibliothèque Charpentier, 1886).

Merjian, Ara H., "'Il faut méditerraniser la peinture': Giorgio de Chirico's Metaphysical Painting, Nietzsche, and the 'Obscurity of Light,'" *California Italian Studies Journal* 1, no. 1 (2010), http://escholarship.org/uc/item/12d9s5vb.

Messing, Scott, *Neoclassicism in Music: From the Genesis of the Concept Through the Schoenberg Stravinsky Polemic* (Ann Arbor, MI: UMI Research Press, 1988).

Milnes, Rodney "Navarraise, La," in *Grove Music Online*, http://www.oxfordmusiconline.com/subscriber/article/grove/music/O008723 (accessed April 15, 2011).

Mitchell, Timothy, *Flamenco Deep Song* (New Haven and London: Yale University Press, 1994).

Mitjana, Rafael, "Acerca de algunos libros que tratan de música y músicos españoles," *Revista de filología española* 1, no. 1 (1914): 151–162.

———, *La música contemporánea en España y Felipe Pedrell* (Madrid: Librería de Fernando Fé, 1901).

———, "La musique en Espagne: Art religieux et art profane," in *Encyclopédie de la musique et dictionnaire du Conservatoire*, ed. Albert Lavignac and Lionel de la Laurencie, vol. 4 (Paris: Delagrave, 1920), 1913–2351.

———, *¡Para música vamos! Estudios sobre el arte musical contemporáneo en España* (Valencia: Sempere y Cía., 1909).

Un Monsieur de l'Orchestre, "La soirée. A l'Opéra-Comique," *Le Figaro* (February 27, 1908).

Moradiellos, Enrique, *1936: Los mitos de la guerra civil* (Barcelona: Península, 2004).

Moreau, Philippe, *La Iglesia de San Pedro de Ansó* (Huesca: Instituto de Estudios Altoaragoneses, 1988).

Murga Castro, Idoia, *Escenografía de la danza en la edad de plata, 1916–1936* (Madrid: CSIC, 2009).

———, "Escenografía y figurinismo de los bailarines españoles de principios del siglo XX," in *Congreso internacional imagen y apariencia* (Murcia: Ediciones de la Universidad de Murcia, 2009), 1–15.

Murphy, Kerry, "Carmen: Couleur Locale or the Real Thing?" in *Music, Theater, and Cultural Transfer: Paris, 1830–1914*, ed. Annegret Fauser and Mark Everist (Chicago: University of Chicago Press, 2009), 293–315.

Musk, Andrea, "Aspects of Regionalism in French Music During the Third Republic: The Schola Cantorum, D'Indy, Severac and Canteloube," (Ph.D. diss., Oxford University, 1999).

———, "Regionalism, Latinité and the French Musical Tradition: Deodat de Severac's Heliogabale," in *Nineteenth-Century Music: Selected Proceedings of the Tenth International Conference*, ed. Jim Samson and Bennett Zon (Burlington: Ashgate, 2002), 226–249.

Nattiez, Jean-Jacques, *Music and Discourse. Toward a Semiology of Music* (Princeton, NJ: Princeton University Press, 1990/1987).

Nematollahy, Ali, "Nietzsche in France, 1890–1914," *Philosophical Forum* 40, no. 2 (June 1, 2009): 169–180.

Nichols, Roger, *The Harlequin Years: Music in Paris, 1917–1929* (Berkeley: University of California Press, 2002).

———, and Richard Langham Smith, *Claude Debussy, Pelléas et Mélisande* (Cambridge: Cambridge University Press, 1989).

Nietzsche, Friedrich, *Le cas Wagner, suivi de Nietzsche contre Wagner*, trans. G. Colli, M. Montinari, and Jean-Claude Hémery (Paris: Gallimard, 1991).

Nin, Joaquin, "Un compositeur espagnol. M. Felipe Pedrell," *Le courrier musical* (February 1905).

———, "Les musiciens espagnols anciens et le clavecin," *Le courrier musical* (November 1925).

———, "Les musiciens espagnols anciens et le clavecin (II)," *Le courrier musical* (December 1925).

———, "*La vie brève* de Manuel de Falla," *La tribune musicale* (February 1914).

Niño Rodríguez, Antonio, *Cultura y diplomacia: Los hispanistas franceses y España de 1875 a 1931* (Madrid: Consejo Superior de Investigaciones Científicas, 1988).

———, "El hispanismo científico y los intereses franceses en España a finales del siglo XIX," in *España, Francia y la Comunidad Europea: Actas del Segundo Coloquio Hispano-Francés de Historia Contemporánea, celebrado en Aix-en-Provence los días 16, 17 y 18 de junio de 1986*, ed. Jean-Pierre Etienvre and José Ramón de Urquijo y Goitia (Madrid: Casa de Velázquez, 1989), 31–56.

Nommick, Yvan, "*La vida breve* entre 1905 y 1914: Evolución formal y orquestal," in *Manuel de Falla: La vida breve*, ed. Yvan Nommick (Granada: Archivo Manuel de Falla, 1997), 23–52.

Nora, Pierre, "Between Memory and History: Les lieux de mémoire," *Representations* 26 (1989): 7–24.

Núñez, Xose-Manoel, "The Region as Essence of the Fatherland: Regionalist Variants of Spanish Nationalism (1840–1936)," *European History Quarterly*, 31, no. 4 (2001) 483–518.

O'Flynn, John, "National Identity and Music in Transition: Issues of Authenticity in a Global Setting," in *Music, National Identity and the Politics of Location*, ed. Ian Biddle and Vanessa Knights (Aldershot: Ashgate, 2007) 19–38.

Olmeda, Federico, *Folk-lore de Castilla ó cancionero popular de Burgos* (Sevilla: Librería Editorial de María Auxiliadora, 1903).

Orledge, Robert, *Debussy and the Theatre* (Cambridge: Cambridge University Press, 1982).

———, "Evocations of Exoticism," in *The Cambridge Companion to Ravel*, ed. Deborah Mawer (Cambridge: Cambridge University Press, 2000), 27–47.

Ortiz de Urbina y Sobrino, Paloma, *Richard Wagner en España: La Asociación Wagneriana de Madrid (1911–1915)* (Alcala de Henares: Universidad de Alcalá, 2007).

Osma, Guillermo de, "Sert, Gris, Pruna y Miró," *Los Ballets Russes de Diaghilev y España*, ed. Yvan Nommick and Antonio Álvarez Cañibano (Granada and Madrid: Fundación Archivo Manuel de Falla, INAEM, 2000), 47–56.

Pagden, Anthony, *The Idea of Europe. From Antiquity to the European Union* (Washington, DC: Woodrow Wilson Center Press, 2002).

Pahissa, Jaime, *Vida y obra de Manuel de Falla* (Buenos Aires: Ricordi Americana, 1956).

Palacios, María, *La renovación musical en Madrid durante la dictadura de Primo de Rivera: El Grupo de los Ocho, 1923–1931* (Madrid: Sociedad Española de Musicología, 2008).

Palacios Garoz, Miguel Ángel, *Federico Olmeda, un maestro de capilla atípico* (Burgos: Instituto Municipal de Cultura de Burgos, 2003).

———, *El hispanismo musical de Raoul Laparra y Henri Collet: Dos discípulos franceses de Federico Olmeda en Burgos* (Burgos: Institución Fernán González, Academia Burgense de Historia y Bellas Artes, 1999).
Parakilas, James, "How Spain Got a Soul," in *The Exotic in Western Music*, ed. Jonathan Bellman (Boston: Northeastern University Press, 1998), 137–193.
———, "The Soldier and the Exotic: Operatic Variations on a Theme of Racial Encounter Part I," *Opera Quarterly* 10, no. 2 (1993): 33–56.
Parejo Delgado, José, *Gerónimo Giménez: Un precursor de Manuel de Falla* (Sevilla: Padilla Libros, 1997).
Parnac, Valentin, "Ballets espagnols de l'Argentina," *La revue musicale [ReM]* 9, no. 11 (October 1928).
Pasler, Jann, *Composing the Citizen: Music as Public Utility in Third Republic France* (Berkeley: University of California Press, 2009).
———, "Deconstructing d'Indy, or the Problem of a Composer's Reputation," in *Writing Through Music: Essays on Music, Culture, and Politics* (Oxford and New York: Oxford University Press, 2008), 101–139.
———, "Race and Nation: Musical Acclimatisation and the Chansons Populaires in Third Republic France," in *Western Music and Race*, ed. Julie Brown (Cambridge: Cambridge University Press, 2007), 147–167.
———, "Theorizing Race in Nineteenth-Century France: Music as Emblem of Identity," *Musical Quarterly* 89, no. 4 (December 21, 2006): 459–504.
Payne, Stanley, *Basque Nationalism* (Reno: University of Nevada Press, 1975).
Pedrell, Felipe, "Les artisans du folklor musical espagnol," *La revue musicale* 2, no. 11 (October 1921).
———, *Cancionero musical popular español*, 4 vols. (Valls: E. Castells, 1922).
———, *Por nuestra música: Algunas observaciones sobre la magna cuestión de una escuela lírico nacional motivadas por la trilogía (3 cuadros y un prólogo) Los Pirineos, poema de D. Víctor Balaguer, música del que suscribe* (Barcelona: Henrich, 1891).
———, *Tomás Luis de Victoria, Abulense. Biografía, bibliografía, significado estético de todas sus obras de arte polifónico-religioso* (Valencia: M. Villar, 1918).
Pérez Gutiérrez, Mariano, *Falla y Turina a través de su epistolario* (Madrid: Alpuerto, 1982).
Persia, Jorge de, *En torno a lo español en la música del siglo XX* (Granada: Diputación Provincial de Granada, 2003).
Piquer Sanclemente, Ruth, *Clasicismo moderno, neoclasicismo y retornos en el pensamiento musical español (1915–1939)* (Sevilla: Doble J, 1910).
———, and Michael Christoforidis, "Modernist Representations of the Guitar and the Instrument's Classical Revival in the 1920s," *Proceedings of the First Conference on Interdisciplinary Musicology* (Paris, 2009)
Plessier, Ghislaine, *Étude critique de la correspondance de Zuloaga et Rodin de 1903 a 1917* (Paris: Éditions Hispaniques, 1983).
Porras Medrano, Adelaida, "Toledo o el secreto de Maurice Barrès," *Thélème. Revista complutense de estudios franceses* 14 (1999): 11–22.
Poueigh, Jean, "Critique musicale: Opéra-Comique," *La rampe* 2, no. 472 (March 1, 1928): 12.
Pouradier-Duteil, Bertrand, *Les musiciens et les Hauts-de-Seine* (Paris: Sogemo 1991).
Pougin, Arthur, "La légende de la chute de 'Carmen' et la mort de Bizet," *Le ménestrel* (February 1903).
Prat de la Riba, Enric, *La nacionalitat catalana* (Barcelona: Tipografía L'Anuari de la Exportació, 1906).
Preston, Paul, *Las tres Españas del 36* (Barcelona: Plaza & Janés, 1998).
Prod'homme, J.-G., "Jean Chantavoine. Nécrologie," *Revue de musicologie* 34, no. 103–104 (December 1952): 166–167.
Prudhomme, Jean, "L'interpretation," *Comœdia* (December 1913).
———, "Opéra-Comique," *Le temps*, May 7, 1911.

———, "Les premières. Théâtre de l'Opéra-Comique," *Le matin* (March 13, 1928).

Quiroga Fernández de Soto, Alejandro, "La idea de España en los ideólogos de la dictadura de Primo de Rivera. El discurso católico-fascista de José Pemartín," *Revista de estudios políticos*, no. 108 (2000): 197–224.

R. C., "Concert de musique catalane," *Le courrier musical* (May 1905).

R. D., "La vie brève," *Excelsior* (January 1, 1914).

Radomski, James, *Manuel García: 1775–1832: Chronicle of the Life of a Bel Canto Tenor at the Dawn of Romanticism* (Oxford: Oxford University Press, 2000).

Ramos López, Pilar, "The Construction of the Myth of Spanish Renaissance Music as Golden Age," in *Early Music: Context and Ideas. International Conference in Musicology* (Cracovia: University of Cracovia, 2003), 1–6.

———, "Mysticism as a Key Concept of Spanish Early Music Historiography," in *Early Music: Context and Ideas. II International Conference in Musicology* (Cracovia: University of Cracovia, 2008), 1–14.

Riquelme Sánchez, José, "El pintor Gustavo Bacarisas. (Gibraltar 1873–Sevilla 1971)," *Almoraima: Revista de estudios campogibraltareños* 1 (1989): 73–76.

Robledo Estaire, Luis, "Estructura y función de la capilla musical en la corte de Felipe II," in *La Capilla Real de los Austrias: Música y ritual de corte en la Europa moderna*, ed. Juan José Carreras and Bernardo García García (Madrid: Fundación Carlos de Amberes, 2001), 195–206.

Rodríguez del Castillo, Jesús, *Ignacio Zuloaga el hombre* (Zarauz: Icharopena, 1970).

Rodríguez-Picavea, Enrique, *La corona de Aragón en la edad media* (Madrid: Ediciones Akal, 1999).

Roland-Manuel, *Manuel de Falla* (Paris: Éditions "Cahiers d'art," 1930).

Rolland, Denis, "L'Action Française et l'Amerique Latine," in *L'Action Française et l'étranger: Usages, réseaux et représentations de la droite nationaliste française*, ed. Catherine Pomeyrols and Claude Hauser (Paris: L'Harmattan, 2001), 99–115.

Rolland, Romain, *Musiciens d'aujourd'hui* (Paris: Hachette et Cie, 1908).

Romero Ferrer, Alberto, "Un ataque a la estética de la razón. La crítica ilustrada frente a la tonadilla escénica: Jovellanos, Iriarte y Leandro Fernández de Moratín," *Cuadernos de ilustración y romanticismo* 1, no. 1 (1991): 105–127.

Ros-Fábregas, Emilio, "Historiografía de la música en las catedrales españolas: Positivismo y nacionalismo en la investigación musicológica," *Codex XXI. Revista de la comunicación musical*, no. 1 (1998): 68–135.

———, "Música y músicos 'extrajeros' en la España del siglo XVI," in *La capilla real de los Austrias: Música y ritual de corte en la Europa moderna*, ed. Bernardo J. García and Juan José Carreras (Madrid: Fundación Carlos de Amberes, 2001), 101–126.

———, "Musicological Nationalism or How to Market Spanish Olive Oil," *Newsletter of the International Hispanic Music Study Group* 4, no. 2 (1998): 6–15.

Ross, James, "*Messidor*: Republican Patriotism and the French Revolutionary Tradition in Third Republic Opera," *French Music, Culture and National Identity, 1870–1939*, ed. Barbara L. Kelly (Rochester, NY: University of Rochester Press, 2008), 112–130.

Rossell, Antoni, "Le pregón: Survivance du système de transmission oral et musical de l'épopée espagnole," *Cahiers de littérature orale* 32 (1992): 159–177.

Rougnon, Paul, "Latinisme et germanisme," *Le ménestrel* (September 1920).

Rowden, Clair, "Paris-Londres: *La Navarraise* face à la presse," in *Le naturalisme sur la scène lyrique*, ed. Jean-Christophe Branger and Alban Ramaut (Saint-Etienne: Publications de l'Université de Saint Etienne, 2004), 107–128.

Sahlins, Peter, *Boundaries: The Making of France and Spain in the Pyrenees* (Berkeley: University of California Press, 1989).

Said, Edward W., *Orientalism: Western Conceptions of the Orient* (New York: Vintage Books, 1978).

Salazar, Adolfo, *Modesto Mussorgsky y su Boris Godunof. Boceto histórico artístico* (Madrid: Antonio Matamala, 1923).

———, "Lettre d'Espagne," *Le courrier musical* (April 1918).
Sánchez, José Antonio, "'The Impossible Theatre': The Spanish Stage at the Time of the Avant-garde," *Contemporary Theatre Review* 7, no. 2 (1998): 7–30.
Sansone, Matteo, "The Critics' Response to 'Cavalleria Rusticana,'" *Music & Letters*, 71, no. 2 (1990): 198–201.
———, "Verga and Mascagni: The Critics' Response to 'Cavalleria Rusticana,'" *Music and Letters* 71, no. 2 (1990): 198–214.
———, "Verismo," in *Grove Music Online*, http://www.oxfordmusiconline.com/subscriber/article/grove/music/29210 (accessed April 15, 2011).
Santana Burgos, Laura, "La traducción de un pregón callejero: La ópera El retablo de maese Pedro de Manuel de Falla," *El genio maligno. Revista de humanidades y ciencias sociales*, no. 3 (2008): 130–137.
Schaeffner, [André,] 'Concert Manuel de Falla,' *Le ménestrel* 89, no. 20 (May 20, 1927).
Schmid, Marion, "À bas Wagner!: The French Press Campaign Against Wagner During World War I," in *French Music, Culture, and National Identity, 1870–1939*, ed. Barbara Kelly (Rochester, NY: University of Rochester Press, 2008), 77–94.
Schneider, Louis, "Le 'Gaulois au théâtre.' Les premières," *Le Gaulois* (March 11, 1928).
———, "La mise en scène et les décors," *Comœdia* (March 1911).
———, "La mise en scène et les décors." *Comœdia* (December 1913).
Scott, Derek B., "Orientalism and Musical Style," *Musical Quarterly* 82, no. 2 (1998): 309–335.
Sherman, Daniel J., "Art, Commerce, and the Production of Memory in France After World War I," in *Commemorations: The Politics of National Identity*, ed. John R. Gillis (Princeton, NJ: Princeton University Press, 1994), 186–211.
Simpson, Sally S., "Caste, Class and Violent Crime: Explaining Difference in Female Offending," *Criminology* 29 (1991–1992).
Sinclair, Alison, "Spain's Love Affair with Russia: The Attraction of Exotic (Br)others," *European Review of History* 11, no. 2 (June 1, 2004): 207–224.
Smith, Angel, "Sardana, Zarzuela or Cakewalk? Nationalism and Internationalism in the Discourse, Practice and Culture of the Early Twentieth Century Barcelona Labour Movement," in *Nationalism and the Nation in the Iberian Peninsula: Competing and Conflicting Identities*, ed. Clare Mar-Molinero and Angel Smith (Oxford and Washington, DC: Berg, 1996), 171–190.
Smith, Anthony D., *Nationalism and Modernism: A Critical Survey of Recent Theories of Nations and Nationalism* (London: Routledge, 1998).
Smith, Leonard V., Stéphan Adouin-Rouzeau and Annette Becker, *France and the Great War, 1914–1918* (Cambridge: Cambridge University Press, 2003).
Smith, Richard Langham, "French Operatic Spectacle in the Twentieth Century," in *French Music Since Berlioz*, ed. Caroline Potter and Richard Langham Smith (Aldershot: Ashgate, 2006), 117–160.
———, "Laparra, Raoul," *Grove Music Online*, http://www.oxfordmusiconline.com/subscriber/article/grove/music/16011 (accessed April 15, 2011).
Soubies, Albert, *Histoire de la musique. Espagne, I. Des origines au XVIIe siècle* (Paris: Librairie des Bibliophiles, 1899).
———, *Histoire de la musique. Espagne, II. Les XVIIe et XVIIIe siècles* (Paris: Librairie des Bibliophiles, 1899).
———, *Histoire de la musique. Espagne, III. Le XIXe siècle* (Paris: Librairie des Bibliophiles, 1899).
———, *Histoire de la musique allemande* (Paris: May & Motteroz, 1896).
———, *Musique russe et musique espagnole* (Paris: Fischbacher, 1894).
———, *Un problème de l'histoire musicale en Espagne* (Paris: Librairie Fischbacher, 1896).
———, and Charles Malherbe, *L'oeuvre dramatique de Richard Wagner* (Paris: Fischbacher, 1886).
Soubies, Albert, and Charles Malherbe, *Mélanges sur Richard Wagner* (Paris: Fischbacher, 1892).
Souday, Paul, "A l'Opéra-Comique," *Le temps,* March 23, 1911.

Spies, André Michael, *Opera, State, and Society in the Third Republic, 1875–1914* (New York: P. Lang, 1998).

Spivak, Gayatri Chakravorty, "Can the Subaltern Speak?" in *Marxism and the Interpretation of Culture*, ed. Cary Nelson and Lawrence Grossberg (Urbana: University of Illinois Press, 1988), 271–313.

Staël, Germaine de, *De l'Allemagne* (Paris: Charpentier, 1839).

Steingress, Gerhard, *Sociología del cante flamenco* (Sevilla: Signatura Ediciones, 1991).

———, *…y Carmen se fue a París: Un estudio sobre la construcción artística del género flamenco (1833–1865)* (Córdoba: Almuzara, 2005).

Stoecklin, Paul de, "Chand d'musique," *Le courrier musical* (April 1909).

———, "L'esthétique allemande," *Le courrier musical* (January 1909).

———, "Le germanisme et la musique," *Le courrier musical* (November 1909).

———, "Musique allemande et musique française," *Le courrier musical* (June 1923).

———, "Salle Pleyel. MM. Granados et Jacques Thibaud," *Le courrier musical* (June 1909).

Stoianova, Ivanka, "Concerto por clavecin: Tradition et découverte artistique," in *Manuel de Falla, latinité et universalité. Actes du colloque international tenu en Sorbonne, 18–21 novembre 1996*, ed. Louis Jambou (Paris: Presses de l'Université Paris-Sorbonne, 1999), 277–296.

Storm, Eric, "The Rise of the Intellectual Around 1900: Spain and France," *European History Quarterly* 32, no. 2 (2002): 139–160.

Suschitzky, Anya, "Debussy's Rameau: French Music and Its Others," *Musical Quarterly* 86, no. 3 (2002): 398–448.

Sutton, Michael, *Nationalism, Positivism, and Catholicism: The Politics of Charles Maurras and French Catholics, 1890–1914* (Cambridge and New York: Cambridge University Press, 1982).

Taruskin, Richard, "Back to Whom? Neoclassicism as Ideology," *19th-Century Music* 16, no. 3 (1993): 286–302.

———, *Text and Act: Essays on Music and Performance* (Oxford and New York: Oxford University Press, 1995).

Taylor, Timothy D., *Beyond Exoticism: Western Music and the World* (Durham, NC: Duke University Press, 2007).

Tenroc, Charles, "Les cinquante ans de Carmen. Un anniversaire," *Le courrier musical* (March 1, 1925).

———, "M. Raoul Laparra nous parle de 'La jota'," *Comœdia*, March 26, 1911.

———, "Opéra-Comique: Les ballets espagnols de Mme Argentina," *Le courrier musical* (June 1928).

———, "Opéra-Comique: La vie brève, L'amour sorcier, Les tréteaux de Maître Pierre," *Le courrier musical* (April 1928).

———, "Théatre Fémina: Les ballets espagnols de Mme Argentina," *Le courrier musical* (September 1928).

Thiesse, Anne-Marie, *Écrire la France: Le mouvement littéraire régionaliste de langue française entre la Belle Époque et la Libération* (Paris: Presses Universitaires de France, 1991).

———, *Ils apprenaient la France. L'exaltation des régions dans le discours patriotique* (París: Éditions de la Maison des Sciences de l'Homme, 1997).

Thorpe, Frederick J., "The French Press and the Franco-Spanish Convention of 1904 on Morocco," *French Colonial History* 3, no. 1 (2003): 157–173.

Tiénot, Yvonne, "Soubies, Albert," *Grove Music Online*, ed. Deane Root, http://www.oxfordmusiconline.com/subscriber/article/grove/music/26281 (accessed August 2, 2011).

Tiersot, Julien, "Bizet et la musique espagnole," *Le ménestrel* (September 1925).

———, "Bizet et la musique espagnole, I," *Le ménestrel* 87, no. 39 (September 25, 1925), 394–395.

———, "Bizet et la musique espagnole (II)," *Le ménestrel* 87, no. 40 (October 2, 1925).

———, "Bizet et la musique espagnole (III)," *Le ménestrel* 87, no. 41 (October 9, 1925).

———, "Bizet et la musique espagnole (IV)," *Le ménestrel* 87, no. 42 (October 16, 1925).

———, "Bizet and Spanish Music," *Musical Quarterly*, no. 4 (1927): 566–581.

———, *Promenades musicales à l'Exposition* (Paris: Fischbacher, 1889).
Tomás, Mariano, *Ramón Cabrera (historia de un hombre)* (Barcelona: Juventud, 1939).
Torchet, Julien, "Opéra Comique. Carmen," *Comœdia* (December 1907).
Torres Clemente, Elena, *Las óperas de Manuel de Falla. De* La vida breve *a* El retablo de Maese Pedro (Madrid: Sociedad Española de Musicología, 2007).
———, "La presencia de Scarlatti en la trayectoria musical de Manuel de Falla," in *Manuel de Falla e Italia: Estudios*, ed. Montserrat Bergadà et al. (Granada: Archivo Manuel de Falla, 2000), 63–122.
Trenc, Elisé, and Edmod Raillard, "Les relations franco-espagnoles pendant la guerre. La question catalane vue à travers les activités culturelles françaises à Barcelone," in *Españoles y franceses en la primera mitad del siglo XX* (Madrid: Consejo Superior de Investigaciones Científicas, Centro de Estudios Históricos, Departamento de Historia Contemporánea, 1986), 129–150.
Trend, John, *Manuel de Falla and Spanish Music* (New York: Knopf, 1929).
Trevitt, John, "Landormy, Paul," *Grove Music Online*, http://www.oxfordmusiconline.com/subscriber/article/grove/music/15950 (accessed April 15, 2011).
trilogía La, "Los Pirineos" y la crítica (Barcelona: [s.n.], 1901).
Turbow, Gerald D., "Art and Politics: Wagnerism in France," in *Wagnerism in European Culture and Politics*, ed. David Large and William Weber (Ithaca: Cornell University Press, 1984), 134–166.
Turina, Joaquín, "Les 50 ans de Carmen," *Le courrier musical* (March 1925).
———, "Manuel de Falla," *Chesterian* (May 1920).
Turina Gómez, Joaquín, *Historia del Teatro Real* (Madrid: Alianza, 1997).
Turner, Malcolm, "Chantavoine, Jean," *Grove Music Online*, ed. Stanley Sadie, http://www.oxfordmusiconline.com:80/subscriber/article/grove/music/05417 (accessed April 15, 2011).
———, and Jean Gribenski, "Curzon, (Emmanuel) Henri (Parent) de," in Grove Music Online. Oxford Music Online, http://www.oxfordmusiconline.com/subscriber/article/grove/music/06977 (accessed January 31, 2012).
Tyre, Jess, "Music in Paris During the Franco-Prussian War and the Commune," *Journal of Musicology* 22, no. 2 (April 1, 2005): 173–202.
Unamuno, Miguel de, *En torno al casticismo* (Madrid: Espasa Calpe, 2001/1905).
V., "Un spectacle lyrique espagnol à Paris," *L'illustration* (March 17, 1928).
Velletaz, E.-F., "A l'Opéra-Comique: La vie brève, L'amour sorcier, Les tréteaux de Maître Pierre, de M. Manuel de Falla," *Journal des débats* (March 1928).
Victoria, Tomás Luis de, *Opera omnia, ex antiquissimis, iisdemque rarissimis, hactenus cognitis editionibus in unum collecta, atque adnotationibus, tum bigliographicis, tum interpretatoriis*, ed. Felipe Pedrell, 8 vols. (Leipzig: Breitkopf und Härtel, 1913).
Viñas, Ángel, "Apertura exterior y modernización económica," in *España, Francia y la Comunidad Europea: Actas del Segundo Coloquio Hispano-Francés de Historia Contemporánea, celebrado en Aix-en-Provence los días 16, 17 y 18 de junio de 1986*, ed. José Ramón de Urquijo y Goitia (Madrid: CSIC, 1989), 265–277.
Vuillemin, Louis, "'Le voile du bonheur.' 'La jota,'" *Comœdia* (April 27, 1911).
Vuillermoz, Émile, "A l'Opéra-Comique: La jota," *S.I.M. Revue musicale mensuelle* 7, no. 5 (May 1911).
———, *Musiques d'aujourd'hui…* (Paris: G. Crès et Cie, 1923).
———, "Théâtre des Arts—Opéra-Comique," *Revue musicale S.I.M.* 9, no. 12 (December 1913).
Walsh, John K., "España y los Ballets Russes de Serge Diaghilev. Contexto histórico: España durante la Primera Guerra Mundial," ed. Yvan Nommick and Antonio Álvarez Cañibano, *Los Ballets Russes de Diaghilev y España* (Granada and Madrid: Fundación Archivo Manuel de Falla, INAEM, 2000), 23–30.
Washabaugh, William, *Flamenco: Passion, Politics, and Popular Culture* (Oxford and Washington, DC: Berg, 1996).
Weber, Eckhard, "Falla y Lorca: Entre la tradición y la vanguardia," in *Falla y Lorca: Entre la tradición y la vanguardia*, ed. Susana Zapke (Kassel: Reichenberger, 1999), 117–154.

Widor, Charles-Marie, "La Villa Velasquez à Madrid," *Le ménestrel* (September 1920).
Wright, Julian, *The Regionalist Movement in France, 1890–1914: Jean Charles-Brun and French Political Thought* (Oxford: Oxford University Press, 2003).
Wright, Lesley, "Berlioz's Impact in France," in *The Cambridge Companion to Berlioz*, ed. Peter Bloom (New York: Cambridge University Press, 2000), 253–268.
———, *Georges Bizet, Carmen: Dossier de presse parisienne (1875)* (Weinsberg: Musik-Ed. Galland, 2001).
Young, Robert, *Colonial Desire: Hybridity in Theory, Culture and Race* (New York: Routledge, 1995).
Zeldin, Theodore, *A History of French Passions 1848–1945: Intellect, Taste and Anxiety* (New York: Oxford University Press, 1993).

INDEX

Académie des Beaux-Arts, 51
Academy of Beaux Arts, Madrid, 136–137, 199
Acción Española, 10 n. 31, 52
Action Française, 9 n. 30, 10, 14, 16, 25, 49, 52, 57, 62–63, 65 n. 75, 79
Adam, Adolphe, 164
Aderer, Adolphe, 116
afrancesados, 182
Alarcón, Pedro Antonio de, 196
Albaicín, 140–141
Albéniz, Isaac, 21, 23, 29, 61, 81, 91, 136, 138, 146–147, 151, 185, 194 n. 11, 205, 223
    as an anti-German composer, 11–13, 15, 24–25, 120, 209
    and Debussy, *see* Debussy, Claude
    as a noble savage, 25–26, 30, 32–33
    and racial otherness, 26–28, 31–32, 71
    at the Schola Cantorum, 14, 26–28
Albingensian Crusade, *see* Cathar Crusade
Albright, Anne Cooper, 218
Alfonso XII, 51
Alhambra palace, 140–141
Alhambra Theatre, London, 44, 196
Altermann, Jean-Pierre, 48
Ambros, August Wilhelm, 67
Amsterdam, 194
Ancien Régime, 8, 59, 62, 103, 134
Andalusia, 7, 48, 74, 76, 86, 128, 132, 150, 196, 198, 203–204, 206, 210, 214, 220–223
Ansó, 102, 104–105, 112, 126, 128–132
anti-clericalism, 51, 60
anti-Semitism, 9, 27–29, 59, 63, 125–126, 134, 227
Apaches, Les, 20
Appia, Adolphe, 221, 224 n. 149
Aragón, 53, 85–86, 102, 104–105, 111, 129–130, 132–134, 214
Arana, Sabino, 106
Argentina, 153

Argentina, La (Antonia Mercé), 193, 203, 212–219, 222–223, 225, 235
Argentinita, La (Encarnación López Júlvez), 203
Arlésienne, l', 174–177, 183–184
art-nouveau, 80
Association française d'Expansion et d'Echanges Artistiques, 192
Ateneo de Madrid, 10, 51
Athens, 8, 12, 82
Auric, Georges, 44
Austria-Hungary, 57, 109
Austria, 22, 152
authenticity, discussions of, 58, 129, 146–152, 155, 171–172, 177–178, 180, 182–191, 197, 213
Ávila, 64, 67, 69, 71, 93–94, 220

Bacarisas, Gustavo, 203–204
Bach, Johann Sebastian, 18–19, 189
Bailly, Alfred, 129, 141
Balaguer, Víctor, 85–86
Balearic Islands, 95
Ballets Russes, 43–45, 197, 203, 213–214, 223
Barcelona, 39, 43, 71, 73, 76, 78–82, 86–91, 187, 194, 196
Barrès, Maurice, 25, 52, 59–77, 112, 125–128, 175, 191, 222
Barrios, Ángel, 223
Bartók, Béla, 120, 141 n. 33, 184
Basque Country, 61, 64, 79, 102–103, 105–106, 110–111, 176, 180, 220
Baudrillart, Alfred, 50
Bayreuth, 7, 86, 170
Beethoven, Ludwig van, 19, 34–35, 151 n. 75, 189, 212, 225, 229
Benjamin, Walter, 122
Bergson, Henri, 51
Berlin, 225

263

Bernini, Gian Lorenzo, 70
Bertrand, Paul, 48
Bilbao, 110
Bizet, Georges, 44, 101, 123, 143–144, 157, 161, 163–191, 204, 208
  and *Carmen*, 13–15, 36, 107, 114, 123–124, 138, 143–144, 161–193, 204, 208, 213
Black Legend, 4, 108, 209
Boieldieu, François-Adrien, 164
Boito, Arrigo, 138
Bonaparte, Joseph, *see* Joseph Napoléon
Bonaparte, Napoléon, *see* Napoléon Bonaparte
Bordeaux, 5–6, 65–66, 70, 73, 101
Bordes, Charles, 26, 82
Boulanger, Nadia, 207
Boulogne, 101
Bourbon dynasty, 4, 22, 55, 103
Brahms, Johannes, 172
Brailoiu, Constantin, 36
Brass, Tom, 124–125
Breitkopf und Härtel, 22, 55, 71, 145
Bretón, Tomás, 234
Britt-Arredondo, Christopher, 65, 143
Bruneau, Alfred, 106–107, 109, 114, 117, 139
Burgos, 73, 78, 95, 101, 234
Butler, Judith, 39

Cádiz, 137, 182, 222
Cage, John, 116
Campo, Conrado del, 29
cante jondo,*see* flamenco
Canteloube, Joseph, 112, 175
Capuana, Luigi, 140
Caravaggio, Michelangelo Merisi da, 68
Carlism, 79, 99–100, 102–106, 110–111, 131–134
Carlist Wars, 99, 102, 104, 110, 133
Carré, Albert, 102, 117–118, 129–131, 138–139, 166, 168
Carreras, Juan José, 56
Carroll, David, 126
Carvalho, Léon, 107
Casa Velázquez, 50–51, 66
Casadesus, Henri, 44
Casals, Pau, 223
Casella, Alfredo, 10
Casino Municipal, Nice, 138–139
Castile, 49, 53, 69, 74–75, 86, 95, 104, 127–128, 150, 209–210
  and centralism, 64–67, 76, 78, 89–90, 105, 197, 204, 220–223
  music from, 96, 214
  and mysticism, 77
  in Spanish painting, 64
Castro, Américo, 28, 63
Catalan music, 24, 49, 64, 73, 75–77–92, 95–96, 113, 220–221, 231

Catalonia, 24, 49, 77–79, 81, 84–86, 89–90, 95, 221
Cathar Crusade, 85
Catholic Kings, 53, 130
Catholicism, 5–6, 8–9, 49–98, 103–104, 106, 115, 130, 132–134, 148, 199, 206, 222, 229
Caucasus, 48
Cerdannes, 139
Cervantes, Miguel de, 25, 100, 195, 208, 218–219, 226–227, 230, 234
Chabrier, Emmanuel, 26, 43, 146–147, 157, 185
Chambonnières, Jacques Champion de, 232
Champclos, Davin de, 166
Chantavoine, Jean, 211–212, 217, 224–225, 230, 234
Chapí, Ruperto, 137
Charlemagne, 85–86, 230
Charles-Brun, Jean, 13
Charpentier, Gustave, 142, 165–166, 200
Chausson, Ernest, 26
Chopin, Frédéric, 24
Christoforidis, Michael, 142
Cid, El, 74, 110
Cimarosa, Domenico, 44
Cirot, Georges, 70
Civil War in Spain, 99, 118, 143
Cixous, Hélène, 217
Clark, Linda L., 198
Clark, Robert L. A., 163
Classic Antiquity, 7–9, 14, 81, 114
Clément, Catherine, 217
Cocteau, Jean, 15, 20, 23, 207
Coeuroy, André, 199–201, 206, 215, 227
Collet, Henri, 3, 36, 46, 48, 59, 61
  and anti-German propaganda, 6–7, 10, 11, 13–15, 19–33, 120, 206, 209
  and anti-Italian propaganda, 49–57
  and French hegemony, 12, 34–43, 153, 185, 210, 215
  and mysticism, 65–77
  and regionalism, 77–84, 88–101
Combarieu, Jules, 35
Comité Catholique de Propagande Française à l'Etranger, 50, 59, 70
Comité de Rapprochement Franco-Espagnol, 51
Comité International de Propagande, 50, 60
Concerts Colonne, 193
Conrad, Joseph, 21
Constitution of 1812, 79, 102–103, 182
Costa, Joaquín, 64
Council of Trent, 69
Couperin, François, 145, 225, 230, 232
Covent Garden, 110
Craig, Gordon, 221
Cuba, 24, 52, 80, 149, 180
Curtiss, Mina, 164

Curzon, Henri de, 88, 194–195, 200, 216, 225–226, 230, 234

Dadaism, 28
Dama de Elche, 66
Darwin, Charles, 198
Daudet, Alphonse, 175, 184
Debay, Victor, 114
Debussy, Claude, 43, 169
  and Albéniz, 12–13, 21, 27
  and Falla, 10, 138, 142, 146–147, 150, 151, 154–157, 195, 202, 206, 208, 211, 227–228, 231–232
  and French music history, 57
  influence of, 28, 35, 38–40, 185, 189
  and Russian music, 48, 207
  and *verismo*, 109, 111, 117
Défense de la Musique Française
Delaunay, Jean-Marc, 23
Delthomas, Maxime, 223, 235
Demarquez, Suzanne, 142
desastre, 51 n. 11, 52, 80, 82, 143, 149, 220
Deschanel, Paul, 22–23
Dezarnaux, Robert, 226
Diaghilev, Sergei, 43–44, 196, 203, 223, 227
Diémer, Louis, 101
Diocletian, 64
Don Carlos, 102, 133
Don Quixote, 6, 25, 64–65, 74, 95, 195, 208, 218–221, 226, 229, 231, 233–235
Dorsch, Juliane, 226, 233
Dreyfus affair, 10, 27, 29, 59, 99, 126, 134
Dubois, Paul, 164
Dufranne, Hector, 229
Dukas, Paul, 26, 27, 29, 38–40, 117, 138
Dumas, Alexandre, 26, 61

École des Hautes Études Hispaniques, 66
École des Hautes Études, 172, 174–175
El Escorial, 22, 63
Elias, Norbert, 122
Ellis, Katharine, 57
encyclopédistes, 57
England, 22, 52
Enlightenment, 16, 99, 102, 121, 124, 132, 182
Ernst, Max, 44
Escudero, Vicente, 203
Esplá, Óscar, 29
exile, 16, 28, 38, 42, 63, 81, 103, 136, 153, 193, 206, 223–224
exoticism, 3–5, 12, 30, 35–37, 41, 43–44, 52, 56, 104, 123–124, 143–146, 162–163, 166, 172, 179–180, 194, 200, 205, 230
Exposició Universal, 80

Falla, Manuel de, 13, 20–21, 29, 35, 44, 54, 81, 91–92, 95–96, 111, 120, 134, 136–157, 182, 184, 186–187, 192–239
  and *El amor brujo*, 150, 192–193, 196, 203–210, 212–215, 220–221, 225, 228–229, 235, 238
  and Debussy, *see* Debussy, Claude; and the *Harpsichord Concerto*, 95, 146, 150, 192, 196, 232
  and German music, 10, 45
  and *El retablo de Maese Pedro*, 21, 95–96, 146, 150, 152, 192–193, 195–197, 218–235, 238
  and *La vie brève*,111, 134, 136–137, 139–144, 146–147, 149–151, 153, 155, 157, 184, 192–197, 199–205, 207, 220, 227, 229, 235
Faull, Katherine M., 219
Fauré, Gabriel, 12–13, 26–27, 29, 39–40, 44, 101, 115, 117, 165–166
Fauser, Annegret, 168
Féderation Régionaliste Française, 79
Félibrige, 13–14, 78, 89
Ferdinand VII, 79, 103
Fernández-Shaw, Carlos, 137–140
Fernández-Shaw, Guillermo, 138–139
Fesser, Joaquín, 45
First World War, 4, 7, 9, 15, 20–23, 29, 43–44, 49–52, 120, 138, 156, 161–162, 166–168, 196, 199–201, 206–207
flamenco, 44, 46, 120, 128, 141, 180, 184, 195–196, 204, 214, 216, 220, 223, 234–235
Flemish school, 54, 67, 69, 77
Fokine, Mikhail, 44
Foucault, 122
Francis Xavier, 76
Franck, César, 20, 33–34, 176
Franco-Prussian War, 3, 107, 168, 198
Franco dictatorship, 28, 42, 63, 96, 103, 224
Frankish empire, 86
French Revolution, 8, 10, 23, 35, 78, 103, 112–113, 134, 169
Friedländer, Max, 225
fueros, 103, 106

Galicia, 95, 214
Gallet, Louis, 107
Galli-Marié, Celestine, 163–165
Gambetta, Léon, 215
García Lorca, Federico, 184, 196, 222–223
García, Manuel, 177, 180–182, 208
Gaudi, Antonio, 80
Gaudier, Charles, 164, 167–172, 177, 180, 190–191
Gauthier-Villars, Henri, 110, 189
Gauthier, Théophile, 138
Generation of 1898, 51–53, 59, 61, 64, 73–75, 77–78, 82, 95–96, 100, 117, 127, 128, 132–134, 197, 221–222

Generation of 1914, 51–53, 59, 61, 64, 73, 75, 77, 82, 127, 197
German music, 50, 117
  and critiques of civilisation, 31
  and critiques of dehumanization, 18, 23, 61
  and critiques of formalism, 16–17, 32
  and critiques of rationalism, 23
  and critiques of universalism, 34–35
  and critiques of virtuosity, 18;
  and critiques of seriousness, 18, 224
  reactions against 5–7, 9–11, 13–17, 20, 24–25, 42, 45, 51–52, 59, 65, 70, 87, 168, 211
Gevaert, François-Auguste, 54, 76
Gheusi, Pierre-Barthélemy., 194, 198, 202–203, 206, 215–216
Giménez, Gerónimo, 142
Giraud, Ernest, 169
Gluck, Christoph Willibald, 172
Goehr, Lydia, 169
Golden Age in Spain, 54, 67, 74, 76, 89, 95, 145–146, 220
Gómez Renovales, Juan, 45
González Cuevas, Pedro Carlos, 84
Goode, Joshua, 122
Granada, 78, 140–142, 151, 157, 184, 196, 204, 223
Granados, Enrique, 19–20, 23–24, 26, 29–33, 51, 68, 81, 90–91, 147, 185, 229, 238
Great Britain, 57
Greco, El (Doménikos Theotokópoulos), 25, 62–71, 77, 222–223
Greece, 14, 62
Grieg, Edvard, 24
Gris, Juan, 44
Grupo de los Ocho, 204
Guam, 52, 220
Guerrero, Francisco, 54, 67, 145
gypsies, 26, 30, 47–48, 123, 134, 138, 140–143, 162–165, 171–172, 182, 184, 190, 196, 204, 210, 213–215, 218, 220, 235

Habsburg dynasty, 67
Hahn, Reynaldo, 117
Halévy, Ludovic, 163, 190
Halffter, Ernesto, 146
Händel, Georg Friedrich, 18
Hannah, Martha, 199
Harney, Lucy D., 143
Haydn, Joseph, 18
Hegel, Friedrich, 18
hegemony, 12, 29–30, 33, 36–37, 48, 68–69, 123, 136, 153, 170–171, 177
Herder, Johann Gottfried, 16
Hérold, Ferdinand, 164
Hess, Carol, 45

hispanistes, 5–6, 12, 36, 38 n. 171, 49, 56–57, 61, 73, 99–100, 172
Huebner, Steven, 107
Hugo, Victor, 26
hybridization, 28, 63, 69, 71, 93

Iberian Peninsula, 63
Ignatius of Loyola, 76
imperialism, 52–53, 74–75, 84, 143
Imperio, Pastora, 193, 213–214
India, 124
Indy, Vincent d', 26–27, 29, 38–40, 117
Inquisition, Tribunal of the Holy, 109
Institut Français de Madrid, 50, 60, 62, 66, 70
intrahistoria, 127–128
Isaac, Adèle, 164–165
Isaba, 105
Isabella II, 102
Italian music, 7, 10, 17–19, 21, 23, 37, 49–98, 101, 106, 111, 117, 137–138, 144, 165, 187–188, 193, 199–200, 232, 235
  and accusations of paganism, 58, 75, 77
  reactions against, 38, 49, 54–56, 75, 109, 139–140, 182, 190, 201–203, 205, 228

Jacobins, 134
Jankélévitch, Vladimir, 32
Javanese gamelan, *see* gamelan
Jean Wiener Concerts, 194
Jean-Aubry, Georges, 20–21, 23, 35–36, 47
Jews, 8–10, 27–28, 32, 53, 63, 69, 94, 126
José Martínez Ruiz "Azorín", 10 n. 31, 52, 64
Joseph Napoléon, 4

Kamen, Henry, 53
Kamienska, Olga, 226
Kant, Immanuel, 120
Kochno, Boris, 44

Lalo, Charles, 73
Lalo, Edouard, 43, 146–147, 157
Lalo, Pierre, 116–117, 140
Laloy, Louis, 35, 57, 72–73
Lambert, Constant, 44
Landormy, Paul, 172–178, 182–184, 187, 191
Landowska, Wanda, 196
Langdon-Davies, John, 130–131
Languedoc, 73, 85
Laparra, Raoul, 36–37, 73, 99–135, 139, 144, 146, 150, 153–155, 157, 166, 177, 179, 184–186, 191, 197, 208–210, 212, 215

and *La habanera*, 73–74, 100–102, 107–114, 117, 128–129, 132–133, 135, 139, 143–144, 150, 166, 171, 197, 210
and *La jota*, Raoul Laparra, 99–135, 166, 212, 238
Laparra, William, 101
Latin America, 9, 53, 65, 124, 180
Latin race, *see* Latin Union
Latin Union, 5, 7, 9–10, 14–15, 17–24, 30
  and Russian music, 21–22, 34, 45–46, 206–207
  and Spanish music, 24
Ligue de la Patrie Française, 126
Legendre, Maurice, 50–51
Legitimism, 103–104
Leipzig, 11, 22
Lejárraga, María, 196, 221
Les Six, 6, 20, 176, 227
Linor, G., 144–146
Liszt, Franz, 157, 212, 225
Lliga Regionalista, 83
Lliurat, Frederic, 78
Llobet, Miguel, 223
Locke, Ralph P., 181
Locle, Camille du, 190
London, 20, 25, 40, 44, 110, 196
Longuet, Charles, 79
López Júlvez, Encarnación, *see* Argentinita, La
Lorraine, 3, 107
Louis XVI, 62
Louvre, Musée du, 66

Machado, Antonio, 52, 64
Madrid Conservatoire, 90
Madrid, 12–13, 39, 63, 91, 95, 101, 136, 137–139, 142, 151, 153, 182, 187, 193, 196, 199, 206, 213–214
  as compared to Barcelona, 90
  and French propaganda, 51, 66, 71, 78
  and Russian musicians, 44
Madrid, Alejandro, 29
Maeztu, Ramiro de, 52
Mahler, Gustav, 21
Malherbe, Henry, 129, 194, 197–199, 202, 205, 207–212
Malibrán, María, 208
marca hispánica, *see* Spanish March
Marne, 60
Marnold, Jean, 35, 47
Martínez Sierra, Gregorio, 196, 221
Mascagni, Pietro, 106, 110, 138
Massenet, Jules, 106, 110–111, 115, 135, 138
Massine, Léonide, 44, 196
Maurras, Charles, 10, 21, 23, 59, 81–83, 112, 126, 176
  as an anti-Republican thinker, 14, 52, 113
  and anti-Semitism, 28, 126

and German culture, 16, 21, 49, 63
and the Latin Union, 8–9, 30
and regionalism, 13, 24, 77, 79, 89, 175
McClary, Susan, 123, 124, 143, 163
Mediterranean race and music, 13–15, 24, 81, 83, 167, 174–176, 212, 228
Meilhac, Henri, 163
Mendelssohn, Felix, 34
Mendès, Catulle, 17
Menéndez Pidal, Ramón, 70–71
Menéndez y Pelayo, Marcelino, 52
Mercé, Antonia, *see* Argentina, La
Mérimée, Ernest, 50, 60, 62, 66, 70
Mérimée, Prosper, 61, 163, 178, 183, 190
Mexico, 29
Meyerbeer, Giacomo, 46
Meyerhold, Vsevolod, 221
Millerand, Alexandre, 23
Milliet, Paul, 138–139
Miranne, Jacques, 139
Miró, Joan, 44
Mistral, Frédéric, 13–14, 78, 83, 112, 176
Mitjana, Rafael, 83, 88, 93–94
modernisme, 80–81, 83, 85
modernization, reactions against, *see* nostalgia
Montéclair, Michel de, 44
Montserrat, 86, 231
Morales, Cristóbal de, 54, 67, 145–146
Moriscos, 53
Morocco, 22, 150
Mozart, Wolfgang Amadeus, 18–20, 212, 217, 225
Musk, Andrea, 112
Muslim culture, 53, 63, 71, 86, 93
Muslim invasion, 63
Mussolini, Benito, 223
Mussorgsky, Modest Petrovich, 22, 48
mysticism, 6, 43, 64–78, 82, 88–89, 93–96, 220–222; *see also* Catholicism

nacionalcatolicismo, 96, 103
Napoléon Bonaparte, 16, 102, 182
Nattiez, Jean-Jacques, 116
naturalist opera, 73, 100, 106–110, 112–114, 141, 165
Navarra, 102–103, 105–106, 109–111, 115, 202, 214
navarraise, La, 106, 109, 110–111, 115, 202
neoclassicism, 15, 20, 42, 145, 167–168, 174, 176, 191, 195–197, 204, 207, 211–218, 225, 232–233, 235
New York, 194
Nietzsche, Friedrich, 13–16, 117, 167–168, 172–174, 176
Nijinska, Bronislava, 44
Nin, Joaquin, 29, 232
Nommick, Yvan, 156

nostalgia, 69, 75–76, 80, 89, 103, 119, 124–132
noucentisme, 24, 81–83, 85

Occitania, *see* Languedoc
Olmeda, Federico, 73–74, 76, 78, 89–92, 95, 101, 133
Opéra Comique, *see* Salle Favart
opéra-comique (genre), 165, 167–170, 190, 191, 215
Orquesta Bética de Cámara, 153
Ors, Eugeni d', 24, 82
Ortega y Gasset, José, 10 n. 31, 52, 64, 220

Pactes de Famille, 22–23
Pahissa, Jaume, 153
Palais Garnier, 100
Palestrina, Giovanni Pierluigi da, 54–55, 69–73, 75, 82, 93
Parakilas, James, 123–124
Parejo Delgado, José, 142
Paris Commune, 3, 14, 78
Paris Conservatoire, 101, 115, 189
Paris, 3, 28–29, 52, 70, 79, 100, 112, 123, 135, 139–144, 148, 151, 157, 162, 169, 177, 182, 206–207, 217, 237–239
 and centralism, 79, 112, 128
 and critiques of civilization, 39
 and the construction of French hegemony, 12, 22, 40–41, 82, 123, 136, 146, 153, 155, 205
 presence of *verismo* in, 142, 165
 Spanish musicians in, 13, 26, 38, 54, 81, 136, 138, 147, 151–152, 182, 192–196, 202, 214, 223, 232
Paris, Pierre, 66, 70
Pasler, Jann, 134
Pedrell, Felipe, 26, 45–46, 54–56, 58, 69, 71–73, 75, 77–78, 82–96, 138, 145–146, 151, 182, 196, 229
Pere el Grande, *see* Peter III
Perpignan, 81
Peter III, 85
Peters, 22
Petronilla of Aragón, 86
Philip II, 63, 66–67
Philip III, 85
Philippines, 52, 220
Phillip V, 55
Picasso, Pablo, 44, 214
Pirineus, Els, 83–88, 87
Plato, 39
Polignac, Salon, 194, 218
Polignac, Princess Edmond de, *see* Singer, Winnaretta
Ponce, Manuel María, 29
Pope, 10, 63, 66, 85, 87, 88

Poueigh, Jean, 197, 200–201, 205–206
Poulenc, Francis, 232
Prat de la Riba, Enric, 83–84
Primo de Rivera, Miguel, 96
Prix de Rome, 101
Proske, Karl, 67
Protestantism, 9, 49–50, 62–63, 148, 207, 229
Proudhon, Pierre-Joseph, 168
Provençal, 13, 78–79, 175–176, 184
Prudhomme, Jean, 211–212, 216
Pruna, Pedro, 44
Prussia, 7, 198–199
Puccini, Giacomo, 140, 173
Pyrenees, 38, 79, 85–86, 88–89, 102, 110, 126, 185–186, 231

Querelle des bouffons, 57

Radomsky, James, 181
Rameau, Jean-Philippe, 57, 72, 145, 232
Ramón Berenguer IV, 86
Ravel, Maurice, 39, 43, 111, 117, 146–147, 150–151, 157, 185, 189, 195, 202, 223–224, 230–232
Reconquista, 53, 63
Reformation, 69
regeneracionistas, 64
regionalism, 7, 13–14, 40, 49, 64, 66, 74, 76–77, 80, 82–84, 88–89, 95–96, 110, 112–113, 124, 128, 132, 134, 175
renaixença, 79, 85, 87
republicanism, 5, 10, 50–52, 62, 66, 78, 99, 113, 134, 199
Respighi, Ottorino, 44
Ricard, Louis-Xavier de, 79
Ricordi Publisher, 138
Ricou, Georges, 222, 234
Rimsky-Korsakov, Nicolay Andreyevich, 21, 26, 48, 146–147, 185, 202
Rivas Cherif, Cipriano de, 203, 222
Rocreuse, 107
Roland-Manuel, 35–36
Rolland, Romain, 70
Roman empire, 50
Romanticism: 24, 117, 141
 reactions against, 8–9, 16, 24–25, 52, 81, 207
Rome, 8, 14, 50, 54, 62–63, 82, 106
Romea, Julián, 142
Ropartz, Guy, 112
Rothschild, Fondation S. de, 192
Rousseau, Jean-Jacques, 30, 57, 209, 228
Russia, 17, 20–22, 26, 34–35, 40–48, 124, 148, 206, 227

Russian Revolution, 42
Russolo, Luigi, 116

Sacromonte, 141
Said, Edward, 148–149, 154, 177
Saint John of the Cross, 64, 67, 71–72, 94, 220
Saint Maurice, 63–64
Saint Teresa of Avila, 64, 67, 71, 220
Salamanca, 59, 76
Salazar, Adolfo, 13, 42, 229, 232
Salignac, Thomas, 229
Salle Favart, 74, 99–100, 107, 116–117, 130, 134, 136, 139–141, 147, 150, 162–169, 175, 192–193, 203, 207, 215, 218–219, 223
Salle Pleyel, 192, 196
San Sebastian, 223
Sánchez, José Antonio, 221
Sanz, Gaspar, 232
Satie, Erik, 223
Scarlatti, Domenico, 232
Schaeffer, Pierre, 116
Schneider, Louis, 200, 202, 217, 226
Schoenberg, Arnold, 39, 229
Schola Cantorum, 14, 19, 21, 26, 28–29, 40, 70, 80, 168, 189
Schopenhauer, Arthur, 16, 117
Schubert, Franz, 18, 208
Schumann, Robert, 24, 34, 172, 185, 217
Scott, Derek, 150
Second Empire in France, 3, 8, 104, 107, 177, 198
Second Republic in Spain, 52, 96
Sedan, *see* Franco-Prussian War
Semaine espagnole, 22–23
Sepúlveda, 223
Sert, José María, 44
Setmana Tràgica, 80
Séverac, Déodat de, 112, 175
Seville, 12–13, 44, 73, 76, 153, 194, 203
Shakespeare, William, 80
Sicily, 23, 85–86
Sinclair, Alison, 43
Singer, Winnaretta, 223
Sociedad Nacional de Música, 10, 13, 153
Sorbonne, 6, 65, 70
Soriano Fuertes, Mariano, 53, 55
Soubies, Albert, 46–47, 58, 62, 72, 73
Souday, Paul, 115
Spanish March, 86
Spanish music
    and anti-German propaganda, 28–29
    and anti-Italian propaganda, 54–55
    and discussions of authenticity, *see* authenticity
    and marginality, 25, 30–33, 37, 39–40, 47–48, 69, 86, 210
    and the noble savage, 30–31, 39–30
    and Orientalism, 25, 41, 47–48, 69
    as popular music, 35, 179–184
    and racial otherness, 28, 30, 69, 76, 162–164, 182; 189–190, 218
    and Russian music, 40–48, 206–207
Spanish Royal Chapel, 67
Spivak, Gayatri, 211
Staël, Germaine de, 16–18
Stoecklin, Paul de, 15–19, 25
Straeten, Edmon van der, 54
Strauss, Richard, 17–18, 21, 25, 33, 44
Stravinsky, Igor, 39, 44–45, 116, 120, 176, 195, 206–208, 210–211, 227, 231
Suresnes, 101

Taylor, Timothy, 162
Teatre del Liceu, Bacelona, 87
Teatro Lara, Madrid, 193
Teatro Real, 137
Teixidor, José de, 54
Tempranica, La, 142–143
Tenroc, Charles, 114, 133, 164, 190, 198, 201, 205, 227–229
Théatre de la Monnaie, Brussels, 138
Third Republic in France, 7–9, 14, 104, 109–111, 134, 198–199, 235
Tiersot, Julien, 178–184, 191
Toledo, 63
tonadilla escénica, 55, 181
Torres, Elena, 142
Tortosa, 82, 86
Toulouse, 60, 66, 70
translatio studii, 8
Trianon Lyrique, 193
Triple Alliance, 49, 57, 109
Triple Entente, 4, 11
trufaldines, 55
Turina, Joaquín, 20, 29

Unamuno, Miguel de, 52, 59, 61, 64, 127–128, 220
United States, 52, 143, 149, 220

Valencia, 75
Valladolid, 63
Vallas, Léon, 139
Vallin, Ninon, 193, 201
Varèse, Edgard, 116
Velázquez, Diego de, 231
Velletaz, E.-F., 203, 207, 215
Venice, 62–63, 87, 223
Verdi, Giuseppe, 82
Verga, Giovanni, 140